TANGLED TRAILS

A Memoir

Best Wishes to My Readers!
W. Floyd Elliott

W. Floyd Elliott

The opinions expressed in this manuscript are solely the opinions of the author and do not represent the opinions or thoughts of the publisher. The author has represented and warranted full ownership and/or legal right to publish all the materials in this book.

Tangled Trails
A Memoir
All Rights Reserved.
Copyright © 2016 W. Floyd Elliott
v3.0

Cover Photo © 2016 W. Floyd Elliott. All rights reserved - used with permission.

This book may not be reproduced, transmitted, or stored in whole or in part by any means, including graphic, electronic, or mechanical without the express written consent of the publisher except in the case of brief quotations embodied in critical articles and reviews.

Outskirts Press, Inc.
http://www.outskirtspress.com

Paperback ISBN: 978-1-4787-6908-8
Hardback ISBN: 978-1-4787-6993-4

Library of Congress Control Number: 2015920599

Outskirts Press and the "OP" logo are trademarks belonging to Outskirts Press, Inc.

PRINTED IN THE UNITED STATES OF AMERICA

INTRODUCTION

Welcome to this collection of my "little stories." My motivation in writing these stories of my growing up in East Texas, and the other places of my childhood, for my descendants and others who may be interested was to put my memories on paper — hence Tangled Trails. Simply memories, not intended to be history or literature, just my "little stories" so they won't be lost in the years following me. Yes, they are about me — call that egotistical if you wish, but who else could do this? And besides, they are also about my family, friends and the times of my youth — which I want to share with others. So I have — and I will not apologize for neither the quality nor quantity.

Why did I want to do this and when did I get started? This is a little story of its own. All my life I loved to read history and even historical novels where talented authors could put feeling and thinking into the characters of history. When I had to decide on a final major in college — I chose history. And what do most people do with a history major? They teach — so that is what I did for a career. But I strayed from history and wandered around in other fields of study for a long career in teaching and educational administration— from 1950 till into the early 1990s, and enjoyed it very, very much.

After retirement from teaching and a few years in some other activities, I found I had some free time on my hands. I became interested in and active in the Texas Folklore Society, the East Texas Historical Association and the Texas State Historical Association. Because of these activities I decided I wanted to record some of my "family lore" and this led me to writing my little stories. I did not begin writing these until well into my eighties, with most of them written after the age of eighty-five. When constructing my stories, based on my memories, I have found many instances where it was necessary for me to connect events and happenings from rather shadowy glimpses into the past. I have supplied some parts to my stories on what I think would have happened, should have happened or could have happened. In a few places I gave the reader glimpses into the future to tie the past to coming events. If this was confusing, or seemed self-satisfying on the part of the author, to the reader, I then offer my apologizes. I was attempting to make the experiences seem more meaningful to my life.

I have debated with myself (and maybe others too) as to when a person is "grown up." Some argue that a person is grown when they graduate from high school. Others declare when they finish their education, and still others say when they are self-dependent financially — with many others using different measures. In my case I am selecting the beginning of my teaching career — September, 1950. Joyce and I were married, had completed enough education to make us financially independent of our parents and we were then employed as teachers. And there we will end my little stories of growing up.

Some may disagree with them — remembering differently from me. That is fine, let them do their own stories. But I truly hope you enjoy mine.

TABLE OF CONTENTS

ALBERT'S FAMOUS MEXICAN HOT SAUCE .... SINCE 1940* 1
VISITING IN THE 1930S* 7
HOW I CAME TO BE IN EAST TEXAS 13
THE HOUSE AT LEVERETT'S CHAPEL 29
RAYMONDVILLE 39
LEBANON, TENNESSEE 63
TYLER 85
GRANDMA'S FARM 127
WORLD WAR II 177
CORPUS CHRISTI IN 1942 187
THE SUMMER OF 1943 193
THE 1943-44 SCHOOL YEAR 215
THE SUMMER OF 1944 241
THE 1944-45 SCHOOL YEAR 271
R. L. GOOD JR. AND MY FIRST YEAR OF COLLEGE 289
AND, THEN 297
GOING ON 341
AND ON 367
EPILOGUE 407

# ALBERT'S FAMOUS MEXICAN HOT SAUCE .... SINCE 1940*

An afternoon a week or so ago, I was rummaging around in the refrigerator looking for a snack when I spied a container of Albert's Famous Mexican Hot Sauce. I pulled it out and went to the cabinet for a box of crackers. I got a fresh glass of unsweetened iced-tea and sat down at the kitchen table — all set. As I savored the semisweet sauce spooned onto the crackers, I looked at the container. It was a relatively new type; not the old familiar glass pint and quart jars which I was used to, but what caught my eye was "Since 1940" printed on the label. This date started me thinking — could that be correct?

Now I have to do some explaining. Being eighty-six years old this last August, I thought I remembered Albert's hot sauce before that date. I also remembered what the French writer Marcel Proust once wrote "Remembrance of things past is not necessarily the remembrance of things as they were." So I carefully recalled my acquaintance with Albert and his hot sauce as I munched cracker after cracker heaped with hot sauce.

My first remembrance of Albert is when we were living at Leverett's Chapel and I must have been in the first or second grade. This was in 1934 and 1935. But then again, it could have been in 1938 or 1939 when we lived in Tyler and I attended the fourth and fifth grades at Gary Elementary School. I prefer to think it occurred during the earlier period. The year in between, we had lived in Tennessee.

At this time Albert was living in a house on the north side of Longview St. in Kilgore. It was near where the antenna manufacturing plant is now. A little toward town is where my wife's grandparents, the Sheppards, had a grocery store until into the 1980s (now it is a church). I don't know when or how Albert got to Kilgore but at this time he prepared food in his kitchen and served it in the front rooms of the house. I never ate in the front rooms but I had a few meals in the kitchen. Years later (in the late 1940s after WWII) I remember eating at his nice restaurant downtown on North Kilgore St.– with my parents and in-laws — and then in the 1960s there and his restaurant on East Hwy 80 in Longview while I was teaching at Kilgore College and living in Kilgore (1962-1964). Albert's Mexican Village served this delicious hot sauce with saltine crackers as a warm up to your meal. This was before Mexican restaurants started serving chips with the hot sauce. My mother-in-law once laughingly accused Albert of putting something addictive in his hot sauce but he only laughed and assured her it was only good wholesome food.

Now I will tell you why I ate in the kitchen and not the dining room of Albert's oldest place. As I have mentioned we were living at Leverett's Chapel but I spent Sundays, holidays and summers at my Grandma Jernigan's farm — about ten miles due west of Kilgore. They had moved into Kilgore about 1928 in order for my Mother's younger sister to go to high school — she graduated from Kilgore High School in 1931 and Grandpa Jernigan died soon after that. Their house was on Main St. about where the Presbyterian Church has a large parking lot today. This house was later moved around the corner to Lawrence St. for the city to build a hospital on the site — the hospital before Laird Memorial. With the coming of the oil field to Kilgore, the character of Kilgore changed so much they moved to the farm at a community called Browning where the family sawmill business was located. I recall hearing Grandma tell someone that the town was terrible then due to the oil boom — she would go out to the chicken house to gather eggs and people would be in there sleeping. After moving from Kilgore she remained on her farm until her death in the 1960s.

I promise I will get back to the hot sauce in a little bit, but first I need to give you a little more background. My Mother's middle brother Walter was working at the sawmill and running the farm, but during slack times, such as bad weather and slow sales, he hung around the sheriff's office in Tyler. In jail was a young black man named Buddy Thomas who was headed to prison for murder. Evidently the government didn't like to send blacks to prison in those hard times (due to the cost of feeding them I guess) so a system was in place where a responsible white person could have them paroled to them for work. Walter had this arrangement made for Buddy and moved him to the farm and had him working on it when Grandpa, Grandma and the two youngest kids moved there. Despite Buddy's "story" he turned out to be a very dependable, honest and deserving fellow, much liked by the older members of the family and greatly loved by us of the younger part.

Buddy's story was that he had married young and after only a year or two he came home early one day and found his wife "entertaining" another man. He took a gun from his car and shot the man five times in the face. When asked why five times Buddy is reported as saying "that was all the bullets that I had."

Buddy more or less became kind of a member of the extended family. Soon a young girl from the community entered the picture as Grandma's cook. It wasn't long until Buddy and Ruby married. They never had any children but both treated the grandkids (my generation), great-grandkids, and even great-great-grandkids, and their spouses as their own.

A part of Buddy's work was to feed and care for the working stock — the many horses, mules and oxen (yes they still used some oxen then) that were worked at the sawmill. In fact the first memory I have of Buddy was at the barn and pens for the oxen. I must have been about three years old and my Dad had taken me with him to go see about something. He and someone were looking over the solid strong fence at some oxen — the fence was about five feet tall and they peeping over it. Dad was holding me in his arms and I was trying to climb up on top of the fence — made out of thick timbers like crossties. Finally Dad set me on top of the fence and continued talking with the other person. I was inching my way down the fence and after a couple of feet I came to this ox looking up at me — we locked eyeball to eyeball. I said something, I don't remember what but evidently this huge red beast with a white face didn't like it. He lowered his head and rammed the fence with a bang — it knocked me off the fence backward and I did a full flip and made a six point landing, on my heels, butt and hands. Dad had reached for me but he wasn't quick enough to break my fall. The next thing I knew, I was ear to ear with Buddy with me clinging to his neck as he had scooped me off the ground. I remembered his saying "you's got to be careful around them oxies — they's slow but they's powerfull." From that day till he died, Buddy and I were "buddies."

The working horses and mules were fed a lot of corn so Buddy shucked many ears a day for them. Somehow he and Albert had made a connection and a deal on corn shucks. Buddy would save the shucks and every week or two he would take some tow sacks full of them to Albert's place in Kilgore, usually on a Saturday afternoon. About the time I started to school Buddy would take me and sometimes William or Robert, my cousins, with him. We would help Buddy take the shucks to the back door of Albert's house. After paying Buddy, Albert would have us sit down in the kitchen and treat us to a Mexican plate with all the trimmings. Of course this included crackers and hot sauce. This is how I came to eat in Albert's kitchen and not with the other "whites" in the dining room.

After leaving Albert's, Buddy would make a couple of stops on the way back to the farm and put several sacks and boxes in the car trunk. It was Buddy that let us begin driving his old brown mule Kate to the cart and sled while doing hauling on the farm. Later he taught us to milk cows, plow and to work a team to a wagon. From him we learned to break and train our own horses and a few for other people. I think Buddy had more patience with kids than anyone I ever knew except my Grandmother Elliott (our Ma). He taught the kids how to farm, ranch and make things "do." The last time I saw Buddy he was on his death bed in the Overton Hospital. I was in my midlife by then, but it was very difficult to tell an "old buddy" goodbye. He was just as sweet, caring and cheerful as ever.

A few years ago Robert (my "closest" cousin) and I were sharing old times and I asked him if he remembered us going with Buddy to deliver corn shucks to Albert's. He laughed and said he was telling Modena about them just the other day when they were eating Mexican food at El Charro in Tyler. I told him it was only after my last visit with Buddy that I realized why he took us kids with him on those trips. He looked at me and asked what I meant by that. I told him that Buddy was bootlegging and we were his cover. Having a couple of white kids with him looked like he was running errands for their folks and he could stop at the liquor stores in Kilgore and not look suspicious. Robert looked surprised and said he had never thought of that.

Buddy worked for our family from the time Walter brought him to Grandma's farm until he passed on. After Grandma Jernigan died Buddy went to work for my youngest uncle, Fred, in his sawmills, lumberyards, and fixture shop. He was well past retirement age when I saw him for the last time, but he told me he was still piddling around some for Mr. Fred when he was able to do a little.

Ruby?** At a 100 plus a couple or so she was still living — on her old home place less than a quarter of a mile from Grandma's farm. After Grandma died Ruby went to work for my cousin Robert and his family. Robert bought the Browning place adjacent to Grandma's farm and developed it into a first rate ranch — Jernigan's Double R Ranch. Robert is gone now but his wife, Modena, some of their children, grandchildren and great grandchildren still live on the ranch. He is buried there in a family cemetery they have started.

Grandma's farm? Yes, it too is still in the family. When Grandma died, Auntie inherited it. On her death it passed to her only surviving child, Jack Spear. Our family tends to hold on to property. At my old home place, I have children, grandchildren and great grandchildren living there. The great grandchildren are the sixth straight generation to live on that property and the seventh generation to live at Leverett's Chapel.

My, my, what memories a taste or two of hot sauce can bring back.

Could be they started selling Albert's Famous Mexican Hot Sauce in grocery stores as a staple in 1940 — I have heard tell it is sold in maybe nine states now.

*Adapted from the story as read by the author at the East Texas Historical Association meeting in Nacogdoches, September, 2013

**Ruby Square Thomas passed away in a nursing home June, 2014

 # VISITING IN THE 1930S*

As a child growing up some of my fondest memories are those of my family and some aunts, uncles and cousins loading up and going visiting. My maternal grandmother was the ringleader, deciding when where and how. Her big Buick was the lead car, and then probably ours and maybe another one, determined by whom all were going. Grandma never learned to drive so someone in the family always drove her where she wanted to go. These visits were usually for at least two or three days at a time. We took a lot of special food and things — especially bedding for the kids to sleep on the floor.

One of my favorite visits was to see the Hinkles. They lived a little way out of Carthage on a farm. The visits I remember extended from when I was a small boy of four or five and lasted until the last visit I remember when I was about twelve — the beginning of World War II.

Two or three times when we visited the Hinkles, he was operating his syrup mill. This was a special treat for the kids. I looked eye to eye with the old red mule that walked around in a circle that made the press work which squeezed the juice out of the ribbon cane. I wondered what the mule was thinking but he never gave me a hint.

I also enjoyed watching Mr. Hinkle work in his blacksmith shop. To me it was like watching an artist at work. He seemed so engrossed in the task at hand that you felt as if you needed to hold your breath while you watched. Each movement was so sure, precise and accurate. As the result of the work emerged you felt as if you had contributed.

Mr. Hinkle also had a large woodworking shop where he made all of their furniture, handles for tools and things like that. He also had a little sawmill where he cut lumber which he used to build things such as his house, barns, workshops, sheds and pens. I think Mr. Hinkle must have made everything on that farm. When he was working on a project, you knew you were watching a master craftsman at work.

Quilting was also a big thing at the Hinkles — she had a special room for sewing and quilting with a quilting frame hanging from the ceiling. Both of my grandmothers had a similar set-up in their homes where the women sat around the frame, quilted and talked.

I'm sure the Hinkles had first names but I never heard any. She always called him Mr. Hinkle and he always called her Mrs. Hinkle as did our family.

I always thought the Hinkles were related to the Jernigans, Elliotts or Griffins since we visited them as other relatives of my Mother and Dad's. In 1991 my Mother passed away. The night before the service, we had family visitation. Cecil (a Hinkle son — the one we were closest to) his wife and a sister (Kathryn) came through the receiving line. As I introduced them to my wife I told her these were dear family members but I really didn't know how we were related. At this point Kathryn surprised me saying that we were not related at all but were closer than family! She then proceeded to tell my wife and me how our families had become so entangled.

My grandfather had a sawmill near Overton and was in town to get supplies for the mill and food to feed the hands. As he was coming out of the general store he was approached by a young man who had just gotten off the train and still had a suitcase in his hand. He asked my grandfather if he could recommend a rooming house where he could stay while he was looking for work. My grandfather looked him up and down and said if it was work he was looking for he had plenty of that at his sawmill. He could help Grandpa put the supplies in the wagon and they would go to the mill — where there were living accommodations for the workers. Mr. Hinkle left with Grandpa and a strong bond was made. A few years later my Grandpa died and Mr. Hinkle started his own family and prospered but the families always stayed close.

Another favorite trip was the one to Houston to visit my Mother's uncle Willis Jernigan and family. This was the only brother or sister of Grandpa

Jernigan's that I remember ever seeing. Evidently uncle Willis and Grandpa had been very close and the families remained so since Grandpa died in 1931 and the visits to see uncle Willis that I remember were during the mid and late 1930s. The Jernigan son and daughter's families from Houston continued the visits to the July 4th picnics at Grandma's Farm until the end — about 2005.

Since uncle Willis lived in the city of Houston, there wasn't the spread like at the Hinkles — but they had a large house and a very interesting garage with an attached workshop. There was a good sized backyard fenced with a chain link fence which they called a "hurricane fence." There were lots of trees, grass, and tables with benches and chairs.

Uncle Willis was a streetcar conductor/supervisor. The kids loved loading up in a streetcar on a Sunday and uncle Willis driving us on a ride around town. He would tell us stories about people and places as we discovered Houston.

It would be hard to decide if the streetcar rides were the highlight of our trips to Houston or the trips to the Houston Ship Channel where he taught us to "crab" — as he called it. Back in the 30s Houston was large but nothing like today. It didn't take long to get to open spaces along the Ship Channel where kids could run wild.

Uncle Willis would load up his car with kids, tie the crab net to the passenger side door handles and off we would go. He would find a place to park which would look like a bank on a lake and here we would crab. He always had a big ball of twine, a large piece of dry salt pork, and of course the crab net. He would cut pieces of string about ten or twelve feet long, then cut off pieces of the pork. We always had to taste of it to be sure it was really salty. Then he tied the pork to the string and found a good place to tie the other end to a tree, rock or bush. He would let one of us take the meat and throw it into the water. As the string got wet the line sank in the water.

After all the lines were in the water he would get the old wooden box (like an apple crate) out of the car trunk and we were ready to run the lines. He showed us how to gently lift the line to see if a crab was attached and, if so, continue to raise the crab to just below the surface of the water

— then ease the net under the crab and lift it up on the bank. What fun we had getting the crab in the box. Evidently uncle Willis knew where the crabs were since we could always fill our box in an hour or two before the youngest kids tired of the fun and we headed for his house.

In his backyard he had an old cast iron wash pot with a gas heating ring underneath the pot. He would put water from the garden hose in the pot, light the gas under the pot to heat the water. We all crowded around wanting to see the water boil but he would say that a watched pot never boils and then take us into the workshop to wash up — he had a lavatory with the hottest water and big bars of smelly soap that we learned to use regularly.

We would go into the house and report to our parents and tell everyone what had happened and soon someone would announce that the water in the pot was boiling and we would all rush to the backyard. Uncle Willis would carefully rinse off each crab with the garden hose and drop it into the boiling water. Sometimes the squeamish would gag but we enjoyed it in the main.

After a few minutes of boiling the crabs, uncle Willis would pass out plates. Then he would use a set of long metal tongs to carefully place a crab on each person's plate. After he placed the crab on our plate we would take it to the picnic tables which were covered with oilcloth and set with silverware. There was an assortment of tools on the table for each person to crack the shells and pick out the meat. We had salad and saltine crackers to go with the crabmeat. Of course the older people would dip their crabmeat in bowls of melted butter and some would squeeze lemon juice on it but most of us kids ate the meat plain and loved it. What fun!

These crab feasts weren't our dinner — which usually came about dark and consisted of sandwiches, potato salad and cookies. Instead of cold drinks as with the crab, we had cold glasses of milk with our dinner.

At least once during each visit — whatever the season — we had a fish fry. For this meal uncle Willis would take the kids to a fish market a few blocks from his house where "we" would pick out a few large whole fish from the display case with the fish lying on a bed of cracked ice. Uncle Willis would point out why one fish would be better than another and not always dependent on the size. It usually took two or three of us boys to "tote" all the wrapped fish to the car and then to the backyard. Uncle Willis did all the preparation and cooking in the backyard. He would always explain that the lady of the house did not allow fish to be cooked in her kitchen since it smelled up the whole house.

Uncle Willis got his wash pot ready — but instead of water as he used for the crabs, he used cooking oil. We mostly just watched as he got things ready to prepare the fish for cooking — but he explained what he was doing and why. Believe me he kept our attention as he used his cutting board and big knives. We watched him cut off the heads, cut up the fish, wash each piece and flop it around in his pan of corn meal which he had sprinkled in all kinds of seasoning to flavor the fish. Every few minutes he would drop some batter or a fish morsel into the pot to see if the oil was hot enough to begin cooking. Uncle Willis always cooked the fish out in the backyard in the spring, summer and fall. We ate there also — picnic style on the tables with their oil cloth coverings and the benches — much like our crab feasts.

When the weather was too bad to eat outdoors, we would eat our fish in the house. The older adults ate at the large dining room table which must have seated about twelve. The rest ate at card tables in the living room with the youngest ones in the kitchen. The host family women didn't sit much because they were busy serving food and seeing after the children. There was always a lot of talking and laughing — happy sounds except maybe a dissatisfied little kid every now and then.

During World War II, my Dad was in the Marine Corp and stationed at the Navy Blimp Base in Hitchcock as the brig warden. In the summer of 1944 Mother and I worked on the Naval Base — she in the Civilian Personnel Office as a secretary and me, at the age of fifteen, as a clerk in the Public Works Warehouse. We were relief workers for the regular people to take a summer vacation. We didn't get to nearby Houston much due to the gas situation but one time we were there and I noticed a road that looked familiar. I asked Mother if that wasn't the way to uncle Willis' house. She said it was but it would be better if we didn't just drop in. She went on to explain that uncle Willis was having trouble with his memory and it upset him to see people he should know but couldn't recognize. He also lived in the past and told long boring stories — he could have been suffering from the then unheard of Alzheimer's.

And speaking of long boring stories — just remember, after all, I am related to Uncle Willis!

THANK YOU!

*As read by the author at the Texas Folklore Society meeting in Fort Worth, February, 2014

HOW I CAME TO BE IN EAST TEXAS

I have never been really interested in the genealogy of my family as usually practiced by most people, but I have always been very interested in the family stories that have been passed down in our family — I call this my family lore. I remember hearing my great uncle Harry (Grandma Jernigan's brother) tell us stories he had heard from his parents and other relatives about the Civil War. He could relate stories hours on end to us children when we would be at Grandma's. Uncle Harry lived with Grandma Jernigan for several years after the death of his wife. He had been injured in a sawmill accident many years before that, and was almost blind with his vision deteriorating further when Grandma took him in to care for. I think the accident had occurred while he was working for Grandpa so she felt some responsibility for him other than just family. I think she supported him for a long period of time even before his wife died because they were living in "their own house" on Grandma's farm when I first remember him.

My Mother told me that she had also gathered much of her information from Uncle Harry about her grandparents and others. She also told me that when she was a little girl and they still lived at her birthplace at Leverett's Chapel, her grandmother Griffin lived on a piece of property next to them and Uncle Harry with his wife and a child or two sometimes lived with his mother. Across the road on a large farm lived her aunt Ida (her mother's sister) who was married to Charlie Christian. The three siblings were very close and would spend time visiting together with their mother. My Mother said that as a little girl she recalled them sitting around the fireplace and talking. She would stretch out nearby on the floor and listen to them. In the summer time they would sit on the front porch during the evening and talk. From my Mother I learned most of my family lore.

Besides Grandma's brother Harry and her sister Ida, I think there were at least two other brothers and one sister (sometimes I get the Jernigan and Griffin relationships confused). One brother lived in San Francisco and was a policeman. Some of the family visited him and his family in California during the 1930's but lost contact after that. They said he wasn't much interested in family ties so they didn't push it. The other brother was Henry and a veteran of the Spanish-American War. He never married and had health problems from his military service the rest of his life. He spent most of his time in veteran hospitals and just hanging around the rest of the family. The other sister, whose first name I don't recall, married a man named Barber. I know she had a daughter named Grace (after Grandma Jernigan) and a son named Ernest. Grandma helped raise Grace and Mother said that after Grace married (a Woolley) that Grandma always helped support Grace and her family. I remember a son of hers named Horace that came and lived with Grandma while he attended high school in Tyler (and maybe some business college) until he went into the military service for World War II. Mother's cousin Ernest is the one I remember most.

She had at least four cousins in the Christian family. There was Gordon who lived on their old home place at LC and had a feed store in Overton. I worked at the ice house next to his store (in the office and on the dock) while going to Kilgore College. I found out he had a reputation for hitting the bottle regularly but evidently he hid it pretty well and took care of his business. The other male cousin was Clarence and seemed to do pretty well with his investments but died fairly young. He and his wife lived in Henderson (close down-town) and had two girls, one my age and one younger — there was also a still younger boy, but I did not know him.

The two female cousins lived most of the time at the old home place although both were married. One married a man named Dean and had two sons, Charles and Don. I never knew the husband but I knew the boys (taught Don in the fifth grade at Overton). The other cousin, Bonnie, married Esque Proctor, a preacher/teacher. Proctor was a real character and we all liked him. They never had any children and I don't think Gordon and his wife did either. The Dean boys ended up with the Christian LC property and Charles's widow still lives there.

Ernest Barber lived on his Grandma Griffin's place next to Grandpa

Jernigan's farm while his family increased to three children. The youngest was Hazel, she was three weeks older than me — we started first grade together and graduated from high school together. We haven't always been really close but have kept in contact over the years. She now lives at Leverett's Chapel across the highway from my home place on the south side of the school. Sometime during her school years, her family moved to a house on the property east of the school. Hazel has told me that the house they had there was built by my Grandpa Jernigan — I am assuming it was part of the property he had built and developed when he was planning to move his sawmill to LC. Her dad Ernest was an interesting fellow. He volunteered to take the school census for LC for a long, long time — maybe fifty or more years. There is a plaque in the school somewhere that tells how long. I remember him as a school bus driver. Since bus driving was a more or less part time job most of the drivers did something else also like farming, carpentering, house painting, etc. Earnest was a rancher but he ran his cattle on what was called "free range." He didn't have land for them to pasture on and just let his cattle wander. He would drive around in an old battered pickup and check on them — feeding them some hay or fodder in the winter. After many years this was outlawed and he had to find fenced land to lease or buy. Eventually he ended up buying my great grandfather's original farm from my uncle Fred who had gotten it in the division of property following Grandma Jernigan's death. Hazel inherited part of it when her mother died. She recently sold her part as her brother and sister had done so that farm is no longer in the family.

My Grandma (Jernigan) and her sister Ida (Christian) looked enough alike to have been twins except one was larger than the other and now I don't remember which was the larger. I recall a time that several of Mother's family was visiting her aunt Ida — maybe the aunt's birthday — and a bunch of us cousins were there. Grandma and Ida, along with a couple of other adults, were in the living room sitting around talking while the rest were in the kitchen and dining room and the kids playing outside except for me, the oldest "kid" there — hanging around listening to the elders. In came this little kid, probably Auntie's Jack — running straight to Ida and crawled up in her lap. With tears running down his face he told her that the big boys were picking on him. She patted him and said something to console him, he looked up at her and in a shocked voice said "you're not my grandma" — jumped down, spying the other "grandma" across the room ran and jumped in her lap. They may have looked alike but they didn't sound enough alike to fool a grandchild.

Those are some of my memories about my Mother's relatives on her mother's side. How they got to East Texas makes an interesting story about my great grandmother and great grandfather Griffin that came through my Mother and Uncle Harry. Great grandmother Griffin was born and grew up in New Orleans. She was a fourteen or fifteen year old school girl when she began to notice great grandfather Griffin. I didn't say "met" because of the circumstances of their noticing each other. He was a private from Illinois in the Union Army doing his duty as part of the occupation of New Orleans near or at the end of the Civil War. He served as a sentry or guard at an Army office on the route to her school. Every morning on her way to school — and every afternoon on her way home — she saw him and soon he started noticing her. As young girls often do, she started smiling at him and may have let a wink or so slip. After a while he began to make sure he was standing near the fence when it was time for her to go by. They began to pass "good mornings" and "good afternoons." This was South meets North and the intrigue was there. They began to visit after their salutations and he took a smoking break every now and then. This visiting went on for a year or so. When his enlistment came to an end and he was ready to go back home to Illinois, he went to great grandma's home and asked her father for her hand (marriage). Her father told the young soldier that she was not old enough to consider marriage, but to come back in a year and they would discuss it then. Her father probably thought that would be the last he would hear from that Yankee.

Well, my great grandfather Griffin left for Illinois and Iowa — since he had family on both sides of the river. He settled into farming and learning the trade of a foundry man (metal worker, close kin to a blacksmith), preparing a home, etc. A year later he returned to New Orleans and repeated his plea for marriage. This time he was successful, they were married and left for Illinois/Iowa.

Things went well for a while and they had a couple of children. Great grandma (now Griffin) began to miss her home in the South and wanted her children to grow up there. Great grandpa Griffin didn't like the South any better than she liked the North. They finally compromised on Texas. He had a friend who had settled in Tyler so he wrote to this friend asking how well he liked it there and did he think there was opportunity for a foundry man in that area. Receiving a positive response on both counts they made plans to sell out and move there. This was a long move with household goods, tools, farming stuff, etc. — I don't know for sure but I think a lot of it was made on the riverboats of that day and then by wagons. They ended up in Tyler but found that by the time they got there another man had opened a foundry. No way was there enough business for two in the same town.

They looked around and decided to settle in Overton. He purchased a lot to build a home and business on for them to raise their family. He was a hard worker and after getting his business underway, he bought some land near present day Sexton City to develop into a farm. In his spare time he was clearing this land and during one winter he caught pneumonia and died. This left his wife as a widow with six or seven young children, no relatives nearer than New Orleans, and had been in the community for only a few years. She made up her mind to stay put and try to raise her family alone. My Grandma was four years old when her dad died. Times were tough.

There were a few people who didn't want him buried in the Overton Cemetery since he was a Union veteran, but his wife persisted and he now lies there with two other Civil War veterans, both CSA Army. Great grandmother Griffin began working as a nurse for families in order to feed her children. The older children tended the younger while she worked and somehow she did a good job of raising her family. No wonder most of these children were very close for the rest of their lives.

I never knew any of my great grandparents while they were alive. Today Joyce and I have four great grandchildren, two boys and two girls — all offspring of our three Blanton grandsons. They range in age from seven to twelve and not only have we been fortunate enough to know each — but we saw each on the day they were born or the following day — and as far away as Fort Worth and Corpus Christi!

When I was about eleven years old we moved back from Tyler, where we had lived for two years, and be at LC again. Dad had promised Sonny and me that we could have horses when we moved back there. Of course we had spent a lot of time at Grandma Jernigan's during the past two years with Tony and various other ponies and horses but this meant having our very own. Dad had been shopping around the Wagon Yard in Tyler on Saturdays and had bought two horses to be delivered to our place at LC.

We first saw the horses in their pen behind our house at LC, one a three year old black female was to be mine and the other, a two year old black and white male (fixed) paint, was to be Sonny's. Dad said we could name them whatever we wanted so we thought about it for a while. He had explained that my horse was a little pigeon-toed but he would have her shod and this would correct the front feet. I decided to name my horse Pigeon — (like the bird but because of the feet, I guess). Sonny insisted on naming his horse Tony. We also got matching new saddles — called youth size — and bridles. Sonny's horse was raised as a pet so it really took to the idea of being ridden but mine was something else — which could be another story.

We took Pigeon to Mr. Bennett, a blacksmith in Overton. He put shoes on her and she walked fine as long as we kept shoes on her. My Dad talked to Mr. Bennett for some time after he had paid him for the shoeing. I didn't pay much attention to what was being said since I stood by the trailer with Pigeon. After we drove off headed to LC Dad said he had asked Mr. Bennett if he knew the history of his place. He had told Dad that as far as he knew it had always been a blacksmith shop since that was what he had been told when he bought it several years previous. This location was about two and a half to three blocks east of the railroad and on the south side of the highway headed toward Sexton City. Dad said that my Grandma Jernigan had told him once that she thought this was the location of her dad's metal shop and their home where she was born. He explained to me that would have been my great grandfather Griffin's place — probably changing hands several times since my Grandma was born there. I can find no trace of the shop at this location now so I think there is no physical evidence of the Griffins left there now.

I will stop here about the Griffins, my Mother's maternal grandparents, and move on to the Jernigan's story — her other grandparents. The Jernigan grandparents both originated from Alabama. I don't know her story, but he and his siblings were first generation Americans. His father and younger brother (his uncle) had immigrated from England to New York City in 1821, his father being twenty-one years old at the time and the brother seventeen. During their stay in New York they were separated on the city streets and for three weeks the older brother searched for the younger one. He never saw nor heard from the brother. In his searching he found out that his was not a unique case. The people there, including the police, seemed to take it for granted, since it happened so frequently.

While searching for his brother he met a man from Alabama who took a "liking" to him and offered him a job at his place. They returned to the man's home and he worked for him a few years and got his "start." He married, became quite well-to-do, and acquired a plantation complete with slaves and a large family. Mother's grandfather, Stephen Decatur, went to the Civil War at age fifteen or sixteen, he had older brothers that had preceded him and not all of them came back. When the war was over, he and a brother returned together — his brother had left a young family behind. They found their parents had died and everything in ruins. Stephen Decatur married the girl friend he had left behind. He and the brother decided to move to California where the war had not been so devastating and there was more opportunity. They pooled their resources and left via the southern trail for California. When they entered North East Texas, Stephen Decatur began to notice how close the countryside appeared to resemble his old home place in Alabama — the pine trees and red soil. They stopped for a few days near Kilgore to rest their teams and themselves. They had come a long way and had a greater distance to go. The younger Jernigan fell in love with the area and decided to stop there, put down roots and raise his family — it wasn't California but it was TEXAS. The older brother decided to continue the journey toward California. The brothers parted, never to see nor hear from the other.

The older brother got as far as Ranger, Texas when his wagon broke down and it was necessary to rebuild it. While doing the work on the wagon he took ill and was incapacitated for some time. After he was well and able to travel he decided to settle in Ranger since he had come to appreciate the kindness of the people during his illness and liked that part of the country.

He nor his brother were ever in contact with the other but sometime later my Mother's dad (Grandpa Jernigan along with his son Walter) drove an ox wagon from Grandma's to Dallas or Fort Worth for the celebration of some store's anniversary — a publicity stunt with parade and all. Some of the relatives in Ranger read the story in an old newspaper later and contacted Walter to find out if they were kin. They made the connection and the families were in contact with each other. I remember Mother and Dad visited some of them in 1950.

An interesting footnote to the selection of their new homes by the Jernigan brothers is that in both cases the land they chose turned out to be good oil producers. Neither of the brothers profited from the oil but the families of each did in time. My children receive some small income from my great grandfather's land even today — when my Mother passed away my brother and I decided to let the inheritance jump to our children.

Stephen Decatur Jernigan selected a farm site about a quarter of a mile due south of the present day Leverett's Chapel School. Next to families like the Sextons and Christians — today's Sexton City (in name only since there is no town there now) the namesake of the former. He, his wife and children (as they were added to the family), worked and developed their land as early settlers in frontier America had done for generations. The work was hard, the life was tough. In 1882 the wife, and mother of several children, died.

She was buried in Pirtle Baptist Cemetery alongside a previously deceased infant daughter — called Baby Mary by her siblings. My grandfather Jernigan was eight years old at the time.

Leaving his children with neighbors, great grandfather Jernigan returned to Alabama and married an "old maid schoolteacher" who had been a child-hood playmate of his and his deceased wife. They returned to East Texas and she helped him raise his children. After his death in 1924, his widow decided to sell her share of the property (one-half of his estate that she inherited) and return to Alabama.

Grandpa Jernigan and a friend, Charlie Christian, were raised on adjoining farms, married sisters, and each purchased farms adjoining each other some mile or so, as the crow flies, north east of the farms where they were born. In order to help out his stepmother, Grandpa purchased her interests in the estate and eventually bought out the rest of the children's interest. At the time it appeared to be a bad investment but in the long run it turned into a very good one. He and Charlie Christian seemed to be successful in their business dealings.

This original farm remained in the family for another seventy-five years or so. I remember that after we moved back to LC from Tyler, my Dad had a grocery store on our property facing the highway across from the school. Mrs. Carter's restaurant and home combination was on the corner next to the original road (now named Don Leverett Rd) and the store. The old Jernigan farm was about half-way to Sexton City on the opposite side of the highway from our property. Fred, Mother's youngest brother, owned the old farm at that time and had leased it to Dad. As part of the operation on the farm, Dad had several acres cleared and planted in tomatoes. He had them picked, packed in bushel baskets and we hauled them to a packing shed in Jacksonville. As the price soon fell (as produce does when in plentiful supply) it wasn't profitable to pack and ship the tomatoes. He placed a handmade sign on the highway which advertised "Tomatoes For Sale — You Pick .50 BU — We Pick $1 BU" with an arrow pointing to the field. This was my first experience in the world of work. It was my job (after school and on the weekend) to stay in the field, collect money and pick the tomatoes if the buyer desired. It wasn't hard work but it was tiring and boring. I kept a box of Morton Salt handy and ate a lot of tomatoes — some seventy plus years later I still don't care for tomatoes.

Thinking about the business places at LC and Sexton City, I am amazed at the difference in that period of time and today. Currently there is not a single business place at LC. About the time I was selling tomatoes, LC had two restaurants — Mrs. Carter's that served only a family style lunch (the forerunner of the now popular all you can eat buffet) but also Flossie's where you could get almost anything at any time of the day or night (plus a hamburger stand on the school side owned by my Dad), two grocery stores (one that sold gasoline and also ice), a service station (where you could buy kerosene and such), kind of a hardware store that had a mixture of new and used merchandise and a barber shop with two barbers. Sexton City — about a mile south and at an intersection of highways — was even larger. It had three service stations (one with a garage for major car repairs), a large café (and a couple of smaller ones), a barber shop with three barbers, a lumber yard with many tools and hardware, and other types of business that I can't recall at this time. One thing I do remember very well was the swimming pool. It was a private enterprise but rivaled Kilgore's municipal pool in size and quality — it only lasted a few years. Today, not a regular business exists at Sexton City — only a once a month "trade days."

But LC and Sexton City are not the only places in East Texas that have seen radical changes over the years. Pirtle, where the cemetery mentioned above is located, is another prime example. Today's Pirtle community is located about two to three miles due east of LC on both sides of Highway 259. If you go east from Sexton City, you run dead-end into Highway 259. This area, for as long as I can remember, was always called Pitner's Junction. Today there are no signs indicating there was ever a Pitner's Junction. If you go north on the highway, in a mile or so you see a small highway sign that reads Pirtle Community. The scenery is very pastoral and you think — community right. This has not been the case forever.

A recent article in the Longview News-Journal (Vol. 81 No. 317) has a very interesting (to me) story about a Pirtle Community church celebrating its 165th anniversary. When the church was founded in 1847 the community was called Belleview and had a population of 631. Among other things it had an academy, four churches, a cotton gin, four stores, hotel, saloon, and a blacksmith shop. The name of the community was changed to Pirtle when, during Reconstruction around 1869, the post office was being confused with another town named Bellevue. Pirtle's population was later reported to have been much more than many of today's large Texas cities at that time.

Besides having part of my Jernigan family buried in the Pirtle Baptist Cemetery, I have one relative buried in the Pirtle Methodist Cemetery. She was the mother of my great grandmother Griffin. I have lost her name now but was shown her grave by Auntie after my Mother passed away. After she was widowed in Louisiana she moved to East Texas near the end of her life. She was living with a grandson in the Kilgore/Peatown/Danville area when she passed away. They were taking her by wagon to Overton to be buried with the Griffins, but it was in the heat of summer, they decided her body wouldn't make it — so they stopped at Pirtle and buried her in the Methodist Cemetery.

Now you can find the Pirtle Baptist Cemetery pictured on the internet (or go there in person) and looking through the entrance you see the meeting area ahead and on the right are grave monuments. The Jernigan graves are located here. Knowing their headstone shapes, you can easily pick them out since one has a ball on the top. One of the very first times I was there I noticed the ball was loose, could easily get dislodged and lost. I bought some epoxy glue and fastened it securely to the main part of the monument — it is still in place today. Grandpa and Grandma Jernigan with Auntie, my Mother, Dad, Sonny and others (now including my Joyce) are buried in the Jernigan plot in the Overton Cemetery. This plot is located to the right just inside the main entrance to the east section. We have markers in the plot for David and me. Our daughter Susan has another plot, on the front west end, for all of her family. Most of the older Griffins are buried here in the Overton Cemetery but scattered and more difficult to find.

My Dad's relations moved to Texas later and came from closer states than did my Mother's. His mother, always called Ma by members of our family, came with her family from Mississippi by wagon when she was five years old. She told us grandkids stories of her "walking to Texas" with her brothers and sisters. They brought their cows, pigs and chickens with them. The children herded the cows and pigs during the day and the chickens rode on the wagon. Ma, my source of information about her family, told us that she would ride on the wagon with the chickens and take naps. The Reynolds family settled in Central Texas, Robertson County, near present day Franklin. Her family settled in as pioneers and did well as farmers.

Her mother died when Ma was eleven, her father married a younger woman and had a second set of children, making Ma's family rather large. Ma said the children got along fine but she and her stepmother had conflicts as Ma grew older. She never did run away from home but she thought about it.

My Dad's father was born in Louisiana near the border with Texas on property that is now covered by the Toledo Bend Reservoir. This property belonged to my Dad's grandfather Elliott. He told me that one of his uncles showed him the gravesite of his great grandfather in the nearby woods after his father had passed away and before the reservoir was built. His grandfather and all of his uncles with their wives now lie in a large plot in a nice, well-kept cemetery a few miles into Louisiana near where the old home place was located. After Sonny and I were married and away from home, Dad and Mother had been going every year or two to this cemetery for their annual clean-up and dinner-on-the-grounds the Saturday before Memorial Day.

The spring after Dad passed away Mother received a post card addressed to them reminding folks of the week-end event. She showed it to me and said my Dad always looked forward to this get-together since it gave him an opportunity to visit some of his relatives. I told her that I would like to go if she thought she could find the way. After we told my brother Sonny, he too wanted to go. Mother made arrangements with a cousin of Dad's that lived near Carthage for us to go by and pick her up. When we got to her house, one of her sons was ready to go with us also. I remembered both from days when I was a little kid and we used to go to visit Dad's uncle (her father) to spend a week or so fishing on the river. She was better informed about the relatives and knew most of the people at the cemetery — where her father was buried. We had a very good time visiting and sight-seeing. I was very impressed with the cemetery and the people I met. Actually I have never enjoyed eating at a cemetery but I usually "make out." I was really surprised when I saw my great grandfather's headstone — a huge one with a Confederate flag embossed in color and citing him as a defending Colonel of the CSA. He had five sons buried in the same plot — the sixth one and youngest, my grandfather, is buried with Ma in Williams Cemetery in Smith County only a few miles from his home where he had lived with his family.

This trip to Louisiana meant so much to me that I decided I would spend the rest of that Memorial Day weekend visiting the grave sites of my other great grandparents. Spending the night at my Mother's on Saturday, the next morning I made the trip to my great grandparents Griffins' graves in the Overton Cemetery (about four blocks down the street from Mother's house) then to the Jernigan's' in Pirtle. I had lunch with my mother-in-law (Mrs. Petty) in Kilgore and then left for Kingsville. Robertson County was on my way home. I had gotten directions and the cemetery name for my Reynolds great grandparents from my Mother who had been there only a time or two. Her directions were somewhat unclear — yes they sometimes change roads as they have done in East Texas since I was younger. To make it worse, there were two cemeteries with almost identical names — neither exactly matching the name given me by my Mother.

I finally found an older fellow also looking at graves in one of the two and asked for his help. Turned out he knew some of the family and told me it was in the other cemetery. He insisted on showing me how to find the graves. I would never have found them without his help. It turned out that my great grandfather had a wife buried on each side of him — my great grandmother on one side and his second wife on the other. Originally my great grandmother was buried in another plot nearby but not in the Reynold's plot. Some of her children had her moved next to her husband (and their father) after some years. I left for home feeling quite satisfied that I had spent a very worthwhile holiday week end.

Leaving my great grandparents for the time being, we go back to Grandpa Elliott. Being the youngest in his family I guess he had a little more freedom and less responsibility than his siblings. When he was about eighteen he joined up with a small group of young men and followed the "cotton picking trail." They would go by horseback and wagon to the south of Louisiana as the cotton would ripen for picking, and pick for payment by weight. As a group they could do better in contracting the work for the growers and assure themselves steady work during the season. This group would pick east to west and west to east in Texas and Louisiana and end up in the Panhandle of Texas, or as far as Oklahoma.

It was customary for the community to have a dance on Saturday nights while the cotton pickers were visiting their community. While Grandpa Elliott was at such a dance in Robertson County, Texas he met this fascinating girl a couple of years younger than him. It may have been love at first sight.

A month or two later when he finished the cotton picking circuit he returned to Robertson County and proposed marriage. He hung around a week or two then they were married, he acquired a wagon and team for them to use in going to Louisiana for Susan D. Reynolds Elliott to meet her new family. They spent the winter in Louisiana and in the spring they moved to Tyler, Texas. Grandpa had used his cotton picking trip to pick the place where he wanted to settle down. They bought a section of land about seven miles east of Tyler and a little bit south. This property is just east of Chapel Hill (now named New Chapel Hill so as not to confuse it with Chappell Hill, Texas).

Grandpa and Ma had nine children that I know of — two that did not survive into adulthood. One died in infancy — I was named Floyd after this son — and the other as a teenager from the flu during World War I. The oldest, a son, was called Boss by his siblings (nieces and nephews also) but Son by Ma, his given name was Kay. The next was a sister named Effie but called Sister by the siblings (this must have been a custom in East Texas since my Mother was called Sister by her siblings and she too was the oldest daughter). The next four children were boys — Oliver (always known to everyone as Bug), Allen, Albert (my Dad), and Fred. Joy was the baby of the family and Ma called her Baby during her lifetime.

When a new highway was built from Tyler to Henderson it ran about a fourth of a mile north of their farm so the family bought a parcel of land on the north side of their property fronting on the highway. Grandpa built their second home on this land facing the new highway. This is the old dog run house that I remember so well with Ma living there, many times alone. Grandpa Elliott died when my Dad was fourteen so Ma spent a long period of her life as a widow. Sometime in the late 1940s or early 1950s Allen and my Dad tore down the old house and built Ma a new small modern frame one. Alan was manager of a lumber yard at the time and Dad was doing some house building. They were the most prosperous of the siblings and wanted to help their mother. Not all but some of both pieces of these properties still belong to different members of the family. My Dad still owned a few acres up until a short time before he died and asked me if I wanted it. I had several properties scattered around at that time and didn't need more to worry about so I encouraged him to sell it off, and he did.

Ma lived to be ninety-five years old but spent the last couple of years in a nursing home. While we were living in Kingsville, Joyce and I were at Tyler for some reason and decided, on a spur of the moment, to go by the nursing home and see Ma. She had no way of knowing we were coming by since we didn't until a few minutes before we got there. We asked directions to her room, knocked on the door and walked in. Ma raised her head, her eyes brightened and she said "Well, Joyce and Floyd, what a nice surprise." We were astonished that she recognized us — and so quickly. That was the last time we saw her alive, she died just a few months later. We were certainly glad we made that decision to visit her when we did.

THE HOUSE AT LEVERETT'S CHAPEL

Leverett's Chapel always seemed to me to be a busy place, especially since it was so far out in the country. The East Texas Oil Field was in full swing by the time we moved back there from South Texas (some 500 miles plus). When I started to school there in 1934 mud was everywhere you looked. I guess I was a little used to Raymondville where it seemed dry and dusty all the time. We had lived almost in the middle of town in Raymondville and there were dusty streets for blocks in all directions from our house. There were oiled roads everywhere at LC but not many paved ones. Those that were not oiled were muddy most of the time due to the fact that heavy equipment was always being hauled over them and deep ruts were formed.

I don't have any memories of the LC House from the first time I lived there since I was very, very young when we moved there and left before I was three. I do remember a lot of things after we moved back since I was there for the first and second grades. I remember sitting on our front porch and watching the highway department pave what is now State Highways 42 and 135. It had different numbers then but the highway ran from Gladewater to Kilgore, then to Laird Hill, LC, Sexton City, New London, Turnertown and then intersected with what is now highway 79 running from Henderson to Jacksonville. This road ran through a lot of the East Texas Oil Field.

The LC House was built in 1928 — the same year I was born. We were living at my Grandpa Jernigan's sawmill about seven miles east of Tyler at that time. The sawmill was not only the business but was also called a lumber camp where most of the employees and families lived together. The nearest community to the sawmill, as far as I know, was Bascom. Now most of that area has been taken into the town of New Chapel Hill. As was the business procedure for most sawmills in those days, it was necessary to relocate them after a number of years so the logs for the sawmill didn't have to be hauled so far. Grandpa Jernigan had decided to move the sawmill to Leverett's Chapel — which would be the third location for the mill (the first was Jamestown about a mile northwest of Overton). LC was "home" to his family since his original farm was about a mile northwest of there — where his children were born — and he was born and raised about a short mile southeast of there at his dad's original farm. Grandma had been raised in Overton and one of her sisters and family lived across the lane from their farm and her widowed mother on a twenty acre plot on the south side of their farm.

In preparation for the relocation of the mill, Grandpa bought from the Leveretts the thirty acres in the southeast corner of the Overton/Kilgore road and the west boundary of the school property — which the Leveretts had donated to the school.

He also purchased additional land on the east side of the school with a creek running through it. This was to be the location for the sawmill since it was necessary for water to operate the boilers for the steam engines of the sawmill. He started construction on a new home on the thirty acres — this was so the new home would be on the main road. By this time Grandpa had two mature sons taking over responsibilities for the sawmill and a very dependable son-in-law (my Dad) who he depended on a lot. His time was spent in locating and buying timber, selling lumber and contracting building projects.

When the new house at LC was about finished, a man came to see him at the mill and told him he had a section of land covered with a lot of timber he wanted to sell. The location of the property was about twelve miles west of Kilgore. At this time Grandpa didn't want any more land but he did need timber and this was only about eight miles from the mill. Grandpa found the place did have a lot of good timber on it and surprisingly a great creek on it that could be dammed in a couple of places for very good mill ponds. He liked this property very much and began to see the possibilities it offered for a sawmill site due to the location. There were other factors at work also that he was taking into account. Moving the mill eight miles rather than twenty-five by wagons pulled by oxen and mules was one factor. But there were others.

His father, my great grandfather, who originally settled at Leverett's Chapel from Alabama, had passed away. Before he died he had asked Grandpa to build him a house in Kilgore since his health was failing and he would be near a doctor if he lived there. Great Grandpa bought the northwest corner lot at the intersection of today's Main St. and Henderson Blvd. and Grandpa was building him a house on the property. As the elder Jernigan's health was deteriorating during the construction of the house, he and his wife moved into a rooming house on the southwest corner of the intersection of Houston St. and Henderson Blvd. — now on the campus of Kilgore College. Just before the house was completed the father passed away. He was buried in the Pirtle Baptist Cemetery — south of Kilgore and east of LC. This death at that time had presented some legal problems for Grandpa due to the family history. His dad left half of his estate to his then current wife and half to the children.

Grandpa's mother (the mother to all his siblings) passed away when the children were quite young. This left his dad with several children to raise, just a few neighbors and no family he knew of closer than Alabama. He left the children with neighbors while he went back to Alabama. He looked up a childhood friend (now an "old maid" school teacher) of his and his deceased wife, married her and brought her to Texas. She did see to the raising of the children and the duties of a farmer's wife. But evidently she had enough of Texas and wanted to go back to Alabama and see after her widowed mother. She asked Grandpa to buy out her interest in the property so she would be free and endowed enough to leave for good. Grandpa agreed and they were able to work things out to her satisfaction. Now Grandpa was the majority owner in his father's estate but it took a few years to buy out the other siblings. After this was settled, he found that he had a sawmill that needed moving, a newly acquired thirty acres of prime property at Leverett's Chapel with a newly completed home, his large family farm about a mile to the northwest and his father's farm about the same size to the southeast about the same distance — as well as property for the sawmill site about a half mile east of the thirty acres. Then there was the Kilgore property that sat vacant for a number of years while he cleared up his individual ownership.

One of the other factors at work was that Auntie (Mabel) the youngest girl wanted to go to high school. The closest high school to the current mill site was Tyler and none closer to Leverett's Chapel or the now being considered mill site than Kilgore. None of the older kids had been interested in high school until Auntie had finished Bascom and now wanted to go to high school. Fred, the youngest son (a couple of years younger than Mabel) would be following her if he was interested. Mom said Grandpa told them many times he would help the kids get as much education as they wanted or could use.

Grandpa's work role had changed from the day to day running of the mill so he didn't necessarily have to live there since he was in and out. Also he saw he was going to need some help with running the two farms at LC, whether or not the mill was moved there. This was taking place during the spring of 1928 as best I can tell now — looking back — since I wasn't born until August that year and my sources of information have all passed away. The plan developed from this situation was: Grandpa, Grandma, Auntie, and Fred would move to the new house at LC when school was out so they would be closer to Kilgore; during the summer they would see to finishing the house in Kilgore; and then move to Kilgore in time for the kids to start school for the fall semester. Grandpa went ahead and bought the new place and firmed up the plan to move the mill to it. Walter and Charley (the two older brothers) and their families would stay at the old mill place until ready to move the mill and then they would also move to the new mill place and run it. Ruby, the middle daughter, had married by this time and moved away. Dad was still working at the old mill site and he and my Mom were living there. After I was born in August we would move to the LC house after Grandma and Grandpa moved to Kilgore. Dad would run the two farms at LC and help Grandpa with the lumber business. This plan took some time since a new mill site with housing for most of the employees had to be developed as well as move the sawmill equipment. Most of the housing and buildings from the old site was torn down and hauled to the new site.

I am sure the mill move was a huge undertaking at that time. I just never talked much about it with anyone to know the details. It was only the last few years of my Mother's life that I found out a lot of family history. After she passed away I got most of my information from Fred and Auntie. They told me about their short stay at LC while they were getting the house in Kilgore ready to move into. Today that Kilgore property is in the middle of town, but at that time they built chicken houses, a barn and horse pens for Fred's pony and Grandpa's team of mules he had for the wagon, as well as, a garage for the car. Auntie said that they went back and forth to Kilgore in the wagon from LC while they were working on the house. They got to paint their own rooms and part of the house — and Fred said he guessed they did a pretty good job since Grandpa had him paint the barn, chicken houses and garage.

When the Kilgore house was completed they moved into it and Auntie attended Kilgore High School, graduating in 1931.

When Grandpa and his family moved from the LC House to the Kilgore house, we moved into the LC House (which would later become more or less our permanent home) after I was born and the move from the old mill site to the new one.

Unfortunately for our family, my Grandfather died rather young (1931) and Grandma was left with two children at home. Fortunately though, Grandpa had accumulated considerable property and the East Texas Oil Field covered a lot of it. Some was to produce oil for over eighty years. But Grandma was living in town — Kilgore — and it was a wild boomtown as the stories have been told. She said she couldn't take the things that were going on around her house so they packed up and moved to the new mill property — and she never moved again. Grandpa had built a new house on the west side, a mile from the mill site, about a year before he died. This was to be a permanent farm home for the property since the housing at the mill was a more temporary type. At this time the oil field had about taken over the properties at LC. This home, near the new mill site and on the new farm, came to be known as Grandma's — all the grandkids spent many happy summers and holidays there. The two big events each year — Christmas and the July 4th picnic — saw the very extended family gather there from near and far.

The house in Kilgore remained in the family until after World War II — I remember my aunt Ruby living there in 1946 — but eventually it was moved a little north on Lawrence St. and the Kilgore Hospital was built on the site (this building does not exist now after the new Laird Hospital was built on South Henderson Blvd). The house still stands — if you turn north off Main St. on Lawrence it is the first house on your right. The house on Grandma's farm, the LC House and the Kilgore house all started as the same basic plan — today none of them resemble each other. The house on their old home place, as my mother called it — the original farm home for Grandpa Jernigan and his family — no longer exists. It was destroyed by fire a few decades ago as it sat vacant.

So my little story about my "home" at Leverett's Chapel actually turned into a story of three identical houses that each has its own story. Most of these properties still remain in the family. Grandma's farm is now owned by a first cousin and the LC House by my daughter. At this time all my children and grandchildren live on the property at LC. My great grandchildren now living there are the sixth generation to live on that piece of property and the seventh generation at Leverett's Chapel.

At some time there had been a house a little north of our LC House — also facing the Overton/Kilgore road. One time when I was about eleven or twelve years old, we were working in the yard on the north side of our house and I found some old bricks just below the surface and my mother told me that was where an old well had been filled in many years before. The well had been on the back porch of a house which had burned around the beginning of World War I and was never rebuilt. I was told this was where some of the Leveretts lived at that time.

The road on the north side of our property began to lose importance as the oil field developed and the one on the east side of our property took on more importance.

This being the one that was paved by the Highway Department and became a primary artery for oil field traffic and continues to amaze me with the amount of heavy traffic it carries today.

Not long before the highway on the east side of our property was paved, mother had my dad build a large concrete porch on the east side of the house and here he placed the main door into the house. When they paved the new highway, mother was ready with her new entrance. It was a number of years before she got her colonial columns and roof on the porch but she was patient.

When the front porch was completed — it really did dress up the house. Not long after, the brick and wrought iron fence was built in the front of the house. We also had a concrete fish pond in the front yard with a waterfall over native rock and "goldfish" that grew to be as large as a foot in length. In 1939 when we moved back to LC from Tyler, a lot of remodeling and improvements were made to the house. It was not until 1957 that the large den was built on the west side of the house and the entire house was bricked. The house structure has remained about the same since that time.

About the same time my Dad made the main entrance on the east side of our house, he also extended and closed in the front porch on the north end and made three bedrooms and a bathroom from the space. This was done so they could rent rooms to the single school teachers who needed housing out in the country. At this time all the men teachers had to be married and all the women teachers had to be single — in line with the school district policy. The school board also had rules about dating when it came to the women teachers. If a teacher had a date, it had to be on a Saturday or Sunday, and Sunday dates could only be to attend church services.

There were a lot of rules and regulations concerning teachers back in those days and seem a little foolish now but evidently made sense at that time.

It would have been necessary for the school to provide a teacherage if families had not been willing to help out by providing rooms for teachers and in some cases also provide "board." My family was blessed with the companionship of many young teachers as a result of this arrangement. Many of the teachers who lived in our home while teaching there, later married or moved closer to their hometowns to teach but many of them remained lifelong friends of my parents and they kept in touch for many, many years. One of our dearest friends, Ellen Rhode from New Braunfels, came fresh out of college to teach at LC and a few years later married Randolph Watson, a principal at Laird Hill School. World War II came along and Randolph went into the armed forces, Ellen followed him when she could. After the war he came back and taught at Kilgore College, then was dean and served for a long period as president. Ellen still lives in Kilgore and we see her every now and then at the grocery store. There are many more that have a similar story to tell because the oil field schools had the money during the big depression to pay good salaries to teachers to come there and teach. The oil field drew some great teachers, as well as great individuals, from south, central and west Texas to our schools and colleges that benefited all of East Texas.

As I indicated above, the LC House was more or less our permanent home from the time I was nearly a year old until I married. After living there a short time we moved to Raymondville for a period of three or four years where my younger brother Sonny (Albert Minor Elliott) was born. We moved back to the LC House sometime in the spring or summer of 1934 and remained there until I finished the second grade. We then moved to Lebanon, Tennessee for Dad to attend Cumberland Law School for a year. We then moved to Tyler where I attended the fourth and fifth grades at Gary Elementary and we lived on Glenwood Blvd. We then moved back to the LC House and lived there through the Second World War except for the year we lived in Corpus Christi while my Dad was serving in the Marine Corp. I was away attending college some of the time after I graduated from high school but came back home a time or two. After Joyce and I were married in 1948, we lived in the garage apartment for the summer and then went away to college. When my Dad reached retirement age they built a new home in Overton (now the parsonage for the First Baptist Church) and moved there for the rest of my Dad's life. Joyce and I purchased the LC property from my parents in 1972 and now it has gone into the hands of our children.

The LC House, along with approximately ten acres on the north end of the LC property, is home to our daughter Susan and her husband John Blanton. Our son, three grandsons and five great grandchildren live on other portions of the LC property. This week, July 15, 2014, we buried my beloved wife of sixty-six years. I will be moving into the apartment in the north end of the LC House so my daughter and son-in-law can "see after" me. Did someone say you can't ever go home?

RAYMONDVILLE

How or why we ended up in Raymondville, Texas around early 1931 I don't really know. I remember hearing stories about living in Raymondville after we had moved back to East Texas in 1934 and I have some remembrances of my own about living in Raymondville, but I don't remember my parents or any other family member explaining why we moved there. So I just take it as part of life and go from there.

Actually, the more I think of it, I have quite a number of remembrances from the three years plus that we lived in the Valley. Sometimes I have trouble as to which to refer to — the Valley or the Wild Horse Desert. Raymondville was both to me since we had a farm in one direction from town that was irrigated for raising vegetables and in the opposite direction a large ranch, neighboring the great King Ranch, for raising cattle. I used the term large because in just the last few years my cousin Robert Jernigan and I were talking about our memories of Raymondville. He said his dad made many references to "Albert's (my Dad) seven thousand acre ranch" and that he wished he had been able to get it back from the purchaser. My uncle Charley and his family took over the management of the farm, house, and service station when we left Raymondville but evidently not the ranch. I remember visiting them later when I was eleven or twelve years old and he also had an Oliver tractor dealership. Later when I was about fourteen or fifteen, he had sold out in Raymondville and moved to a large ranch near Blanco where I went to deer hunt some until about the time I got married.

To me the farm was the Valley and the ranch was the Wild Horse Desert. The remembrances that first come to mind for each are not pleasant. As for the farm, I remember wagonloads of onion and cabbage piled up rotting — the smell terrible — and my Dad telling the foreman to quit harvesting the vegetables because there was no market for them. I didn't understand then, but later I learned that the Great Depression had reached the Valley by 1933. As for the ranch, it is riding my pony in the heat, clouds of gnats about my head (the animals also), the choking dust and the mesquite thorns tearing at your arms, legs and head. Every now and then you would suck in and swallow a few gnats trying to breathe in the dusty air.

Maybe these memories from when I was five years old are reasons that I never wanted to be a farmer or rancher. But there were others, many others that were happier and more pleasant. I try to dwell on these as I remember this part of my early childhood. It seems that most of my early childhood memories come from when we were living in Raymondville — little snatches or vignettes in no order or time arrangement. For instance, I have this clear memory of my sleeping on the backseat of our car and us on the way to East Texas for a visit. In Refugio they had some drainage ditches in downtown which were effective speed deterrents also. Dad failed to slow down for one and I was pitched off the seat to the floor. I was reported to have asked him was he trying to bump me out of the car. Was this really a memory or have I heard this story told so many times that I could remember it as a memory? There are many more like this but they are remembrances so we will treat them as memories.

Another "memory" that I can visualize due to the retelling of the story in front of me many times involves me in the barber shop with my Dad. Dad was in the barber chair getting a haircut when the local Texas Ranger entered without my Dad seeing him. The barber was stropping his razor getting ready to shave around my Dad's ears and neck. The Ranger and Dad were great friends and he wanted to play a prank on Dad. He motioned to the barber to be quiet and took the razor from his hand and went to Dad's back. Fortunately he turned the razor over with the dull side against my Dad's ear and said, in a much disguised voice, "I'm going to cut your ear off." Well that was enough for me — I jumped up, ran to the Ranger, grabbed his leg and buried all my teeth in the back of one of his thighs. My Dad was motionless with a razor pressed against his head, the Ranger let out a yell, dropped the razor to the floor and turned to see this little four year-old clinging to his leg. Everyone had a good laugh but me and the Ranger — the prank turned out to be on him. Well, as the story goes, he and I did get to be buddies later and his nickname for me was "holy terror."

That story reminded me of another law enforcement officer friend of my Dad's. Luther Snow ended up as the long time sheriff of Willacy County. He was not yet the sheriff when we first lived in Raymondville and evidently was in business with, or worked for, my Dad. I remember hearing that he lived with us for some time before he was married. In the late 1960s, after we had built a new home and moved to Kingsville, my Mother and Dad came for a visit to see our new home, school, etc. Besides a tour of the campus and King Ranch, dinner at King's Inn, and other local attractions, I usually took visiting fireman to Brownsville, crossed the border and had dinner at the "Drive In."

We wanted to give my folks the full treatment — but of course the name led the guests to expect an American style drive in. This "Drive In" was really something else. It was a very special upscale family type dining club that you entered through a very nice shop — and here was an elegant supper club restaurant, tuxedoed waiters, an orchestra, a small dance floor — the works. The décor was colonial Mexican (somewhat elaborate) with many brightly colored birds in cages built into the walls. The food was great — all the border specials served just right. Of course the surprise was part of the treat — but let me get back to the Snow story.

As we were driving south on 77 through the sand dunes of the Wild Horse Desert and nearing Raymondville, I asked my Dad how long had it been since he was in Raymondville. He said that in 1950 he and my mother bought a new car and took a driving vacation to Mexico City and stopped for a visit in Raymondville. Mother spoke up and said they had spent a couple of days in Raymondville and Dad had nearly talked his head off while they were there. I then asked him if he wanted to drive through town or go around on the bypass. He eagerly said it wouldn't do any harm to "look around," so we did. As we were going through downtown he said if we had time he would like to stop and get a Coke at a run-down looking restaurant he pointed out. We stopped, went into the business, sat at a table near the door and ordered our drinks. Dad looked around a minute or two and then was up talking to the cashier. When he came back to the table we saw her pick up the phone and call someone. Mom asked him what that was all about and he replied that he simply asked her if Luther Snow still came in there for coffee.

In less than five minutes in came this elderly gentleman with a big six-shooter on his hip, this large western hat and came straight to our table. He grabbed Dad in a handshake, put his left arm around Dad's shoulder and they beamed at each other. He then turned to Mother, kissed her on the cheek and said "How are you Miss Lillian?" He pulled up a chair and Dad introduced me and my family to him. In a couple of minutes in came another man similarly attired and came to our table and we saw the same act repeated. This gentleman — didn't sit down — he suggested that he, Dad and Luther move to a larger table over behind us. They did and in just a few minutes at least five or six more old timers were at that table after they had spoken to Mother and been introduced to us. Mother's only comment was that news of the older set surely did get around fast in Raymondville.

After about an hour of this my kids and wife were getting restless but Mother was used to it since my Dad visited with everyone no matter where he went. So I took it on myself to go over to this group and suggest that we needed to be going on our way. We did get away pretty soon and had a lovely evening in Mexico. That night on the long drive back to Kingsville I asked Dad how he had liked his dinner. He said it was probably the best meal he had had in in at least a decade or two but nothing could be better than getting to see Luther Snow. That was his way of thanking me for making the stop in Raymondville.

It was, and still is, a long trip from Raymondville to East Texas. At that time it was longer since there was no highway down through the Wild Horse Desert across the King Ranch from Kingsville to Raymondville. We had to go west from Raymondville to a little place called Red Gate and then go north. But we made the trip at least four times a year — Christmas, Easter, 4th of July and early fall — Thanksgiving being so close to Christmas.

Members of my Mother's family visited in between these times. My grandfather Jernigan passed away not long after we moved to Raymondville so when Grandma came to visit she was accompanied by at least one aunt or uncle — usually more since Fred was only about fourteen or fifteen when we moved to Raymondville. One of the stories Dad used to tell on Fred was that when he learned we were moving to Raymondville Grandma saw him out in the yard cryng. When she asked him why he was crying he told her that with us way down in Raymondville without him to protect Floyd, Sister (my Mother) would beat him to death. No wonder Fred was always my favorite uncle. My Mother was very strict with me but not mean. My cousin W. A. (Elliott) and I used to argue about whose mother was the strictest — I usually conceded that Aunt Maggie had Mother beat a little since I used to visit with them and see her in action with W. A. and Kelley — she would sometimes also get after me with a switch — of course I always needed it.

When Grandpa, Grandma, Auntie and Fred moved to Kilgore for Auntie to go to high school in Kilgore, we moved from the sawmill to the LC house. Fred had a horse that he kept at their house in town. Mother and Dad would tell that it was nothing unusual for Fred to ride his horse out the six miles to LC two or three times a week to see us.

Right after we moved to LC, I was about eighteen months old, Fred came out one day to get Mother to bring me to town since there was a man with a Shetland pony making kid's pictures on it. She did and that picture is one of my all-time favorites. But the story didn't end there.

Fred was so taken with the pony that he convinced Grandma that she should buy the pony, tack and all, so that she would have it for all the grandkids to share. He promised to care for it and help all the little ones (that would be coming along) when they rode it — and on and on. After a couple of days of begging, Grandma gave in and bought the pony, tack and all.

Tony, as he was already named, was well trained — could do tricks too. He became part of our extended family and when Grandma and Fred moved to Grandma's farm, Tony went right along. By the time this took place, the two girls had married — Ruby to Carl Jeter and Auntie to Margene Spear (both from old families in Kilgore). Tony lived on Grandma's farm for the next twenty-five years teaching thirteen grandkids and scads of small friends a little horse sense.

It wasn't long after we moved to Raymondville that I ended up with another pony. I don't know for sure but I think someone offered it to Dad because their child had out grown it and Dad didn't want to hurt their feelings by refusing to take it. Compared to Tony this new pony wasn't much to look at. Where Tony was about forty inches tall, a sleek shiny black coat of hair, a tail that nearly drug the ground, a beautiful mane and a forelock that tumbled down his face on a large blaze, this new pony was about six inches taller, thinner and strung out more — kind of gaunt looking. She was rather a mousey color with a scrubby mane and tail of some kind of dirty, moldy brown color. And to top it all off, she was lame in one hind leg. She kind of drug this one hind leg and it kept her from trotting or running at all. Of course this turned out to be a blessing for a three year old who didn't want anyone to lead "his horse."

It was love at first sight on my part when Dad brought this mangy looking pony to our house. She had the most tired and lonesome looking eyes I still believe I ever saw. Somehow she must have sensed that her feedbag depended on me so she made friends very fast. I called her my Tony and Dad explained that Tony was a male name and she was a female. That was pretty deep for me but Mother came to my rescue. She said that Toni was a girl's name and she could be my Toni — and that was settled, then and there, she was my Toni. She came with a bridle, saddle and blanket; ready to ride right out of the box, rather the truck. Dad led us around the block before he put her in the barn for the night as it was supper time. I could hardly eat due to my excitement. I wanted to sleep in the barn with my Toni but for some reason my parents wouldn't hear of it.

We lived right in the middle of town — or so it seemed — a block or two north of the main street (highway) running east/west and maybe two or three blocks east of the main street (highway) running north/south — as well as I can remember. Town wasn't much back then, mostly strung out along the two highways which seemed to be paved while the other streets were made of a mixture of caliche and oyster shell. Our house sat on a lot that must have been at least a half block in size. Besides the house and double garage on the front part, on the back we had a barn with pens on three sides, a chicken house with at least two pens and a machinery shed with about four slots for vehicles and implements. My Dad always kept at least one horse in the barn and a truck with cattle frames to haul horses in — I don't remember seeing horse trailers back then. We had chickens as most people did in those days and I ended up with an orphan lamb that someone gave me — but more about that a little later.

Of course there was no way a three year old could take care of a pony, much less saddle, mount and ride by himself. I spent a lot of time pestering my adults and anyone else I could find to saddle my horse and put me on her. It wasn't long after getting the pony that I was turned loose on the town — could go all over the place unescorted after I was mounted. It was a different world then and can never be the same. My mother was a stay-at-home mom (as most wives then) but also the bookkeeper, payroll clerk, and secretary/receptionist for my Dad's businesses which included the farm, ranch, Texaco service station and I don't know what all else. We had a cook/housekeeper who cooked lunch and cleaned the house a little six days a week. She had a family of her own and a husband who worked when he could get some. She came to work about nine in the morning and left about three in the afternoon. She didn't have much time to mess with me and my play.

This is where Marveena entered the picture through the back door, literally. Christina, our cook, was Marveena's aunt (her mother's sister) and the two families lived next door to each other about two blocks from our house on the same street headed away from town. The mother of the two sisters, a widow I presume, lived with Marveena's family but they were so close and back and forth all the time it was difficult to tell who lived where. I think the grandmother took care of the kids most of the time. Marveena's mother did ironing at home for several families — including ours — and may have worked some for other families in their homes.

Christina had a rule that her kids could not come to our house where she worked and any messages would be delivered back and forth by Marveena. Marveena soon found a lot of excuses to come to our house and entertain me. She was a skinny eleven or twelve year old when we moved there, very active and my parents told me later that she was rather attractive as she got older. I soon came to adore her and she wanted to take care of me all the time. She was a big help for my Mother, especially when Mother was pregnant with my younger brother. Her English and manners were very good so Mother felt she was a good influence on me although the rest of her family spoke Spanish in front of me and I began to pick it up. She called Christina "Tia" and I soon picked that up too. I'm sure some visitors in our house that heard me call her Tia (aunt) thought "no way." I came to be kind of a part of Marveena's extended family and spent a lot of time at her house with them.

Marveena helped me do things that I couldn't do myself, such as saddle my horse, feed and care for it — and other things such as feed my baby lamb its bottle. She taught me how to get on my pony by leading it to the front steps, walking up three or four steps at the end and getting in the saddle. To get off, I rode up to the end of the steps and stepped off on them. I had a place by the water trough in the barn where I could tie Toni and she was ready for a ride as long as someone saddled her for me in the mornings and unsaddled her in the evenings. Things were really going my way. I felt like I was conquering my world.

My lamb grew into a young ram and he got quite rough in his play that Marveena and I taught him. I still called him Lamb since that was the name I had given him. After a while he started butting people for no good reason other than just to be ornery and get attention. This was the same time that my Mother was expecting my brother. As soon as he was born my uncle Charley (Mother's oldest brother) brought my Grandma Jernigan down to "take care" of Mother and the baby. This was when my world began to come apart. Everything was revolving around that baby. My Mother, my Grandma, my Dad and MY Marveena only had time for the newcomer and pushed me aside. Charley, noticing that I was rather unhappy one evening, took me out to check on my Lamb and my Toni. While we were at the barn Lamb butted Charley not once but a couple of times and my uncle got really mad at him.

That night as Dad and Charley were talking about Charley's leaving the next morning to go back to East Texas, I heard Dad say he would appreciate it if Charley would take care of Lamb when he left. Charley said he would put him in the trunk and drop him off at the ranch on his way. I was still surprised the next morning to find my Lamb gone as was Charley. No one would tell me what happened until finally the next day Tia told me that Mr. Charley had taken him to the ranch so the hands (cowboys) could have a bar-b-que. Of course she had no idea how much that crushed me. I cried for hours. Finally I got Marveena to saddle Toni for me. I took off on my horse for the ranch as best I knew how to go.

I went by my Dad's service station and didn't stop for a soda pop as I usually did and was headed out of town instead of toward home. Fortunately the man who ran the service station saw me go by and phoned the house. Mother got word to Dad and by the time I was out of town a little way, here came my Dad driving up behind me. Well you can well imagine what happened when I told him I was going to the ranch to live with Lamb and not coming home. After my spanking he made me ride Toni back home with him following us in his truck. I think the thing I remembered most was that my Mother told me later that night that the next time I wanted to leave home just tell her and she would pack me some clothes. Life can be tough on a five year old. But things can also get better.

I recall that it was in Raymondville that I made my first friend and playmate other than relatives. About a year after we had moved there, one afternoon as Marveena and I were playing in the yard a maid from one of the houses from the block behind us walked up with a little boy by the hand about a year younger than me. She told Marveena that her employer (she called the name but I can't remember it now) wanted her to ask Mrs. Elliott if her little boy could come over and play with Joey. Marveena ran into the house and got Mother while I starred at the two through the fence. I had seen the little boy in his yard as I rode by on Toni but he would always run and hide from me. Mother came out and there was a three way discussion among the maid, Marveena and Mother. It was decided I would go play and that Marveena would go with us and bring me back home after thirty minutes.

From then on Joey and I were great friends. I am reminded of this friendship frequently by reading Dennis the Menace in the newspaper with his friend Joey. Joey, being younger, followed me around and wanted to do whatever I wanted. Of course I let him ride Toni, pet Lamb and other of my big boy things — even sharing Marveena. We had lots of fun and many adventures. You don't easily forget your first real "best friend."

Sonny, my brother Albert Minor, was born on April 1 and by the time Marveena's school was out for the year, she was tired of the baby and back spending most of her time with me. My world was filled again with whirl wind activities. We had a lot of things going on around home, Marveena's house and other activities. One thing I remembered many years — even dreamed about it for a long time — occurred about this time. Mother took me with her to a party and left the baby at home under the care of Marveena. I think it must have been a party for Mother's Sunday school class, or some women's club — that was held on a ranch out in the country. It was all women and some children. While the women were in the living room of the ranch house a teen aged girl took us children out in the front yard to play — leaving the infants in a bedroom under the care of another teenager.

The caretaker showed us a horse pen to the side of the house and told us not to go near it since the horses in it were wild. She then took us back to the front yard and we started playing as kids naturally do. The girl became interested in what was going on in the living room and sat on the front porch watching those activities through an open window. One of the boys — about eight or nine and probably the oldest one — looked at me and said "let's sneak around to the pen and watch the horses." I reminded him we weren't supposed to and my Mother would probably spank me if I did. He called me a sissy and headed for the pen.

I followed him as far as the corner of the house and watched him as he crawled through the fence and did something to make the horses run around in the pen. I saw him walk toward one of the horses standing and looking at him. The horse let him get fairly close then wheeled and kicked with both hind legs. One of the hoofs struck the boy on the side of the head and he slumped to the ground and the horses went to the far side of the pen. I was so frightened I didn't know what to do. Finally I ran to the front porch to the girl and pointed toward the pen. She jumped up, ran to the fence, saw the boy on the ground and ran screaming into the ranch house.

It was sheer bedlam for a few minutes, everybody running every which way asking what had happened. I told them the best I could. From somewhere two men appeared, opened the gate and ran to the boy. Three women were at the gate sobbing, two of them were holding back the third to keep her from going into the pen. The two men carefully picked up the boy, carried him out the gate and eased him down on the ground again with the women crowded around. The rest of us stood around and watched in silence. In a minute or two one of the men stood up and walked toward us and said for us to get out of the way for he was going to drive a car up to the boy. We all went toward the porch and watched as the man drove the car to the pen. Again the two men gently picked up the boy and placed him on the backseat as a woman slid in from each side and sat on the edge of the seat. The two men jumped in the front. They turned the car around, drove down the lane to the road and sped off in a cloud of dust. We could see the dust cloud for a mile or so. As people began to go back into the house, get their things together and leave, I asked my Mother where they were taking him. She told me they were taking him to the hospital so the doctors could take care of him. We didn't say anymore but got in our car and headed home. After a long silence and lots of driving, I finally got up enough nerve to ask my Mother would the boy be alright. She reached over with her right hand, grasped my left knee and with tears in her eyes said we certainly hoped he would be alright and that we would pray for him tonight.

When we got home Mother told Marveena what had happened at the party. She went home and I am sure she spread the word to her family. She was back in a few minutes and said that my Dad had come by while we were gone and left a message with Marveena that he had to go somewhere for some feed or something and would be late coming in so not to wait supper on him. She had forgotten the message when we got in due to all the excitement. Mother asked Marveena if she wanted to stay and eat with us and she readily agreed. I think Mother was in need of some company.

After we ate our meal, I dressed for bed. Marveena went home and Mother had the baby in her arms and went with me to my room. She knelt by the bed, laid the baby on the side of the bed in front of her and motioned for me to kneel beside her. As I got in position she started praying. I think this was the first time I ever heard my Mother pray. She paused and asked me if I wanted to ask God to help Daryl get well. I asked her what do I say and she said I could just repeat after her. She said this short little prayer, letting me repeat after her — Dear Lord….please use your power….to help Daryl….get well. Amen. I had not heard what his name was until we had this little prayer session.

This must have been the first time I had prayed anything other than the child's Now I Lay Me Down To Sleep… prayer. I think I must have gone to sleep saying his name to myself, over and over again. I never did find out what happened to Daryl. I didn't remember anything about a funeral. I did ask my Mother about this incident a year or so before she passed away, but she did not remember the details — too much water under the bridge by this time I guess. That kind of pushed me in the direction of trying to recall as many memories from my childhood as I could. Most of my "family lore" had come from my Mother during her later life as we visited at her retirement home after my father had passed away and I had semi-retired. I intended to write some of it down before it was lost but I should have started sooner while my parents, aunts, uncles and other family members were still alive. Now I have to rely on the stories I have heard from the past.

When I was trying to recall if I remembered anything about a funeral for Daryl, I realized I couldn't remember going to any funeral until the fall of

1944. In August of that year I turned sixteen while I was working at the Hitchcock Naval Air Station where my Dad was stationed at the time. When Mother and I returned to East Texas for my senior year at L C, I enlisted in the Texas State Guard. The minimum age was sixteen and I served for the last year of high school until I left for the University of Texas. My company was located in Overton and I was the only one from L C in it but I served with several boys from Overton that we played football against each other my junior and senior years. Pete Fuller was one of these and we were active in the First Baptist Church as kids and then again after we were both retired and moved back to East Texas. We renewed our friendship and spent some time recounting tales of our exploits as soldiers in the TSG. One of our memories was the many funerals we took part in as part of the honor guard. By this time in World War II the armed services were returning many of the fallen service men to the US for burial. Our company had the responsibility (and honor) to supply the men for the military part of the services in a good size area of East Texas. We talked about the great number of services we were a part of and that we missed a great deal of school. Of course we also remembered the numbers of times we stood in the rain with water running down our backs or in our faces looking toward heaven and firing our rifles (loaded with blanks) pointed at the sky.

The first "civilian" funeral I actually remember attending was for Gene Weaver. Gene and I started school at L C together and graduated together. But graduation was where our paths separated forever. Gene and I were the two youngest boys — as well as smallest — in our class and due to this we kind of stuck together. His dad was also our scout master. Gene, Lester Hickman, Perry Taylor and I were kind of a group in our class because we all went to the same church in Overton while most of the other boys were Laird Hill or Kilgore oriented. I was the only one of our four that participated in sports. Lester, Perry and I were the only boys in our class to go off to college after graduation, most of them going into the service or for a semester or two at Kilgore. Perry and Lester both went to Baylor while I went to the University of Texas in Austin.

Gene's parents gave him a Model A Ford for graduation. Where they got it I have no idea — but it was a beautiful little roadster, looked like new. Our graduation ceremony was in the afternoon so our evening was free and activities were limited. To prove his manhood Gene somehow got a bottle of whisky and about nightfall was drinking on a street corner in Overton. Some of our friends tried to take Gene home. Being quite drunk by this time he said he would drive himself home to show them he wasn't drunk. He made it about a half mile out of town, ran off the road, the car hit a culvert and tossed him on his head. His service was held at our church in Overton and he was buried in a cemetery at Corsicana. I was a pallbearer and we went as a group in Glendee Honzel's car for the burial. Glendee drove exceedingly fast all the way there and back; but I will always remember it being one of the longest trips I ever made.

I am pretty sure most of my memories about our living in Raymondville are during the last year we were there since we moved soon after I turned six years old in August. One of the very vivid memories I have was never told, as far as I know, by my Dad to me or anyone. But — I remember it very well. One day my Dad asked me if I would like to go with him the next day to help "work cattle" at the ranch. This got me very excited and of course I wanted to go. He explained that we would take our horses, leave very early in the morning and not come back till after dark. After I had settled down some he explained that the ranch foreman's wife had suggested it to him and wanted us to come out and have a ranch hand breakfast with them. He also explained to Mother that she said as soon as I tired I could stay with her in the ranch house. This made everyone happy.

The next day before daylight, Dad saddled and loaded "our" horses, waked me and we went to the ranch. It was just getting daylight when we parked near the ranch house where the hands had gathered with their horses and gear ready to go to work. We all went into the ranch house and sat around a long table while the lady brought out the food. Everything was going great and we were putting food on our plates when Dad, helping my plate, put a biscuit on it. I looked at it, turned it over, and looked at it again.

It didn't look anything like my Mother's fluffy buttermilk biscuits. I looked up at my Dad and probably in a very clear voice asked what was wrong with this biscuit. I still remember the silence and then my Dad asked that we be excused for a minute. He took me by the hand and led me to the front porch. He squatted down in front of me, looking me straight in the eyes, he explained to me that we were guests in this home and the family was giving us the best they had — we should be grateful to them and not hurt their feelings. I thought it was time for my spanking, but he patted me on my shoulder and said lets go eat breakfast. I was so ashamed I wanted to duck my head and run to the truck. Instead, Dad took me by the hand back in, we ate, and everything went well the rest of the day. I tried to be as nice to that lady as I possibly could that day and every time I was around her. This memory has popped up so many times in my life I know it certainly served a useful purpose for me and I hope it did not hurt or affect anyone else as deeply as it did me. I have not been kind to everyone during my life, but in most cases I have surely tried.

In trying to piece my memories of Raymondville together I have found many gaps and now I have no one to turn to for help. I have patched together a little scenario; based on my recollections, which I hope does not injury the truth or memories of any one too much and will share it with the reader.

I am assuming that Grandma Jernigan was involved financially with Mother and Dad in the business activities in Raymondville. This partnership was probably begun by Grandpa before his death and it continued after he passed away. There were a lot of financial situations that he had dangling when his early death occurred. Mother's oldest brother, Charley, took over the control, more or less, of the estate and for a while ran Grandma's share. The estate consisted of the sawmill and farm where they were living, at least two farms at Leverett's Chapel as well as the property on both sides of the school, a few other tracts of land scattered around that he had purchased for the timber on them, and the investment in the Raymondville properties. Walter, the middle son, was farming and supervising some of the sawmill activities. Fred was still in school and Mother's two sisters were involved in being married and starting families.

With the oil field coming in big, it started producing some income for all the children and quite a bit for Grandma.

My Mother began to be somewhat dissatisfied with living in South Texas. Being in East Texas at our "place", which she had inherited on Grandpa's passing, was a great pull. The schools in East Texas, due to the oil field, had become some of the richest in the world while those in South Texas were some of the poorest in the state. The family was very close and she wanted to be near them. I am sure my Dad had many of the same feelings. He was deeply involved in Raymondville but by this time the economy there was getting pretty rough on everyone — if it had not been for my Mother's oil income they would have probably gone bankrupt. Evidently the operations in East Texas were not going too well either since the economy was in a poor condition at that time except for the oil. Grandma was losing confidence in Charley's handling of the business — she had to bail him out on a deal or two — and she began to make the decisions.

By 1934, Mother and Dad had decided to sell out in South Texas and move back to East Texas. I would start school in September and Mother had made up her mind it would be at L C. Grandma and they decided to split up the property in South Texas and she would retain her interest and move Charley and his family to South Texas to manage it. He had been involved with it some with Dad. Mother and Dad took the ranch and service station while Grandma took the farm and house in town. Charley ended up buying the service station from Mother and Dad and they sold the ranch to someone else. We moved back to L C in time for me to start school in Miss Percy Lander's first grade classroom. Charley, his wife Evie, sons Richard and Robert and Mrs. Smith moved to the house in Raymondville. At that time they had been living in a home in Tyler, which they returned to off and on over the years. Richard was about four and a half years older than I and the oldest of my Jernigan cousins. I was next in line after Richard; then William, Walter's son a year younger than me, and Robert just four months younger than William.

The three of us — Robert, William and I — became very close over the years, more like brothers than cousins. Richard had been attending school in Tyler. Robert, due to how his birthday fell on December 24th, started two years behind me and one year behind William. Maybe I was a little slow developing and small in size because we all seemed to be "right along together."

After we moved back to East Texas in 1934, I was not sure what took place in the Valley until sometime, probably in 1939 or 1940, we went to visit in Raymondville — Mom, Dad, me and Sonny. I was old enough to know some of what was happening during the visit. I knew that Robert and his mother were at Grandma's and had been there for a while. Charley and Richard were living in Raymondville and had a live-in housekeeper who seemed to run things around the house. I was aware that Mother, Dad and Charley were being careful as to what they said in front of us kids. Richard was either fifteen or sixteen at the time, driving a beat up old car that they called their fishing machine and seemed pretty much to me to be on his own. He personified to me what every boy wanted to be as a teenager.

I wanted to see Marveena as soon as we arrived on this visit. I was very disappointed to find out that her whole family had moved to North Texas a couple of years before our visit. I never heard anything from or of her.

After sending Sonny and me to bed the first night there, Charley, Mother and Dad were talking in the living room, just across the hall from the bedroom we were in. I'm sure they thought we were asleep, but being in a strange place and kind of excited with the new adventure, I lay awake a long time hearing what was being said in the living room. In a little while, I heard my Mother say to Charley that what she really wanted to talk to him about was his drinking problem and why he had dumped Evie and Robert on my Grandma. Boy — things got lively for a few minutes and I was afraid a fight was going to take place. Things got quiet for a minute or two and then someone stomped down the hall and slammed the front door. I heard Mother say she guessed they might as well go to bed. I think Charley didn't come home until the next morning.

The next day things were arranged so that Richard and I would go to their cabin on a bay near Port Mansfield, spend a couple of nights there and fish. This was great sport for me. They had a bay cabin set up with a fishing pier and had a motorboat for fishing or riding around on the bay. We had loaded the fishing machine with groceries and did our own cooking — or at least Richard did. We mostly rode around on the bay, swam some and lay on the sand listening to the radio. Richard said the fishing in the bay wasn't very good and the way to catch fish was from the pier at night under lights. We didn't get around to doing much fishing. Richard kept me entertained with his stories about school, sports, girls and such. He bragged about bringing some of his friends (boys and girls) to the fishing cabin and the things they did. It surely did make me want to jump the next four years or so in a hurry so I could live the life he described.

When we got back to town Mother and Dad said we were leaving the next morning. We got up really early and on the road before good daylight. This trip was a little different from most of our long trips. Our usual procedure was for Mother to get up really early, fry a batch of chicken and pack us a picnic basket with all kinds of goodies. We would eat our breakfast and be on our way by daylight. This time, not being at home or at a family relative with a regular family, we left early and ate breakfast on the way — as well as lunch and supper.

Since we stopped to eat a few times, gas up and restroom breaks there was some relief during the trip, but the two kids were restless except when taking a nap. Mother and Dad were never really the talkative type and were extremely quiet on this long trip. I was all ears when awake but did drop off asleep a few times. With what I picked up on this trip home, had learned in the past and found out in the years ahead, the story went something like the following. Charley had a partner in the tractor business in Raymondville. He had mortgaged Grandma's farm there as his capital and the business was sinking. Grandma was pouring money into the enterprises there and the rest of the family was very alarmed. Mother and Dad were sent on this fact finding mission and asked to see if they could straighten things out. It seems Charley had agreed to get grandma out of this endeavor as best he could by selling the properties (even at a big loss) to stop the drain on Grandma's money. He was to go on his own. It would take a year or so but this would give Richard time to finish high school in Raymondville and then go off for college. This seemed to unfold as planned (or forced) and this is when, I am guessing, that Charley moved to Blanco to start his ranching activities. I think he leased the ranch there and operated on borrowed capital. Evidently he was good at appearing better off financially than he really was.

Charley's family life was rather unsettled most of the time until later life when he married Corine — his third wife, who got him involved in her church and curtailed his drinking. Things went well for them during his first marriage until Robert was born. Evidently Evie had a bad delivery, became addicted to pain killers and was a semi-invalid the rest of her life. For some reason, after their family had been in Raymondville until Robert was about ten years old, Evie and Robert moved in with Grandma (Evie's mother-in-law). I think this was about the time Mrs. Smith passed away. Mrs. Smith, the other grandmother, had lived with them and taken care of the boys since Robert's birth. Evie remained there until she passed away a few years later. Robert was there through high school and moved out when he married.

His marriage to Modena lasted all of his life and they were a great pair. Robert, who chose not to go to college, was very bright. His grades qualified him as valedictorian of his graduating class from Tyler High School but since he had attended there only two years he was not eligible — since four years there was required. He had transferred in from a nearby country school having only ten grades.

Auntie told me in her later life that Robert was like a son to her — that near the end of Evie's life she had given Robert to her to mother. Auntie's marriage was not very successful, but she never was divorced. She spent much of her married life living with Grandma and was very close to Robert and his young family as they developed. Robert and his family (two kids at the time) moved back in with Grandma to help with the place after being out on their own for several years. Suzette, the third child, was born about this time. Robert had started a dairy herd on a farm owned by Kidd Dairy in Tyler and with the help of his high school vocational ag teacher, Mr. Ford, he financed it through the bank. When he moved back to Grandma's he built a dairy barn on her place and moved the cows with him. After several years of getting up so early (it seemed like the middle of the night to him) for the morning milking and repeating it again in the afternoon, he tired of the dairy business. He was able to buy the Browning farm next to Grandma's and went into ranching — raising beef. He eventually got involved in raising purebred cattle and was very successful. In fact both Robert and Richard were very successful in their endeavors during their lifetimes.

Robert and Modena became quite involved with French Charolais cattle breeding and as they developed their program, they began auctions at their ranch. These productions were so successful that other breeders asked them to do the same for them. This led to Jernigan Charolais Sales Management. They were very successful growing into an international operation. They hob-nobbed with a lot of well-known people — such as Bunker Hunt, John Connally and others. Some of their clients in Texas asked them to also handle ranch property sales for them. In order to do so Robert had to be licensed as a real estate agent. He went into partnership with a broker in Fort Worth who was also a Charolais breeder, learned the ropes and this too was very successful.

About this same time — late 1980s — I took early retirement at the university, teaching half-time. I had become somewhat involved in rental real estate — at LC, Austin and Corpus Christi. My son, David, was managing the LC properties after my Dad passed away. My brother-in-law Ed Petty was back in Kilgore, a licensed real estate broker doing his own developing and selling. Joyce and I had bought back our house in Kilgore from the estate on the death of her mother. I decided that we would open a real estate office in the Kilgore house under Ed's broker license and David as an agent — he had gotten some experience while working for an appraiser in Corpus Christi. At that time I started on the path for a broker license and got it in the minimum time while associated with American Realty in Kingsville. About this time Ed passed away and we moved the office to the LC properties under my license and broadened our sales activities in that office.

Robert's broker wanted to retire to the ranch and forget the real estate business. Robert, due to the educational requirements, did not want to get a broker license. He came to me with a proposition for me to cover his operations under my license. We ended up forming a partnership — under the name Lone Star Realty — housed at their ranch office in their home. Modena was a whiz with the paper work and client relationships — as in their other businesses. This too, ended up being not only successful for them but for me also. As the sales management business declined as a result of the downturn of popularity in the Charolais breed the real estate business filled the gap for them.

This arrangement lasted until 2005. In 2004 I had another heart attack, a stroke that cost me the sight in my right eye, and I decided I needed to cut down on my activities. Robert and Modena had wanted their daughter Judy to get a broker license but she wasn't interested in real estate. It ended up that Bob, the son, did and I disengaged myself from their activities. As Robert's health declined, Modena and a grandson-in-law kept up the business with Bob — who kept a full time job in computers and the printing trade along with the real estate activities.

Richard, after graduating from high school, went to the University of Texas. While he was in college, World War II cranked up. He was able to join the Navy V-12 program, graduated from UT and went on to the UT medical school in Dallas. When the war was over and he graduated from UT Southwestern Medical University, he served in the Navy for a couple of years or so due to his obligations under the V-12 program. He came back to Fort Worth and did his residency in surgery. He opened his practice in Arlington — there being no hospital there at that time for surgery, he admitted his patients to hospitals in Fort Worth. It wasn't long until they had a new hospital in Arlington and he was in on the ground floor. Several of our family members would go to Arlington to have surgery done because they felt that Richard would see that it was done right.

His girlfriend at UT was Pat and a year behind him. When she graduated they married and she went to work to help support him in medical school. Their marriage lasted through the Navy service and the rough part of his practice in Arlington — then they drifted apart and divorced. It wasn't long before he married his second wife — his nurse. They had two children and the marriage lasted for their lifetimes. Richard died in his early sixties. I have been told that this scenario is not rare among physicians. I remember my Mother was very critical of Richard when he divorced Pat but later she forgave him. She said Richard wanted a family and Pat couldn't have children — so to her he was justified.

In 1965 I began teaching at Texas A&I University in Kingsville. Joyce had been teaching at Schanen Elementary School in Corpus Christi while I was at the University of Corpus Christi. She was offered a counseling position at Wynn Seal Jr. High for the 1965-66 school year enabling her to take advantage of her certification in that field. We decided to stay in Corpus Christi for the school year and I would commute. We leased a home on Southern St. for a year and began the planning of building a new home in Kingsville — which we moved into on September 1, 1966. Before we moved she was offered her choice of three counseling positions in Kingsville for the coming school year. She chose the one at Gillett Jr. High School and served there the next twenty-five years.

During my first year at Texas A&I, my dean asked me to develop a proposal for a program to submit under the guidelines of the Teacher Corp. I did and when I took it to Washington D.C. it was accepted and funded. This turned into quite a lucrative contract for the university. Since I had developed it, I was asked to run it (probably no one else would have dared to take it on).

Since this was a large endeavor the president named me his assistant and said he wanted me to direct the research and development that was going on at the university and to expand our activities in that area. As a result I had two new titles (Assistant to the President and Director of Research and Development) and set up a new office next to the president's.

My new duties brought me into the area of university finance. We had a man in the business office that carried the title of Auditor but to me he seemed to be the head bookkeeper or financial manager. I spent a lot of time with Spike Boyle in setting up accounts and watching where the research grant money went, etc. Spike could tell me how much money we had in any account and how that not there had been spent. He taught me the ropes in spread sheets, financial reports and state regulations, etc. I became included in the business office coffee group after a few weeks of this activity. Spike was a bachelor, walked with a pronounced limp (from polio) and had his little odd mannerisms. Unlike many of the people who came in contact with him, he and I got along fine. I found out he had been crippled since a little boy and that he was from Raymondville. After graduating from high school he came straight to Texas A&I, completed B.S. and M.S. degrees, went to work in the business office and had been there ever since. His work was his life.

One afternoon about five as I was about to leave (Spike never left until six or later and was always the first in the Administration Building for the start of the work day) I asked him if he knew my cousin Richard Jernigan when he was in Raymondville. He kind of snorted and said, "Old Jernigan, yes I knew him quite well and he was some fellow." I sat back down because I could tell Spike wanted to talk about Richard. He told me his story.

Richard was a year or two ahead of him in school and evidently kind of his idol. Spike was the water boy for the football team and Richard one of the key players. They called him the Nullifier. This came about because when they were getting ready for a game the coach would say to Richard that he wanted him to nullify this or that player on the opposing team. Spike said Richard was good sized (not extra-large but big enough to take on any player in their league) fast and strong — especially good on defense. Spike said he was surprised that Richard didn't play college football because he knew Richard was offered scholarships at two or three, but Richard had told everyone that he was going to college to get an education and not to get his brains knocked about. Spike couldn't remember which but he knew Richard graduated either first or second in his class. Spike said that most of the guys thought of Richard as one of the rich kids — maybe two or three in the whole school. This was because he had his own car, always had money to eat and party on and did much as he pleased. Most of them were like Spike, hardly had enough to eat. He ended up saying that Richard was very popular with both the boys and girls.

I remembered the fishing trip Richard and I took some twenty-five or so years before and the stories he had told me. I thought much of it was probably baloney at the time and he was just trying to impress me, but after hearing Spike's story I think that most of it must have been true. I even remembered the story that Richard told me about a football game. He said during a time out the coach motioned for him to come to the sideline. The coach told him that number forty-eight was killing them

— they had to do something so take care of him. Richard said he went back in and the next play he knocked the kid out, they carried him off the field and he didn't come back in. I didn't relate any of my experiences with Richard, or the stories he told me, to Spike — but I brought Spike up-to-date on what had happened to him. I told Spike I would get Richard up-to-date on him too, and Spike wanted me to tell him the water boy sends his warmest regards to the Nullifier. At Spike's funeral a few years back, all this came to mind.

LEBANON, TENNESSEE

After spending about two years at Leverett's Chapel while I was attending the first and second grades, we made a big change. When school was out for the summer at the end of my second grade, we loaded up our car with clothes and headed for Lebanon, Tennessee. This was the location of Cumberland University. I learned that we would be there while I attended the third grade and my Dad was going to attend the Cumberland University Law School.

Cumberland University was an old and revered university, according to the Announcements for the Sessions 1936-7 — Ninetieth Year of Law School — brochure (which I still have, along with my Dad's diploma, class picture and yearbook). The university was founded in 1842 and the law school began in 1847. It, especially the law school, had a very successful history with many noted graduates. Today, if you go to the internet, you will find that Cumberland University still operates in Lebanon, Tennessee as a liberal arts university, but no law school.

Now the Cumberland School of Law is an American Bar Association accredited law school at Samford University, Birmingham, Alabama. It is the 11th oldest law school in the United States with over 12,000 graduates during its more than 160 years. I give this background information because two questions have always remained unanswered in my mind: Why did Dad go to law school at this time of his life and why did he choose Cumberland University? I didn't ever recall it being discussed by our family so I was in the dark. Being in the education business most of my life, I was particularly interested in the answers. It was not until a few years after my Dad's death that I brought up this subject with my Mother. Based on her information I have pieced together the following little story.

When my Dad finished the eighth grade at Bascom, he went to live with his Elliott grandparents in Louisiana — I think this was after his father passed away. He spent a couple of years there working on their farm and some other jobs. Evidently he didn't go to school there or after he returned home. Eventually he got a job at Grandpa Jernigan's sawmill and worked there for several years. This was the beginning of the courtship between my Mother and Dad. His work experiences, through the mill activities, brought him in contact with a wider group of people in business.

When we moved back to LC in 1934 he was in business for himself — building homes and other structures. He was working on projects in Tyler & Smith County through the Jernigan mill (Grandpa now deceased) and in Rusk and Gregg counties through Moore Lumber Co. in Kilgore. Mother felt it was the influence of one of his associates, Judge Fisher, in Tyler that encouraged him to go to college. He was thirty years old at that time and very few people that old started a college career in those years. This is where law school entered the picture. I don't know if Judge Fisher was a graduate of Cumberland University or not (in fact I know very little about him) but it evidently was well known in this area for I have found that at least three of Dad's later acquaintances were graduates. They were: James Allred (a Texas governor), Crawford Martin (a Texas attorney general and secretary of state) and Wright Patman (a U S representative from Texas). Mother insisted that Dad was not interested in practicing law but was interested in learning more about business, especially real estate, and Judge Fisher may have convinced him that law school would prepare him for this. As far as I know, he never used the law degree to seek employment or advancement.

Cumberland University admitted mature students on an individual basis and their degree program at that time was only a little over a year in length. This met with my Dad's desires and he made application and was accepted. He was successful and graduated in 1937. His never prepared for, nor took the Texas bar exam — as far as I know — seems to verify Mother's belief that he had no interest in practicing law. To me, this endeavor was for his personal satisfaction: to prove to himself that he could accomplish this goal and at the same time to improve his chances for success in the business world.

So, in the early summer of 1936, we told friends and family good bye and dropped Jack (our dog) off with a neighbor and headed to Tennessee. Evidently Dad had already made a trip or two there for the admission exams and to make our living arrangements. Now some seventy-seven years later, I am amazed at the memories that come to mind as I think back — and most of them are happy but a few sad ones too. I don't remember the trip up there or others coming back but I remember leaving LC and arriving at Lebanon.

Mother and Dad had Sonny and me stay in the car as Dad took Jack from our arms and handed him to the neighbor. Sonny, Jack and I had tears rolling down our faces as we left the neighbors. Before we were out of sight of the neighbors Sonny started crying very loud and then I couldn't hold back. Mother joined in and it was all Dad could do to keep from crying also. No one said anything for a while and the crying finally faded out and we began to talk — much more than we usually did when in the car. As we began to leave familiar sights behind we watched the scenery go by and began to ask when we would eat lunch. The trip had begun.

I don't know how long it took us (I think we spent the night on the way so we wouldn't arrive late at night) but finally Dad said we were now getting into Lebanon. I was all eyes. We drove down to the middle of town, turned one block to the left and then to the right for a couple of blocks then crossed the railroad tracks. After passing some large coal bins and an empty block on the left, Dad pointed to a large red brick home and said this is where the Bones live and we are going to be next door in the smaller two story house.

As he turned into the driveway he told us that the Bones had built the little two story house when they first got married and built the larger one as their family got bigger and they could afford a larger home. They had rented the two story over the years to others, mostly to law students at the university. He parked the car and said for us to stay in it while he got the key from next door. In a few minutes he returned with Mr. and Mrs. Bones, an elderly couple and very friendly looking. We were all introduced and the Bones escorted us to our "new home." We toured the house with the Bones serving as guides. The first floor had a living room, dining room, kitchen with a breakfast nook and an opening off the hallway led to a half-bath. Upstairs were two bedrooms and a bathroom.

The thing that interested me most was the cellar. Mr. Bones took Dad and me down some steps from a door in the kitchen and we saw chunks of coal piled against one wall, a big cast iron furnace in the center of the room, with a kind of workshop on the wall opposite the coal bin. He explained the workings of the furnace to my Dad but said it would be a while before we needed it. He then walked over to the work bench and said there were a lot of tools he kept there so if dad needed them he would have them handy. He then pointed to a leather strap hanging from the wall and said that was what he used when his kids were bad but he looked at me and said he doubted if Dad would need that tool.

While Dad and I were in the cellar with Mr. Bones, Mrs. Bones was showing Mother and Sonny the kitchen and how to work the stove. It was furnished with pots and pans, silverware, and everything needed except for linens. We noticed that Mrs. Bones had even put out bowls of fruit, snacks and flowers to welcome us. The Bones certainly treated us like family and were very close to Mother and Dad for years after we had moved from Lebanon — but I don't want to get ahead of my story.

We started unloading the car and putting things in place. When that was done, Mother said she needed to go to the grocery store and get things necessary to "stock" the kitchen. Mother wanted to buy groceries alone so it was decided that we would drop her off at the large downtown grocery store and Dad would show us some of the sights. We rode by the campus where Dad would be going to school. He pointed out the building where his classes were held and wanted to know if we would like to go up in the tower at the top of the building. Of course we did, so we climbed the steps up to the open part of the tower and looked out on the campus. The view was shared with many pigeons that didn't seem to really welcome us to their roost. After seeing as much as we cared we went back to the car and drove to the store again, picked up Mother and all of her bags of groceries. She then wanted to make a stop at the hardware store for a few things and then we returned to the house. Mother and

Dad were busy putting up things while Sonny and I played in the backyard and looked around. It wasn't long until we were called and told to wash-up for supper.

For many years after that I vividly remembered the first night we spent in this house. Now the memory has faded somewhat and I can't remember all the details but I do recall having this dream. Our family was having a picnic out in the open country — kind of like Death Valley (remember at this time most of the movies we saw were shoot-um-up westerns). We heard this sound and Mother said "what is that?" We all listened and Dad yelled "Indians!" We all jumped up and ran in every direction. As this group of Indians rode down on us astride their paint ponies, their screams were piercing my ears. As one leaned over and was grabbing me, my screams woke me up and I realized that I was having a bad dream. I looked around and figured out I was in a strange place and then the Indian screams started again. I jumped up ran to the door of my room and Dad grabbed me. He assured me everything was alright and it was just the train whistle I was hearing. By this time Sonny was awake and Mother was standing in the hallway. We all went down to the kitchen and had milk and cookies while we all "calmed down." What a way to spend the first night in a strange place.

In a couple of days our box of household items arrived by Railway Express. As Dad unpacked the things from the big wooden box he had built for this special purpose, Sonny and I were delighted to find that some of our toys were also in the container. We really began to "settle in" for the "duration."

There were no houses behind our house but the street was lined with houses and there were several with children living in them. It wasn't long until we had many friends in the neighborhood. We really started to enjoy our "new home." Since it was summer time I did not go to school yet, but after a week or two Sonny and I attended vacation Bible school at the

Methodist church — which was only a block or two up the street from our house.

Only a day or two after we arrived in our new house, a couple of ladies from that church came by to visit us. They welcomed us to the neighborhood and invited us to visit their church. Mother explained that we were Baptist and would go to the Baptist church but thanked them for being so nice to visit us and invite us. After visiting a while longer they asked would Sonny and I like to attend their vacation Bible school starting in just a few days. They explained that the school was for all the children in the neighborhood and that most of the children went to three or four during the summer. Of course we readily agreed when they told of the fun we would have — especially the refreshments part. So the next day another lady came by and walked Mother and the two of us to the church, showed us around and enrolled us for vacation Bible school. She explained to Mother that a big boy like me probably could walk his little brother with him to the church each morning for the school.

Monday morning, soon after Dad left for his school, Mother got us ready for our vacation Bible school. Sure enough Sonny and I left the house, holding hands. Not far behind us came Mother to be sure we got there safe and sound. As we started up the church steps, we turned and waved. This was my signal that I didn't want her to come any further.

We all went to the general assembly first, were warmly welcomed and then the teachers were introduced. Then each teacher called out the names of the members of her class that had already been enrolled and took them to the assigned rooms. They started with the youngest so Sonny reluctantly left with his new teacher. I assured him I would be there when it was all over and we would go home together. Those that had not been pre-enrolled were assigned to the proper classes and some came down to my room. As I looked around I saw several faces that I recognized from my neighborhood.

The vacation Bible school was a great experience for us since it gave me an opportunity to meet a lot of new kids and grownups. I remember this one especially well, I guess, because it was our first that summer. I know we went to others but I really don't remember anything about them. I do remember going to "our" church and Sunday school but I don't remember the vacation Bible school there. Most of what I remember about the church we attended was the "outside" activities.

About the second time we attended the Baptist Church on a Sunday we didn't go to the church building in town but met at the "river." This was an experience I have never forgotten. I remember we drove up to a big park like area on the side of the hill — in Tennessee I guess it would be a mountain — parked the car and got out. Dad took me by the hand down the hill while Mother followed us with Sonny in tow. Soon we saw this big stream rushing by. It was kind of frightening at first but was at the same time very fascinating. Dad explained that we must never go near the river without one of them being with us. We took a right turn and walked beside the river a little way and saw this swimming area with people splashing and having loads of fun. It had a big yellow rope with floats attached that separated the swimming area from the river. We learned that we would be able to go swimming there some other time but now we needed to go back to the park area where "church" would be held.

When we got back to our car there were others parked nearby and a lot of people gathering around in a seating area. I was learning that when I went anywhere with my Dad to expect to be among the first to get there — my children later said I must have inherited this from him since I always pushed them to be "on time." Dad pitched his hat in the car, slipped on his coat and told us we would have church first and then dinner on the grounds. We then joined the group that was now singing hymns as others were coming.

Well we didn't really eat on the ground but sat at the picnic tables and really had a good time eating the delicious foods that the people had brought. I remember how the people bragged on Mother's fried chicken. After this experience, she was known as the champion of fried chicken preparers and people talked about her Texas style fried chicken. I always remembered it as being very close in taste and appearance to what we later began to know as Colonel Sander's KFC. She, to her "dying days", was very proud of her fried chicken — and she had a right to be because I have never eaten better fried chicken in my eighty-five years.

After lunch the kids ran around playing in the park, the teens did what young people do and the older ones sat around and talked. Babies and toddlers were placed on quilts spread on the ground for their naps. We all had a great time, especially the kids. It began to get pretty warm so people started to bid each other goodbye and head for home. We were some of the last to leave.

After this experience, we took many family outings to the river for swimming and picnicking. One Sunday afternoon when we went to the swimming area we found that a church was having a baptismal service and many people were standing around on the beach area watching. We joined the watchers and when the service was over, as the participants came ashore, the crowd clapped their hands, called out amends, and such. Then we went swimming.

That summer seemed like a magical time. We made so many new friends and had so many new experiences that I really didn't want to think about school starting. Mother told me that school would be just as much fun because I would meet more new friends, have a lot of other new experiences, and learn many new things. Then I found out that my best friend and I would be in the same class. Billy lived across the street with his family from West Virginia. We both had birthdays in August but he was a year older than me. That is why I was surprised that we were in the same grade. I asked him if he had failed a grade and he assured me that he had not. He explained that he didn't start school until he was seven and his brother, Bobby, did the same way two years later. I always wondered about this because Billy wasn't small for his age — a head taller than I was since I was on the small side — and seemed really smart to me. I told him about my best friend Novis Davis back home who had been "held back" a year because he could not read on the level he should after the second grade. I told him the other kids said he had failed because he was dumb but I didn't think so. Mother explained to me that he had a reading problem and might catch-up when he learned to read. Billy told me that he had a friend back in West Virginia that couldn't read either. We decided that we were very lucky and not like them since we both could do pretty well at reading most things. We agreed that we would help each other in our school work when school started because we didn't want to be "held back."

Billy's house was an old frame structure with huge porches on the front and rear. On the front porch was a large swing in which Billy and I spent many happy hours swinging, talking and thinking. We took on world problems, philosophy of life and a lot of other topics during long summer days, afternoons after school and weekends. Sometimes when Sonny and I would go over to their house, Billy and Bobby — his younger brother — would be swinging and Billy would make Bobby get out of the swing for me to sit with him. Bobby would sit on the front steps and entertain Sonny and sometimes their little sister Betty. Betty was two years younger than Bobby, making her very close to Sonny's age.

No one ever called Betty by that name — it was always Littlebit. I asked Billy about that and he told me that when she was born the family called her Little Betty; but Bobby, just learning to talk, had trouble with that and it ended up being "Littlebit." The name stuck. The only time she was called Betty was when one of the family was mad about something she did. I guess when she started school she would go by her real name, but one never can tell.

I also asked Billy about the name or term "Hillbilly." I wasn't very diplomatic when I did it, I just came out and asked him one day as we were swinging why he was a Hillbilly. He looked at me in a surprised way and said "I'm a Billy but I ain't no Hillbilly." Then he wanted to know who had called him a Hillbilly. I told him I didn't know the boy's name and explained that it was during vacation Bible school that he had asked me where I lived. I told him the best I could and he had said that it must be across the street from the Hillbilly. Billy could tell I didn't have any idea what a Hillbilly was so he explained that Hillbillys were mountain people that wore old clothes, black floppy hats and the men chewed tobacco while the women dipped snuff but both smoked corncob pipes.. They made and drank white lightning liquor and carried on a lot of feuding. He said he guessed the boy's family had called his family Hillbillys because his family was from West Virginia where there were a lot of Hillbillys. He also let me know in a nice way that it wasn't very proper to refer to people as Hillbillys. He said it would be like someone calling me a Cowboy because I was from Texas; but that most people thought that Cowboys were good where Hillbillys were considered dumb and no good. I told him I was a cowboy in a way. Then I told him about Tony and the things we did at Grandma's where there were cows and such and about our ranch we had in Raymondville. He told me that since I was a Cowboy he would let me in on one of his secrets — he had a place that he called his "Cowboy Land" and he would show it to me.

We crossed the street, went beside our house and out the back yard through an old fence. Billy said to come on to the top of the hill and then we could see it and another time we would come back and play Cowboys and Indians there. Sure enough, as we topped the hill we could see a large, dry over grazed pasture with a valley and a little creek running through it. It did look like a scene out of a western movie — I expected to see Tom Mix come riding his horse across the view at any time. I wanted to go explore it but Billy said we couldn't because he had promised his mother that he wouldn't go there without first getting her permission. I decided I wouldn't tell my Mother about it and would just say that I was going to play with Billy at his house — which would be true in a sense — since we would always leave from his house and slip by our house to go to cowboy land. I was learning that some things were better kept to yourself. We did go there many, many times and played all over the hills, valleys and some patches of woods. Of course Mother did eventually find out as mothers usually do.

We spent a lot of time at Cowboy Land and found many treasures such as pieces of old farming equipment and rotted pieces of harness that was in a junk pile where evidently there had been an old tool house or small barn. The building was gone but the remains were a "find" to us. We made us a lean-to in the edge of some trees along the creek and stored our "articles" in it. The only times we ever saw anyone on the property was at a distance, on a hill observing us but they never did approach us. We decided it was alright to play there so we considered it to be our exclusive territory and never told any of our friends about it. One day I found a cow skull along the creek — it was a very interesting object with holes for the eyes, holes in the nose place and teeth in the upper jaw. It even had horns sticking out of the forehead. Billy said it was his since he had found cowboy land, but I claimed it since I was the one who had found it. We almost had a fight over it but I realized Billy was bigger and older than me and could easily beat me up so, as I usually did, I made a trade with him. I said it would be ours together but I had a good place to keep it at the back of my house where there was a little shed with lift up doors that they used to dump the coal into the basement. It had a shelf on one side where some buckets were sitting. Billy said he didn't see why we didn't just leave it in our lean-to with the rest of our stuff. I convinced him that the skull was too valuable to leave in cowboy land since anyone spying it would certainly take it with them.. He finally conceded; we took it to my house and carefully placed it among the buckets. Nearly every day I checked on it to be sure my prize was still safe.

It was still warm weather but school had started and one day as I crossed the street from Billy's house to ours, I went around to the side of the house to check on my cow head. As I was knelling down, bending over and looking at the cow head something made me look up at the window above where I was kneeling. There stood my Dad framed in the window looking down at me. He tapped on the glass and motioned for me to come in where he was. When I got there he was standing in the living room doorway and told me to come into the living room. He sat down on the sofa beside my mother and then asked me what I was doing at the cellar hatch. By the look on his face and the tone of his voice I knew this was no time for me to say anything but the truth. As I explained he had other questions ready. Mother never said a word but followed our questions and answers by turning her head and looking at the one speaking. I didn't think I had done anything wrong so I told all. After I had answered all of Dad's questions, he said that he and I would go return the cow head to the place where I had gotten it.

As we headed toward cowboy land with the cow head — I was given the opportunity to hear a lecture about property ownership and what all that entailed. It boiled down to the fact that I had taken someone else's property and we were returning it. I didn't agree with all this but I didn't have a say since dad was the boss and the judge in this case. The lecture was just ending as we topped the hill and looked down on the valley in cowboy land. I was surprised to see a group of cows scattered around about the stream getting their late afternoon drinks. As we came down the hill they started climbing up the facing hill, going away from us. When we neared the stream one turned around and headed back, eyeing us. He was bigger than the others, had a black face and shoulders with the color kind of fading to a dark brown and then still lighter to a tan at his tail end. Dad told me he was the bull and this was his herd of cows. The bull stopped a little way toward the stream and pawed the dry ground making a little cloud of dust. Then he just stood there looking at us. I told Dad that was the first time I had seen any cows in cowboy land when we came there. He said the land owner had probably just moved them from another pasture to this one for the winter. He imagined the owner lived on the other side of cowboy land and had a barn there for his cattle where he could feed and care for them during the bad weather we would have during the winter which was just around the corner.

Dad asked me where I had found the cow head so I pointed off to the right toward the stream and said it was just before that big tree with the yellow leaves. We headed in that direction and Dad kept an eye on the bull that was watching us. As we walked in that direction up the stream the bull lost interest in us, turned around, got in front of his cows and they headed over the hill in the opposite direction from where we had come. We replaced the skull in the spot that I remembered as being its original resting place and then headed toward home. On the way home, I received another lecture about taking someone's property — even if it didn't appear to me to belong to anyone. At the supper table Dad filled Mother in on what had transpired and it was decided that I was forbidden to enter that pasture in the future. After seeing that bull I gladly agreed.

After school started we got into a more or less fixed schedule. Billy, his little brother Bobby — who was in the first grade — and I walked to school and back every day as long as the weather was nice. Our dads shared rides together to their school since they had similar hours. When the weather was bad and it got cold in the winter, one of our moms took us to our school and picked us up in the afternoon. This made our families pretty close. Billy and I spent a lot of time together as usual during the school year. I came to know a lot about his family during our swinging and talking time. One night, as we were eating supper, I told our family something Billy had related me about his family. Mother said that Billy was a "big talker" and sometimes it wasn't a good idea to tell other people all of your family business. For some reason that made a big impression on me and afterwards I always was very careful about what I told other people.

Billy did like to talk. He had told me all about how his family had ended up in Lebanon. It seems that his dad was ever older than my Dad and was a veteran of the World War (there was no World War II yet). He had enlisted in the army when he was only sixteen or seventeen and spent about twelve years as a soldier. He had been to many places in the world during his army days. After he and Billy's mother married and she was expecting Billy, they decided he had to leave the army and for them to settle down like a real family. They moved back to West Virginia where Billy's grandparents lived and his dad went to work as a clerk in the office of a lawyer uncle.

Somehow Billy's mother had "come into some money" and they decided that the dad would go to law school and become a lawyer. They planned to return home and he would be a lawyer in the same office where he had been working. He and my Dad had started to law school at the same time and were on about the same schedule. It was good that our dads and families got along so well because it was a lot easier on our mothers to have such good neighbors. Our families did not go to the same kind of church but that did not seem to make much difference in our relationship.

One of the amazing things about Billy was his bicycle riding ability. His family had this old beat-up bicycle that was always lying around the front steps, or if it happened to be raining it might be on the front porch. Billy told me it had been his dad's when he was delivering telegrams. I guess that was before he went into the army. It was about the tallest and thinnest bicycle I ever did see. My bicycle today is called an adult 26 inch one and I think theirs must have been a thirty incher. Its tires weren't much bigger around than my thumb is now. When Billy was astride it he wasn't tall enough to keep his feet on the pedals as they went around. With the pedals level he could just barely reach both at the same time with his toes. Watching him ride the bike was quite a show.

Billy would hold the bicycle upright along the front steps, loop a leg over the bar from the front seat to the front fork, push off and pump the bike with his body going back and forth across the bar and then coast with the pedals level and him standing on tip toes. He would go up and down the street in this manner for quite a while. When he was ready to stop he would slow down in his yard, let the bike fall over as he nimbly stepped off it. I tried to ride his bicycle only once — that was enough since I was even shorter than Billy and not as strong.

When we went to East Texas for Christmas Santa Claus brought me the prettiest bicycle I had ever seen. It was a Roadmaster and the top of the line — it had a tank covering the bars to the front fork, fancy fenders with a headlight on the front and a taillight on the rear, a luggage carrier and what they called balloon tires with white sidewalls. When we took it back to Tennessee tied on the car, I was the envy of all the neighborhood kids. There were several new bikes around, but none like mine. Billy and I made quite a sight riding down the street together — I was reared back pedaling my Roadmaster and Billy bobbing back and forth on his tall, thin bike.

I am unable to decide whether it was during the fall or spring semester, though I tend to favor the later, that my brother Sonny became ill with scarlet fever. It was a terrible shock to our family. In the 1930s this disease was evidently a misunderstood one and the treatment was very drastic since this was well before our modern day drugs. The very first thing the doctors did was to quarantine our house and treat Sonny at home rather than in a hospital.

The quarantine was to last for three weeks. My Dad told the doctors there was no way that he could miss three weeks from his classes and continue his studies on schedule. They worked out a compromise — Dad was to stay downstairs when at home while Sonny would remain in bed upstairs in Mother and Dad's larger bedroom and I would use our bedroom. Mother was the nurse, cook and housekeeper that took her little bit of rest when she could — which was usually in a chair in the "sick room" while Sonny slept. Dad had to do the shopping and run most of the errands but Mrs. Bones helped out a lot in that area because she would come to the backdoor during the day with some food she had prepared, set it inside the door and collect the empty and washed bowls, trays, etc. She and Mother talked over the telephone several times during the day.

The doctor and nurse came to our house together once each morning and the nurse came back in the late afternoon to check on Sonny. There were many rules and agreements about how we lived during the quarantine. I don't remember all of them but many I do. I couldn't go into the room where Sonny was "kept" and I couldn't go down the stairs. I could go to the head of the stairs and see my Dad coming and going, we could yell back and forth a little but Mom usually kept me pretty quiet. Luckily my room was on the front of the house which allowed me views up and down the street, our front yard and part of Billy's house and front yard. I would watch my Dad drive off in the mornings and wait for Billy's mom to drive her boys to school and return with Littlebit. Every morning and afternoon when they were going or coming, Billy would stand at the curb in front of their house and wave at me. I would return his waves and hoped that he could see them.

My Dad would eat breakfast on his way to school each morning and then have lunch at the university cafeteria. I don't know if this was one of the rules or if it was to help Mother with her many duties. Dad and Mom usually ate together in the evenings. Sometimes she would eat breakfast and lunch in my room with me. I thought this quarantine was great at first — no school and I could play all day in my room — then on the second or third day I realized that I was lonely. The days dragged by — hour by hour — Mom busy with Sonny and me watching what was going on. I even started looking forward to the nurse and doctor visits because he looked me over in the morning and she in the afternoon. They both would say I was doing great and seem so surprised that I never developed the "fever."

I could not go into the room where Sonny was in bed but I did go by the door, slow down and peek in as I went by. One of my duties was to sit at the head of the stairs so Sonny and I could talk back and forth when Mother was downstairs preparing meals or hanging up clothes on the clothes line in the back yard. Sometimes, when the weather was bad, she hung the clothes to dry in the basement. At times Mother would ask me to read a little story to Sonny from one of his books while I sat on the top of the stairs and he lay in bed. He would want me to read his stories to him over and over. This led to my reading some of my books to him also.

This brings to mind my favorite book of all time, which caused me to stop writing for a minute and walk over to my "other desk" — the one with my desk top computer on it. I keep this third grade reader on the shelf over my big computer — at this time I am writing on my laptop. This book is one of my treasures — having it for well over seventy-five years. I had to take time to look through it again — which I do every now and then. It is the first book I "loved" and has led me to thousands more, many of which I am now trying to give away to friends, family and libraries. But back to IF I WERE GOING, The Alice And Jerry Books — Reading Foundation Series — by Mabel O'Donnell and Alice Carey, illustrated by Florence and Margaret Hoopes. At this point you might rightly ask why I still have a reader from my school days after so many years, so I will take time to explain.

In Tennessee, unlike Texas, the students in public schools were not furnished their textbooks by the state — they had to buy their own if they were to have a personal copy. Each classroom had a few copies of the "required" books and supplementary readers for those children to share that the parents could not afford to purchase their books. Thankfully, my parents were able to purchase my books for me. When we left for Texas at the end of the school year my Dad wanted to donate my books to the school for the next group of students. I wanted to keep IF I WERE GOING and he agreed — after all who cared about the spelling, math and those other hard books that you struggle so over. Anyway, I kept my third grade reader — and still have it.

This book not only told great stories but has such good illustrations (many paintings in color and such great sketches) that even today I still find myself daydreaming as I study the pictures. A few days ago I showed this book to my oldest great grandson — who is twelve and in the sixth grade. His comment was that it read more like a fifth grade book than a third grade one to him.

But back to 1936-37, my Dad went to school to confer with my teacher as soon as we were quarantined to work out a plan for my missing three weeks (or more) of school. He thought they may have a visiting teacher program or some plan for such circumstances. He was told that due to being quarantined the school did not allow any bringing back and forth of work for or from me. This meant I could work with my books that I had at home until I returned to school and then the teacher and principal would decide what remedial work needed to be done. Luckily I had my speller and math books along with IF I WERE GOING at home. Mother found time to work with me on all three. When Mother suggested that I read my "book" to Sonny I enjoyed my reading to him much better. By the time I returned to school I knew every word in my reader and kept up with the spelling and arithmetic due to Mother's pushing and work with me.

Another dream I remember from my days in Lebanon is one about the Castle Heights Military Academy located there. I think this boys' boarding school was on the same street (probably a highway running through town) as Dad's university and we drove by it most of the time we were out in the car. It was a large, spacious campus with beautiful grounds, buildings and other facilities. Many of the times we went by in the car we would see the cadets marching in uniforms on the drill field, playing football, baseball and such, as well as riding horses and other interesting activities. For some reason I began to think that going to school there would be the greatest thing ever. I started asking Dad questions about it and his information led me to believe that students could begin there in the sixth grade and it went through high school, maybe two years of college and that it was mostly for wealthy families that wanted to get rid of their kids for some reason — maybe divorce, death of a parent or trouble caused by the boy. I kept thinking that maybe, somehow, I could come back when I got to the sixth grade and go to school at Castle Heights. I told my plan to Billy and he agreed that would be the way to go and he would try to meet me there in the sixth grade.

One day at the evening meal my Dad told us of a happening at the military school which he had heard of in one of his classes. An eighth grade cadet had fallen from his horse and broken one of his arms. The school doctor had set his arm in a cast. A couple of weeks later his parents had him taken to a specialist in Nashville and found out his arm was not mending correctly and the opinion was that the arm needed to be broken and set correctly. Dad said there was going to be a lot of litigation over this incident. Mother said she felt sorry for the little boy having to go through a lot of pain and suffering for not getting the proper medical help in the beginning.

I guess we had read something of the French Revolution and I had seen a picture of a guillotine in a book for that night I had the dream I remembered so well. We, a large crowd, were circled around the drill field at Castle Heights and in the center was a raised platform with a machine resembling a guillotine. Two or three men in uniform marched this kid — also in uniform — to the machine and placed his arm through the opening. As a band played one of the men gave an order and a block dropped on the boy's arm and he screamed out with pain. Then his parents rushed on the platform and took him away. I heard someone yell "Put the doctor in the machine and drop the block on his head." I started yelling "Yes, yes! the doctor." About that time Sonny started crying very loud and my Dad was shaking me awake saying "It's just a dream — a bad dream."

After things quieted down somewhat; we all crawled into bed again. My Mother said "I shouldn't have let him eat that second plate of sausage and sauerkraut." I did lose my taste for sausage and sauerkraut for a while but it wasn't long before I regained it. After I told Billy my dream — several times I am sure — we both cooled on the idea of going to a military academy.

One of the strongest memories I have of our year spent in Tennessee is that of visiting the Hermitage, President Andrew Jackson's home, and the city of Nashville. I must say that I enjoyed our visits to the Hermitage much more than those to Nashville. Now the Hermitage is considered to be a part of Nashville (having a Nashville address) but back during the time we were in Tennessee it was several miles out of Nashville. Also the Hermitage now seems nothing like I remember it as a child. The last time I visited it was in the 1960s. At that time it was so overly developed as a tourist "sight and site" it was difficult to imagine it as being the same place.

Back when I was there as a child, I remember it being a great big park where we picnicked, played in the orchard groves and ran in and around the mansion and other buildings. Now you even pay for parking. Lines are everywhere — you wait and wait to see only a small part of the plantation at a time. I remember my Dad taking us around the places while explaining the many things he had learned about it from studying the history of them and the people who had lived there. Today you have to go in paid, organized group tours to see any part of it. Those were great visits as a child but things change and I guess the changes are best in the long run to protect our national treasures from some of the careless public.

We also visited many historical places in Nashville but the thing that I remember most about those visits was that all the buildings seemed to be covered with soot. Dad explained that this was due to the coal they used to heat with during the winters. The smoke left soot on the outsides of the buildings as well as on the inside. The spring and summer rains washed some of it off and some people washed their buildings too. I wondered why there was so much more soot in Nashville than in Lebanon and found out that it was due to the heavy concentration of people and industry in the large cities that made it so much worse. I also noticed a change in this condition when we visited there in the 1960s — for the better since heating technology and different fuels had been put into use.

Another great memory I have of visiting around in Tennessee is going to Lookout Mountain. I think we went there twice when we lived in Tennessee back in the 1930s. Since then we have been there at least two or three more times. If I recall correctly, you can see four states from one lookout point. The thing I remember most (well leaving out the grand view) was the train that ran straight from the top platform to the valley below. The first time we were there my Dad wanted us to go on the train.

Again if I remember correctly, it was let down and pulled back up by a cable. My Mother said there was no way she and Sonny were going to get on it. She agreed to wait in the concession area while my Dad took me. After he inquired about the time it would take, he decided they would have to wait too long so we did not take the train ride. I think I have been there five times and have never ridden that train. Some things are not to be — and probably better that way.

As I mentioned earlier, we made a trip back to Texas for the Christmas holidays. As far as I know this was the only trip we made to East Texas during our stay in Tennessee. But for Easter that spring East Texas came to us. Auntie (Mabel Spear — Mother's youngest sister) along with Grandma Jernigan and Auntie's toddler son Kenneth made the long trip to visit us. Jack, Auntie's younger son , was not born yet. As I remember it we had a fine time — showing them all the fine things to visit in our area of Tennessee.

The thing I remember best about their visit is that a large pot plant, with several Easter lily blooms on it, was delivered to Auntie from her husband Margene. This was the first time I recall seeing an Easter lily and I thought it something to get a fresh plant sent all the way from Texas to Tennessee. I guess they had Floral Telegraph Delivery back in those days and I am sure it was expensive. Auntie's and Margene's marriage was an on and off affair, with a lot of restarts, all their lives but they never divorced and were still married at the time of his death. Auntie spent a lot of time at Grandma's during her life, even when the boys were young. Margene had a drinking problem that was stronger than his love for his wife and kids which, or his mental condition, finally got the best of him. I didn't mean to start digging up old family problems so I will try to avoid them in the future.

The visit from our family members was one of the high spots of our time in Tennessee. The second summer we were there must have been much of a repeat of the first since I don't really remember anything in particular. We made our move back to East Texas probably in the middle of the summer in order to get set-up again for a new experience of living in Tyler. Mother and Daddy had been planning it during the year in Tennessee. The first I knew of it was during Grandma and Auntie's visit at Easter. It was during this visit that we were all told what the big plan was when we returned "home."

By this time I had mixed feelings about leaving my friends I had made in Tennessee and wanting to go back to East Texas and our relatives. But Mother explained that things would be changing there too since Billy's family would be moving back to West Virginia and other people would be moving in. And, she made the move to Tyler sound exciting and reminded me of the fun we would have at Grandma's with our cousins, horses and such. So by the time moving time came I was ready. Daddy made a second shipping box for all the things we had accumulated during our stay there and I wished I had "my" cow head to take back to Texas with me.

TYLER

When we returned to Texas from Tennessee in the middle of the summer of 1937, we were busy getting ready for another move from Leverett's Chapel to Tyler. It seems my Dad and Mother had made some big decisions and plans on how our lives would be in the future. They had purchased a new house, being built or just completed, in Tyler at 1410 Glenwood Blvd. It was ready to move in when I first saw it and I liked it very much. Mother and Dad took us for a tour through it and showed us which rooms would be ours.

Sonny and I would each have his own room for the first time since his birth, mine the larger and Sonny's on the other side of our bath. Each room had a door into the bath where you could see from one bedroom to the other. A hall ran between our bedrooms and the kitchen with a door from this hallway leading into the kitchen and living room. Mother's and Dad's bedroom and bath were on the other side of the kitchen from our rooms. A hall also separated their bedroom and bath from the kitchen, with a door into the kitchen and dining room. A utility room (for laundry, etc.) connected the two halls on the back and here was the outside back door opening onto the driveway, on the north side of the house. The living and dining rooms were across the front of the house with the front door opening a little off center toward the dining room allowing for a large fireplace and more space in the living room. The backside of the fireplace and chimney were, more or less, the decorative feature of the front of the house on the outside along with a small entrance front porch. I think this style was called cottage and was very typical of that time. The dark red brick with its white mortar looks today much the same as it did when we lived there. The exterior wood was pained a bright white and the wooden shingle roof was stained a dark green. A sidewalk ran from the front door to the street curb and Mother had a flower bed on each side of the walkway with red verbena growing and blooming profusely.

This floor plan placed the kitchen in the center of activity — I'm sure Mother was the one who planned it that way. Most everything did revolve around or in the kitchen. We had this big (and to me it seemed very old) kitchen table where we ate, did my homework, and listened to our radio programs from the radio on another table where mother kept her papers, books, secret weapons and such. I had a desk in my room also but it was used mostly for building model airplanes of balsam wood and paper. My Dad had a large very nice desk in the living room for his "homework" also but he did a lot of work at night in the kitchen while I was doing my homework or he and Mother were discussing money issues from papers on her table-desk. We kids were not supposed to go into the living room except at Christmas time, when we had company and we were part of the visiting and when invited. Dad told us the reason we had a hallway from our bedrooms to the living room was so we could rush into it on Christmas morning to see what Santa had brought us without our disturbing Mother and Dad. On one Christmas eve while we lived in Tyler Mother and Dad took us to a movie that afternoon and when we drove into the driveway we saw a toy lying there. We ran into the house and Santa had been there while we were gone.

The lot, or maybe two, on the south side of our house was vacant and nearly all the houses close by were relatively new. Today as you drive by this section of town it looks to be pretty old and maybe appears somewhat rundown. Back in the days when we lived there, some seventy-five years ago, it was the latest in housing — except possibly the art deco style. In the house next to us on the north side lived an older couple with an old maid sister of one of them. We didn't have much contact with them and Mother was constantly warning us not to cut across their yard and to keep the noise down on their side of our house. They never said anything to us but the way they looked at us you could tell they didn't much care for children.

The next house north of us was on the corner and contained a family with three daughters. All three girls were older than me and always acted rather snooty toward Sonny and me. That was certainly alright with us because we didn't care much for them either. We had many friends in our little neighborhood and spent a lot of time visiting and hosting them at our home and playing games on the vacant lot next to our house. Mother soon had a reputation for having lemonade or hot cocoa ready, according to the weather, for our visiting friends.

Glenwood Blvd. ran straight north and south where we lived and this was on a good sized hill with the peak about a block and a half south of us. The houses in this block south of us were mostly two story as were the houses across Glenwood from them. The street south of us (running east and west) was kind of the southern boundary of our neighborhood with the northern boundary being about where Judge Fisher's house was — about three blocks north of our block. This hill continued on downward (north) for several blocks until it reached Front St. We loved to coast our bikes down this hill but none of us could pump all the way up it. There seemed to be no boundaries on the east or west for us, since our school was several blocks to the east and the houses played out a couple of blocks to the west of us.

The street on the south side of our block and the one on the north side, both running east to west, dead ended into Glenwood Blvd. There was this street running from the northeast toward the southwest that crossed Glenwood about a half block north of the street on the north side of our block. This was a main street at the time running from the center of town toward the country — maybe even to Palestine. This layout produced two points of land — one pointing north with the tip kind of in front of our house and the second pointing south with the tip a block or so north of our house. I will use this description of the area so that I can relate some things that happened in this location.

All the land formed in the triangle north of our house belonged to Judge Fisher. His house (some people called it a mansion) was about three blocks north of the tip down Glenwood. The house didn't face Glenwood but north toward a street running east and west about two blocks north of the house just before you got to Front St. You drove or went to his house on a block long driveway from Glenwood or the angle street on the east side of his property. I remember these directions very well because I made many trips between our house and the Judge's with messages.

It seems the Judge was in business with Dad or was his attorney in his business. My Dad told me once Judge Fisher didn't like to talk over the phone (being a little hard of hearing) so they sent handwritten messages and papers to be signed back and forth by me. Sometimes, especially if the weather was bad or at night, Judge Fisher's big black car would drive up in front of our house, either with or without Judge Fisher in it, and Jacob would come to our back door. Jacob was a tall thin black man with very white hair and was the Judge's driver, personal assistant and handy man. If the Judge was in the car, always sitting in the back seat, sometimes my Dad would go out to it and get in the back seat with him and they would talk for a while and at other times Dad would walk up the driveway a little way with Jacob and wave at the Judge. When I delivered or picked up at the Judge's house, Jacob was always the one who answered the front door and he would give me a peppermint stick from a bowl near the door as I was leaving. I always liked to go to the Judge's house — I guess it made me feel a little important.

Most all our activities were located in a north, northeast or east direction from our house. Downtown was northeast and our church, First Baptist, was located there also as was Dad's business office. Most of our relatives living in, or near, Tyler were on the east side. As best I remember, three of Mother's siblings lived in Tyler when we moved there. Charley, who had taken over in the Valley when we moved back to East Texas was back and forth between Tyler and Raymondville. The boys, Richard and Robert, along with their mother Evie and grandmother Mrs. Smith had been spending the summers in Raymondville but the school terms in Tyler. Charlie had a home in the northeast section of Tyler — located a couple of blocks north of East Erwin and a couple of blocks east of Sam R. Hill Lumber Co. It was either after Christmas or the end of the school term during the first year we were in Tyler that the whole family moved to Raymondville for some years and then Robert spent summers and holidays at Grandma Jernigan's until later when he and Evie moved in with Grandma. This may have been when Mrs. Smith passed away for she seemed to be the one who took care of the boys.

Not far from this house was Fred's (Mother's youngest brother) and Carl Jeter's (Mother's brother-in-law married to her sister Ruby) Indian motorcycle shop. It was either on East Erwin or just a block or so north or south. Here they sold a few motorcycles, repaired some but mainly involved in racing them all over the United States. When Carl was injured racing in Indiana — broken leg and damage to his back — they decided to give up this "business." While operating the shop, Fred — recently married — was living in a garage apartment at Grandma's that she had built for him for a wedding present. Carl and Ruby had a house on East Front that she kept after they were divorced several years later (probably bought with her money to start with). When they closed the shop Fred went into a partnership with one of the Brookshires with a grocery and feed store (Brookshire & Jernigan) a block east of the downtown courthouse square. He operated this store until he sold out and went into the Marine Corp during World War II. Carl and Ruby went to California and Carl started working for Douglas Aircraft. At the end of the war they divorced and Ruby returned with their two children to East Texas and later married Charley Jackson. Carl stayed in California, remarried and started another family.

Walter, Mother's middle brother, with his wife and two sons lived at Liberty Hill on a property next to his in-laws (the Florences) a couple of miles east of Tyler on the Kilgore highway. He was busy with the family sawmill and farming activities. Auntie, the other sister, had also married (like her sister Ruby) a Kilgore man — Margene Spear. They lived in a new house, a wedding gift from her in-laws, in Kilgore on a part of the Spear property. Auntie, and later with her two boys, spent most of the time at Grandma's with her busy driving and taking care of things for Grandma. Grandma never had any interest in learning to drive and always had a family member do her driving. At this time in the garage under Fred's apartment was this big, long black Lincoln limo that was never used after Grandpa died. I remember it had a V-12 or sixteen cylinder engine in it that was taken to the sawmill during the war to replace some of the power to operate the mill. We kids would play in the car, with its roll up and down window between the front seat and the back where there were seats that pulled out of the front one. There was a radio between the driver's front seat and the back where we could talk back and forth. I think Fred kept the battery charged so we could play in it and talk over the radio. This car was always a mystery to me but no one ever told me the full story — if they knew it. I think maybe Grandma and Grandpa had a big fuss when he bought this car and everyone decided the less said about it the better. He died shortly after getting it and Grandma never wanted to get rid of it after that, but never used it.

Mother was not the only one with family members living nearby because Dad had a bunch too — just not in town. His mother, my grandma we called Ma, lived at their old home place which was about six or seven miles east of town on the Henderson highway — the old highway since the new one later cut her property into two pieces. Her youngest child, Joy was still living at home with her and Ma called her "Baby" all their lives. Her oldest son Kay, who all the family called "Boss" but Ma always called "Son" lived in his house on Ma's property with his second wife Laura and daughter Lavern. His first wife had died young and their daughter, Marie, was living with her other grandmother and two aunts in Tyler. The aunts, Minnie and Winnie (a school teacher and a telephone operator), had a big hand in raising Marie. Dad had another brother, Oliver — everyone called him "Bug" — living nearby on another farm. Dad's older sister Effie, the family called Sister, also lived nearby on a farm with her husband, Leon Stamps, and several sons.

Dad had two other brothers that I always thought he was "closer" to in terms of relationships and probably age had a lot to do with it. Allen, just older than Dad, lived on a piece of property across a country road from his in-law relatives the Hills. This place was about halfway between Tyler and Overton and only about three miles from Ma. At that time he was working at a lumberyard in Arp and later spent many years as manager of Wm. Cameron Lumber Co. in Overton. The last and youngest brother was Fred who lived and had a country style grocery-filling station (the forerunner of today's convenience store) on the Henderson highway near Bascom — about three miles from Tyler.

So, we had a lot of relatives close by to visit, which we did frequently. Sundays, holidays and summers were designated as "at Grandma Jernigan's" — after "Sunday Dinner" the rest of the afternoon was usually spent visiting Elliott relatives The whole Jernigan clan gathered at Grandma's farm if at all possible at these times. The summers were devoted to canning — the fruits, vegetables and other produce from the prolific farm. Grandma even had a special, large house only a few steps from the porch off the huge dining room for the purpose of family canning. All the families loaded their storerooms with canned goods for the periods when fresh foods were not available. This was the time before home freezing became possible, the big super markets and fast foods. Meats were either smoked or cured — with many procedures and products for this. Grandma's smoke house was on the other side of the house from the canning house — just a few steps from the kitchen outside door.

The biggest celebration of the year was Grandma's Fourth of July picnic. This was the time when distant relatives from distant places made the trip to Grandma's. Christmas was also very big but just a few less people.

The Saturday, or maybe two, before we moved to Tyler, the four of us went over to visit Dad's new office and take care of some other business. Dad's office was located in the multi-storied building in the southwest corner of the block lying kattie-korner north east of the Courthouse Square. His office was on the second or third floor and his brother Boss worked in a barbershop in a semi basement in the same building. We rode the elevator up — a big deal for Sonny and me — to Dad's office.

The door was open and when we entered the office we saw a large room with a reception area, a couple of desks on each side of the room and at the back was a wall, the bottom half wood paneling and the upper portion glass. There were two doors in this wall and one was open with a smiling man standing in the doorway. He said "You Elliotts come on back." Dad introduced Sonny and me to Mr. Gentry — Dad's new partner. Then he explained that he and Mr. Gentry would take time about working on Saturdays so this was Mr. Gentry's Saturday and next Saturday would be Dad's to work. The receptionist and secretary were not there since they only worked Monday through Friday. Mr. Gentry showed us in his private office then Dad opened the other door and took us into his office. It looked the same as Mr. Gentry's but we were surprised to see our pictures on my Dad's desk. After our "inspection" of the office we took the elevator down and went outside the building.

To our left was a set of steps down a few feet. At the top of the steps was a barber pole and at the bottom was a door into a barber shop. As we went down the stairs we could see into the barbershop through the large window. Just inside the window was an elevated shoe shine chair and then down one side of the long room was a line of six barber chairs and along the other side a line of chairs for customers to sit in if they had to wait for their favorite barber. Both walls above the chairs were solid mirrors. Behind each barber chair was a work station with the barber's tools and bottles of stuff along with his license and picture hanging for all to see. It was Saturday and it looked like every seat was taken.

The barber at the first chair was our uncle Boss — evidently he was the "official" greeter and warmly welcomed everyone coming into the shop — most by name or something like neighbor or friend if he didn't know the name. Boss was always very friendly but extremely so at work. As soon as we got inside and was also "warmly welcomed" he took us to the back barber chair and introduced us to "his partner" — with all the other barbers nodding and speaking to us as we passed by their chairs. We walked back to the front, Boss went back to work on the customer in his chair, Mother excused herself to go do some shopping, the shoe shine man placed a small straight chair and stool from behind his shoe shine chair to near the door for Sonny and me. Dad climbed up in the big chair for a shoe shine. While the shoe shine man worked on his shoes Dad and Boss visited, I listened and carefully watched the progress on the shoes.

Dad was telling Boss about his and Mr. Gentry's real estate and insurance business and our upcoming move. Boss was taking in Dad's report and talking to and finishing up on the customer. As soon as Boss finished that man another came forward and got in the chair and the barbering and shoe shinning went on. I think the shoe shine man was the blackest person I have ever seen. At times his skin seemed to have a purple sheen to it as he worked his arms, legs and head back and forth — with a light coating of perspiration covering his exposed skin. I wondered if he used the shoe polish on his skin in order to make it so black and shine so — but I never did get around to asking anyone. He wasn't really very fat but plenty plump, with gleaming white teeth and a great big smile that never left his face. When he finished, Dad paid him and remained in the chair since no one was waiting for a shine. The shoe shine man sat down on the edge of the platform for the chair and took a rest. He asked "Mr. Albert" several questions about insurance and certainly appreciated finding out about those things that had been bothering him.

When Boss finished with this last man he reached behind him, retrieved a board which he placed across the arms of his chair and motioned for Sonny to climb up. Sonny looked at Dad and Dad nodded his head so Sonny took the seat offered. I followed Sonny after his hair was cut. Dad said he would wait till a weekday when Boss wasn't so busy. We left and went to the car and Mother appeared in just a few minutes. She still needed to go to a fabric store and another stop or two before we headed for home at Leverett's Chapel.

There wasn't one big moving day — most of the furniture and appliances were bought new and delivered to the new house by the stores from which they were purchased. Most of the other stuff was moved in our car — a load or two a day — by Mother, Sonny and me while Dad worked in his office. We put the stuff up as we carried it into the house. Usually we would make a load in the morning with the four of us in the car, drop Dad off at the office and go unload what we had packed. Go back down to the office at noon for Dad and we would eat lunch with him at Kidd's Café on the Square. The three of us would depart from there for another load, leaving Dad at the restaurant to visit for a while and walk across the Square back to his office. The next load would be much larger since we had the whole back seat to pile stuff in. After a few days of this moving we had everything we needed and started spending the nights in Tyler during the week. One or two Saturdays Dad hired Buddy with one of Walter's or Fred's trucks and the two of them moved some bigger and heavier stuff. We kept the LC house furnished and liveable all the time we were in Tyler so we could spend a weekend there every now and then — until we moved back there in a couple of years.

One day, while still straightening things up after our move, the three of us were sitting around the kitchen table taking a break and drinking lemonade. We heard a knocking on the front door and I, always wanting to be a help, jumped up and headed for the dining room. Mother reached out, caught me by the arm and said "Remember, you nor Sonny answer the door unless Dad or I tell you to." She got up, took Sonny by the hand and went to the front door with me close on her heels. When she opened the door there stood a boy about my size with another smaller boy about Sonny's size. Each had a hand on the tongue handle of a red Radio Flyer wagon loaded with tan colored bricks. The larger boy, without hesitation, spoke right up with "Good afternoon Mam, would you like to buy some good new bricks? They are just five cents each."

Mother was a little taken back at first by such a good sales pitch from the boy that she looked at the two boys and then the loaded wagon and said "We don't need any bricks and does your mother know you are out selling bricks?" "Yes'um" was the reply and then "she sent us out and said we could have half the money we got to go to the movies each week." You could tell Mother didn't much care for this situation so she questioned the young salesman further. I'll admit that I admired the kid for how he handled himself. It turned out that his name was Johnny Patten, his little brother Jimmy, and they lived across Glenwood in the last house (tan brick) in the next block north which was adjacent to some heavily wooded vacant land. Johnny looked at me several times while talking to Mother but I never said anything. Finally Mother told the boys she hoped they had good luck with selling bricks and goodbye. As she closed the door she looked at me and then asked if I knew that kid. I told her I didn't but I thought I had seen him riding his bicycle down Glenwood a time or two. That was all that was said about the sales call until supper and then I found out how Mother really felt about it.

When Dad came in from work we had supper. While we were eating Mother recounted the visit that afternoon by the Patten boys to Dad and ended up asking if he could imagine a mother sending the boys out to sell bricks. Dad took a little bit of a different view of the situation and suggested that Mrs. Patten probably didn't "send the boys out" — maybe they were warting her to go to the movies and she said that cost money and they had none for that. One thing led to another and they thought up the brick business. I remember Dad said something about times being hard and a lot of grown men were selling apples on street corners. Mother said she still couldn't believe a mother would let such young children go out on that kind of business. That was the last I remember being said about the incident but I could always tell that Mother didn't care much for Mrs. Patten — all during the two years we were in the neighborhood.

Up to this point Johnny and I had not exchanged a single word but I felt a warmness toward him and this feeling developed into a very close friendship between two boys of a young age that is hard to explain. I had this friendship with Billy in Tennessee and two or three others as time went by. It is very close to brotherly love but possibly not quite as strong — maybe more like my bond with my two Jernigan cousins William and Robert and on the other side of my family with W. A. Elliott. There was a lot of love in these relationships — and now I am the only remaining cousin.

A few days after the brick incident Dad came home for lunch and when we had finished eating he told me to go wash my face and hands again, and to comb my hair, for he was going to take me to meet Judge Fisher. I wasn't sure whether this was good or bad but I did as I was instructed. As we rode past the Patten's on the way, I saw Johnny and Jimmy in their front yard kicking some kind of ball around the yard. I didn't say anything because Dad was getting ready to turn at the Fisher driveway. We walked to the front door and Dad pulled on a chain that rang a bell inside the house. Jacob, a black man in a black suit, white shirt, black tie and very shiny black shoes opened the door, then greeted Dad with a "Please come in Mr. Albert." We stepped inside, Jacob closed the door and then Dad introduced me to Jacob. Jacob said "Pleased to meet you Master Floyd." I was wondering if I should stick out my hand or not and could only say "Me too." Dad said for him to just call me Floyd as everybody else did for master sounded too formal and that would make it easier on every one. Jacob replied with a "Yes sir." Then Jacob told us the Judge was in the library and wanted us to come on in. Dad led the way and we found the Judge seated at a big desk and he pushed his chair around to face us. He didn't get up but put his hand out and shook Dad's. Dad went through the introduction thing again and the Judge shook my hand also. All through our conversation he referred to me as "Young Man" whether he was talking to me or Dad. As best I can remember the Judge never called me by my name — it was always simply "young man."

When we left the Judge's I saw Johnny and Jimmy were still playing in their yard so I asked Dad if I could ride my bike down to see them when we got to the house. He said he thought that would be fine but go in and tell Mother he had brought me back and had gone to the office. I did as instructed — but I just told her that Dad said I could go ride my bike for a while if she had no objections. She said that would be O K but don't go too far or stay very long. I made a point of not telling her where I was going because I thought I should save that for another time.

As I neared the Patten house on my bike, Johnny and Jimmy ran to the curb to meet me. Before I completely stopped Johnny greeted me with a "Hi Floyd." I was surprised and asked him how he knew my name. He told me that he had ridden his bike by my house a day or two ago and saw Sonny on the front porch so he stopped and asked him his name and my name. After answering his question about the names Sonny told him that he was getting the mail out of the box and had to take it to Mother so that was the end of their conversation. Johnny and I both had a lot of questions and answers that we exchanged as we three sat on the curb with Jimmy turning from one to the other and just listening. We had a good visit and found out a lot about each other and our families. In a little while I saw Mother and Sonny walking out our driveway and looking around. I decided they were looking for me so I told my new friends I had better head for home. As I left the Patten's I could see that Mother saw I was headed home so she and Sonny turned around and went into the house.

When I got inside the house Mother said she needed a couple of things for supper from the neighborhood grocery. She started to write them down on a piece of paper but I assured her I could remember them without a list. She had me repeat them a couple of times to be sure I would remember. I got back on my bike and when I turned the corner headed for the store I saw Johnny, still in his front yard, waving at me. The store was just two blocks east from the corner on the left hand side. As I opened the door to the store I saw Johnny on his bike turning into the parking lot. I picked out the things Mother wanted and gave them to Mr. Smith to charge to our account. He wrote it in the sales book, put them in a sack, handed it to me and said thank you. When I walked out the door Johnny was straddling his bike next to mine and grinning. I put the sack in the wire basket attached to the handlebars of my bike. The first thing said between us was his asking where I got the basket on my bike. I told him I didn't know since one day last week Dad came home with it and put it on my bike. He had told me that it would be needed for me to carry things in since we moved to Tyler. Johnny said he had a luggage rack on the back like mine that he tied stuff on. I had to then explain that Dad had said that sometimes I would need to pick up important papers at Judge Fisher's that would be in folders. These folders would fit flat in the basket without folding or crimping. It also came in handy for small packages, sacks and books without having to tie them on. I could see Johnny was thinking that maybe he also needed a basket.

We left the store side by side on our bikes and when we got back to the corner, where my house was up to the left and his was down to the right, Johnny pulled over to the curb and said "I'll be seeing you." I asked if he didn't want to come to my house and see my room. He said he wanted to very much but his mother had told him not to push himself on us after he had told her that he thought my mother didn't like him. I explained that I thought Mother liked him just fine. It was just that she was surprised to see him with his little brother out by themselves trying to sell bricks. Johnny studied me for a minute and then said that his mother told him that she wanted him and Jimmy to learn to be independent but at the same time very dependable — so she let them do things on their own and expected them to do things that were needed to be done. I told him that it sounded like a good idea to me but without saying any more I really didn't understand it all too well. We agreed that we would see each other tomorrow and then parted in our different directions.

A little later at supper we talked about the visit to Judge Fisher's and the Patten family. After Dad told Mother about our visit I had some questions about Jacob. I found out that he wasn't married, lived in a small apartment attached to the garage at Judge Fisher's and had worked for the Fisher family since he was a small boy — starting out opening gates for the Judge's elderly father. I told them I didn't understand the term "master" he had used with my name. Mother explained that it was a title used for young men instead of Mister. She said it was kind of "old timey" now but occasionally used on envelopes addressed to boys. (A few years later I received a school graduation letter and gift from an elderly distant relation so addressed and I vividly recalled old Jacob and this conversation)

When the conversation got around to the Pattens, I told my family that I had found out that Mr. Patten worked for the railroad but didn't drive a train or take tickets. The best I could make out was that he just worked in an office. Dad explained that he was an accountant and one of the higher up officials in the railroad office. Mrs. Patten had been a teacher but since they had the children she stayed at home. With this information I think Mother started feeling a little better about the Patten children. I finally worked around to the point where I explained that Johnny was afraid to come to our house without an invitation from Mother. At this point she volunteered to invite him in the next time he rode his bike by the house. The next day I made a point of arranging an "accidental" meeting with him at our driveway at which time Mother "invited him in." From that time on Johnny and I were very close — both as friends and neighbors.

My bike, the one I had gotten while we were in Tennessee, and Johnny figured in many of my adventures while we lived in Tyler. Johnny's mother was a little more lenient with allowing Johnny to roam around than mine. Several times Mother expressed a fear that Sonny or I would be kidnapped after all the publicity about the Lindbergh case. She would say that people would think our family had money and could pay a ransom to get us back. We weren't exactly poor but Dad would say we weren't rich enough to worry about kidnappers. I guess I really did get around town on my own a lot while we were in Tyler.

One of our first adventures after Johnny and I connected was to explore the sand and gravel road on the north side of his yard that separated the houses from the wooded area on the west side of Glenwood — across from Judge Fisher's. This old road ran west and connected to some other country–like roads with just a few houses scattered about. We would ride west on it and then take one of the others to see where it went and what was there. We found that the first road, leading north took us to the baseball field — in the area near the current fair grounds and football stadium. Tyler had a pro or semi-pro baseball team at that time and we became frequent visitors to practices and even some afternoon games that first summer. The second summer, with our parents' permission, we spent a great deal of time there. Not only kids but grownups too came to watch the practices when the gates were wide open and everyone could come in free. We began to know the players and they would notice us. Tyler had a player named Floyd and Johnny wasn't bashful in telling him that it was my name too. Soon he took us under his wing and would let us in the playing area to help the batboys chase balls. When there were games, Johnny could usually talk our way in through the player's entrance by saying that Floyd so and so wanted us in. It usually worked and if not the gate keeper would go ask him and he would O K it. We had great times and talked about our being batboys in two or three more years. After we moved back to LC I always wondered if Johnny stayed in Tyler and became a batboy.

One afternoon as I rode in the driveway coming home from school, Mother opened the back door and called me to come inside. She said Dad had called and he was going to be late for supper and he wanted me to ride down to Judge Fisher's to pick up some papers for him. I had learned that this would mean a peppermint stick for me. I took off right away.

After Jacob handed me the papers, the Judge called to me to come into the library. I did and I got the feeling he just wanted to visit with me for a few minutes. It was mostly just him asking me how I was getting along, how I liked my school and such. He asked me if I was one of the boys that played in the woods across the street. I told him that Johnny and I had gone over there a couple of times but some bigger boys had run us off saying that those were their woods and for us to keep away. He looked at me a little while and then asked if Johnny was the Patten boy about my size. I told him he was and that we were good friends. He told me to tell those other boys that you had the Judge's permission to play there and if they gave us any trouble he would have the police take them home to their parents. I thanked the Judge and took off with my candy as soon as I could. When I got home Mother wanted to know how my visit went and I told her about visiting with the Judge this time. I omitted any reference to the part about the woods — which I also did when I recounted it to Dad after he came in.

I could hardly wait to tell Johnny about my visit with the Judge but it was supper time and I had to wash up and get ready to eat. Since it was only a week or two since school had started, the weather was still very warm and the days fairly long. After supper and my homework it was still daylight a little and I got permission to play outside a few minutes before getting ready for bed. I was told not to leave the yard and to play with Sonny. We played catch in the driveway and in a few minutes Johnny came riding by and saw us. He turned around and came back to talk with us. I hinted that I had something important to tell him but didn't want to do so in front of Sonny. I told him it would wait until tomorrow when we rode our bicycles to school. Johnny and I were in the same grade but not in the same room. Our schedules differed enough that we didn't have time to visit any during the school day so most of our "talking" was done on the way to and from school.

Johnny was very eager to hear my news when we met at the corner the next morning. I related what had happened during my visit to the Judge's and Johnny let out a little whistle. He smiled and said "That paints a whole new picture on the woods and those big boys." I asked him how many there were of the big boys. Three or four he replied. Then I asked him if he had seen any of them at our school and he said that he hadn't so they must be eleven, twelve or maybe older and they would go to Hogg. I didn't know anything about Hogg so he explained that it was the junior high that you went to after the sixth grade and it was two or three blocks on the other side of Gary. We rode on in silence for a few minutes and Johnny told me that his family was scheduled to go to the movies right after supper but since this was Friday we could go to the woods the next morning. We both agreed that would be our plan. I knew the next day was Dad's Saturday to keep the office so we would be home. That afternoon, on our way home, we firmed up our plans and laughed a good deal thinking of the surprise we had for the big boys.

Bright and early the next morning I was up and dressed in time to go into the kitchen while Mother and Dad were eating their breakfast. They both wanted to know what I was doing up so early on a Saturday since Sonny and I usually ate breakfast every morning later than they did even on school mornings. I told them I didn't want to waste any of my day off from school. After some more questioning about my plans, I explained that Johnny had gone to a movie with his family and I wanted to know all about it. This seemed to satisfy them so the conversation shifted back to what they had been discussing and what I wanted for breakfast. I decided on my usual two eggs over easy with bacon and some of the hot biscuits — and Ovaltine to drink. Normally Mother split a left over biscuit from their breakfast for Sonny and me, buttered and toasted it in the oven. Sonny usually had scrambled eggs.

My Dad always got up about 5:00 AM and after getting ready (which included looking through the newspaper) liked to eat at 6:00 on the nose. He usually left home about 6:30 and was at his morning activities by 7:00 — whatever he was doing. At this period of our lives on Saturday mornings I knew he would go to the Wagon Yard (just a couple of blocks south of the Square) where he would visit and drink coffee for an hour or so with his farmer friends camped out the night before to be ready for a Saturday of trading — buying, selling, swapping, etc. Monday through Friday he would spend this hour at the Kidd Café and be at his office at 8:00 AM. Not only was his timing very predictable, but his eating habits too. He never cared for eggs at his breakfast — preferring instead Mother's buttered golden buttermilk biscuits with ribbon cane syrup from a half gallon can and meat on the side. The meat was usually bacon in warmer weather and big juicy sausage patties in colder weather. With the change in weather and meat sometimes in the colder weather he would eat sorghum syrup in place of the ribbon cane. He was also very particular about where his meat and syrup came from and who made it. Dad usually ate lunch at a restaurant with some of his associates and it was normally Kidd's when we were in Tyler. Breakfast and "dinner" (now called lunch) was his two big meals. He always ate a light "supper," his favorite being a piece of cold cornbread crumbled up in a glass of milk (buttermilk preferred). Mother had her favorites also but she leaned toward salads and lighter foods to help control her weight. But all in all we ate well all the time.

After Dad left and Mother consented to my going on my bicycle to see Johnny, I left also. Johnny was nowhere around his house and I didn't want to disturb them, so I sat down on the curb in front of their house — our usual meeting place. I kept an eye on the woods, wanting to see any activity in that direction. For about thirty minutes everything was quiet, then Johnny emerged from his front door. We talked about what we should do and decided to ride our bikes up and down the road next to the woods for a couple of blocks until we saw someone in the woods.

After some several back and forth trips we heard some talking in the woods. We parked our bikes in Johnny's driveway and boldly walked from there into the woods. After only a few steps in the woods we saw two boys standing under a tree looking up. Standing on a platform attached to the first limb, about six or seven feet high, was a third boy. When we were only a few feet from them it was the boy on the limb that first noticed us. He let out a shout "What are you turds doing in our woods?" The two boys on the ground turned to face us and Johnny and I looked at each other. Johnny then looked them in the eye and said "We have a message from Judge Fisher for you," then looking at me said for me to tell them what the Judge had said. In my weak and stuttering voice I recounted my visit to see the Judge again and what he had said about them. One of the boys on the ground used the "F" word "to you" — I think this was the first time I had heard this word and had no idea what it meant but I knew it must be bad since it sounded so ugly (I didn't like it then and I have tried never to use it).

Johnny responded with a "Right back at you," turned and looked at me — I am sure I was very pale — then he took off in his fastest run for his house with me close behind. We ran into the house and then his bedroom. His mother yelled to quit running in the house. We quietly looked out his bedroom window toward the woods — we saw no one. Then in very low voices we discussed what had happened and Johnny gave me a lesson on "bad words." We decided to go play at my house for a while. His mother wanted us to take his little brother with us so he could play with Sonny — the little brother was about a year younger than Sonny but they got along fine and Mother always encouraged their visiting — so we consented. We rode our bikes with the little brother straddling Johnny's luggage rack and clinging to Johnny's waist.

Mother offered Johnny and me a cup of hot chocolate which we gladly accepted. We three sat down at the kitchen table and Mother had a cup of coffee while we drank our chocolate. Sonny took Jimmy to Sonny's room and showed him his board games for him to choose one to play. While they were playing and we had finished our drink, Johnny and I went outside to play — and keep an eye on Johnny's house and the woods. Everything looked quiet down that way. After an hour or so, Mother called us in and asked Johnny if he and Jimmy would like to stay for a lunch of soup and sandwiches. Johnny readily agreed since he was sure Mother's soup would be homemade and not just from a can like his mother used. Johnny had developed into a fan of my Mother's cooking. Johnny phoned his mother for permission and Mother readied our lunch.

After lunch Johnny and Jimmy left for home so Jimmy could take a nap and I rode with them. As Johnny took Jimmy in, I studied the woods and listened for any voices. I couldn't see nor hear any activity so when Johnny came out we decided to park our bikes and walk to the woods. Not finding anyone there, we explored around the tree where we had seen the three boys. Sitting nearby were two boxes, one an apple crate seemed to be in good condition while the second was nearly crushed flat. We then noticed that there was a second platform on another limb some five or six feet above the lower one. They were about the same size, each about six feet by six feet, but the higher one had a wall between three or four feet high enclosing it except for an opening in the short wall about three feet wide for entrance to the platform. Connecting the two platforms was a ladder from the floor of the lower to the opening in the side of the higher one. We looked more closely at the tree trunk and saw a board nailed on it about six feet off the ground. After studying this situation a little longer we figured the boys had boards nailed to the tree trunk and climbed these to the first limb, stepped from the limb onto the lower platform and then climbed the ladder to the second platform.

Johnny decided the big boys had taken the missing boards from the tree trunk so we wouldn't be able to climb up to the tree house. We thought about putting the apple crate under the board nailed to the tree and try to pull up the trunk, mount the board and step onto the limb and platform from it. But instead we figured we needed to explore the woods some more before we did anything else. Darting from tree to tree, as we had seen the Indians do in the movies, we made a circle in the woods. It appeared to be about a block wide from west to east and two blocks long from south to north. There were a lot of big trees and bushes in spots. We didn't find any signs of people or buildings — it was just woods. As we circled back toward the tree house we discovered a board very similar to the one nailed on the tree trunk. It still had the nails in it. A little further on, we found another matching board. Johnny figured it would take three boards to get up the tree trunk so we separated a little and searched the area. Sure enough we found a third board where it had been tossed. We took the three back to the base of the tree.

We sat down on the exposed roots of the tree and did a lot of discussing. It was Johnny's thinking that the big boys decided to abandon their tree house rather than take the risk of getting in trouble with the law but wanted to make it hard for us to use it. He said that they probably threw the crates from the upper platform where they were used for seats. That sounded right to me because I could imagine sitting on the apple crate and looking over the sides of the upper platform. The plan we developed was to leave everything as it now was and see if they came back and did anything. During the week we would keep a watch on things to see if there were any changes. As we walked back to Johnny's house we decided we had a good future with our woods.

When we got home from school Monday we each went in and changed from our school clothes to our play clothes. For school clothes nearly all the boys wore nickers made of corduroy or a similar material that reached just below the knees. Mine all had a band of elastic material on the bottom that fitted them to my leg. Some of the kids had a buckle and strap on theirs but Mother preferred the elastic ones so I wouldn't have a strap hanging down a lot of the time. Our shirts were usually made of flannel and the kind that slipped over our heads. We usually just wore the same shirt with a pair of old overalls for our play clothes.

We met at Johnny's curb and walked into the woods. As far as we could tell no one had been back to the tree with the tree house since everything looked the same as when we left it on Saturday. We explored the woods some more to become familiar with the paths, etc. We repeated that procedure the rest of the school week and made plans to go up and in our tree house in order to do some work on it that coming Saturday. We were feeling quite possessive of the woods and tree house by now since it seemed apparent the big boys had abandoned it and moved on to some other things.

Saturday morning was a very warm and sunshiny day for the last half of September and we were all ready to "work" on our tree house. When I got to Johnny's house I saw where he had put a hammer, some rope and a coffee can about half full of nails on the curb in front of his house. I saw him coming out of the side door of his house with something white in one hand. As he got closer I could tell it was some toilet paper folded up. I pointed to the paper and looked up at him. He said if we had to go to the bathroom we would be prepared. I said when we went to the bathroom in the woods at Grandma's we just used the leaves off some bushes or weeds. He said he knew some people did that but he broke out in a rash once when he was camping out with his family and he wasn't taking any chances. I drug my bike closer to his front door — so it would look like I was inside visiting — and we divided the load of supplies, heading for the woods.

The first thing we did was to nail the three boards on the tree trunk as best we could and then Johnny tested them by carefully climbing up to the first limb. He stood up on the limb, holding on to the trunk, and then he stepped onto the platform. He balanced himself with his arms held out from his sides and proudly proclaimed "That is the way to do it." Then he took another step over to the ladder leading to the second level, clutched one side in his right hand and motioned with his left for me to follow him. I did very timidly, testing every movement very carefully. I caught hold of the other side of the ladder and we looked around — studying our domain.

My legs felt a little rubbery but when Johnny asked if I was ready to go up to the second level, I just nodded. He climbed the few steps up the ladder, crawled through the opening in the railing and stood up holding on to the railing. He looked down on me, smiling broadly, and said to come on up. Again carefully, I did. As we stood side by side holding the railing we again looked all around the woods as far as we could see in all directions. Even though we were higher now it felt safer than the first platform, due I am sure to the railing around the higher one. We wondered if the big boys planned it this way or it was just luck that standing on the second level you had a good view down the paths that crossed the woods. After studying the sights a while longer, Johnny said we needed our seat up there so we could sit down. He said he was going back down to get the rope we had brought with us and for me to wait for him.

I watched as he climbed down and got the rope. He put one arm through the coiled rope, looped the rope over his shoulder and quickly scrambled back up to the second platform. He went to the side of the platform opposite the opening in the railing, tied one end of the rope to the railing and tossed the other end down to the ground. He pointed at the apple crate and said for me to go down and tie the rope to it. Then he added that I better climb back up to help him pull the apple crate up to the platform. I could see nothing wrong with that idea so I nodded my head and climbed down to the ground. I had carefully watched Johnny tie the rope to the railing so I used the same procedure to fasten the rope to one of the planks on the end of the crate. I climbed back up to the top platform as quickly as I could and saw that Johnny was pulling the rope up with the crate swinging on the end of it. When he got the crate just past the floor of the platform he said for me to catch ahold of it and drag it on the platform. I did and Johnny laid the rope down on the floor, untied my knot on the crate and laid the other end of the rope on the floor also. He turned the open side of the crate down on the floor, sat down and patted the crate beside him for me to sit down also. We sat there grinning at each other very happy with our work. About the same time we each decided that we were very thirsty and had nothing with us to drink. I said it was too bad that we didn't have a lunch packed also so we could have a picnic. Johnny agreed that this would be a great place to have a picnic so we decided to go home, get us something to drink and talk our mothers into packing a lunch for us. We gathered up our tools and headed home.

Since it was such a nice, pretty day our mothers agreed that a picnic would be fine and also agreed for us to have it in the woods. Each packed her son a sack lunch and put in a cold drink. We put the lunches in the basket on our bikes and this time we rode right up to "our" tree. We tucked our paper sack lunches in the bib of our overalls and the cold drink in the hip pocket. After climbing up to the top level we spread out our lunches on the apple crate, sat on the floor around this table and prepared to enjoy our meal. Luckily Johnny's mother had included a little bottle opener in his sack or we would not have been able to open our cold drinks — mine a Dr. Pepper and his a root beer. As we ate our peanut butter and jelly sandwiches, munched on potato chips and downed our drinks, we began to stretch out on the floor with our faces looking up at the tree above us. We saw a squirrel peeking at us from a much higher limb. Johnny said we should leave some breadcrumbs and potato chips on the platform for him and his family. As we closed up our sacks we made sure there was plenty left for Mr. Squirrel. We were tempted to stay stretched out and maybe take a nap but naps were for little kids so we would move on.

We had noticed on the trunk side of the upper level that there were some grape vines hanging down to the ground. Johnny tested them carefully and decided they would hold his weight so he hung on them and slowly let himself down all the way to the ground hand under hand. He looked up at me and motioned for me to follow suit. I did so very slowly. We walked around our tree a couple of times looking up and decided to climb up and slide down the vines a few times. It wasn't Tarzan swinging through the trees but it was fun. And it was warm so we decided to take off our shirts, shoes and socks. Before long we were running around in the woods feeling free and wild. All of a sudden something grabbed my right foot and I fell over on my left side. With both hands I lifted my right leg by the ankle and a piece of wood about two feel long was stuck to it like a ski. It hurt terribly so I eased my foot and leg back on the ground with the board still attached.

I yelled for Johnny and he came running wanting to know what had happened and I managed to point at my foot. He got down on his knees beside the board and carefully caught hold of the board and I screamed. He looked at the board, my foot, leg and face. Then he said he thought I had a nail stuck in my foot. I told him it hurt something terrible. For a few seconds Johnny looked very frightened and I was afraid he was going to run away so I grabbed his arm and said please don't leave me. Looking me straight in the eye he said he could jump on his bike go tell my mother and she would have help quickly. That really frightened me so I said no — for us to see if we could get my foot off the board. So again Johnny lightly touched the board with both hands — I didn't scream but I wanted to, it hurt terribly. As soon as he moved the board a little I did scream and Johnny let go.

I told him I thought he was going to have to yank it off. He studied the situation a little further and with a little grin on his face he said it was too bad that we didn't have a bullet for me to bite on. I looked him in the face and could tell he was dead serious. I said go ahead so he squatted down with the board crosswise in front of him and told me to hold my leg with both hands and not let it move. He caught the ends of the board in his hands and yanked. Evidently the board came off easier than we had expected for Johnny fell back and nearly hit his head with the board. My foot which had been hurting so much started to throb, I felt sick at my stomach and the trees begin to slowly spin. I could hear Johnny talking but I couldn't understand what he was saying and everything was kind of a blur. This went on for what seemed like a long time but according to Johnny only a minute or two until I looked up and asked if the board was off. He assured me it was and my foot wasn't bleeding much.

I could tell Johnny didn't know what we should do now so I said my uncle Harry had told me once that when you stuck a nail in your foot or cut it that you should soak it in coal oil. Johnny wanted to know what coal oil was and I told him it was the same thing as kerosene that you could get at the store. He said that his dad had a can of kerosene in his shop that they used in a lantern when his family went camping. We decided to go use the kerosene at his house. I walked on the heel of my right foot with my foot hurting terribly every time I touched the ground as we hobbled back to our bikes with Johnny helping me balance by holding onto one arm. We put our shirts and shoes in our bicycle baskets and pushed them to Johnny's house.

Johnny got the gallon can of kerosene and found a pan in his dad's shop. He poured the kerosene in the pan and had me sit on the floor and put my foot in the pan of kerosene. As the liquid soaked into the puncture it seemed that my foot began to feel better with just a little stinging. Johnny stood there with his hands on his hips and said that maybe he ought to be a doctor for his work. I laughed and said maybe he might make a better veterinarian. He wanted to know what that was and I told him a horse doctor. He laughed too and said all the same. After a while we decided we had soaked my foot long enough, Johnny poured the kerosene back in the can, put the pan and can up. We put our shirts, socks and shoes on and I got on my bike and headed for home — using my heel on the pedal rather than the ball of my foot to pump.

I tried to walk as normal as possible when I went into the house. Mother and Sonny were in the kitchen so I walked as usual through the kitchen on the way to my room. I was walking into the other hallway when Mother called for me to come there. I turned, walked back and stood between them as they sat at the table. Mother wanted to know why I smelled like kerosene and, of course, Sonny had to add a phue-ee. I thought fast and was ready to tell her that Johnny was showing me how to work their kerosene lantern and spilled some on us. But the look in Mother's eyes told me to think better of it and tell the whole, true story.

Mother didn't get excited, mad or anything like that which surprised me. She said to go to the back porch, put my shoes on the steps, take off all my clothes, put them in the washing machine and go take a bath. While I was in the tub with a lot of bubbles, she came in and inspected my foot. It still ached some and hurt when she felt of it. She told me to wash good and then to dry off, put my pajamas on and lie down on my bed. As I was getting ready for bed I could hear her talking with someone on the phone in the kitchen. I thought it was probably my Dad and then I thought it might be the doctor. I went to bed — wondering what was next.

I must have dozed off for the next thing I knew my Dad was standing beside my bed telling my Mother that the kerosene treatment ought to take care of it but if she wanted the doctor to see it to go ahead and call him. Mother said she thought she should and it was better to be safe than sorry. Dad sat down on the side of my bed and had me repeat the story I had told Mother. After I finished he asked me a bunch of questions and evidently was satisfied with my answers. He didn't scold me or get on me about anything and seemed quite sympathetic. Again I was surprised because I expected to be in trouble for what I had done.

Mother called from the kitchen for us to come to supper. Sonny had been standing in the bathroom doorway listening to Dad and me so he walked into my room and went with us to the kitchen. When we were seated Dad asked Mother what the doctor had said. She said he would be over right after he had his dinner. After supper I got back in my bed and was there when Dad called me to come into the dining room.

Mother and Dad were seated on one side of the dining table and a man was seated on the opposite side. Mother introduced me to the doctor and he asked me to sit in the chair on the end between him and Mother and Dad. He had a black bag beside his chair and he reached down and opened it. He then said for me to let him see my hurt foot. I sat back in my chair and lifted my foot up to his lap. He looked at the red place on the bottom and felt around on my foot and watched my face as I flinched each time he squeezed on my foot. He then took out a little flashlight from his bag and shined it in the puncture as he again mashed around on the bottom of my foot. He then said, looking back and forth from Mother and Dad to me, it is a pretty deep puncture and would probably be infected by now except for the kerosene treatment — so I figured Mother or Dad had told him about that. He then explained that if we were to get infection up in the top of the puncture he would probably have to open up my foot from the top to clean it out. This time I saw Mother flinch and Dad kind of patted my arm that was on the table. The doctor added that hopefully it would not come to that.

He said that for now he was going to clean the wound, put some medicine up in it and give me a tetanus shot. He put his black bag in his lap and began to take stuff out of it and put them on the table in front of him. He asked Dad to get him a straw from a broom. He told me he was going to give me a shot in my foot so it wouldn't hurt while he was doctoring my foot — which made me worry more about the shot than the "doctoring" did. Mother moved over to the chair where Dad had been sitting and caught hold of my hand and held it tightly. The shot didn't hurt much but I did let out a little yell. About that time Sonny appeared at the table to see what was going on so Dad motioned for him to come over to Dad and sit in his lap. The doctor reached over, took the straw from Dad and cleaned it with a cotton ball he had saturated with alcohol. He looked in his bag again and looked up at me and asked if I might have some airplane glue. I said yes — on my desk and Mother went for it. While she was gone the doctor cut some tiny strips of gauze and lined them up on another cotton ball. He took the tube of glue from Mother and very carefully applied some to the gauze strips and glued them to the end portion of the straw. He explained that he needed the gauze to stay on the straw when he put it in and took it out of the puncture. He said that on an open wound you could use a cotton ball between your thumb and forefinger but with a puncture of this type you had to stick it in and pull it out — and not leave anything up in the wound. At this I kind of gaged but he looked at me and assured me I would be fine while we did it.

He said my foot should be numb by now and began to work on it. I looked over his head so I couldn't see what was happening while he cleaned and doctored my foot — it took only a couple of minutes. He took another cotton ball, wet it with alcohol and cleaned the bottom of my foot. He said we didn't need to bandage it but we did need to keep a clean white sock on it so dirt wouldn't get in the wound. Then it was the tetanus shot. The doctor said he would be back tomorrow night about the same time for him to check my foot and decide about school on Monday. He said in the meantime he wanted me to soak my foot in warm Epsom Salt water for about fifteen minutes in the morning and again in the afternoon. He rummaged around in his bag and found a small box of the Epsom Salt and handed it to Mother. Then he sent me off to bed.

The next morning Dad volunteered to stay home with me while Sonny and Mother went to Sunday school and church. Just before she left Mother put a roast on to cook so it would be ready for our Sunday dinner when she got home. We usually ate at Grandma Jernigan's on Sundays but this time we would eat at home. I stayed in bed all day except to eat, soak my foot and go to the bathroom. Up in the morning Johnny knocked on the back door and Dad brought him in for a visit in my room. Dad complemented Johnny on doctoring my foot with the kerosene and told him the doctor said he did a good job of it. This made Johnny feel very good because he expected Mother and Dad to be mad at us for getting a nail stuck in my foot. After Dad went back to reading his newspaper in the kitchen, I told Johnny all about the doctor visit. When Mother and Sonny came home after church Johnny left for his house.

That evening as I lay on my bed reading a comic book the doctor came into my bedroom and sat on the side of the bed. He asked me how I had been doing, how my foot felt and such. He then examined my foot and told me it looked good and that I could go to school the next day but to be careful with it. If it got to hurting very much during the day or that night to have someone call him and he would have some medicine sent to me for pain. I started to tell him school was a pain anyway so maybe he needed to give me some medicine now but I decided he would think I was trying to be a smart aleck so I kept my mouth shut. I liked this doctor and I didn't want to risk him giving me more shots. Mother, Dad and Sonny were all standing behind the doctor taking it in. When the doctor stood up to go Mother told him she had put on a fresh pot of coffee if he wanted to have a cup of coffee before he left. He said that would be good to sit and visit while they had coffee. As he turned to go he looked back and said if he hadn't heard from me for two or three days he would drop back by and check my foot. With that they all trooped into the kitchen where Mother served them coffee and then put Sonny to bed while he insisted he needed to visit also.

I could hear Mother, Dad and the doctor conversing in the kitchen — sometimes having to strain to hear what was being said. From their talk I gathered that the doctor was either the son of the doctor that delivered me in their little two room house at Grandpa Jernigan's sawmill or the preacher who married them. I heard both stories that night for the first time. Dad had shown me where the sawmill had been located when I was born but there wasn't much there then but a few bricks, decaying sawdust piles and things like that. But the preacher's house was located on old highway 64 and nearly every time we drove by Dad would say that is where your Mother and I were married.

The story about their getting married was that one Sunday after dinner Mother and Dad, with another couple, rode in a horse drawn buggy a couple miles from the sawmill to the preacher's house. The other couple was to "stand up" for Mother and Dad as was the custom then — but in this situation they "sat up." The preacher and his wife were sitting on the front porch in rocking chairs. When Dad drove the buggy into the lane to the house the preacher came out to meet them at the front gate, and finding out their intention to get married, he yelled to his wife to bring his glasses and Bible from the living room and assist him. The ceremony was performed with the preacher and his wife standing by the side of the buggy, Mother and Dad sitting in the front seat and the couple seated in the back seat. You could tell Dad loved to tell this story while Mother didn't seem to enjoy it very much. Over the years I heard Dad tell this story many times. They returned to their "new house" at the sawmill, then had cake and coffee with a few friends. The next morning Mother helped her mother prepare breakfast for the single sawmill hands and Dad was at his job as usual. The only thing I remember Dad ever added or deleted, according to who was listening, was that he was in his "shirt sleeves" and that Mother had a bridal bouquet in her lap when they were married. If he added this little bit he usually also added that the bridal bouquet later decorated the coffee and cake table back at their house.

As Mother, Dad and the doctor laughed and talked my eyes got heavy and I drifted off to sleep. The next morning I went to school without any problems and sure enough in two or three nights the doctor came by one evening and gave me a clean bill of health. This was not the last time we had this doctor at our house for medical attention. He made several trips during the two years we were in Tyler. There were some for sore throats, upset stomachs and such but one other for a cut foot.

For Christmas that first year in Tyler Santa Clause brought Sonny a sidewalk bike that looked like a miniature motorcycle with a shaped metal motor above the pedals. The edges of the fake motor were pretty sharp and once when Sonny was riding it barefooted he fell with his bike and it cut the bottom of his foot rather deep. Again the doctor administered medical attention. Sonny's experience was very similar to my nail deal except he had his foot bandaged for a week or so. It seems Mother and Dad did not need the doctor as much as Sonny and I but enjoyed having him over to visit.

As a result of my school work we had another doctor that took care of Sonny and me. My reading must not have been very good at this time since I was placed in the yellowbird reading group in my room at school. Everybody in the class knew that the yellowbirds were the poor readers and the redbirds and bluebirds were much better and faster readers. The school had a nurse that came to the school about one day per week and one day my teacher sent two or three of us down to the nurse's room to have our eyes tested. A letter to my parents followed which suggested that I have my eyes examined by a doctor. In the office building where Dad worked there was an ear, eye, nose and throat doctor located. Mother took me there to see him.

After getting my medical history he tested my eyes. After that he talked to Mother about her medical history. He said that since she had the measles when I was six months old and had transmitted them to me, he felt that they had weakened my eyes and yes I definitely needed glasses. He ordered and fitted me with glasses. I was to wear them only at school and when doing my homework since he thought I would have trouble with them during more active times. I think I was the only kid in my room that wore glasses and maybe the only one in the fourth grade. I had glasses from then on but would sometimes go for long periods without wearing them. I, more or less, quit wearing them about the eighth or ninth grade and didn't seriously wear them until about the time I got married. Later my wife said she didn't know I needed glasses until after we were married. She would kid me sometimes by saying "see what not wearing your glasses got you into." Somehow I got by for many years with my very limited eyesight.

Due to our frequent sore throats, our regular doctor and the specialist I went to for my eyes decided that we both should have a tonsillectomy. This was a fairly common practice in that day and arrangements were made for the specialist to do the operation on both of us in his office, one following the other. In his office suite the doctor had a surgery room equipped with a big leather chair that reminded me of a picture of an electric chair I had seem. I asked him if he was going to electrocute us and he laughed and said no that he was just going to take out our tonsils which were giving us trouble and we didn't need them anymore. He said he wanted me to go first and show my little brother that it didn't hurt. I reluctantly climbed up in the chair and he and the nurse started strapping a lot of equipment on me and soon I was smelling this funny odor. I didn't remember much after that until I was sitting in another chair in another room with Mother holding my hand and a nurse talking to me. In a few minutes the doctor and another nurse brought Sonny in and sat him on the other side of Mother. He looked dead to me but I was afraid to ask so I just watched as they revived him. Mother continued to hold my hand and put her other arm around him.

The main thing I remember after we were out of the "fog" was that a nurse brought each of us a dish of ice cream. Mother helped Sonny with his and I ate a little of mine. We were told that it was all we could eat the rest of that day but I don't remember complaining about that since I didn't even feel like eating much ice cream. A nurse gave Mother a page of instructions and read them over with her as Sonny and I listened very carefully. The nurse asked if there were any questions and Mother said she thought we could handle it all right. Dad met us at the doctor's office and drove us home.

Tony played a big part in my school life while we were living in Tyler. Anthony was his real name but only the teachers ever called him by that name. If any of the kids called him Anthony you could see he was taking it as an insult and would redden considerably. Tony was in my class in both the fourth and fifth grades and in the yellowbird reading group until I got my glasses and moved up to the redbirds. I was first attracted to Tony due to his funny talk. I told him that he sounded like the people in the movies from Brooklyn. He liked that and said he wasn't from Brooklyn or New York but he had relatives there and had visited them several times. Tony was what I would later term "typically Italian." He told me that he had moved to Tyler with his family from a large city, either Detroit or Chicago — I couldn't ever remember which — and had been in Texas a year when he was in the fourth grade.

Tony was large — probably the largest in our class — tended to be loud and was a leader. Since I was one of the smaller kids — and tended to be quiet and hang back a little — I decided it would be a good idea to be friendly to Tony. Most of the kids would shy away from him — some even called him "the Diego" to his back — but the closer you got to him the nicer he seemed. My friendship with Tony paid off several times since he would always come to my rescue when another bigger kid would try to push me around. This backup encouraged me to hold my own on the playground and on the way to and from school (it even continued somewhat after we moved from Tyler because I found others that took up for the little guy sometimes). So as it turned out, Tony was my best friend at school and Johnny was my best friend at home and around our neighborhood.

Tony lived on the other side of town from us and I only rode my bike to his house one time. His was a big old house in one of the older neighborhoods. His mother and older sister were at home when we arrived. He took me into the house, reported to his mother and introduced me to them. His mother fixed us some hot chocolate and the four of us sat around the kitchen table and talked. His mother asked me a lot of questions and the sister laughed a good bit. Tony wanted me to go upstairs to his room and see his things. I told them I should go on home since I didn't have permission to go visiting and would be missed in a little while. I left with his mother's blessing and hurried home.

On the way home I saw Johnny at Smith's Grocery and turned in to park beside him. I could tell he was a little cool toward me and then as he told me he had seen me riding off with Tony after school, I realized he was jealous of my friendship with Tony. From then on I was always careful to not mention Tony to Johnny — he resented my friendship with Tony so I decided the less said about Tony the better. Tony came to my house a few times — usually uninvited — so I was careful to keep Tony out of sight if possible.

One time when Tony was at my house and we were going down to the store on our bikes to get something to snack on, we rounded the north corner and Tony glanced back at the corner as if he was looking for something. When we got to the store he said he had just noticed that we had storm drainage sewers on our street. I didn't know what he was talking about so he said he would show me when we got back to the house. After we returned to the house, had our snack and drinks, Tony said to come on and he would show me the sewers. On the way to the corner he explained that in the city where they lived before coming to Texas he had watched the big boys going in and out of the storm sewers. One time a big friend of his had put him in one and let him look around.

As we stood at the corner, Tony pointed out that the street had a small dip at the corner and an opening a little over a foot tall extended for four or five feet on each side of the corner. You could see how the dip would turn water from the street into the cutout and funnel it into the opening through the curb. Tony went on to explain that under the curb and sidewalk there were concrete tunnels that carried the water to a creek, gully or even larger tunnels so that when it rained the streets would not flood. I was amazed that Tony knew all this without even looking into the openings. Then he said look at this and pointed at the sidewalk over the corner. There was a larger section of sidewalk over the corner and in the center was a big metal disk about two feet in diameter. Tony said this is the manhole cover. When the workers need to go down in the tunnels, they lift this off and climb down. Then he motioned for us to lie down in the gutter and put our heads in the opening.

As we lay on the concrete gutter we poked our heads in the opening in the curb. At first it was just darkness but as our eyes adjusted we could begin to see around underground. We could make out the outline of the tunnel and a little spot of light in a couple of places down the tunnel. Tony said it wasn't very far to the floor of the tunnel and he would let himself down and then for me to follow him. He had convinced me he knew what he was doing so I nodded and kind of grunted. I watched as he lay on his stomach and edged his feet and legs into the opening. When he was all in up to his waist, he grinned at me and slipped on into the tunnel. He kind of fell over but then his face popped up in the opening with a big grin on it. He then said for me to come on and do as he had done. I hesitated and asked how we would get out. He said don't worry, I'll show you. Well, this was no time to back out now so I followed his example and dropped into the tunnel. Since Tony was about a head taller than me my eyes just reached the bottom of the opening in the curb. I could see out the opening but I had to stand on my tiptoes to see the street. Tony could stick his face in the opening and turning it back and forth see both directions up and down the street.

Since I couldn't see much outside, I began to look around inside the tunnel. As our eyes became more adjusted to the darkness we could see the tunnels running down under the streets. We didn't go far in any direction but did a little exploring and found this underground layout amazing. There was a lot of junk and trash scattered around so we were careful to walk around or over it. I was still worried about how we were going to get out of the tunnel but each time I said something about it Tony would only say that he would show me in a minute or two.

As we were standing near the place where we had come into the tunnel, Tony said it would take the two us working together to get back out so we should never go into the tunnels without a buddy. As I looked at him he could see the anxiety building on my face, so he patted me on the shoulder and then motioned for me to stand just below where we had come in. He looked me in the eye and said that he was going to reach up into the opening and for me to give him a boost so he could then pull himself through the opening. I caught him around the waist but he said to get lower down and I reached around his knees. He said lift up and I did but instead of going up much we went over and both tumbled on the ground. I said since he was bigger and stronger maybe he should lift me up to the opening. He said that wouldn't do because then I wouldn't be strong enough to pull him through the opening. Now I really was getting worried but Tony just said come here right under this opening and get on your hands and knees and hold as firm as you can. I did and as he held to the edge of the opening, stepped on the middle of my back and pushed through the opening to his waist and squirmed on through. I jumped up and looked out the opening — there was Tony on his hands and knees looking into my face grinning. He said give me your hands which I did as he gripped me around the wrists and said for me to grip his wrists. He said he was going to start pulling and for me to keep my head in the opening as I came up. He pulled and I slowly slid up to my waist in the opening and then kind of rolled out into the street. I was shaking all over and very happy to be in the street. Tony sat down on the curb and I crawled over and sat down beside him. I thought that would be the last time I would ever get in those tunnels but Tony had other ideas.

Several times after that Tony would come over to my house for us to explore the sewers. During these expeditions we covered two or three blocks in all directions. We found an outlet a little way past Smith's Grocery on the other side of the street and we would use this route to go to the grocery store when we didn't want to ride our bikes. Of course this secret was just too good to keep from Johnny so after a while I told him about it — not telling him of Tony's role in it. I had already planned a modified escape method when I told Johnny. We would gather and build a platform of rocks, broken bricks and the like so that we could climb out without assistance.

Johnny decided that he would be King of The Woods and I would be King of The Sewers. We would each make up the rules for our play in each of the areas. This sounded good to me so I agreed. Eventually we decided to include a few friends from within our neighborhood as long as they swore to follow our rules. This arrangement worked all right as long as my family was in Tyler. I never visited back in this neighborhood after we moved back to L C or saw anyone I knew there so I never found out how well it worked after I left. I always wondered who took my place as King of The Sewers — finally deciding that, knowing Johnny the way I did, and him, the way he was, I was sure he also claimed the title of King of The Sewers.

In the summer between my two school years in Tyler we spent a lot of time at Grandma's farm — especially during canning season. One day after coming back home from spending four or five days at Grandma's, Mother asked me to go to the grocery store and get us a fresh loaf of bread so we could have sandwiches for supper. I jumped on my bike and went to the store. Since it was so sandy around Grandma's we never rode our bikes there — preferring to ride our horses or drive old Kate to the cart. Mr. Smith had missed me and we visited a few minutes while he caught up on the news as to what we had been doing.

I put the loaf of bread in my basket and headed toward home. As I neared our corner I started my cut across the street to go up a driveway and ride on the sidewalk around the corner to our house as I usually did.

Just as I started to the left, I felt this tremendous surge of my bicycle forward and it was all I could do to stay on it. Instead of turning into the driveway, I hit the curb across the street head on and went flying over the handlebars into the ground on the other side of the sidewalk. The last thing I remembered was flying over the sidewalk. The next thing I remembered was a lady standing over me saying "Poor little thing he had gotten a loaf of bread for his mother when someone hit him with a car from the back side." I wondered if I was dead but decided to see if I could move so I got up on my hands and knees and looked around. A young man was standing astraddle the front wheel of my bike holding onto the handlebars and looking at me. Two or three other people were standing around me and I saw a couple of cars parked in the street.

I was a little dizzy but couldn't tell that I was hurt much so I took the few steps over to my bike. The man holding it stepped aside, still holding it up, and said that he had straightened the handlebars and the braces on the back fender where the wheels seemed to turn all right. I remembered to say thank you and took hold of the handlebars. As I swung my leg over and sat on my bike, the lady holding the loaf of bread said that maybe she should take me home. I told her I was all right and could make it by myself. She put the loaf of bread in my basket and I rode off and turned the corner. As I looked back I could see they were all watching me as I went out of sight around the corner.

Evidently the car that had hit me did not even stop from what I had heard one or two of the bystanders saying as I was trying to get away. I was afraid I would be blamed for it so I just wanted to get home and forget about it if I could. I made it home fine and Mother never knew what had happened as far as I knew. I think I was one lucky kid that time since I didn't get seriously injured. Later I wondered how any driver could knock a kid off his bicycle and not stop and tend to him as the child lay helpless on the ground.

During the summer Mother always insisted that I spend a good deal of time reading so I would not lose ground in this area while not in school. She was always agreeable to my going to the public library with someone else or even by myself when we were at home in Tyler during the summers. Johnny liked to go to the baseball park and the playground on Broadway but he never was much interested in going to the library with me. I usually ended up going to the library by myself. The library was just a block or so southwest of the Square — which was a little distance from our house but an enjoyable bike ride for me.

One summer afternoon I had finished the current National Geographic at the library and didn't find anything else I wanted to read so I decided to ride up to the Square and look around there since I still had time to burn. At one of the corners on the Square I noticed a sign with an arrow pointing north with Tyler State Park on it. I had been to Tyler State Park a couple of times with my family for church picnics or such and then it seemed just out of town going in the car. I knew it was an interesting place and would probably be a nice bike ride to it. Of course it was in the opposite direction to home.

I had no trouble finding my way since there were a lot of signs to mark the way, but the distance stretched out and got longer and longer. Every once in a while I thought maybe I should turn around and go back from where I had come but I kept on. Finally I saw a sign that said Tyler State Park One Mile. Since I had come that far I couldn't turn back without getting to the park. I made it to the park and took a short loop and headed back. By this time I was very tired and very, very thirsty. Thankfully I found a water fountain near the entrance and got a good drink before I started back. By now I didn't look forward to the return trip with much relish but I knew it had to be done. I had to remember the route I had taken for there were no signs to direct me back I made it back to the Square and was really tired by then. I stopped off at the library for a rest and another tank of cold water with a restroom break.

I got home and I was exhausted, probably the most tired I had ever been. I dragged in and Mother wanted to know why I was so late. I told her I got interested in my reading and forgot about the time. She said she was glad I was putting my time to good use and nothing more was said. After supper I went to my room and to bed. Mother came in to check on me but I told her I was just tired and wanted to go to bed. She said fine and left me to sleep. The next morning I felt fine but decided not to recount my adventure to anyone. I did think that I needed to look at a little longer plan the next time I left on an excursion.

Also during that summer we played a lot of unorganized baseball on the vacant lot just past Smith's Grocery on the opposite side of the street and just before you got to the railroad track. This was where I cut my right hand as I was sliding into third base. This section of the field was pretty rough and somehow a broken bottle had gotten just outside of the baseline. I put my right hand on the ground as I slid in to the base and it hit on the bottle and cut from my little finger up past my wrist. My hand was bleeding pretty good so someone wrapped their T shirt around it and ran over to Smith's grocery and told him. He phoned my Mother and got his car. He picked me up at the ball field and then we went to our house for my Mother and Sonny. Then he drove to the doctor's office. Since our doctor had always come to our house before I had never been to his office.

It was a large two story house with his office downstairs and the family lived upstairs. When we got there, Mr. Smith went into the office with us but then he left to go back to his store. By the time we were in the examining room my Dad showed up. The doctor looked my hand over and had the nurse clean it up. He assured us that it was going to be O K. He took me and Dad to the room next door and the nurse took Mother and Sonny back to the waiting room. The doctor had me sitting in a large leather seat, pulled some bright lights down from the ceiling and put my hand on a shelf he pulled across the arms of the chair. The nurse came in and put some instruments and supplies on the shelf. The doctor and nurse bent over my arm and began working on my hand. He rubbed some deadening on my hand, little finger and wrist. He told me to hold very still while he sewed up my cut.

I felt sick at my stomach and was afraid I was going to throw up. The nurse saw the expression on my face and handed me a large aluminum pan to hold across my stomach with my left hand. She didn't need to tell me what it was for but I never did throw up. The doctor patted me on the shoulder a couple of times and reassured me I was doing fine. After he finished with the stitches the nurse bandaged my hand for several inches above my wrist. The doctor said that should do for a couple of days and for me to come back to the office then and he would check it and the nurse would bandage it again. He also said for me to sit on the side of the bathtub to bathe and not get that hand wet. Dad thanked him and we all went home. After I cleaned up some, I went to bed.

Then the kids started coming by to see me. Later that evening at supper, Mother said she thought every kid in the neighborhood had come by for a few minutes. Each would only stay for a minute or two but the word must have gotten out that it was the thing to do — come by and see me.

My hand healed well and I had a good scar from the finger digit next to the hand, up the outside edge up my hand and two or three inches past my wrist. Today, some seventy-five years later, you can still see a scar on the outside of my wrist for a couple of inches and about an inch from the heel of my hand toward the little finger.

The railroad tracks past Smith's Grocery and the makedo baseball field was another area which the neighborhood kids loved to explore. We could go north and would curve to the west and meet up with other tracks near downtown, but going south was our favorite path. There weren't many trains on this track which I am sure led to Bullard and probably on to Jacksonville. As we headed south we began to leave houses behind. There was a large dairy and then a little further on a pond — we called it a lake but it wasn't very big. We never really went swimming in it but we did wade in it a lot and splash around some. One time a few of us tried to gather enough poles and pieces of lumber to make us a raft. This wasn't very successful so we left it about fifty feet out in the pond with one end in the mud and the other sticking a little out of the water.

No one ever bothered us around the pond and we had free run of that area. One area of the pond had the bottom covered with mussels so we gathered a lot of them and had nothing to do but prize them open and look inside.

We never knew that people ate raw mussels like oysters at that time so we never tried to eat any raw. One time some of us boys decided to camp out overnight there and after we built a fire we decided to boil some of the mussels to see what they tasted like. No one wanted more than a taste but everyone did or you would have been a scardycat. About ten o'clock we watched a freight train go through and our fire was about burned out with our wood all gone. We decided to go home so we followed the tracks back to our neighborhood. I suspect the other parents, like mine, were still sitting up expecting to see us come in by midnight.

A week or so after that, as three or four of us were going to the pond late one afternoon we saw a small group of men gathered around a fire cooking their supper. We saw them and they saw us but neither let on. We sat on the side of a small hill and watched them for a while. After a while Johnny said that must be a hobo camp that he had heard his dad telling his mother about. The railroads were having trouble with them moving closer into town. He said we should steer clear of that place because there could be robbers and murders in that group. That was enough for us to quit going down south on the railroad tracks and stay closer to home.

The second school year we were in Tyler Sonny was in the first grade. I usually rode my bike to school as long as the weather permitted and in bad weather I would ride with Dad as he took Sonny to school. Mother wouldn't let me ride Sonny on my bike, as we called it double, for fear of an accident. But occasionally he would want to walk and I had to walk with him. In the pretty weather there would be a string of kids on their way to school but Mother did not let Sonny unless I walked with him.

One morning as we were walking we rounded our corner and headed east. When we got to the first house facing that street, a lady with Mary the little girl that lived there called to me and I looked her way and stopped. She asked if Mary could walk to school with us and I said sure. I could see this boy, about my age, sitting on the front steps where Mary and the lady had come from. The lady said that she was Mary's grandmother and she would pick her up after school. She thanked me and as I looked back at the boy on the steps and he could tell I was looking at him he ran into the house. We walked down the sidewalk with Mary between Sonny and me. Mary was a year older than Sonny but I knew he had played with her both at her house and at ours.

As we walked along I asked her about the boy. I said I had seen him there but every time I look at him he runs in the house and I had never seen him going to school. Mary said simply that he didn't go to school. I wondered why so I asked more questions. She explained that he and their mother were in the London explosion. He was waiting in the car for her when the New London School exploded in 1937 and evidently killed the mother and he witnessed the horrible aftermath. He and Mary came to live with their grandparents and her brother couldn't bear to see or be near a school building after that. When they went to a school he would start shaking and having a fit. The doctors said it would be better if he stayed home from school and maybe he would outgrow it.

Since Joyce, my wife, started to the New London School right after the explosion and graduated from it, we go to the reunions. I always remember this boy and the frightened look on his face — and wonder if he ever did go to school again.

When school was out that year, Sonny had finished the first grade and I had finished the fifth. We had heard Mother and Dad talking about moving back to L C and Dad was going to start a new business. Just as we had hated to leave our friends in Tennessee, we hated to leave our friends in Tyler. But we knew we had some old friends at L C and there would be some new ones too. And of course, there were our very own horses that would be waiting for us at L C.

GRANDMA'S FARM

One of my most loved places on this earth is what we always called Grandma's farm. If you were to draw a line from Kilgore straight west to Tyler and put an X in the center of this line you would have marked near where Grandma's farm was/is located. It became a part of our family about 1928 I think (around the same time as me) and still is today. This purchase was a part of Grandpa's involvement in his sawmill business. He first bought a section of land here for the timber and as the third location of his sawmill. He extended the size of it by purchasing several smaller adjacent pieces of property. Over the next couple of years he had a lot of farming activity going on also in addition to moving the sawmill there. Grandma liked this location so much that he built a new home there also for them. They were living in Kilgore at the time for Auntie to finish high school but with the advent of the East Texas Oil Field Grandma yearned for the country. Some of this is covered in the story about the house at Leverett's Chapel.

Not long after the house was finished at Grandma's farm, Grandpa passed away. As part of his and Grandma's estate they owned three identical homes (build from the same plans), as well as, several other properties. With the division of the estate, Mother received the house and the thirty acres it was located on at Leverett's Chapel — while Ruby received the house in Kilgore. Later when Grandma Jernigan died in the 1960s, Auntie gained the property we call Grandma's farm. I think she told me that it consisted of 625 acres about the time she received the property. Her son, Jack Spear, is the owner now. So, two of the three houses are still owned by family. Our daughter now owns the Leverett's Chapel house. The Kilgore house is still there but has been sold and moved around the corner — located on Lawrence St. It was originally moved in order to construct the Kilgore Hospital before Laird Memorial was built a few blocks south on Henderson Blvd. Today the spot it was first built on is the

Presbyterian Church parking lot. Each house has been remodeled several times and none resembles the other two.

About once every week or two I see the back of Grandma's house driving to or from Kilgore and Tyler. This came about when the new Highway 31 was built and is now a mile or so south of its original route in that area. This change made it run through the middle of Grandma's farm from east to west. Now the back of the house (north side) — on the west end and south portion of the property — is visible from the new highway, but the old mill site — on the east end and north portion — lies hidden among the new growth of pines. I see the Kilgore house when I drive to my dentist or the public library — about four blocks from our Kilgore home. We go by or to the Leverett's Chapel properties several times a week — where our children, grandchildren, and great grandchildren now live.

When I was growing up and spent a lot of time at Grandma's farm, everything looked quite different driving there then and now. The old sandy road has been replaced with a more modern paved asphalt road with signs proclaiming Jernigan Road in honor of Grandma Jernigan. Back then as you left the highway and turned south, there was only one business actually facing the highway. This store was named Meadows Grocery & Feed and operated by two midget brothers. They had another brother, regular size (actually a little taller than average), who did most of the heavy lifting but seemed to have another regular job some other place. The Meadows also sold gasoline, oil and such for cars, trucks and tractors. In the feed department they also had a lot of seeds, fertilizers, livestock medicine and supplies. We kids usually kept track of most everything in the store. The two midgets never married and I don't think the other brother did either but we noticed that he had a girlfriend every now and then.

 As you went about a block south the sandy road made another ninety degree turn east for about three blocks and then sharply curved again until it was running south. In about another block there was another small store building that changed hands every now and then and was kind of a secondhand clothes, furniture, and tool store. They may have also loaned money on items kind of like today's pawn shops. Most of their customers were black and/or very poor. Another road ran directly west from in front of this store. The only thing down that road was a small sawmill and farm. The sawmill was operated by the farmer when he wasn't planting, plowing or harvesting. He usually had only one or two men helping him when he was working the sawmill. Most everyone in our family referred to it as the peckerwood mill.

The main road ran on due south for about another half mile. The first building in this section was the Browning General Store — belonging to one of the Browning family for which the community was named. Across the street was the Baptist church and a little further down on the right side of the road was the Methodist church. Neither of these churches was very large and probably didn't have services every Sunday. There were a few houses scattered along both sides of the road until you got to another ninety degree bend to the east.

Just past this turn on the south side of the road was a large church that every Sunday afternoon there would be a large crowd of blacks for singing and preaching. Many Sundays Robert, William and I would ride our horses over to this church and in the middle of the afternoon sit on our horses while the singing, preaching and "carrying on" was in full blast. We never did go in but were tempted when someone we knew would invite us in. There was always a lot of coming and going during the services. We did buy us a soda pop sometimes at the little concession stand they had outside under the shade of a tree.

After this turn, the road just kind of meandered along for another mile or so and then made a turn and ran straight south for two or three miles until it ran into another road running east and west. There were a few houses on small farms scattered along the road but at this turn south there was a nice, large dog run type of farm home. This was where another member of the Browning family lived and farmed. Some thirty or so years after Grandpa's original purchase of Grandma's farm my cousin Robert bought the Browning farm, and some smaller parcels adjacent to it, and developed a very nice ranch where his wife, Modena, and some of their offspring still live — and have raised purebred cattle all this time.

Grandma's farm was next to the Browning's on the northeast side (the only white neighbors for a mile or more in all directions) but about one-fourth of a mile from the road. Evidently the previous owner had bought a lane about thirty yards wide from the Brownings to connect Grandma's farm with the road. To get to Grandma's we drove down a fenced lane — with the sandy soil kept plowed up and packed down wide enough for one car.

The south fence line that formed the lane continued on east as it joined her property and ran straight east for a little over a mile — the length of the property — being the south boundary. The west boundary of the property ran due north for about a mile. The north and east boundary lines were not straight since pieces of property had been added after Grandpa had purchased the original section.

Even thinking about these scenes, and especially when I see them, I am flooded with memories of growing up there. As I described above the location of the small sawmill in the area around Browning, I was reminded of my first "contracting job" when I was about eleven or twelve years old in partnership with my two cousins Robert and William.

One morning we borrowed old Kate and her cart from Buddy to go looking around. William was always our driver of draft animals hooked to all sorts of conveyances — carts, sleds, wagons and such. His specialty was harness and mules, while mine and Robert's were more toward horses — with or without saddles. Looking for different territory, we decided to head Kate for Browning — about two miles away. It was probably about nine in the morning when we got there and looked around some. We saw that the little sawmill was operating so we rode down that way. Since we had no money William suggested maybe we could work for the sawmill and make some — since he knew the man who ran it.

William drove Kate up to the trunk of a small tree, I jumped out of the cart and tied her to the tree with the small rope attached to her bridal and looped around her neck. William, usually the most timid of the three, led the way over to a large man standing near a heap of slabs. He was carefully stacking them in a neat pile. As we approached he took off his hat with one hand and wiped his forehead with the gloved back of the other hand. We could see his overalls and shirt were dripping with sweat. Looking straight at William, he asked "What you boys up to?" William told him that we were wondering if he had any work that needed to be done that we could do to make some money. He looked at Robert and then me, wiped his forehead again — this time with the other hand — and glanced over his left shoulder before he looked back again at William. With a broad grin he said, "I just might have." We looked at each other and began thinking how lucky we were today.

The man motioned for us to follow him and walked toward three piles of sawdust at the end of the shed covering the sawmill works. Each pile was roughly about eight feet tall with their bases overlapping each other. He pointed to the piles and said that he needed to move one of them to have room for another pile or else he had to build an extension to the exhaust chute. He figured it would be easier to move some of the sawdust than construct more piping. He said with our cart we could load the sawdust and haul it over to that bare spot about fifty feet from where we were standing. As he talked we began to nod to indicate we understood his plan. He then told us that he paid a grown man two dollars for a full day's work so he felt he could pay us three dollars to move one of the piles.

The looks on our faces pretty well gave him his answer when he asked if that was agreeable. He pointed to one of the piles and said it was the closest to the area where he wanted it and would be the easiest for us to load and unload with our cart. Again we nodded. He walked under the main shed and came back with two shovels in one hand and two pair of heavy leather gloves in the other. One of the shovels had a short handle but a big scoop on the other end like the one we had watched Buddy use to feed the milk cows the cotton seed hulls in the winter time. The other had a long handle but a much smaller load capacity. The man said we could take time about with the shovels. We left the shovels and gloves at the pile and got Kate, led her with the cart back to the pile and went to work. One of the black men working under the shed also knew William and came over to visit for a few minutes.

Within minutes we were also soaked with sweat. The gloves were so large that they slipped around on our hands and instead of helping they made it worse. The blisters began to appear and then break. We were in the direct sunlight and it kept getting hotter. The same black man came back by and told us that when we got thirsty there was some cool water under the shed. We all three went over for a drink out of a wooden barrel with a single tin cup on a string to drink with. For the rest of the time the third man (boy) not shoveling spent his time under the shed by the water barrel. After about two hours we were worn out, tired and hungry. Robert got the bright idea that maybe the man would give us some money so that we could go get us a soda water and a snack. William said he would check it out with the black man and he did. The next thing we knew the black man took William to the boss and William came back with a fifty cent piece.

We loaded up and rode down to the Browning store. We each had a soda, a moon pie and a candy bar — with a nickel left over. Boy was that good eating and drinking. We were so tired that we could hardly stand so we draped all over the cart in the shade of one of the big trees at the end of the porch. Mr. Browning came out, pulled up a straight cane-bottomed chair at the end of the porch and visited with us a while. A customer or two came to the store while we were resting and Mr. Browning would go in and take care of them — then return to his chair on the porch. He found out what we were doing and the details of our working deal. He seemed concerned and finally said that he was afraid we were working too hard and might have a heat stroke. He suggested we go on to Grandma's and he would tell Mr. Gothe when he came down at his usual time around one o'clock. He said he knew Mr. Gothe well and he would feel they had earned the fifty cents for the work we had already done. We thought that was a great idea and were immediately ready to go. We thanked Mr. Browning for his help and headed for Grandma's. Old Kate must have understood the conversation because as we turned toward her "home" she wanted to trot all the way.

About half way from the black's church and the turn of the road at Grandma's lane, there was a small stream usually running across the road.

This stream had no bridge but was running over rocks and gravel as it funneled water from the bottom land into a kind of slough south of there. As we rode over the stream Robert and I began to recount — again — the story about when we had our big adventure there. It had occurred a few months before but we still liked to tell William about it. The story was that one evening just about dark in the wintertime, our uncle Fred was taking us with him in his pickup over to the Meadows to get something for Ruby, Grandma's cook, to have for the next morning's breakfast.

We were riding along and Fred was telling us a scary hunting story. As we neared the stream a black panther jumped across the road from one side to the other just above the hood of the truck. As he sailed through the air, he turned his head to look at us — his eyes gleamed red which made the hair stand up on the back of our necks and a chill run down our spines. Uncle Fred turned to us and said "Did you see that?" We both gulped and I finally stammered "yyyess." As we finished our story William, being easily scared, tapped Kate with the reins to pick up the pace a little more.

The lane to Grandma's Farm always reminds me of two incidents concerning birds. The first is when I was probably about six years old and got my first BB gun. It was a Tom Mix model, for I think my second one was the Red Ryder with a leather thong attached to it. After being warned to be careful where and how I shot, I went out the front of Grandma's to go bird hunting. I walked down to the lane and went up it a little way toward the Browning house where I spied a bird sitting on the top wire of the lane fence. I think it was a dove due to its full rounded breast. I took careful aim and pulled the trigger. Even with one eye still closed, I saw the bird topple over and kind of glide to the ground. I was overjoyed and ran to the fence and looked over at the bird on the ground.

I carefully climbed through the barbed wire fence and stood over the bird. With the toe of my boot I pushed the bird around a little and it fluttered, raised its head and squawked at me with a wide open mouth and a steady stare into my eyes. My heart was pounding and I could hear the blood pumping in my temples as I just stood there kind of shaking. I recalled something about God knew when every sparrow fell or something like that which made me look all around but saw no one — just a few cows eating grass on the hillside. They didn't pay me a bit of attention. After a few moments in this disturbed state, I decided to take the bird with me and try to help it recuperate — undo the harm I had done. I was afraid to touch the bird for I was sure it would peck me in its current situation so I laid my gun on the ground, took off my cap and dropped it over the bird. The bird quit squawking and settled down at once in the darkness of the cap. I picked up the cap carefully being sure it was closed over the bird and clutched it to my chest. Holding the cap with one hand I picked up my gun and retreated to the fence. Here I slid my gun under the fence and carefully worked myself through it.

I retraced my steps back to the house carrying my bundle. When I came to the front yard gate opening to the brick sidewalk leading to the front door, I decided not to take the bird any further. I laid my gun aside again and gently placed the cap under the edge of the hedge close to the gate so that I could lift my cap off the bird. As I removed the cap I saw the bird squatting down, its wings about half extended on the ground and its eyes staring straight into mine. Then the squawking began again. With tears in my eyes, I tucked my cap under one arm, picked up my gun with the other hand and rushed into the house.

As I passed from the front porch into the hallway I could see through the open doorway to Grandma's large bedroom/sitting room where Mother and Grandma were seated in front of the fireplace. Mother called to me "Back from your big hunt?" I answered yes and that I was going to get a drink of water and kept headed for the kitchen. Ruby was working in the kitchen so I got my drink and visited with her for a while trying to get my mind off the bird. It was no use so I told Ruby I had seen a crippled bird out front and thought it probably needed something to eat and drink. She got a small bowl, filled it about half way with water and covered it with a saucer. Then she got a leftover biscuit and crumbled off a few crumbs into the saucer and handed the stack to me. She cautioned me to be careful so as not to spill any. I found the bird where I had left it and carefully placed the bowl and saucer next to the bird. It didn't seem any happier than before, but I left telling it I would be back later to check on it.

Before supper I remembered the bird and went to check on it. I found the bowl overturned and the saucer empty — no bird. I looked all around but no bird. I decided it had gotten better and flown away which made me feel good and I would be able to eat my supper and sleep that night. But two or three days later as I was walking on the other side of the hedge to get to the back of the garage, about ten or twelve feet from the gate, I saw this little bunch of feathers on the ground just under the hedge. With my boot toe I scooted it out and realized it was a bird wing. Then it dawned on me that one of the cats on the farm had probably eaten the bird. I walked over to one of the yard chairs, sat down and had a good cry. I have never enjoyed bird hunting.

The second memory was some ten years later. A few months before Joyce and I were to be married I took her to Grandma's for Sunday dinner — to meet the "family." As we turned into the lane toward the house several buzzards flew up that had been feeding on a rabbit or squirrel that had probably been struck by a car. Joyce asked what kind of birds were those big ones. I, feeling kind of in a kidding mood at the time, replied that they were wild turkeys and that there was a lot of wild stuff around those parts. She said "Oh" and I let it go at that thinking I would correct her later since we were turning into the front area at Grandma's.

It seemed everything went well during the introductions, dinner and then the visiting afterward. The women sat on the front porch and talked about women things and the men and boys went out front under the shade trees, smoked and discussed male things. In a little while we started dividing up, getting in our cars and leaving. As we got to the car I could tell Joyce was a little cool toward me when I tried to help her with the car door. She said not a word until we topped the little hill as we neared the Browning house. She sat up straight and glared at me which made me ask what the matter was. She said "As if you wouldn't know!" I said I didn't have any idea what she was talking about. So boy, did she tell me. She said all the ladies were sitting and visiting when Grandma turned to her and asked what she thought about what she had seen of the place. All eyes and ears turned her way so she tried to come up with something so she said that she had enjoyed everything especially the wild turkeys. Grandma looked at her questioningly and asked where that was. Joyce said just as we turned in to come to the house several flew up. Grandma laughed and said those must have been buzzards since there had been no wild turkeys in those parts for decades. Then everyone laughed and Joyce told me "I was never so embarrassed in all my life!"

I apologized over and over but she was still mad when we got to her house where she got out and went in. It was our custom to go to evening service at the Overton Methodist Church — due to it being very short compared to any of the Baptist ones. I drove over to her house at the regular time and she was ready to go. She didn't mention the incident again so I surely didn't. Everything smoothed out and we were married on schedule and have completed nearly sixty six years of married life. Many times I have wondered what happened in the three hours between when I left her at home and when we left for church. I think she told her mother, a very sensible woman, and she must have advised her to overlook it since most men are bound to do such stupid things every now and then. I think I had as good a relationship with my mother-in-law as anyone I have ever known has had with a mother-in-law.

As you neared the end of the lane entering Grandma's place there was a large gate in the fence line running north. A little before you got to the gate the little road Y'd off to the left where a car could drive across a cattle guard through an opening in the fence which went into the large area in front of the house. There were a lot of fences and gates at Grandma's. Behind the gate was another lane continuing on east for about seventy-five yards to another fence and gate. This fence, made of wooden boards, ran on north and met the south east corner of the yard fence. This fence served as the separating line between the living area of house, garages, yard and the acre or so in front of the house from the barns, livestock pens, garden, farming areas and sawmill. It was in the open area in front of the house that we had our picnic tables, room for our children's playground and plenty of parking area for the many cars there on July 4th, Christmas and other special times.

The house was fenced in with a green picket fence — the fence being about fifty feet from each outside wall of the house. About midway of the house on both sides there was another short fence running from the house to the outside picket fence — effectively forming a front yard and a back one. This layout created the need for several gates which were well placed and matched the picket fence. The gate in front of the house opened onto a brick paved sidewalk to the front steps leading up to the door. On each side of the walkway was a flower bed — bordered by bricks stuck in the ground at a forty-five degree angle —in which grew all sorts of flowers, according to the season. Just inside the front, west and east sides of the fence grew a neatly trimmed privet hedge the height of the fence.

When Fred, the youngest son, married Thelma they didn't want to move into the same house with Grandma — which she wanted — so they compromised. Grandma had a second floor added to the two end garages to make a garage apartment for them. They lived here for a couple or three years — while Fred and Carl ran the motorcycle shop — until Thelma was expecting Peggy. Then they bought their first home on the southeast side of Tyler.

I was about six or seven years old when the carpenters were doing the work on the garages. One Sunday before dinner William and I were inspecting the progress on the building when I discovered a pair of carpenter's overalls hanging up in the garage. Naturally curious, I checked the pockets and the built-in nail apron and discovered a plug of Brown Mule chewing tobacco. I offered to share with William, but he was not the adventurous type so he refused it. To show him how brave I was I chewed off a good sized bite. I tried to look nonchalant but after a couple of big swallows of tobacco juice I must have turned green. William said maybe he should go into the house and left me right away.

I walked — or maybe it was more of a wobble or stagger — to our car, opened the door on each side of the back seat and lay down on the seat. The car seemed to kind of spin around so I stuck my head out one side and spit and spit trying to get all of the tobacco out of my mouth. I finally gave up, tried to relax and closed my eyes. The spinning did not stop so

I just imagined I was in an airplane swooping around through the sky. Maybe I went to sleep for the next thing I knew someone was calling my name. I couldn't tell who it was or the direction from which it was coming. As my eyes began to focus some I decided the calling was coming from the front steps and it was my Dad. I answered and he said to come on in and eat dinner.

I went into the house the best I could, through it to the dining room on the very back and took the seat that was pointed out for me. No one paid much attention to me and after I was seated, thanks was given. The very thought of eating made me want to throw up. I thought maybe the iced tea would help so I took a swig. The very sweet tea seemed to make it worse. I was more or less forced into a serving of chicken pot pie, which normally I loved to eat. I nibbled around on it a little and forced some down. I finally got to the end of the meal without throwing up and excused myself. I headed straight for the car again.

When I closed my eyes this time I couldn't keep it down. I hung my head out the open car door when everything came loose and up — and up and up. It was the sickest tasting stuff I had ever experienced — and it was chicken pot pie. It was seventy-five years before I dared eat chicken pot pie again.

Several buildings clustered around the house in addition to the garages. On the west side of the garages extending to the fence on the western side of the property was a large machine shed where the many farm implements were stored when not in use. As farming waned the use was switched to hay storage to support the ranching which replaced the farming. The front of this building, as did the garages, was lined up with the picket fence in front of the house. In the northwest corner of the yard fence was the smokehouse. Extending south off the smokehouse was a floored shed open on the side facing the house. Here was stored the yard and maintenance tools and supplies along with a lot of seasonal equipment and things only used on special occasions such as folding chairs, tables etc.

On the outside of the yard fence west of the smokehouse and shed, extending to the garages, were the several chicken houses and pens for the different ages, types and breeds. Grandma kept quite an assortment of chickens and always had a surplus of fryers and eggs even after feeding large groups at her house. She supplied some in her family with eggs and eating chickens all the time as well as some of her neighbors that were having "hard times." She never turned down one who said they needed some food for their children. To most of her friends and neighbors she was known as Miss Grace (Grace being her given name).

Inside the backyard fence, going around the northwest corner, you saw some barrels and equipment where Buddy and usually a friend or two did some outdoor cooking. Usually there was wood stacked up against and along the fence to the gate going out. They called it "cooking 'n smoking" like people nowadays use the term Bar-B-Qing. Past the gate, going east, was a little windowless building about eight by twelve feet with its back to the fence, it was called the power house. I always liked to look inside whether it was operating or not. In the center was a motor mounted on a concrete platform. It had an exhaust piped through the back wall and when running it sent puffs of black smoke out behind. Fred called it a donkey engine. All sides in the interior were lined with shelves from floor to ceiling with glass batteries a little larger than today's car batteries. The only place there weren't batteries was where the front door opened. This was the way they had electricity long before the REA brought it in. Later I learned that the electricity produced from the power house was DC as used on ships and not the high voltage AC type that we normally use in homes. I don't know what happened to the power house but one time I realized it was gone. It may have been put to use during World War II when they gathered up a lot of old stuff including junk for the war effort.

In the northeast corner of the backyard you found the "canning house" — or at least half of it. The building was about twenty-four feet wide (W to E) and thirty-six feet from south to north. The north half stuck out through the backyard fence while the south half was inside the backyard fence. The fence was attached to the building where it butted into the building which kept the backyard fenced in. The canning house was built specially for the family's canning use. The door was in the middle of the south end which made it open into the backyard. The walls were enclosed with wooden siding all around except for the doorway. The walls were constructed so that the top half of each wall could swing out and up then be held in position leaving an opening for cross ventilation. There was no air conditioning back then but the canning house was equipped with large fans to circulate the air on those hot still days. These wall sections were about four feet tall and eight feet long and went all around the building. These openings were screened to keep out bugs just as the doorway had a screened one. When closed up the building was an all-weather one but never used except during the summer when family from all around came and canned together. I'm sure all grandchildren and some greats had a few baths in the #3 tubs with the warm water left over from cooling the hot cans coming out of the pressure cooker.

Just a little past the short fence that separated the backyard from the front yard on the east side was where the pump house was attached to the east end of the front porch. A double door made an opening in the pump house wall about six feet tall and four feet wide which allowed access to the water well workings. The electric motor and pressurized water tank sat on a concrete foundation at ground level. This shallow well served the house for many, many years but was finally replaced by a community water system after some time.

Dividing the house and living area from the rest of the property was still another lane. On the west side of this lane was the house and living area as described above. The north end of the lane was the south fence and gate into the orchard which covered several acres. The west side of the orchard was the boundary line of the property, the north side the milk cow pasture and the east side bordered on a small stream that was running from the north to the south. The whole orchard had a single fence around it with a second gate on the north side that led into the cow pasture. Standing at the north end of the lane in front of the orchard gate, looking south, you could tell there was a slight rise as it neared the house and from the backyard fence to the front yard fence it was level and then went a little downhill toward the south side of the property. There was an open area to the right of the lane about twenty yards wide from the orchard fence to the backyard fence. The lane itself was also about twenty yards wide so it made a ninety degree turn around the backyard fence making the lane kind of L shaped. This made it convenient to have access by wagon or truck to the backyard, smokehouse and chicken facilities.

On the east side of the lane, the different fences going south all lined up to make a straight line opposite the straight west side of the lane. From the south fence of the orchard a corral board fence ran about forty feet until another one ran up from the east into it and formed a little pasture which in turn was divided into about three pieces with gates placed so you could turn livestock from one to the other or into the cow lot on the south side where the milk cow barn was located.

The barn had feed rooms for the bulk cotton seed hulls and others for sacked feed, fodder and sometimes baled hay. There was a feed trough running down the middle of the barn about half its length. One side of the trough had milking stalls on it and the other side where groups of cows and calves could be fed and penned. This lot was also divided into three or more sections so livestock could be sorted and placed where needed. It was here that Buddy taught Robert, William and me to feed, water, handle calves and milk cows. By the time we were eleven or twelve years old we could fill in for Buddy when he would "slip off" for a couple of days (with permission).

From the cow barn and lot a lane ran east to the little stream where there was a gate — that was left open most of the time except when you needed the lane for a pen or small pasture. This lane connected to the pasture for the cows which was on the east and north sides of the orchard. The cows knew to come up in the late afternoon for milking and feed. The milk cows were usually kept penned up overnight after milking in the evening for the next morning. The dry (or non-milking) cows along with the bull would be turned back out to pasture. The cows got most of their water from the little stream in their pasture, but there was a water line run from the house to all the pens so that we didn't have to carry water to any animals penned up in the barn or corrals. There was a large water trough in the main area of the barn where the milk cows were held overnight so they always had access to plenty of fresh water as were the calves that were kept penned up in a corral.

On the south side of the cow barn and lots was the garden. This was a large and very prolific place with a large variety of vegetables growing most all of the year. It was completely enclosed by a wooden fence made of six to eight inch vertical boards about five feet tall. The bottom of the boards were buried in the ground for a few inches to discourage small animals from digging under the fence and also helped to keep out snakes. The garden extended north to south about the same distance on the east side of the lane as did the yard fence of the house on the west side of the lane. From west to east it extended down almost to the stream but left the water enclosed into another small pasture which was dependent on this stream for the livestock contained in it.

Recalling this garden site stirs up a picture of my Grandmother with her large straw hat on her head and a soft blue man's shirt with sleeves down to her knuckles and shirttail nearly to her knees. The shirt was buttoned up at the collar hiding her pinafore or similar dress with the skirt down to her ankles. She always had a hoe or small basket in one hand and the other holding a plant or vegetable for examination. She loved working in the garden and could tell you what and where everything was growing according to the plan in her head.

The only time I remember that Grandma disciplined me with a couple of swats with a hand to my rear was here in the garden. One morning when I was about six or so Robert and I were "helping" Grandma gather some vegetables. I put a couple of okra in my hat band to look like horns. Robert followed my lead and before we knew it we were throwing okra at each other. I, being the older and within reach of Grandma, had my arm jerked and seat warmed with the proclamation that "You are too old for that foolishness."

There were two gates for entrance into the garden — both opening off the lane. The walkway gate was opposite to the backyard gate into the lane near the door of the canning house. The second gate was near the south end of the garden and had a double gate wide enough for a team to pull a wagon through but mostly used to get Kate with her plow, cart or sled in and out. Buddy used Kate and her cart to gather vegetables from the garden and haul them to the backyard gate and carry them into the canning house. A lot of field peas, beans and that sort were raised in the corn field up the hill on the east side of the cow pastures with the little stream in them. A lot of watermelons, cantaloupes and that type were raised in the deep sandy soil of the orchard. Grandma always had as a goal to have plenty of big watermelons ready for her July 4th picnic with enough to send some home with all the attendees. The canning house saw a lot of activity for most of the summer.

Joining the garden on the south side was the big barn and pens originally built for the oxen. By the time I was four or five the oxen were no longer being used at the sawmill. There were a few old retired oxen still hanging around the place for several years — probably up until I graduated from high school — looking through the cracks in their sturdy fence and keeping an eye on everything that went on in the lane. As they died off the grandkids claimed a portion of the barn and pens for their horses they kept at Grandma's. There were three or four log wagons that had been retired also and were parked along the north side of the lane running on the south side of the property. The grandkids played on these wagons for probably twenty or more years. They were done away with as they rotted and collapsed. There were other relics there too, such as running gears with wheels attached, yokes with bows and heavy chains. Some of this stuff was given away to a museum or two, as well as a few collectors. On a visit back to Grandma's farm after I was married and had children, I realized that much was missing and Grandma's farm would never again be as I remembered it as a child.

There was no water line to the oxen barn or water well to draw water from, so the pens extended down a little past the little stream. A dam made a little pond for the animals to drink from and had a fence through it so that those on the north half of the barn were separated from those on the south side. This little pond was also home to a flock of ducks, and sometimes a few geese, that had access to the barn where they could eat left over feed for the oxen and horses. One of our favorite evening activities was to watch the families of ducks parade to the barn for the night.

Next to the oxen barn was the mule barn and pens. Where the oxen barn ran east and west (narrow end on the east and west) with the west side in line with the lane fence (for access to unload feed); the mule barn ran north and south with the south end in line with the south side of the pens. There was an open area on the south side of the mule barn and this allowed access to the barn to unload feed into it. In the south west corner of the mule barn pen was a water well that had a bucket, rope and pulley for drawing water to water the mules. A trough was built into the lane fence where animals could also get water from the lane as well as the mule pens. The mule pens did not extend down to the little stream so the mules were depending on the well and Buddy for their water. Sometimes us thirsty boys would draw up a bucket of water rather than walk all the way to the house for a drink — it surely was cool sweet water from that bucket.

Attached to the mule pens on the east side was a hog pen built across the little stream with another small dam which caused a hog wallow to the delight of the pigs in the pen. The little stream usually ended here in the hog pen but after a good rain or wet weather it would flow on down south into the Browning bottom. A few pigs were raised each year for butchering in order to supply plenty of pork to always be available at Grandma's table. A few calves were also raised around the cow barn for butchering each year to supply the table with beef — especially veal (Grandma's favorite).

About the time the oxen were retired, the mules that worked for the sawmill were moved from here to the sawmill and placed in barns and pens near "old man" Strange's house. That was how everyone referred to Mr. Strange — except to his face. He was the "muleskinner" (also oxen driver) and quite a character. He taught William, Robert and me how to make whips (with snappers) and pop them over the backs of teams without actually hitting them. When they didn't respond properly then you flicked them on the rump without the pop. We learned from him to harness a team of two or four and drive them while sitting up on the wagon seat or walking beside them. William excelled at this and by the time he was eleven or twelve he could handle a team hitched to a turning plow and "break ground." He ended up farming for a vocation and did rather well.

After the mules were moved to the sawmill, only Kate and usually a team of two were kept in the mule barn and the pigs had free run of their pen and the mule pens also. The pigs kept clear of the mules most of the time since Kate would chase them, kick and bite if they bothered her. It was amazing to see such a mild mannered old mule get so worked up. She would put her ears back on her head, let out a squeal and take after the pig. She would chase it round and round until the pig went under the fence to its pen where it was safe from Kate. The other two mules would usually just stand and let out a hee-haw or two, but if the pig came their way they would try to take a nip too.

The open area south of the mule barn extended to the lane running west to east. In it, a short distance from the mule barn, was the harness house — a small building about twelve by twenty feet — in which hung the mule harness and saddles belonging to us grandkids, Buddy and a few others. On each side of the harness house was a small pen about the same size as the harness house. It was used to hold the horses and mules while being saddled or harness applied, doctored, shod and such. Usually we just tied our horse to the fence while we saddled it — if it wasn't taught to ground hitch.

Behind the harness house, backing up to the lane, was what we referred to as Fred's stables. It was by far the best looking barn and pens on Grandma's farm. Fred had this constructed for the horses he kept there even after he and Thelma bought their home in Tyler. His barn had about six stalls in one area of it and a couple more in another area for the "studs." It also had a tack room, feed rooms, etc. There were several paddocks connecting to the stalls for the horses kept in them.

The saddles and equipment were always kept in very good shape since Fred and Thelma both did pleasure riding. Fred always had one or two very nice studs for breeding that were exposed to outside mares for a breeding fee. Fred rode the train to Kentucky three or four times where he would select a couple of horses and ride with them in a cattle car as part of a freight train back home. Once he promised to take me with him on his next trip, but this never happened due to the coming of World War II. Before he went into the Marine Corp he sold all his horses except one which he left with me. I will tell you more about "George" later in my recounting the summer of 1943 and my "last trail drive." During and after the war I think Walter used Fred's stables in a mule breeding operation.

Most of these facilities are long gone, either the lumber used for other purposes or have rotted down and the dust trampled into the ground or blown away. But the dirt will cover me before the memories are blown away. The house still stands but yesterday I pulled over on Hwy 31 and looked at the rear of the house from the two or three hundred yards away. Could be I saw portions of the roof that appeared to have fallen in and decay all around. Today I realized that I will never be in Grandma's house again.

Of course the house, with its grounds, garages, smoke house, poultry facilities, canning house, garden, orchard, barns, pens, etc. was only one part of Grandma's farm. There was Uncle Harry's house with its barn and other improvements, the woods that held such enchanting things to see and do, the fields with their crops and devilish crows, the creeks with their crawdads, dragon flies, minnows and small perch and then, of course, The Sawmill. Each has so many stories I could probably write a book on each but for now we will just spend a little time on each.

Coming down the lane from Grandma's house past the garden, ox barn and mule barn and turning east before the harness house you crossed beside the pig pen in the low area and went up the hill. About halfway up you came to more pens on the left and a barn contained in them. On the right was a yard fence enclosing Uncle Harry's house. Uncle Harry was Grandma's brother and they were very close. I think this house was the first one built on the property as soon as Grandpa bought the land and they got ready to move the sawmill to it. Uncle Harry was kind of the general manager for Grandpa at that time but he was badly injured either at the mill before it was moved or shortly after moving. Charley gradually took over his duties

Uncle Harry and his wife lived in the new house a few years. When she died Uncle Harry moved into the house with Grandma so she could care for him.

Grandma let his daughter and her husband (Pearl and Fonzie) live in Uncle Harry's house as long as he lived. Pearl was very crippled up from childhood and Fonzie all-ways had something wrong with him so Grandma ended up taking care of them also. When Uncle Harry died, I think they moved in with a daughter near Overton. The house was vacant for some time after that.

William was the first of our trio to marry. He and Mary moved in with Grandma in 1947 and lived there until 1949. Auntie was living in Kilgore with Kenneth and Jack going to school there and they (Auntie, Kenneth and Jack) spent the weekends at Grandma's. This arrangement had some of the family with Grandma all the time. As William and Mary's family developed they bought the house toward Tyler that Robert and Modena were living in and Robert and Modena moved in with Grandma.

After graduating from high school Robert had gone into dairy farming with the aid of his high school ag teacher Mr. Ford and Kidd Dairies. After moving in at Grandma's he converted Uncle Harry's house to a milking barn, remodeled the barn and pens and moved his dairy herd to Grandma's farm.

In time Robert decided beef cattle production was more to his nature, purchased the Browning place "next door" to Grandma's where he began his purebred ranching. Somewhat later they build a beautiful home and offices on their ranch to take care of their expanding family and business.

The fenced lane coming into Grandma's farm ended at the gate into the open area south of the mule barn and pens but the little road continued on up the hill between the south side of Uncle Harry's yard fence and the fence on the south side of the property. This formed another short lane between Uncle Harry's and the boundary fence. This was a handy place to run a loose animal into where a couple or three kids could catch it. It was also the entrance to the woods and the road that ran through them to the mill about a mile away. Between Uncle Harry's backyard fence and the pens at his barn was another gate opening into the woods with a lesser road curving off to the left and on up the hill to the fence between the woods and the big corn field in that area. There was a gate where the road ran into the corn field fence and the road turned and ran alongside the fence until the fence turned north forming the east side of the field. A gap was in the fence here for entrance into and out of the corn field and the end of this little road.

Just past the fence corner were three or four chinkapin trees which produced prodigious amounts of the sweet little nuts. William, Robert and I got into the habit when we were headed for the creek or sawmill of entering the woods through the gate between Uncle Harry's house and his barn, looping up to the left and following the fence down to the chinkapin trees. This was one of our regular places to check on. From there we had a trail running north east down the long hill to the bottom (which in wet weather could look like a swamp) till we came to the creek. We would then follow it south to the bridge and the road to the mill. We would cross the creek on the bridge and follow the road on up by Mr. Strange's house to the mill. Very seldom did we follow the lane road on the south side of Uncle Harry's house to the bridge. We considered that road for sissies. It was about half way on our trail from the chinkapin trees to the creek that we three built our log cabin. What an adventure that was. And by the way, what ever happened to all the chinkapin trees in East Texas? The last time I remember eating a chinkapin was when a couple of my Overton fifth graders came to school with their pockets full — over sixty years ago!

The woods behind Uncle Harry's house, mostly large hardwoods and a lot of undergrowth in places, extended downhill for about a half mile until you reached the biggest creek on the place. This creek meandered from the north and made a big loop around and came back to where the mill was located. A good sized pond was formed at the mill which supplied water for the boilers and other needs. There were several houses of the shotgun variety scattered around the mill where the workers lived.

The creek, as we usually referred to it, formed two or three "natural" swimming holes which we loved to take advantage of during the summers. We also fished for perch and brim, as well as, caught "tons" of crawdads by hand. As we got older we learned how to gig frogs (sometimes shoot them) and even cook them ourselves — since Ruby refused to do it for us. We saw lots of snakes, dragonflies and such but I don't remember anyone getting snake bitten or needing emergency care from our playing in the creek. One or two times someone nearly drowned due to our horseplay or carelessness, but we survived. We weren't allowed to hang around the sawmill much due to the danger so we curtailed most of our activities to the area bordered by the creek. Soon after World War II was over, the mill was shut down and we had discovered many other interests beyond Grandma's farm — except for family gatherings and the July 4th picnic.

Grandma's Farm gradually changed its character from its origins as a site for the sawmill in the late 1920s to the center of the Jernigan family activities in the early 1930s with some production of crops. Following World War II it would be more accurate to call it a rural retreat for the family — as Grandma's home and then as Auntie's home.

As the pine timber on the property was used up by the sawmill some of this land was cleared and converted to crop production. This crop land after World War II was eventually converted into pastureland land and then later much of it was replanted in pines by Auntie after she "inherited" the farm. The pine timber area was originally on the east and north sides of the creek and now where the stands of the new pines — primarily on the north side of the new highway 31. The woods and old house site are on the south side of the highway.

From about the beginning of this century Jack and Mollie Sue Spear, living in Longview, have been absentee owners of Grandma's Farm. And during this writing, sadly this week we buried Jack in the old Danville Cemetery. So a new chapter for Grandma's farm will probably begin soon.

But — before we leave Grandma's farm, let me tell you of a few more memories that have been stirred up. Of course it would not have been the same without the many characters who lived and regularly visited at

Grandma's — but not all of these were people. Earlier you met Kate. Grandma's farm was home also to Tony, the pony who became a part of the family when Grandma and Grandpa were living in Kilgore. He moved right along with them to the farm and spent about twenty-five years helping to raise the Jernigan grandkids. Tony had been a traveling photographer's prop to take children's pictures look more like little cowboys — and little cowgirls. Tony had been around the block a few times and was very spoiled, but he knew how to please too so he became dear to everyone, or at least to those who loved horses.

Tony looked like the typical Shetland pony of that era, rather heavy bodied with a long mane and tail and a good heavy coat of hair — but not particularly photogenic. He was black all over with a white blaze down his face. He always seemed fairly alert — keeping an eye on anyone that might be around where he was. Someone had trained him to do a few tricks and he never forgot how to do these, but of course we had to encourage him a little sometimes when he would get a little lazy or wanted to test us. He would try to get away with things too. I would swear that at times he tried to play a joke on one of us — the look in his eyes seemed to give him away.

If you tapped him on the knees of his front legs with the rains or a switch, he would knell down — then if you tapped him in the flanks he would stretch out his hind legs and lie on his belly. When you made a circle with your hand and said "rollover" he would go on over on his side. By tugging one front foot a little and repeating "rollover" he would go all the way over, stand up and shake himself and wait for your approval. You wanted him to be unsaddled for the rollover thing since we did it a time or two saddled and broke the saddle frame. Another trick Tony did was that of "rare up" (sometimes referred to as rearing up — funny how this term came about) and walk around a little on his hind legs — just like circus horses. As long as the rider wasn't too large he would do it saddled with the rider on his back.

One day I had Tony on his front knees and I got down on a knee looking at something on the ground. William was standing nearby, and being of the religious type, said it looks like you two were praying. From then on we had a new trick — one the grownups liked very much.

Some of our tricks with Tony were not very nice. One would take the three of us (Robert, William and me) plus Tony. We would back Tony in a milking stall with one up in the saddle, one holding the bridle and stall door and the other standing in the feed trough. At the signal the rear man would lift Tony's tail and put a corn cob crosswise under it. The front man would open the gate and the rider would try to stay on. In time Buddy told us it was time for us to graduate to big horses and leave Tony to my little brother Sonny, William's little brother W. H. and Carl Jr. There were other grandkids following them too. Probably all twelve has a story or two to relate about their experiences with Tony. I think Richard, being the oldest grandkid, missed the fun the rest had with Tony.

For many years Tony ruled the lane around the house and leading up to the gates into the woods. He always had plenty to eat and tried to mooch treats from everyone who came to the house. All the animals seemed to accept Tony as King of the Lane when they found themselves there also. It was when Kenneth and Jack were little boys — maybe Margene was in the army at this time — and they were living with Auntie at Grandma's that they each received a small pony for Christmas. Kenneth, being the older, got the larger of the two ponies but he was still much smaller than Tony. Jack's pony, Friday, was the smallest grown pony that I had ever seen up to that time. Kenneth's pony, I don't remember his name, was a very dark brown while Friday was as black as Tony. Maybe it was the color, but for some reason Tony took a real liking to Friday — but made no beans about his dislike for the other. The three looked like stair steps when they were together, with Tony usually biting or kicking the brown one. I don't know what happened to the brown one, but he didn't last very long. I suspect that Tony dispatched him to the Great Happy Pastureland, but neither Auntie nor Grandma would talk about it.

Friday hung around Grandma's for a long time. Due to his size just about everyone picked at him and he got downright mean. He didn't want anyone to get on him — not even the very little guys with a parent standing beside him and holding them on. One day Robert and I — who, by then, were way too big to put our weight on him — decided to make him ride and behave. With only a homemade rope halter on him we led him to the deep sand in the orchard where Robert said let him do the riding since he was smaller and lighter. Near the fence and trail were some big clumps of bull nettles so we took him past these for his riding lesson. After Robert got on him, with toes touching the ground, the more he urged him forward and whacked him with the rope the more he dug in and refused to budge. Finally I said "Let me twist his tail — I bet that will make him go." As I reached out to curl his tail, he bolted forward in a little run, ran straight for the bull nettles and stopped up short before he got in them. Robert tumbled over Friday's head and fell spread eagle in the middle of the bull nettles.

About that time we heard Auntie calling to us from the gate — with Tony standing beside her. Friday heard her too and took off in a trot for her. Robert was moaning and groaning from the bull nettle stings and I was having a hard time to keep from bursting out laughing. We slowly made our way up to the gate where Auntie had Friday in tow and Grandma standing at the backyard gate taking it all in. Auntie dressed us down for mistreating little Friday and told Robert to go take a bath in Epsom salt water to stop the stinging. She told me to take the halter off Friday and put him back in the lane with Tony and for us to leave little Friday alone. I swear the two ponies were smiling at each other. Anyway we didn't give Friday any more riding lessons.

Remembering Friday also reminded me of the two sheep Auntie got the boys a little after the ponies. They were little orphan twins someone gave her and she raised them on a bottle in Grandma's backyard and then let them live in the lane under the watchful eye of Tony. They were everybody's pets and learned from Tony to expect treats from anyone in the lane. At night they hung close to the backyard fence where they had first been placed and bottle fed. For some reason Tony and most of the other lane animals usually spent the night a little up the hill close to Uncle Harry's barn.

I was fourteen at this time, I think, since I was driving — back then kids learned to drive about twelve and by fourteen would be sent to town on errands. Mother had sent me into Overton, about five miles from Leverett's Chapel, after some medicine or something. As I was leaving the drug store I ran into Bruce Gillespie — we knew each other from the First Baptist Church Sunday School where we both attended. I stopped and we were visiting about Sunday's incident in church where the dynamic but rather arbitrary pastor "Happy" Holmes had called Bruce down in front of the whole congregation for talking during the sermon. Rev. Holmes was not your typical Baptist preacher — he smoked big black cigars and went to the picture show every day but Sunday. Bruce was telling me he wasn't ever going back to that church with its big fat jerk for a preacher.

About that time a car pulled to the curb where we were standing and a head stuck out the window and yelled for Bruce to come see what they had in the car. These were some of Bruce's Overton friends whom I didn't know but I went to look also. In the back seat lay four fat watermelons. Bruce asked where they got them and they said they had stolen them near Arp and drove off. We took Bruce's regular place on the curb — he spent most of his free time hanging out downtown since he lived only two blocks away. He said he sure wished he could swipe a watermelon or two. I ended up telling him I could swipe all the melons I wanted but it would have to be after dark and I couldn't take our car after dark. Of course I was talking about Grandma's where there were many watermelons in the orchard for my taking but I wanted it to sound dangerous.

Bruce was intrigued. He said he could get a car if I could go with him. Then he went on to explain. I knew his dad was the Overton postmaster but he told me that his dad was also an avid coon hunter. I knew coon hunters hunted coons but he had to explain how that worked. They, the hunting group, mostly sat around a camp fire all night, drank and told big stories while their dogs ran around in the woods, barking and yapping. When a dog or dogs treed a coon the hunters would go and knock the coon out of the tree and watch the dog-coon fight. Most times a dog or so would get lost and couldn't be found when the hunt ended.

Bruce didn't go hunting with his dad so it was his job to go look for lost dogs. Mr. Gillespie's group hunted on Friday nights so Saturday mornings Bruce had to go out "dog hunting." They kept the dogs a little way out of town so it was Bruce's job to feed the dogs every morning too. In order for Bruce to feed and chase dogs Mr. Gillespie had gotten him an old beat up Model A Ford jalopy to drive. This way Bruce always had wheels when he needed them. Bruce also worked at the picture show some as a relief projectionist since he hung around there so much.

Well it was summer time and no school and was getting along about supper time so Bruce came up with this plan — he would come out to my house after supper to see if I wanted to go to a movie with him. We would go by the movie, then head for the water melons as soon as good dark, get us some, go back by the movie and then he would take me home. I still didn't tell him that we were going to my Grandmother's for the melons — since that would take the excitement out of it.

Well, everything went according to plan and we got to the lane and turned down it. I told Bruce to turn off his lights and park against the fence so if someone wanted in or out they could do it and would probably only think the car was a broken down one. I explained in detail what we had to do — go down this lane to the one that ran beside the house and go up it past the house to the watermelon patch on the north side of the house. Bruce wanted to know why we didn't just cut through the pasture on our left to the north side of the house. I told him the Brownings had some wild cattle in it with a really mean bull that I knew I couldn't outrun. He agreed that my plan sounded better.

It was a bright moonlit night but there were big fluffy clouds that passed over the moon and made it very dark about a third of the time. When the moon was out we could see where we were going and when dark we just kept straight ahead on our course. We worked our way to the north/south lane and then up it between the house and garden. About the time we came to the canning house unbeknown to us one of the sheep fell in walking behind us. This sheep seeing Bruce's open hand stuck his nose in it looking for a treat and let out a loud BBAAAA just as his nose touched his hand. Bruce jumped about four feet off the ground and hit the ground running straight ahead. In full stride for about thirty yards, he hit the orchard fence full force. He bounced off the fence backwards and fell flat on his back gasping for breath. I immediately knew what had happened and ran to his side. The wind had been knocked out of him and he was still gasping for breath. As I reached his side the moon came out full and he looked at me and finally got enough air to ask "What was THAT?" About that time we saw lights flicking on in the house. I reached down grabbed both of his hands, pulled him up and said come on before we get shot. We ran to the fence over by the Browning pasture, crawled through the bob-wire and took out across it for the car. Bruce said "What about the bull?" I said not to worry about any bull for he could easily out run any bull in the whole county.

We got to the car without incident, sat in it panting with moonlight flooding the beautiful country landscape. I explained what had happened and confessed I had set it up for his benefit and really there was no danger except what we created. He looked me in the eye and said "I will hate you till I die!" I figured he would forgive and forget in time.

On the way home Bruce was driving rather slowly taking in the moonlit scenes going by. He turned to me and said "I think I will give up watermelons for Lent." I laughed and said that Lent wasn't until spring and it's summer now. And besides you aren't even Catholic. He said "Well, it couldn't hurt." It wasn't but a week or two till the whole Gillespie family started going to the Overton First Methodist Church. For the rest of their lives Bruce and his family were part of the backbone of that church.

As far as I know Bruce never told anyone of our watermelon expedition but I couldn't pass up any opportunities. We remained friends all of our lives — or at least Bruce put up a good show. We married sisters so were somewhat bound together by marriage. When we were both enjoying early retirement we traveled together a lot. One of our best trips was three weeks in Bruce's conversion van in Mexico with my dear friend Bill Holmes. Bruce and Bill were probably the best people to get along with that you could ever find. One night after attending an outdoor pageant at some ruins in Central Mexico the three of us were having drinks at the patio of our hotel. It was a beautiful moonlit night and we were feeling mellow. Something reminded me of our watermelon saga — maybe the moon and clouds — so I launched into it. Bruce caught my arm, looked me in the eye and said "Please don't tell that story again." I stopped and didn't tell it again until after Bruce was gone, some years later. I don't think he would mind now.

I think it was Christmas when I was eleven that I got my first real gun. It was a brand new model Remington bolt action single shot .22 which gave me the choice of shorts, longs or long rifle ammunition. My Dad wasn't much of a hunter — or for that matter not much on fishing either at that time — but being some sort of a rural type, guns fascinated me. I convinced my parents that I was responsible enough to be trusted with a gun after being tutored by several uncles and tested by my Dad. I didn't want a gun so much to hunt as just to shoot. I did a lot of plinking around behind our house at Leverett's Chapel and gradually did most of my shooting at Grandma's farm where there was more space and good targets in the woods, fields and such. Soon afterward William got a small .410 shotgun. This was so he could hunt with his dad who was an avid bird hunter. Walter had some dog pens at Grandma's farm in the northwest corner behind the chicken houses at the edge of the orchard where he kept several bird dogs during bird hunting season so he could hunt Grandma's farm and several places nearby that he had leased for farming and hunting. He kept his dogs at a trainer's place during the off season. These were usually the only dogs at Grandma's except when some of the family brought their pets when visiting. House dogs were not very popular during that era and Grandma didn't care for dogs at her place.

After William and I were "armed" naturally Robert needed a firearm too. He and his mother were living at Grandma's at the time and his mom had a real fear of guns for some reason and held back on Robert having one. Charley got her to agree he could have a BB gun so Charley got him a Benjamin pump that shot BBs but could be pumped up till the BB was a powerful projectile. With Robert and me both pushing it against a post we could pump it until the BB would go all the way through a one inch thick plank. It would take one of my long rifle .22s to match that power.

After we were armed in this manner Uncle Harry told us one day that there was a real problem with crows in the corn field. He said crows were too smart for such things as scarecrows and such so he wanted us to hunt crows for him. He said he would pay us a nickel for each crow we killed. Well it was easy to see how we could get rich off Uncle Harry because the crows were in the corn field by the hundreds all day every day. Since the big corn field produced feed corn for the animals it had to stay in the field and mature or season before it was gathered. This made it great for the crows because they loved the dry corn that had been stripped of its fodder.

We told Uncle Harry to get his money ready because we were going after those crows in the morning. We got a ride over to Meadow's and each got a fresh supply of ammunition. When we got back we asked Ruby to wake us up when she came to work and have our breakfast ready early because we were going hunting. It was hard to go to sleep thinking about all the fun we would have shooting crows and anticipating all the money we would make.

We were at the corn field as the sun was about to rise. We were a little sluggish so early in the morning but we scanned the field as dawn turned to daylight. We squatted along the south fence line about five yards apart so that we could talk without having to raise our voices and watched as the crows began to fly in from the east. One by one they would loop around a portion of the field and then land. A few landed in the tall bare trees that were spotted around in the field. As some began to land closer and closer to us we decided we would ease up so we could see the closer ones and all get a few shots. Robert pointed at me and then to the right, to William and to the left and to himself and straight ahead indicating the direction we would shoot. Then he said O K and rose up with William and me following his move. We didn't make any noise but we heard a clamor from the birds as they took flight as a group. The birds were too fast for us — they jumped up and flew off in a zigzag pattern while each of us took a shot or two but brought down nary a bird. Later William said he saw feathers fly from one of his shots but the bird flew on away with all the other birds. We emptied the field of birds.

We decided to hide again and see if they would come back. In about thirty minutes a few crows looked around again and then a few came down again, and as before we watched a few settle in the tall bare trees. We repeated the same act as before with the same results. After the third or maybe fourth try at the birds we decided to give up and go to the house — tired, thirsty and hungry. We ran into Buddy as we rounded the mule barn and gave him a report. He thought a minute and then said "Them lookouts must've seen you." Then he sketched out a plan for us to follow the next morning. He told us the crows probably wouldn't return much until morning because that was their main feeding time. We were perfectly happy to let it go until the next day.

The next morning according to Buddy's plan we were back at the field before sunup and took our assigned places. Robert and I were a good seventy-five to eighty yards apart and in well–hidden positions so we could shoot over a good deal of field with William in the middle where he could train his shotgun on a stray flying bird or two if we jumped them up in his area. Robert and I were to act as snipers on the lookouts. Our job was to pick them off without exposing ourselves. In theory this was a good plan but it didn't work too well. We had to shoot at the lookouts at great distances for our marksmanship so we missed most shots. Robert's air rifle didn't sound so loud to scare the birds but he had trouble pumping it up enough to hit the birds and when he did it didn't knock them down. My rifle had enough noise that usually I only got off one shot before the birds were disturbed. We worked hard all morning and had two birds to show for our work but we kept the crows out of the corn field all that time. Buddy encouraged us that we would get better and Uncle Harry said he would give us twenty-five cents per day for ammunition. This kept us at it for about three more days before we decided to retire from hunting crows. I don't think Uncle Harry had to pay us over a dollar for dead crows and only a couple of dollars for ammunition in order to keep us at it for about a week.

Crows may walk funny and sound silly but they are no dummies. They decided it was easier to eat someone else's corn and pretty well stayed away from Uncle Harry's corn until it was harvested Back then there were huge amounts of grain produced in East Texas for animal feed but now that land is in pasture for raising cattle. Crows have almost ceased to be in East Texas. The only ones I notice any more are a few alongside the highway feeding on road kill — which I had never observed back in the 1930s.

Hunting crows brought to memory another hunting story which took place a year or two after the crow experience. The three of us hunted

a lot, but not for anything in particular. We just roamed the woods with our guns. This Saturday we had ended up on the north east side of the mill and covered a farm or two that Walter had sharecroppers on. It was after lunch and getting hot after starting out cool that morning. We were well past hungry and a good two miles from Grandma's farm. We had a couple of rabbits and a squirrel tied to our belts and decided to head for home.

We heard a voice off to the left calling to us so we headed to the cabin where it had come from. As we neared the porch we saw this elderly black man with very white hair sitting in his cane bottom chair motioning for us to come on up on the porch. He said, "I thought that was you Mr. William when I saw you walking with that gun on your shoulder just like yo daddy." William greeted him and introduced us to Josh (William knew all the black farmers for miles around as a result of his going about with his dad). William said that we were pretty thirsty if he could spare us a little water from his well. Josh pointed to the well in the side yard and said for us to help ourselves.

We drew a fresh bucket of water and took turns drinking from it. We sat down in the shade on the porch and William let out a big sigh to show he was exhausted. We were just relaxed when Josh said "If'n you boys air hungry, I got some meat and taters in there tat's probably still a little warm if'n yo don't mind eatin my foodstuffs." We were starved and looked at each other and let William do the answering. He said we sure would appreciate some of his food. Josh got up went into the cabin and a few minutes later came out and invited us in.

He had set three places at the table and pointed to them and said "Pick yore place." We sat down and he brought a big, old dented blue roasting pan from the stove and set it down on a cup towel in front of us. He said "Yo can serve yoreselves." The meat was in the center of the pan — kinda cut up in chunks with baked sweet potatoes, onions, carrots, and maybe some turnips, piled around it. We helped our plates and dug in. Josh put out a plate with some cold cornbread in it and we each broke us off a piece. All in all it wasn't too bad — each of us ate a large plate full but stopped there so we wouldn't look too piggish. We left our game kill with Josh after thanking him.

After we left Josh's William said that wasn't bad for pot luck. I agreed. Then Robert said "It was alright except for that greasy grissly pork roast — I could hardly choke it down." William said that the meat wasn't pork roast that it was possum. Robert and I looked at each other and felt sick. That was the only time I, knowingly or unknowingly, ever ate possum — I think.

We three had many, many interesting, and a few times exciting, adventures hunting. Probably the most exciting one occurred close to the same time as the possum experience. We were exploring on horseback a couple or so miles south west of grandma's following a small dirt road one afternoon and saw this old rundown church building a little off the road. I said I wondered if there was a well at the church because I was very thirsty. William said he didn't know but if there was he didn't want to drink any water from it. I asked why and he said that there is a large, old cemetery behind the church and he didn't need any grave water. Well this meant that we needed to go see the cemetery up close. We got off our horses, tied them to the fence around the graves close to the gate and walked about the graves. Robert said he was surprised that he had never noticed or heard about this cemetery before. William said it was where the blacks were buried and they seem to have quit using it some time ago. I said it didn't look full to me so I wondered why they quit using it. William said that it probably was due to the swamp forming just behind it over the years and people said it was full of alligators. He had even heard stories about alligator carrying off black children.

Well that really got Robert and me to thinking. We certainly needed to see that at once. William refused to go any further but then decided he didn't want to stay at the cemetery by himself while we went to look at the swamp. After we promised we would leave if we saw any alligators William consented to going with us. We got back on our horses and rode around one side of the cemetery and looking downhill all we could see from left to right was swamp. As we neared the swamp we could see large trees that had fallen over, big ferns growing and it looked like a scene out of a Tarzan movie. A little way out in the marsh there was water standing which we decided was a lake. We rode one way to the left a little distance and it looked the same so we rode back and then another distance to the right and it still looked the same. We tried to ride out in the marsh a little but our horses bogged down some and they turned back for solid footing. We knew there was such a thing as horse sense so we didn't try to force them. We rode back away from the swamp a few yards and sat on our horses looking about. I decided to get down and walk around some. Robert soon followed. William refused to get off his horse — citing the danger from snakes. We each handed him the rains to our horses so we were able to walk — and maybe run — around better. We walked to the edge of the water letting our boots slosh in the mud. We couldn't see any better than we did on horseback so we walked back to the horses and William. We decided that what we needed was a boat to get around on the water if it was deep enough. Robert reminded us that there was an old wooden boat sunk in the mud at the pond by the mill. Someone had made it to use to get out to the middle of the pond to fish but evidently the fishing wasn't very good so they abandoned the boat. Our plan began to take shape.

Over the years the three of us had many adventures on Grandma's farm but it also served as the base camp for others that took place within an eight to ten mile radius of the farm. My Grandmother Elliott lived about seven miles south and a little west so this was one of our destinations where we were always assured a good meal with great cookies (everyone called them Ma's teacakes) and plenty of good cold milk. Also about the same distance south and a little east was my Uncle Allen Elliott with cousins W.A. (Dub) and Kelly, about our ages, and across the road was their Grandpa Hill's blacksmith shop — a favorite visiting place for boys of our ages. William had a Great Uncle Florence (and an interesting farm) about seven miles east and a little north (almost to Kilgore) was another inviting visiting place for us. He and his wife had no children so a few times he sent word for us to come help him gather crops and such — for which he always paid us more than we were worth. Also about eight miles or so west was William's grandparents the Florences where William's family lived about a quarter of a mile away. What a wonderful area (and era) for us to roam (mostly on horseback) and discover, and believe me, we really did from the time I was seven or eight till I was probably sixteen. There are many exciting and also dangerous stories I could relate, but as I said the alligator hunt was probably the most exciting.

As soon as we got back to Grandma's after our trip to the abandoned church and cemetery, we found Buddy feeding the hogs. We told him we wanted to borrow the wagon and team tomorrow to do some hauling. Of course he wanted to know what we were up to so we told him we wanted to get the boat out of the mill pond and put it in the creek. He said O K but that boat wasn't worth moving — we were welcome to waste our time and energy on it if that was what we wanted to do, just be careful.

The next morning we were at the mill surveying "our boat." Just a little of the front end was showing above the mud and water. We finally got it dug out of the mud and pulled up on the bank. It was in much worse shape than we had imagined but we had a start. Near noon we had all the mud scrapped off and loaded in the wagon. Since it was so water soaked it didn't need any tying down even though it stuck out the wagon bed a couple of feet in the rear. William, our teamster, was hungry so he pushed the mules to take the wagon, load and us back to the house for our dinner. We left the whole rig at the harness house while we ate our lunch. After a good meal and a little rest we were ready to tackle our task again.

Buddy looked it over and said it would take a couple of days to dry out enough to locate the holes and gaps that needed to be patched. He suggested we place the boat crosswise of the wagon bed and then we could get under it and look up toward the sun for areas that needed attention. We left the boat upside down balanced on the wagon hoping no one needed the wagon for a day or two. We then found some other projects that needed our attention for the next two days while the boat dried out.

When we went back to work on the boat Buddy had gathered up a bunch of little pieces of lattice (thin 2" strips), tiny nails and a big bucket of roofing tar. It was crude work but we tacked a lot of strips on the inside of the boat and packed the tar in the outside cracks and gaps. Buddy did an inspection and declared "It might just float — for a little while." He also said that since we were going to be in the creek that we probably didn't need paddles but poles. To our amazement he produced two bamboo poles about six feet long that had come with some carpeting he had installed in the house. We told him we would test it in the water the next day. He kind of hinted around that he could go with us if we wanted him to help. We told him we thought we could manage by ourselves but thanked him kindly for his help and tried to not give away our plans.

The next morning William was our only problem. He had gotten cold feet and balked at going at all. He just kept on making excuses — the snakes, the boat sinking, alligators eating us and on and on. We finally threatened to tie him up in the mule barn where no one would look for him and go ourselves. He decided we were serious so he caved in and eventually started getting ready. We took our arsenal — my .22, Robert's Benjamin pump and William's .410 (for snakes) and covered it in the wagon under the boat. We told Ruby we were going fishing and needed a lunch to take. She fixed us several biscuits with sausage patties in them and a few boiled eggs and added that if we had told her the night before she could have fixed us a better lunch. We told her the lunch was fine but we didn't tell her that we didn't let her know because we didn't want other people to know we would be gone for lunch.

When all was ready, we watched till Buddy was busy behind the house and we took off up the lane to the west — the opposite direction of the creek. Once we were out of sight of the house William got with the program until we got to the swamp and then he again got cold feet. After we got the boat out of the wagon and in the water, he didn't want to get in the boat, he wanted to stay with the wagon and team — saying someone could steal them. We finally convinced him we needed to stay together, there was protection in numbers and we needed all three to hunt the alligators. Finally, but reluctantly, he got in the middle of the boat with his .410 across his lap holding on both sides of the boat. Robert and I both picked up a pole and pushed on the oozy mud. Amazingly the boat moved and we were afloat. We talked in hush tones, warning each about snakes and alligators.

We had moved slowly about thirty yards out into the body of water when William grabbed my right pant leg and pointing off to the left said "L-l-l-ook." I looked toward where he was pointing and could only see a log lying in the water. I said it's only a log and he said "Watch, I saw it move!" All three kept our eyes on it and in a few seconds I saw some circles of water move out from it and William said "See!" Sure enough the log was sliding along slowly away from our direction. Robert said for me to hand him my pole and get my gun ready to shoot. I did and by the time I had my gun pointed in the right direction, Robert said "It's a gator — get him!" I carefully aimed and pulled the trigger — with the crack of the rifle it looked like a mine had blown up, water splashed in all directions and an alligator head popped up, the body shook all over and the water continued to boil around the alligator. I was watching all that activity when Robert yelled "Shoot again!" I worked my bolt action twice quickly getting off two more shoots but I could not tell if I had hit the gator again for he was running and swimming away from us really fast. I was shaking too much to insert another bullet into the rifle, work my bolt action again and I just watched as the gator disappeared in the distance. Robert and I both sat down and gripped the sides of the boat.

We just sat there reliving the experience for some time. We decided the gator must have been at least five or six feet long and the shots upset him but evidently didn't do much damage as he surely did run and swim fast, making a big fuss in the water. We wondered if more were around but decided that if there were they would have been stirred up by all the commotion the one I shot had made. Robert said he thought I had hit him with two of the three shots because of the way he reacted. I said that I was shaking so much on the second and third shots I couldn't tell what was happening.

I told Robert to give me my pole back and for him to take my gun. I would stand up and pole us along and he could sit in the front ready to shoot — maybe getting a head shot to put a Mr. Gator out of commission. I knew Robert was a better shot than me and I knew how I shook the last time. I handed him all the long rifle shells I had in my pocket so he would have them if needed. William was very quiet and kind of pale. Robert got very quiet also as he scanned the water ahead. We poled along for another thirty minutes or so and had seen nothing move except for a few birds playing around in the dead trees. William finally said "I think we need to head back to the wagon, I'm hungry and I think it's time for lunch." We both agreed and turned back toward where we had come — or at least hoped it was the right way because then we realized we could be lost and not know it. It was a bad feeling and as we looked from one to the other we knew we all shared it. We didn't discuss it but kept on in the direction we thought was right with two of us poling as fast as we could. It wasn't long until we recognized the place where we had shot and stirred up the gator so everyone felt better.

With renewed energy we kept on and soon reached our spot. To William's delight the team, wagon and our lunch were all as we had left them. It was then that we noticed we had about six inches of water in the bottom of the boat. I said that's not bad for an old boat — and we all gave a little laugh. But we didn't waste any time getting to our lunch.

After finishing lunch and stretching out in the wagon for a dry rest, we discussed our alligator hunt. William kept saying it was a wonder — even a miracle — that our boat didn't sink and we all drowned. We also kept trying to convince him we were never in water deeper than knee high since we were poling around and pushed with the poles on the bottom. He still wasn't convinced that we didn't just barely escape death and there was no way he was going to get back in that boat again. Robert and I gave up on trying to get William back in the boat for a second go at getting us a gator. We decided that there was no need for snake protection since we had not seen any snakes so far. We could leave William and his shotgun at the wagon. Our only worry about him then would be that he could get spooked after being left behind and take off for home with the mules and wagon. We didn't say anything about this in front of him for fear it would give him ideas.

It took us a while to bail out the water from the boat since we had only one old coffee can to bail with. We were determined to get back in the water and look for us a gator. We went about as far as where we had spotted the other gator with both of us poling. Then Robert sat again in the front with the rifle across his lap while I stood and poled in the back. We looked and looked but saw no gators. After my arms were tired out we just sat and looked around for a while. This place was really spooky with the birds flying around and crying out at us for invading their territory. We decided to make a loop to our left and head back from where we had come — keeping our bearings as we went, the best we could.

In just a few minutes I thought I saw some movement off to our right. I told Robert to look over that way and he too thought he saw something and said to pole in that direction. We began to see some circles on the water in that area from about three different spots. As we got nearer we could tell there was movement in the area. Robert put several shells in his shirt pocket so he could get to them readily and took the safety off the rifle. As we got closer — about thirty or thirty-five feet away — we saw an alligator stand in the water with it coming to about the middle of his body. He wasn't very big, probably three to four feet long. Robert took careful aim and fired — the gator kind of spun around in the water and thrashed about. Two or three more began to thrash about also and were running in all directions from that spot. Evidently they knew where the deeper water was, headed for it, disappearing from sight. Robert had reloaded and trying to get a bead on the wounded one that was still thrashing about. Robert shot again and we heard the gator grunt or snort and slowed down on his thrashing. He got on his legs and ran a few feet to one side and as Robert had reloaded and was ready to fire again the gator disappeared under the water. We looked around and couldn't detect any movement. We sat there a few minutes and decided that we might be surrounded by gators.

Since we had not been able to "knock one out" — or bag it so to speak — we decided we might as well give up on our getting us a gator. We began to realize how dangerous it would be if we found ourselves in a bed of big gators. We decided to pole ourselves in what we thought was the direction to the wagon. In a little bit we began to think we were lost and what a sinking feeling that turned into. We looked at each other but didn't talk much. It was kind of hazy but we could tell where the sun was so we both kept glancing up at it. Robert said "The sun sets in the west and I think it is going that way (pointing to our left) and I think we should go that way." I told him I had come to the same conclusion so we turned our little boat ninety degrees to the left and began to pole in a determined effort to move us toward the west. As we began to get very tired I suggested we rest a few minutes. Robert gave no argument so we sat down — breathing heavily. In a couple of minutes Robert looked at me and said "Did you hear something?" I shook my head and listened carefully. Then I heard a dull thud and I could tell Robert had heard it also.

We started poling our boat again in the direction we thought we heard it coming from. Soon we could tell it was someone chopping wood. The sound stopped but we kept headed in that direction. Then we heard a voice talking in a low tone. We kept poling and then Robert yelled "Hello." Nothing came back in answer for another minute or two and then a weak "Hello." We both looked at each other and smiled. We were sure it was William and so glad to get his hesitant response. We both yelled "William" at the same time. This time he immediately responded with "Yes."

Happy to have found our way back to the wagon, we pulled the boat onto what looked like dry land and ignored the ankle deep water in it. William was as happy to see us back as we were to be back so he immediately began hitching the mules to the wagon in preparation to leave. He asked if we wanted him to back the wagon over by the boat so we could load it. Robert and I looked at each other and shook our heads. Robert said if anyone wanted it they were welcome to it.

I told William I was so glad he was chopping wood so that we heard it and could find our way back to the wagon. He then related what had happened to cause him to chop the wood. It so happened that a black family came in a wagon to the cemetery to look after some graves and the father noticed our wagon down by the water. He walked over to see if everything was all right and found William and the team there. As they visited William explained what we were doing, etc. It turned out that his brother farmed for William's dad. He suggested William build a fire so we could possibly see it and help find our way back to the wagon since he was familiar with how difficult it was finding your way around in the swamp. William thought that was a good idea but he didn't have any matches to light a fire. The man dug about a half dozen from his pockets and gave them to William and waited while William checked the wagon box to be sure there was an ax in it. About that time a couple of kids ran up looking for their dad. The man asked William if he thought he would be all right and when William answered in the positive he and his family left in their wagon.

Robert said we must have heard William talking to the helpful man. William said no the man was long gone before he started chopping wood. What we heard must have been him talking to the mules for in his nervous state he had done a lot of "mule talking."

On our way back to Grandma's farm, we discussed hunting gators and how we could do it better, as well as, also trying to net a young one for a pet. William said to count him out because he had all the alligator business he wanted and would stick to mules and horses for his raising and petting. We both agreed he had a good point there.

The next day word reached our headquarters that some of the Jernigan kids had been seen or heard shooting alligators in the swamp. We were given orders to stay away from that area and to give up gator hunting altogether. We didn't mind this turn of events at all.

About a mile or so north east of the sawmill, just south of Highway 31, lived a pore white family on a few scrubby acres with a lot of kids, a few goats but short on chickens, cows, hogs and mules. Some of their neighbors had been accusing them of stealing chickens and other missing items. Things got pretty hot for them so they loaded everything they could on their old Model T and left one morning — very, very early. They didn't have room for their goats so they just left them to shift for themselves. There were probably six to eight goats to start with but like rabbits, they multiplied. In time there evidently were at least two or three families of goats. One nearby farmer took in one group and a second group kind of took up at our sawmill and in the woods between the sawmill and Grandma's house.

This sawmill/woods group would slip around looking for food all over Grandma's farm. They were as wild as mountain goats and got into all kinds of mischief. They were more or less tolerated until one Sunday when the problem came to a head. We were just sitting down to Sunday dinner when Buddy came in and whispered in my Dad's ear and they both went out front. In a few minutes we heard the front door open, slam shut and in a minute or two a repeat. Then we began to eat again when we heard a BAM! followed by another BAM! BAM! Everyone got up and headed to the front to see what was going on.

We saw Dad and Buddy standing in front of our new car firing deer rifles at something about a hundred yards down toward the south lane. One would fire then the other. We then spied two goats climbing the hog wire fence to get into the Browning property south of Grandma's farm. One of the goats made it over and raced across the pasture but the other was hit as he tried to get through the barb wire on top of the hog wire. He was hanging on the fence. Some of us started out but Mother said for us to wait inside until we were sure the shooting was over.

Buddy handed the rifle he had to my Dad and headed down to take the goat off the fence. Dad came in and told us that the goats were climbing on his brand new car to feed off the tree it was parked under. Buddy had run them off but they came back so that was when he came in and told Dad. He said they shot about six or seven of them but one got away. We went in and resumed our dinner.

After we finished eating Dad, Fred, Walter and Buddy finished bleeding and dressing the goats. They put them in two or three wash tubs in our car trunk. Dad said he would take the carcasses to the ice house for cold storage until we could have a Bar-B-Que. They decided that the next Saturday would be a good time for everyone. My Dad also said since we had so much goat we would have a community event and he would get a bunch of sausage and pork ribs and invite all the neighbors. So, after explaining his plans to Buddy and the others, we headed to the ice house and home.

Dad spent a lot of time the next week getting ready for his Bar-B-Que. Since most of the people had never tasted goat before he wanted it to be special so he had plenty of known meats also available for the less adventurous. Since not all the goats were young, he planned to use the earth-pit method to cook them which he said would cook even an old steer till it was tender. This was the only real pit Bar-B-Que I ever remember attending, seeing or eating — and I have been to quite a number in my eighty-five years. Dad had been introduced to this method of cooking when we lived in the Valley and they would cook out on the ranch for special events. He taught Buddy the basics and later Buddy became rather famous for it. I don't remember any in the Valley but I will always remember the one at Grandma's farm.

I got to be a part of it all, even helping to dig the pits for the cooking. The pits were placed down next to the south lane and the tables to stand up and eat at were built between there and the house. It took Friday night and all day Saturday to get everything ready. The whole community was invited and I think they all came. To go with the Bar-B-Que we had a tub of potato salad and a wash pot full of Mexican style cowboy beans. Sauces, onions, pickles — anything one could want was there and in abundance. No one went hungry that night — nor thirsty either.

There were two two-holers (one for females and one for males) build near the end of the equipment sheds to help handle the heavy traffic during Grandma's Fourth of July picnics These came in handy for the Bar-B-Que also. Grandma did not allow alcohol on the premises (to her knowledge) but her oldest son was a heavy drinker (also her youngest son-in-law) and Charley (the former) always kept a trunkful in his car. For the Bar-B-Que he set up a free drink bar behind the out-houses. There was a steady stream to the men's out-house all night.

I guess this was the first racially integrated affair I remember attending and I was amazed at how nice everyone was to each other. Everyone was so well mannered — even those that were a little tipsy. That evening was also the beginning of the end to the rogue goat era. Now everyone knew how to deal with stray goats.

In this modern age sleek (and expensive) big log cabins have become popular. Back last century in the late thirties and early forties they weren't very popular or much used. The three of us (Robert, William and me) read a great deal in school and pulp fiction about the era of log cabins and like most boys thought it would be great to have your own log cabin in the woods. We were very fortunate to have the necessary materials and place right at hand on Grandma's farm.

We talked about how much we would like to build us a log cabin for some time until one day we were looking around in the harness house and spied an old rusty two man crosscut saw lying across the ceiling joists. We climbed up on the saddle racks and found a one-man crosscut saw along with some more equipment for handling logs as well as cutting and shaping them. That transformed us from thinking to doing. We found us some kerosene and cleaned these tools and located a secure place of our own to keep them.

Robert said we needed to select a place in the woods for our cabin that was out of the way enough that people did not go there much but was easy for us to get to with a wagon or cart — then he added that he thought he knew the perfect place. He didn't want to tell us where but he would show us.

We went to the house, which we had begun calling "headquarters", reported in and said we were going to ride our horses in the woods awhile. We told the headquarters people we would be back in a couple of hours. We caught our horses, saddled them and in a matter of a few minutes we were riding them through the gate between Uncle Harry's house and his barn into the woods. At this point the wagon road angled off a little to the right headed toward the south east and the main road from the south lane going to the creek and on to the mill. There was also a wagon trail that turned left (north) along the fence that led to the corn field near the top of the hill. From there this lesser wagon road turned east along the south fence of the corn field and went to the end (south east corner) of the south side of the corn field.

Robert didn't go in either of these wagon trails but took off just a little to the left through the woods. William said there wasn't anything but brush here in this part of the woods for a long way. Robert said just come on and follow me which we did. I judged we were about halfway between the gate at Uncle Harry's and the south east corner of the corn field when Robert stopped. We both looked at him in a questioning way and he had a funny little grin on his face. No one said anything but we followed his lead in getting off and tying our horses to some brush. He said he had found this place watching a few cows come down here from the trail up by the corn field. As he said this he pushed back a couple of limbs and motioned us to follow him.

We stepped into a clearing that looked almost like a park area. In the center were two huge chinkapin trees and a few other large oaks ringing them in all directions for about twenty yards with some waist to shoulder high bushes scattered about. I didn't know what kind of bushes they were and asked Robert and William if they knew. Neither did and Robert said he guessed the goats really liked them since he thought it must have been those bushes that attracted the goats to this place originally and they had cleared it out so they could eat these bushes as they wanted. After the goats had met their demise the cows had taken it over as their favorite bedding place, hence the numerous cow patties deposited around.

As William looked about he turned to Robert and asked how in the world we could ever get a wagon into this clearing. Robert laughed and said "I'm glad you asked" as he headed to the north side of the clearing. Here was a cow trail winding its way for about one hundred fifty yards up to the fence and wagon ruts at the corn field. You could not see the fence from the clearing or the clearing from the fence. Robert said we probably could get Kate's cart up and down the cow trail now and with a little cutting and trimming probably a wagon but he figured we didn't want much of a road to attract visitors. We both agreed and also commented that it was a very good location for our cabin.

For the next year and a half or maybe two years we spent many hours, days, weeks and months on this project. We would do and then redo our work as it didn't always turn out as we wished. Each of us researched our school libraries and books we had at home to suggest how to do things with the cabin. This was a great learning experience as well as practice in using hand tools to do actual work.

Luckily, we got a lot of help from Buddy which we at first tried to reject but soon found him to be a reliable and trusted advisor in our work. When we were first trying to get started, but stymied with laying of the logs on the slight incline of the site, we looked up and there stood Buddy in the cow path smiling at us. He told us he was plowing Kate in the cornfield and faintly heard this chopping sound and decided he should investigate it. And there we were working away. He discovered our project early and helped us till we lost interest and moved on to girls, cars and the like.

In the end we had us a hide-out with a very usable little one room house where we spent many nights "camped out" learning to cook, fight mosquitoes and rough it like the pioneers. We, of course, had to let our families know what we had made in order to get permission to "live in the woods" as much as we did. As we tired of this and our cabin began to rot and crumble, we had a good laugh when the next trio — Sonny, (my younger brother), W. H. (William's younger brother) and Carl Jr. (the third cousin of this trio) — announced they were going to build them a log cabin in the woods. I can't remember if they ever completed their project or not, but I do know we three had set a high mark to reach as far as log cabins were concerned.

Unfortunately as time passes so do all living things. I have been saddened by the loss of so many people including friends, relatives, and some I just knew of during my lifetime. But the loss of Tony, my first equine love, was a very tough blow. At his passing I had not lost any people really close to me and Tony was really close to me. I felt as if I had neglected him for several of his last years as marriage, a family and career made their demands.

When our son David was born in 1952 one of my many goals concerning him was to have a picture made with him sitting on Tony who at the time was retired to King of the Lane at Grandma's farm and pretty much had free run of anywhere he wanted to go. I made a point of checking on Tony when we were there at Christmas time. I took five month old David out to the lane to visit Tony who nuzzled him and then checked all my pockets till he bumped my coat pocket that held his apple. David watched wide eyed as Tony munched on the apple. Tony's hair was shaggy, off color and his appearance showed much wear and tear. I decided to wait until summer — near David's birthday to take a picture thinking Tony might look better after losing his winter coat and maybe David could sit unassisted on him by then.

In 1953 when school let out I spent the summer working as a night policeman for the city of Overton. In late June, one afternoon I decided to drive by myself up to Grandma's farm before I had to go to work. When I got to the house, Ruby told me that Grandma and Auntie had gone into Tyler for some shopping. I asked her if she knew where Tony was. She looked out the kitchen window and said "No, but you can check with Buddy, he should be out cleaning in the canning house." She didn't look back at me so I headed out the door for the canning house. Buddy and I passed some small talk and finally I got around to Tony. Buddy too looked away and then he told me that during the winter Tony had taken a liking to hanging out in the woods all by himself. He had turned into a real loner. Sometimes Buddy wouldn't see him for several days. Then came a time that he didn't see him for about two weeks he thought. Buddy told Grandma and she agreed that he needed to look for him. Buddy looked at all the places he had spotted Tony over the last year or so, especially along the creek and the gates where he would stand for hours at a time; but didn't find him at any of these places. On about his third loop through the woods Buddy decided to turn his horse toward our old cabin site and check there. He found a pile of horse hair, bones and other horse remains near our cabin site. He went back to the house told Grandma and asked her permission for him to bury the remains where he had found them. She thought that was a good idea and suggested he get some help. Buddy said if she didn't mind he would rather do it alone. She said fine and sent him to do his work.

Buddy turned and looking straight at me with tears in his eyes and said that he had buried Tony's remains and covered the spot with some rocks from the foundation of our old cabin so I would be able to find it. He offered to go with me to see it if I wanted him to. I said no, I would go later.

All the way back to Overton I thought of Tony and all the kids that had been close to him. It was a lonely twelve hours for me from six pm till six am that long night shift. I don't remember anything that happened at work but I do remember making and several times revising plans for the Fourth of July picnic at Grandma's farm.

Finally on the Saturday of the picnic, soon after our meal was finished, I said nothing except to Joyce and quietly slipped away for a few minutes at Tony's resting place — where I stuck a small U S flag among the rocks, said goodbye old friend and cried some.

As I turned between the harness house and the mule lot well into "Tony's

Lane," I heard Auntie ringing her big brass school hand bell. As soon as some of the kids had finished their meal they too had gone to visit Tony, and when they couldn't find him they had made for Auntie. She decided it was time for an announcement. I reached the gate to the yard just as everyone bowed their heads — and I cried a little more — inside.

WORLD WAR II

Today as I sometimes sit on the front porch of my old LC house where I spent most of my school years and gaze at the school across the highway, my thoughts turn back some eighty or so years to when I was a student there. Many are of the period during World War II. I can see the windows of the rooms where I spent so many hours — days — weeks — months waiting for "life to begin" (or so it seemed at that time). I recall that I was in Mr. Wiley's civics class where we heard the President "declare war" on Japan and the other enemies of the USA.

I was thirteen at the time — a tough time in life anyway — but especially so at the beginning of a war. My father had already declared his intentions — he was leaving us for the war and my mother had been crying ever since. I wanted to go fight too but of course I was not anywhere old enough. It seemed later that I spent the whole war waiting to go serve but never got the opportunity. V E Day was the month I graduated from high school and V J Day was the month I celebrated my seventeenth birthday.

My Dad enlisted in the Marine Corp and left on the train at Longview for San Diego, California on February 2, 1942. We waved him goodbye just as we were to see so many Americans do in the movies during and after the war. It wasn't long before the older boys, and a few of the girls too, began to leave school for the war.

The first impact I felt personally from the war was in the summer of 1941. Coach Hill, our high school head football coach and athletic director (as they are now called) was a captain in the Army reserves and was called to duty. He came down to see me one afternoon before he left and said he had a proposition for me.

He was selling his laying hens to the hatchery in Kilgore but they didn't have room for his young chicks and pullets. He wanted to give the leftovers to me to raise and sell from which I would make me some money. The only thing he wanted in return was for me to keep his dogs for a few months until Mrs. Hill could get settled. She was moving back to stay with her parents in the northeast until she decided where she would move their furniture and settle down for a while. Coach Hill's in-laws lived in an apartment complex that did not allow dogs.

These weren't just chickens, these were ROP (record of production) certified White Leghorns. Coach Hill didn't just raise chickens, he bred high production layers! And I knew the difference because both of my grandmothers raised chickens and subscribed to the Poultry Tribune which I read every issue from cover to cover. Coach Hill knew I loved the chickens and that I knew every aspect of raising them since I had been "warting" him about them for years. He had been hiring me to take care of them when he would be away for a few days — also his dogs.

The Hills lived only three doors from us (they owned their house — but it was built on land that my parents leased to them). Since I fed and played with Bugger and Lady (black Scotties) they thought I was their second master anyway. They were pure-blooded (as we called it) or better known as registered and pedigreed. Coach Hill had shown me and explained their "papers," as well as introduced me to Dog World which I also read from cover to cover. I was a big reader even back then.

Anytime I was gone overnight I could depend on my two closest friends to take care of my "livestock" (which usually included a horse or two, a dog or so, banty chickens, etc.). These two were Marcus Carter (whose mother ran a café/boarding house on the corner next to us — also on our land) and Novice Davis (whose family ran a grocery store across Don Leverett Road from us). Marcus, Novice and I were very close from the time we started school until I graduated from high school — I finished a year (1945) ahead of them although Novice and I started the same year. What good times (and a few bad) we had.

It was this experience of breeding chickens that got me into breeding dogs and then ponies and horses. I didn't get over the horses until after I retired from teaching and every now and then I still think about getting a few ponies for pets.

A couple of months after Coach Hill and his wife left in the summer of 1941, Mrs. Hill along with her parents came to LC, picked up Booger and Lady, had a moving van load up their furniture and left. I never heard from them again but I found out that Coach Hill came to the University of Houston after the War as the baseball coach and stayed there until he retired.

Looking back now after more than seventy years, I feel that Coach Hill had a lot of influence on me and my development. Not just during the period I was around him but through the years as I remembered the things he taught me by showing me and letting me help him do things.

Well the chickens did well but I didn't keep them very long. As the pullets began to lay, I sold them to the hatchery and I had a ready market for the fryers through Mr. Davis (Novice's dad) in his grocery store. I would prepare them and he put them in his meat counter — since we were out in the country I guess there weren't many restrictions at that time. It seems I remember that he sold the fryers for twenty-five cents per pound and we split it - ten cents for him and fifteen cents for me. Right alongside the chicken was sliced round steak for the same twenty-five cents per pound. This wasn't a bit unusual for the times but today as I see the price of round steak compared to whole fryers — I am shocked. This was a time when most families in our area ate fried chicken only for Sunday dinner or when having company.

Our family, and most of the people we knew back then, kept a few chickens around their home so if unexpected company appeared close to meal time they always had a meal handy of fried chicken and mashed potatoes to prepare and serve. You didn't have access to all the fast food places we do today. Even the Davises, who had the store with the meat counter in it, raised their own chickens in the backyard behind the store for their family (they lived in the back of the store building). One of the things about their chicken raising and eating that fascinated me was the way they prepared their chickens for cooking. Novice would go into the backyard, catch the intended (usually selected by his mother), wring its head, take it to their tool shed and skin it. There was no picking of feathers at all. They fried their chicken skinless. I must say that is was pretty good since I sampled it many times. They were the only family I ever knew that prepared their "fryers" in this fashion.

About this time, as our nation was preparing for war, we made a trip during the summer to California. We were going to visit my Mother's sister Ruby and her family. Her husband, Carl Jeter, had taken a job in Englewood in the rapidly growing aircraft industry. Sonny, my younger brother, and Carl Jr. were about the same age with LaNell, the daughter, a couple of years younger. One afternoon while we were visiting, my aunt Ruby called me into the kitchen and handed me a couple of dollar bills and said she needed another fryer to have enough for supper. She wanted me to run down to the butcher shop. She added that all I needed to tell the man behind the counter was that Mrs. Jeter needed another fryer and he would know what she wanted. She gave me directions and I took off on foot. I did as I was asked and was I surprised when the man laid a rabbit up on the scales all dressed and ready to be cut up and cooked. I'll have to admit I had a little trouble chocking my meat down that night at supper. I learned that fryer in California didn't mean the same as in Texas.

As I mentioned earlier, I really studied the Poultry Tribune during this time and followed the advances in the poultry industry. It was fascinating for me to read about the tremendous strides being made in the caged layer practices and the developments in the broiler industry. Here was man taking control of environment and heredity and producing animals specially adapted for our use as food. With the broilers it wasn't long until they were producing a pound of meat in half the time and with half of the feed. This was a great example of science put to work.

Another example of the results of my reading the Poultry Tribune was my involvement with capons. Being exposed to life on a farm and ranching, I was familiar with castrating pigs to raise to eat, calves for steers and oxen, horses and mules for work animals, etc. But — chickens??? Yes, the Poultry Tribune told all about it and I studied it all. There was even an ad for a chicken castrating kit. Of course, I ordered it and had my experiments (or rather my applications) going. To everyone's surprise I was pretty successful according to the literature.

This procedure called for going into the body cavity and removing the little bean like organs near the backbone which if left unchecked caused the chicken to grow into a rooster but if removed the chicken developed into a capon. This was a very serious operation for the chicken and needed to be done before it was too big. Since the death rate was quite high you wanted to wait until the young chicken was just large enough to eat so if it perished from loss of blood it could be dressed and used as food.

This first "kit" I had consisted of a sharp cutting tool similar to that used by a surgeon and special clamps for holding the ribs apart and removing the bean. It was rather bloody — hence the high rate of death — but done correctly it was usually successful. Not long after I acquired my first kit there was a new electric procedure which seared the incision and cut down on the bleeding and upped the success rate. With this new procedure I became quite proficient but found it most difficult to get use to the smell of burned flesh.

The capon grows much larger and tenderer than his rooster and hen companions. I ordered day old male chicks of the heavy breeds for this purpose and after some were good sized I took them to Grandma's farm for Sunday dinners. I will never forget the look and reaction from Ruby, the colored cook. She said "Lordee! Chickens big as turkeys — what you younguns gonna come up wit next?"

Another innovation I got involved in from the pages of Poultry Tribune was the use of the Natural Feather Brooder which did not need heat in the brooder itself but you just kept the room temperature in the lower seventy degree range. Most of the chicken brooders at that time involved the use of a large hood the baby chicks hovered under that was heated by natural gas. kerosene or electricity. This new method used a wooden boxlike frame that had a feather board that could be adjusted for height to fit at the backs of the baby chicks as they grew. It had a curtain across one side so the chicks could go in and out for food and water. Of course I had to try it and ordered one. I used it with a couple of batches of chicks and it really did work. But I, as most others I guess, preferred the electric box type more and the natural feather board method was soon gone.

So my magazine reading continued and I ended up breeding dogs (Dobermans in 1946 before they were very popular in the US) as a result of Dog World. I read the Cattleman and became involved in this industry somewhat but I never did have a breeding herd — I didn't like nursing calves and doctoring cows. But horses — that's another story. I won't get into it for now but you can't imagine the time I have spent reading about horses — all kinds of horses. My horse love led to trail riding which I did up into my seventies. And I have had horses all my life it seems — but not now. I got to the point I couldn't "swing up" into the saddle and felt it was time to quit. I took up motorcycle riding — easier to get on and off!

One more little story about my chickens — there are many more but we will stop on this one. Our first teaching jobs were back in East Texas after Joyce and I graduated from college. I was to teach at Overton and her job was at the Gaston ISD (Joinerville). We settled in Overton so Joyce was the one to commute. We lived only a few blocks from my school so in the mornings she dropped me off and went on to her school. In the afternoons I usually walked home — and got in the habit of going through town, checking the Post Office, visiting with the clerks and stopping at the Davis Grocery for what we were going to eat that evening. Yes, this was the same family from LC — they had sold their LC store, moved to town and opened another store. Joyce usually beat me home and we shared the cooking and other duties since we both worked. But about the chickens.

This was in 1951. People ordered their day old chicks by mail then and a lot of times via C.O.D. — which meant they didn't pay until they were delivered to them or they were picked up at the Post Office. Sometimes the person would not accept them (for whatever reason, usually they had run out of money) and the Post Office was stuck with them. The procedure for the Post Office was to auction the item.

Arnold Cohagen was usually in charge of this operation at the Overton Post Office and when I would come by about four in the afternoon he would be ready for me. He had unloaded several orders on me (usually plants and such since we were getting a new house in order). Well, that day it was 100 day old chicks — except they were no longer a day old but maybe three or more and they had to be gone at five for the Post Office to close. Arnold kept after me to bid on them but I said I didn't have any money except for sixty-seven cents in my pocket. He said fine — write it down — there was no minimum. Well I did and went on home. In a few minutes the phone rang and Arnold said I had bought the chickens — the only bid — bring my 67 cents and come get my chickens so they could close the Post Office. I told Joyce I had an errand to run, jumped in the car and picked up the chicks.

I stopped at Davis Grocery for a small sack of chicken starter (they also sold feed and we bought groceries on credit from them) and two or three empty pasteboard boxes they gave away free. Then to Pope & Turner Hardware for some chicken feeders and waterers. I wrote a check for these.

Joyce really got a surprise when I drove to the house with my "chicken farm" — I won't go into the discussion we had except to say she talked to me like she did her second graders when they had done something bad. I made temporary quarters for my animals in the boxes under the kitchen table with newspapers lining the bottom and feed and water spread before them. The table was next to the cook stove so I put the oven on low, left the door open and told them good night. I could hear them cheerfully chirping all night as I tried to sleep — on the sofa in the living room.

The next morning was a Saturday so I had time to make some preparations for the baby chicks. I took Sugar's (our cocker spaniel) doghouse and converted it to a baby chick house — she wouldn't use it anyway because she preferred sleeping on the foot of our bed and wouldn't think about going outside without one of us with her. Strangely enough she refused to pay the baby chicks any attention while they were in the house.

I mounted two light bulbs about six inches above the floor in the converted doghouse for the chicks to have their heat. I had my head in the doghouse when I heard a voice calling me. It was my father-in-law and he had come over for his regular Saturday morning coffee. We went inside and I showed him the chicks — we had lost (died is probably a better word) two or three during the night which was not unusual for baby chicks. I told him I had been in the back making a place for them with the doghouse. He sensed that Joyce was mad (he had been in similar situations before) as she did not show herself.

He and I went to the back yard so I could show him what I was doing. I was to the point I was ready to make a pen around the doghouse to keep the chicks enclosed and other animals out. Mr. Petty said he had the ideal thing — window screens from their house when they had remodeled it the previous summer. He said he would go and get them for me — which he did and was back in about thirty minutes with the screens (they lived only about five miles away). While he was gone I moved the chicken farm from the kitchen to the doghouse. We nailed three or four of the screens together for a fence and went into the kitchen to make our coffee. I was surely glad Mr. Petty hung around awhile so the frost would melt from Joyce and as the kitchen was aired out things got pretty close to normal.

At night the next few days I closed the chicks up in the converted doghouse to protect them from night predators and tied Sugar out by the pen during the day to keep away stray cats. Sugar acted like she thought she had been cast away at first but then began to relish her role as boss and protector of the chicken farm.

I already had the plans in my head for their pen. I would build a frame out of 2X4s four feet wide and eight feet long with the floor elevated three feet and covered with ½ inch welded wire fabric — this sturdy wire made good chicken floors. The 1" chicken wire top would be eighteen inches above the floor and made in two by four foot panels so they could be raised or removed for access to the interior. The sides of the pen were also covered with the 1" chicken wire. The solid portion of the cover for protection from sun and rain would be a piece of 5/8" plywood four feet by four feet. I could mount feeders and waterers around the outside of the pen when the chicks got a little larger and they could stick their heads through the holes in the wire to eat and drink.

For the time being I constructed a brooder out of a sturdy pasteboard box with the two lights I was using for heat in the doghouse and kept it under the solid portion of the roof.

This design would allow two fellows (it turned out that they needed to be strong) to move the chicken farm around the back yard and we could enjoy an automatic grass fertilizing machine. For some reason, I never got around to patenting this idea although it did work rather well. These plans were also devised with the idea where most of the materials would come from (without cost) my Dad's shop and garage. So without much cost by the next Friday we had a great chicken facility in our back yard. Our house was on the last street in a new subdivision and had woods and a creek behind us so I didn't worry about the neighbors complaining — besides back then a lot of people kept chickens even in town.

Everything seemed to be going fine for the chickens, they were eating and drinking in the outside troughs and feathered out nicely (not needing the brooder any more). I was building a fence for a chicken yard and thinking about what kind of chicken house to build, etc. About a month after getting the chicks settled in their movable pen — late on a Friday night, or rather early on a Saturday morning — we had a tremendous storm. It rained and rained, terrible thunder and lightning, the wind blew and blew. We were so thankful we hadn't been caught outside in a storm like this — then we remembered the chickens. They WERE outside and their pen was only a few feet from the bedroom wall where the roof would pour the water down on them. I wanted to go check on them but Joyce would not let me until the rain let up some.

It stopped raining in a few minutes and I peeked out in the increasingly fresh daylight but couldn't tell anything about the chicks so I went to the kitchen and out to the back yard. I was stunned when I neared the chickens — all were stretched out on the floor of the pen and not a chirp or movement in the bunch. I just stared and wondered what to do next. Giving them all up for dead, I went to the tool shed picked up a shovel and went to the back of the yard and dug a ditch about a foot deep, a foot wide and about four feet long. I went back to the chicken pen, stuck my shovel in and picked up four or five of them, walked to the ditch and dumped them in and put a little dirt over them. I then went back for another scoop full. Joyce was standing by the pen. As I reached in with my shovel she caught me by my arm and said to wait — she had seen one moving a little.

She reached in and picked that one up by its feet and a little water ran from its mouth. With the other hand she gently squeezed the small body and a little more water ran out. As she held it in her hands it began to shake and she laid it back on the floor of the pen. To our surprise, it shook some more, stood up and then it began to wobble around. She reached down picked up another and repeated the procedure and she soon had another chick walking around. She told me to quit standing there like a Duffus and get busy. I did and we "raised from the dead" all the rest except maybe eight or ten which didn't perk up. I thought it was a miracle — but Joyce wasn't through by a long shot.

She ran into the kitchen, got a big meat pan, put the chicks in it which had not yet responded to her artificial respiration technique, took them to the kitchen and put them in the oven with the heat turned on low. Again I saw a miracle happen — in a few minutes we began to hear a chirp every now and then. Gradually the chicks came back to life again and we put them one by one back in their pen. The outcome was that the only ones we lost (died) were the ones that I covered with dirt. Joyce always said if she had gotten there sooner she would have saved all of them — and I surely believed it.

It wasn't long before the males were getting big enough to eat, but neither of us felt like eating them. We had been through too much together — we became very generous and gave them away to friends and relatives. We told very few of the receivers the full story. We kept about six of the pullets in our back yard for our supply of eggs and even gave away a few eggs.

CORPUS CHRISTI IN 1942

When my Dad went into the Marine Corp in February, 1942, we thought he might be gone forever and we might never see him again. After finishing boot camp in San Diego, California he was sent to Corpus Christi Naval Air Station and spent the rest of the war in Texas. Not long after his reporting to CCNAS, we made a trip to Corpus Christi to see him. We made the trip in our 1939 Dodge sedan which would last us throughout the war. We used a lot of our gas stamps we had saved for the trip. I was thirteen at the time and had just gotten a new Boy Scout uniform for the first time so I wore it some during our visit to see him. I remember meeting our Dad at Sun Pharmacy downtown where the buses from the Naval Air Station loaded and unloaded. How exciting to see the sailors and marines getting off the buses and reuniting with their girlfriends, wives and families.

We spent about a week there in April and had one room in a run-down rooming house right in the middle of town. I remember my Dad saying how lucky we were to get it since housing was so tight at the time. We had a good visit but I still remember how hard it was for us to leave after seeing our Dad. We tentatively made plans to spend the summer there if he wasn't transferred before we got out of school.

We did spend most of the summer of 1942 in Corpus Christi. We stayed in an old motel on North Beach. What a time we had — living on the beach, a block or so from a carnival and fresh water swimming pool but we loved the salt water and waves better. There were all kinds of attractions — we were too young and naive to fully appreciate them all. There were even news and book stands. Comic books were ten cents new or you could buy used ones for a nickel and sell them back to the newsstand for three cents. Two cents went quite a ways in those long summer days.

The War was beginning to take its toll — on all in many different ways. At that time we didn't have any idea how long Dad would be in Corpus Christi but Mother had decided that as long as he was there we would be there also. During the summer, Dad was able to get us a house for a month or so while we were in line for an apartment in the La Armada, the large navy housing unit in town — still there between Ayers and Port.

When we moved into the La Armada, one of the neighbors approached me about taking over a newspaper route in our area that was being vacated. I was really excited and after going to the newspaper circulation office, putting up a bond, etc. I had a paper route. This same neighbor took me to an out-of-the-way bicycle shop and made it possible for me to buy a brand new bicycle. The newspaper route was great — until it turned cold, rainy weather in the winter. I didn't really mind getting up at four a.m., rolling my papers down at the La Armada office building, delivering the papers, eating breakfast and then to school. After school (I was able to get out of school an hour early due to the paper route) it was the same thing all over — yes morning and afternoon Monday through Friday and once on Saturday and Sunday — the Corpus Christi Caller and the Corpus Christi Times.

This paper route taught me lots of things and I should have learned a lot more from it than I did. It didn't take me long to find out that people — no matter how nice they seemed — will cheat a poor little paperboy out of a few dollars every chance they had and then lie about it. This happened many, many times. I don't know how I could put up with some of the stuff I did but I did do it and survived the experience. But most of the people were very nice and that kept me delivering the papers.

Having the bicycle was great for me — not only did I use it to deliver newspapers but also to go to school, run errands for my Mother and to go to the T-Heads for crabbing. The seawall and T-Heads were relatively new in Corpus Christi when the war came along and boats were not allowed to be at the T-Heads or seawall due to war precautions. The seawall was a great place to go crabbing — tying my lines to the wooden posts along it. I got a crab net like the one Uncle Willis had, found enough strong twine, tied an apple crate on my bike's carrier, got some bacon, dry salt pork or such and away I would go. Crabs were plentiful for the taking

— but I don't remember seeing anyone else crabbing like I was doing it. I did see a lot of sailors and civilians sitting on the seawall watching me and a few times some would come and talk to me about it. Two or three of them told me about their crawfishing back home in the creeks. I told them that my cousins and I did that also in the creek at my Grandma's farm.

When I had filled my apple crate, I would go home and Mother would boil and pick the meat from the crabs. We never ate the meat plain because mother said we needed our vegetables. She would make a salad with the meat and lettuce, dressing, etc. While Mother was preparing the salad, it would be my job to prepare the margarine. Margarine was new stuff then — it was against the law to be sold colored — so it wouldn't be confused with butter, I guess. Anyway the margarine looked like lard (white and creamy) in a plastic bag and you put a pellet of orange coloring in it and squeezed and squeezed it until the color was uniformly butter yellow.

It was then time for me to go on my bike to the Butter Krust Bakery — a few blocks down Ayers — and get a fresh hot un-sliced loaf of bread straight out of the oven and through the wrapping machine. I would race home with the hot bread and we would melt the margarine on it and eat it with the crab salad. This was a real treat — was it really so tasty or was it the fun of doing it to get to eat it?

There was only one high school in Corpus Christi at the time — it later became Miller High School but then it was Corpus Christi High School. There was only one big building for classrooms and offices. It was a three story red brick building with twenty-four hundred students in that one building. Of course there was a gym, stadium and various specialized small buildings on the campus. But to a country boy from a small community — this was something. The first day of school seemed like a roundup on the sheep ranch. We were herded everywhere. The halls were marked off into three lanes — the two outside lanes were one way traffic lanes and the center was for teachers and emergencies. The stairs were in the center of the building around an opening that was from the first to the third floors. You could look from the inner lane of the third floor all the way down to the first floor.

The first day of school my Mother took me and dropped me off at one of the entrances and told me she would pick me up at the same location that afternoon. I was a sophomore (10th grade) but this was really my first year in high school due to the realignment from eleven grades to twelve grades. I wasn't ready for this big-time school business but I made out that first day without passing out or anything like that. When school was over I was going down the stairs to leave the building when I heard this voice calling — "Floyd - Floyd - Floyd." I was almost too afraid to look up and back because I thought it must be God since He was the only one who could know that I was there. To my surprise I saw C. E. Lewis hanging over the rail on the third floor waving and yelling at me. I waited at the door till he got there and we hugged each other to see a friend in such a place.

I couldn't believe it — C. E. Lewis who I had started first grade with and had gone to school with him in all my school days except for the 3rd, 4th and 5th grades. He was the one I had a fight with the first day of the 1st grade and again on the first day of the 6th grade — my Mother had dressed me like a city slicker to start school in the first grade and C. E. made fun of my clothes and we got with it. The same thing happened when we returned from Tyler and I started the sixth grade. But today was a reunion with a buddy.

I told him how I had ended up there in school. He told me that his sister had married a guy in the Navy and he was stationed at CCNAS. C. E.'s family had moved to Corpus Christi to be near the sister and his Dad had gotten a job with the Navy.

We didn't have any classes together but we made a point of seeing each other two or three times a week. We didn't live very close to each other but we visited at one another's home at least once a week. Today the sister lives at LC across the highway from our LC place and we see the sailor she married and her every now and then. C. E. is gone but I remember him each time I look across the highway and see the McLane's house.

Remembering my crabbing experiences above reminded me of my one oystering excursion while I was in Corpus Christi in 1943. I don't remember the boy's name but he and I had two or three classes together and started eating and visiting together during lunch period. Nearly every day he brought the same lunch — Vienna sausages wrapped in biscuit dough and baked — and I know they were very good because we traded lunches a lot of times. Anyway he told me that his father was an oyster man — that he had a boat and "drug" oysters from the bay. This sounded like a lot of fun to me so when he asked me if I wanted to go oystering with him on Saturday — I jumped at the chance. He said his dad had to make a trip or something and was going to let him use the boat. We made plans to meet Saturday morning and I could hardly wait. I just imagined us cruising around the bay in a big boat.

Well, was I surprised when we met at the predetermined place, and the boat turned out to be a twelve foot wooden rowboat that it took two to handle. The way you harvested the oysters was to pull a sled like wooden box with the boat as it plowed up sand and oysters and trapped the oysters in the box. This turned out to be sheer drudgery and in no time I had blisters on the palms of my hands and fingers. Not only was the rowing strenuous — but ever so often you had to pull up the box, take out the oysters and dump the gunk back into the water. What a workout this turned into. After a morning of this we finally went to the bank and he said we would divide the oysters. After looking at the pile I realized they had to be taken apart and the oysters taken out of the shells. This thought made me feel very generous and I told him to keep my share since I didn't really know what to do with them and he did. He thanked me warmly for my help and we remained friends but I never went oystering with him again.

Soon after the first of the year (1943), my Dad was transferred from Corpus Christi to the Hitchcock LTA NAS (Lighter Than Air Naval Air Station). This "Blimp Base" as it was called, was located between Houston and Galveston near Alvin. He was to be the "Brig Warden" (head jailer) at the base. We moved back to LC and resumed life the best we could — very much changed from what we had left.

My boy scout troop was no more, Mr. Weaver (my friend and classmate Gene's dad) had been drafted. My closest uncle (mother's youngest brother Fred, only twelve years older than I) had been drafted into the Marine Corp. Many others were gone to the war also — Mr. Easely (my sixth grade teacher) and others from the school were gone either into the armed forces or some other role in the war. I got another newspaper route — for the Henderson paper — and delivered it on horseback since the roads were not very good for a bicycle out in the country area. I think I had only nineteen customers but every one of them seemed to appreciate my delivering it — several would be sitting on their front porch waiting for me every afternoon after school (afternoon edition only — no Saturday and the big one on Sunday morning).

We had to be very frugal with our gas due to rationing and other items such as tires, shoes, sugar, meat, etc. I heard the "big boys" talking about getting "drip gas" out in the field — about all you needed was a wrench, felt hat (filter) and a container. I told my Mother about this and if we didn't have the stamps for gas I would just go get us some "drip." She told me to stay away from those drips because if I didn't blow myself up I would surely blow up our car with us in it.

THE SUMMER OF 1943

We learned shortly after Christmas (1942) or about New Years day (1943) that my Dad had been selected as part of an advance team to be stationed at a new Navy facility. At that time we did not know where his new assignment would be due to wartime regulations but they were told that for a period of a few months they would be in and out of Corpus Christi NAS and the new location. Mother and Dad decided it would be better if we moved back to Leverett's Chapel and went to school there during the spring semester.

It was good to be back "home" again but not knowing where Dad would be sent worried Mother a great deal. Of course he knew where it was the first time his group flew there but they had been sworn to secrecy and could not even tell their families according to military procedure. In a month or two the married men were told they could tell their families. We were happy to find out it would be Hitchcock, Texas which we were able to locate as a tiny place on our Texas road map. We were delighted to realize it was only about half as far from LC as was Corpus Christi. Dad was to be the brig warden at the new facility.

The Naval Air Station at Hitchcock — about fifteen miles northwest of Galveston — was built by the Navy in 1942 to accommodate lighter-than-air aircraft, commonly known as blimps. The purpose of the base and its blimps was to search for German submarines in the Gulf of Mexico. The most noticeable feature to me was the huge blimp hangar which could hold six of the blimps. It covered an area about the size of a football field and was two hundred feet tall with sliding doors on each end that could be closed and opened. The base was commissioned on May 22, 1943.

As things worked out we made the best of the situation by being flexible all the time Dad was in Hitchcock. It was there that he was discharged at the end of his service with the Marine Corp. in 1945.

Auntie, with Margene away in the army, was living full-time at Grandma's farm along with her two little boys Kenneth and Jack. Robert and Evie were also living with Grandma but Auntie was the one who cared for all of them. Buddy and Ruby were at the farm also to take care of the work in the house and farm.

There was a great need for civilian help at the blimp base and Mother wanted to help the war effort any way she could. At first she felt we needed to move as close as we could to Hitchcock when school was out but there seemed to be no housing available at that time for a family near the base.

Mother and Auntie came up with this plan that maybe Dad could get a room for them in the area and Mother would stay there with my Dad and work on the Navy blimp base for the summer. Auntie convinced her that she would be able to hold "summer camp" for the boys. Dad also agreed to this plan so our summer looked good for everybody.

While Dad was searching for them a room, he met up with a teacher or professor in one of the area schools who said he would rent his home for the summer to a serviceman. This older couple was of retirement age but had agreed to teach on for the duration. They had this little two bedroom cottage near the blimp base and had bought a small piece of property in Colorado where they wanted to retire. They planned to build a log cabin on the property — so they were going to work on it themselves during the summer and return to their jobs in the fall. Dad jumped at the opportunity to get the house for the summer. Sonny and I still wanted to spend most of our time at Grandma's although the house meant we could visit some.

On May 10, just days before school was out for the summer, a storm visited Leverett's Chapel and Laird Hill with severe results. It was early afternoon with me in Mr. Woodall's Algebra I class on the west side of the high school building. Something caught my attention outside and I walked over to the windows to look out. It was lightening, and the sky was full of it. The air seemed to turn a very unusual green color. My attention was pulled to the left and up the hill toward our house. I saw a big chunk of the south east end of the roof fly off as the oil derrick behind the house disappeared. My attention was drawn north with the debris flying in the air. Trash was blowing every which way and signs coming down as Flossie's front porch took flight.

As I visually followed the storm to the right up the next hill two oil derricks lay down on the ground as if to take a nap. The lone house sitting on top of the hill exploded into thousands of pieces just as if it had been dynamited. Mr. Woodall, standing at my elbow, asked "Did you see that?" I turned and looked into his drawn face and was too awed to answer. We both turned again to the windows taking in the terrible scene. In a few seconds he pointed to my house and asked didn't I think I should go home and check on things. Still unable to talk I nodded my head, pushed my way through all the kids at the windows and ran for home.

I didn't go in the front door but ran across the front yard to the driveway — looking up at the roof on the way. I went through the south door, ran down the hall calling my Mother. I ran through the whole house calling and looking for her but could neither hear nor see her. As I came back to the door I had come through into the house I heard her calling from the outside. She was standing in the kitchen door of the Scholar's house across the driveway. I was relieved to see she was unharmed and safe.

I rushed over to the Scholar's just as Mrs. Scholar drove down their driveway. She and Mother met in the baby's room. The baby was still sleeping, happy as a lark. Mother came out and we walked over to our house as she explained what had happened. Mrs. Scholar needed a few things from the grocery store for supper. The baby had just gone to sleep so she phoned Mother (the baby's godmother) next door to see if she could step over and stay with the baby a few minutes while she ran to the store — in the car of course. As she was gathering her groceries the storm struck and she rushed home as soon as she could.

Mother and I surveyed our damages — the missing six by twenty-four foot section from the roof, but could see no other damage to our house or the houses around it. We did find the derrick behind the house lying on the ground and tin from the roof of the barn scattered across the countryside. Mother checked our telephone and it wasn't working so she and I walked across to the school yard and fetched Sonny from the elementary school.

The school was holding the elementary school children till the parents picked them up or time for the regular buses to run. Mother wanted to take Sonny with us to Overton and try to get word to our Dad that we were all alright — anticipating the news would eventually get to him about the tornado. She knew you could make long distant phone calls and pay for them at the Western Union office so we headed for it.

The Western Union man advised Mother to send a telegram since his experience with getting word to servicemen favored this method because Western Union would deliver the message to the base and the military was good at placing it in the hands of the serviceman, no matter what he was doing or where he was. With a phone call you usually had to leave word for him to call back and this would sometimes take hours. So Mother sent a telegram and we went back home.

Before long we found out that luckily no one was at home at the house I saw explode on the hill. But, unfortunately, about half a mile toward Laird Hill the Tuttle home was not so lucky. It was completely destroyed too — taking four lives with it. June, a classmate of mine, lost her mother and a young sister to the storm as well as a neighbor and baby who had gone to the Tuttle's to seek safety. There were many injuries and much heart ache as a result of this terrible storm.

Down in Hitchcock, we found out later, Dad's base commander got word about the storm and it sounded to him as the place Dad had told him was his home. The commander got in touch with Dad and they tried to phone Mother. When they couldn't get through they found out from the phone company the phone lines were down due to a storm. They knew it was the right place then and Dad quickly packed a bag and his commander got his personal car and took Dad to the nearest bus station in Alvin. A few minutes after they left the base the telegram arrived for Dad.

They found out the first bus out would have some layovers in route and wouldn't get to Henderson or Kilgore until the next evening. If they could get to Houston there would be a bus for Henderson out soon that would make it there about ten PM. They rushed to Houston in time and got Dad on the bus. Dad was thinking he would have to hitchhike from Henderson to Leverett's Chapel that night but during war time that was not unusual.

Boy was Dad surprised to see us (Mother, Sonny and me) waiting for him at the bus station in Henderson. Mother had to explain that when the commander got back to the base he found the telegram that had come for Dad and he took the liberty of opening it to find out what had happened. After reading the telegram he tried to phone Mother again and fortunately the telephone line had been repaired as far as our house. While we were eating a late supper the phone rang the two long rings (a party line back then) and Mother talked to the commander.

We celebrated and rejoiced late into the night — with a few moments of sadness thinking what could have been and remembering the other grieving and destitute people. Dad was told to take as much time as he needed but in three days, having repaired the roof, he was on his way back not wanting to go light on his part for the war effort. Who would have ever dreamed that we would go through another "killer" storm that summer in Hitchcock.

We did have a wonderful summer. With the blimp base about halfway between Houston and Galveston we could visit Uncle Willis and his family in Houston and also go to the beach in Galveston. Sometimes Verna & Paul would bring their families to see us and we would all go to Galveston for a picnic. We must have made three trips during the summer to visit Mother and Dad. It was a car load with Auntie (our driver), Grandma, Kenneth, Jack, Sonny and me. Robert stayed at Grandma's with his mother (who was unable to travel) with Buddy doing the driving for them. Robert missed out on all the fun we had on the beach and around Houston but felt like he was doing the right thing staying with his mother.

One of the trips was very memorable due to the weather. We usually stayed about four or five days but this trip in July ended up being for a week or a little longer. Although we experienced the "surprise hurricane of 1943" on the spot, I did not realize the extent of damage until later after the war when the full story was told.

On July 26 the hurricane made landfall at the Bolivar Peninsula on an unprepared population. There had probably been some unpublished ship reports to the Houston Weather Bureau, but wartime security regulations prohibited radio communication due to German U-boat operations off the Texas Coast. A tropical storm warning predicting winds at 30 to 40 miles per hour was published in the local newspapers the day before — which severely underestimated the strength of the storm.

The Navy, through their communications, probably had a good idea of the strength of the storm and was making preparations for it. Late afternoon on the 25th, Mother came to the house and told us a storm was coming and brought us food, water, flashlights, candles, etc. She said they were locking the base down and she and Dad had to stay there until the storm was over. She gave Auntie a little pamphlet with instructions on how to "weather" such a storm. She said for us to stay inside and not to go out until we were told it was safe. She then had to report back to the base — which turned into about a three day stay. Very excited, we hunkered down for the storm.

According to reports, the storm moved slowly through the Texas Gulf Coast area during the late morning and throughout the afternoon of July 26th. Wind velocity was measured at 63 mph on the Galveston Weather Bureau instruments before they were blown away. The wind gauge at Houston Airport registered winds from 80 to 132 mph. Rainfall in Galveston measured 13 to 16 inches. Nineteen people were killed and hundreds were injured. *It was estimated that 95 percent of the buildings in Galveston and Texas City experienced damage. Information about the storm was suppressed so as not to provide information about the hurricane's effect on the war industries to our enemies.*

Luckily for us, the owners of the sturdy little cottage in which we "sat out" the storm had it equipped with a great deal of good books, other types of reading materials and games of all descriptions — ranging from monopoly to Chinese checkers. We spent most of our time, day and night, all together in the combination living/dining room. At night, after we lost our electricity, we all gathered around one candle and played board games — listening to the wind and rain. It was high adventure for all of us — including Grandma and Auntie. Since that storm, I have sat out several other hurricanes but I think I enjoyed this one the most — if you can enjoy a hurricane.

One thing I will always remember was the big ell I spotted on the front porch. I didn't know what it was and got Auntie to look at that baby monster. She quickly decided it had to be an ell so I looked up ells in the handy encyclopedia. Water was about six inches deep over the concrete porch and right up to the bottom of the front door. The water stayed there a couple of days but we never had flooding in the house and that ell would come and go on the front porch — since it evidently liked lying on the concrete, I guess, taking a nap. It was about four feet long and as big around as a man's forearm. He was one ugly fellow — if it was a he.

The second day, after the big winds had stopped, a couple of men came up in a motorboat to the house to check on us. They wanted to know if there was anything we needed. Auntie told them we were doing fine and thanked them for checking on us. Sonny piped up that we were out of candy and could certainly use some. Both men laughed and one said he was sorry but they were out of candy also and they headed down the street in their boat.

The water slowly receded and as the roads opened up Dad came to the house in a Jeep to check on us. He said he had gone by Camp Wallace, an Army base close to the blimp base, and checked on the highways leading north. They told him that the water was going down, thrash had been cleared off the main highways and should be fully passable by sundown. He advised us to pack up and take off early the next morning for East Texas since it would be days before things could get back to normal as a result of the storm. He checked the gas in Grandma's car and said we had nearly a full tank so for us to go until we reached where they had plenty of gas available on our route to refill. It was good news to us that we would be headed for Grandma's farm. And the next afternoon we celebrated getting there and had much to tell everybody about our great adventure.

We only saw William every now and then — mostly on weekends — since he was at home and helping his dad that summer with the crops they were raising. William was always a very responsible and hard-working little kid where Robert and I were more turned toward play and mischief.

As young boys of a certain age are bound to do, Robert and I were always finding things to do to test our limits. We both read a lot and found many mysteries and adventure stories to our liking. I guess it was natural that one of us came up with the idea that we could wait until everyone was asleep, slip out, saddle our horses and go on a night ride. As we discussed and planned an excursion, we decided a ride to Overton and back (about eight or nine miles each way) would be the limit of the distance we could cover. For about a week we carefully planned for this high adventure.

Robert and I were sleeping in the bedroom on the south side of Uncle Harry's. His bedroom was the old kitchen which had been converted when Dad built the new kitchen and dining room across the back of the house. Our room was the old dining room and had two full size beds in it with a couple of large chiffrobes — but no closets. Windows on the outside wall opened to the west side of the house. On the south side of our bedroom was another that had a full size bed and a half bed. Sonny slept in the small bed while Kenneth and Jack slept together in the larger one. All three of these bedrooms opened into the long hallway and ours also had a door into Uncle Harry's — a holdover from the kitchen and dining room set up.

Uncle Harry was very deaf at this time and almost completely blind — so we didn't think we would disturb him during the night as we slipped out of the house through the window and returned the same way. The windows were so high off the ground that we needed help in reaching them from the ground so we located a five or six foot step ladder and pushed it up under the house for us to use. We checked one of the window screens to be sure we could unlatch it and it would swing freely for our exit and entry. We stayed up pretty late one night and found that the moon came out pretty soon after complete darkness and lasted most of the night. So we decided the next night would be "it."

We watched everyone after supper and as they settled down we made out like we were getting sleepy. We announced we were tired and going to bed. With our yawning, stretching and such we moved off to our bedroom hoping to get the others in a mood for bed. Uncle Harry was the first then gradually everyone dressed for bed and began slipping into their rooms. Robert and I kept our eyes peeled and went to the bathroom or kitchen several times checking the lights and snoring. Finally we decided everyone was down for the night and we dressed for our trip.

Going out the window we slipped down the side of the building the three or four feet our legs didn't reach to the ground and would fall in a heap. Then we got up and headed for the harness house. We had put our things there with our saddles — a little flashlight and a small baseball bat about 15" long from the Texas 100 year celebration in 1936 that kept turning up around the house. I was going to tie the little bat behind my saddle to use on dogs that might jump at our feet and legs. We both kept a coiled rope tied to our saddle horn as well as a leather whip on the other side. We didn't want to carry any firearms since people might think we were robbers.

Our horses weren't exactly pleased to see us and snorted and groaned a lot while we saddled them. Once we were underway they seemed to rather enjoy the novelty of this experience and we covered some ground at a brisk walk. We had discussed that we would ride steady but not fast and be ready to get out of the road when we saw a car coming from either direction. We tended to let the horses pick the path in the dirt road but were ready to take over in an instant. We didn't believe the old story that the knots on horses' legs were "night eyes" but we felt they did have a special sense about where they were putting their feet.

There were very few cars and we were making good time toward Overton — east and a little south. It wasn't long till we saw the glow in the sky formed by Overton and then two or three minor ones from oil refineries scattered about. It was wartime but we didn't have blackouts like some places did. The moonlight held pretty well and only a few times did it go behind a big cloud and the darkness closed in completely around us. We would slow down and let the horses pick their way carefully. When we were about two or three miles out of Overton as we passed a little side road we both noticed moonlight reflected off a car parked in the middle of it only about 30 or 40 feet from the main one. We didn't stop but did discuss it some since it was a strange place to park a car since there was no house around close.

As we came closer to Overton we decided that we should not go into the town since we might cause some excitement. People weren't accustomed to seeing horses in town, especially at night, except for parades or celebrations so we picked us a spot on a little hill on the edge of town.

We watched what we could see of the goingons in town — which wasn't much at that time of night. As our horses got rested up a bit they began to get a little restless. We decided it was time to get moving so we turned around and headed home. When we got to the place we had noticed the parked car we stopped for a good look and sure enough it was still in the same spot. Robert said we ought to see if anything was wrong so we turned in toward the car. As we neared it our horses' hooves made some noise on gravel and two heads popped up inside the windshield with surprised looks on their faces. I said let's get out of here and we wheeled around and got back on the main road and went trotting off toward Grandma's. We slowed back to a walk in a few minutes and both laughed since we knew we had disturbed some lovers and they wouldn't be very happy over our presence. That was the only excitement we had on the way home and there was even less traffic on the road on our return than earlier. Robert told me a story that Richard had told him about an experience he and a buddy had with a couple parked on Boca Chica Beach. Richard's friend suggested they drive up close to the parked car and try to look in as they slowly passed. Richard agreed and as he drove by slowly past the car a man stepped out with a rifle and fired a couple of shots above their car so they sped off. He said they decided it wasn't very bright to disturb parked lovers so he had passed this on to his little brother. Maybe we benefitted from this advice.

The next day we "drug around" and took a nap every opportunity we had. It took us about two or three days to recover from our night out but after a week or so we needed some more excitement. We decided this time we wouldn't bother with sliding down from the window instead we would just slip through Uncle Harry's room into the kitchen, unlatch the kitchen door screen and go out. When we returned we would retrace our steps and latch the screen back. This plan worked fine but we did worry some that someone might latch us out of the house if they came to the kitchen and found that the screen was unlatched.

This time the night turned out to have much less moonlight and we had a lot of difficulty seeing our way and the horses weren't as eager this time as before. We stopped at the same hill top as before and had not been there very long when a car drove up behind us and stopped with its lights on and in a few seconds a spotlight shinned on us. A man with a flashlight in his hand approached us and as soon as he got in the headlights we could see he had a gun on his belt around his waist. We both wanted to run for it but we knew that wouldn't work so we sat still and patted our horses to keep them calm, while our hearts raced. The man told us his name and that he was a deputy sheriff for Rusk County. He said we were about on the boundary of Smith and Rusk Counties but he had gotten a call from one of the neighbors about something going on that didn't look right so he was investigating what was happening. He had us get off our horses and he looked us over good with the aid of his flashlight and had us tell him our story. We were shaking and stuttering but we got it out to his satisfaction. He told us in no uncertain terms that what we were doing was very foolish and causing people trouble for no good reason. He told us to get on our horses and head for home and not to stop on the way except to get off the road for cars. Believe me, we didn't waste any time in mounting, turning around and headed out of town.

We didn't talk much on the way home except when a car came up on us from behind. We got off on the side of the road to let it pass but it slowed down and took a good deal of time to pass us. We could tell they were taking a careful look at us. They drove on slowly and about a quarter of a mile ahead they pulled in a side road and turned around. When they neared us from the front they stopped and waited for us to split and go on each side. Robert was on the driver's side of the car and I was on the passenger side. When we were even with the car the driver called to Robert to stop so they could talk. We both stopped but neither said anything since we were getting very scared about this time. The driver asked Robert what we were doing out that late at night. Robert said we're just out riding. After a little pause the driver asked him who we were and where did we live. Robert answered "I'm Robert Jernigan and that's my cousin Floyd Elliott." The man then wanted to know if that was Jernigan like in Mr. Walter. Robert replied that he was our uncle and we were staying at our grandmother's. Another pause and I saw the two in the car exchange glances. Then the driver said that there were a lot of rough characters out and about with sharp knives that would slit our throats for our pocket change and our horses and saddles. I could see the expression — a mean looking sneer — on the face of the passenger and thought he was surely one of them. The driver said we had better get home and not be knocking about at night anymore or we would probably come to a no good end. Robert said thanks and we took off at a trot headed to Grandma's. We kept looking back for the car stayed parked in the road for a few minutes and then drove off toward Overton.

Even though it was fairly dark without much moonlight we pushed our horses on as fast as we could. We were still shaking a little by the time we reached Grandma's. We hurried to the harness house, unsaddled, put our horses up and got in the house as quickly as we could without disturbing anyone. We didn't talk much in bed but saved it for the next day. All day long we discussed our big adventure and kept saying we were certainly lucky that night. I said I was sure the passenger was black since there was a little light on his face. Robert said he thought the driver was white based on his speech, but he couldn't get a good view of his face. When I described the expression on the face of the passenger Robert said the driver was probably just as mean looking. We decided that was the end of our night riding.

The summer of 1943 provided us with a lot of horse riding activity. It was during this time that I participated in my one and only cattle drive. It was only one day long, but what a long day it was. It started before daylight and lasted until dark — and the days in summer are long. Uncle Fred was away in the South Pacific taking islands with the Marine Corp. while Walter and others were looking after his cattle for him. Walter had made arrangements for Fred to lease another place he had been trying to get before the war and let the one he had go. This Walter had done and now it was time to move the cattle to the new place.

Buddy was handling the day to day work of the cattle with his brother-in-law's help under the supervision of Walter. The brother–in-law was Sam Square, Ruby's brother, and a mentor (somewhat like Buddy) to us grandkids and a real character. As little kids all of us had read, or read to us, the story of Little Black Sambo, the umbrella, shoes, tigers, butter and such. Some kid said they wondered if Sam was the Sambo the story was about or something of that nature and Sam became Sambo to all us kids.

Sam wasn't the brightest fellow around but he was one of the biggest and kindest. To us kids Sam was huge — he was probably close to 6'5" or so, weighed in maybe a good 300 lbs. with long arms that were very strong. He could pick up five or six of us kids and carry us around or toss around a good sized calf at will. It was his dress that set him apart also. He was always attired in worn out blue bib overalls, one bib undone and the strap hanging down his back — shirtless, shoeless and hatless. If snow was on the ground, or ice hanging from the trees, he might don a worn out red flannel shirt and an old pair of dilapidated shoes without laces or socks. Someone told the story that Sam went to the draft board and asked them to send him with Mr. Fred so he could "look after him" in the war.

The cast of people for our trail drive for somewhere between seventy-five to maybe ninety head of cows and calves consisted of: Uncle Walter, the trail boss and leader of the herd; Buddy, next in command and the tail of the herd — a spare rider too if needed; Sam, the handler of the herd with his feed bucket and cow sense — on foot (bare feet); William, wagon driver, supervisor of supplies and spare rider; Robert, a rider (herder); and me, also a rider.

There would be no bulls since the two (the old one and the young one) had been trucked ahead of time from the old location to the new one in order that we would not need to handle any bull fights on the way. Also the cows would not hesitate to go into the new pastures with their bulls standing nearby and watching.

A couple of days before the cattle drive, the day after the bulls were moved out, all the crew, wagon and team, horses to be used, the pickup with cattle frames to be driven by Buddy and Walter's car were used in rounding up and penning all the cattle. All the equipment was parked next to the cattle pens with the mules and horses penned close to the cattle. The feed and hay had been loaded into the wagon that was to be fed to the cattle the next two days. Buddy said this was so the cattle would get "cozy" with everybody and everything.

After the cattle were all penned, the horses and mules in their corrals, the wagon in place, and we were putting our saddles and such in the pickup I walked up behind Walter and Buddy talking over their plans. I heard Walter ask Buddy was he sure they didn't need a couple of adult riders in addition to the two boys (referring to Robert and me) to handle the cattle. I heard Buddy reply with "Mr. Walter dem two air as good as you kin hire and better than most, thays'll do us a good job — I'll bet my dinner on it." Then they heard me coming up and said no more about extra help.

By now you know something about the people of our trail drive but I would like you to meet some of the equine involved — specifically the team of mules and the horse I would be riding. In addition to these three there would be three other horses: one for Buddy, one for William, and a spare in case Robert or I needed a replacement. These three were just ranch horses, well trained to ride and could be trusted somewhat to work cattle. Robert's horse was a good looking chestnut, excellent cow horse he would depend on for his life. The first three are the ones I would call "characters" with plenty of personality.

The team of mules belonged to Walter — whom he was very proud of and William always in "high cotton" every time he got to drive them. They were a matched pair of show mules that Walter had purchased in Missouri to have a "good looking team." Since mules are hybrids (can't reproduce) you have to crossbreed in order to produce them. Walter was going into the mule breeding business and had gone to the mule country to get him a jack to breed to his mares for mules. He found his jack but he also found this team and had to have them also. They weren't really big mules, as Missouri mules go, but they were about the size of a good cow horse, very well matched even to the brown and white on their muzzles and white stockings. They always had sleek and shiny black coats that were stunning. The main difference in looks was sex — one a male (Henry) and one a female (Henrietta) — they could have been a full brother and sister, at the least very closely related. Most people could not tell them apart without a close examination but if you were around them very much all you had to do was look them in the eye.

As much as they were alike on the outside, they were very much unlike on the inside. Henrietta was the best working and behaving mule I think

I have ever seen — or hoped to see. She seemed to look for ways she could please you. On the other hand Henry had a mischievous look in his eyes that told you he was trying to out think you. He was always seeking ways to get into trouble. Once Henry knew you meant business he could get with the work as well as the best of them. He knew Walter always meant business but when we were using the team and wagon he would be trying to play tricks on us. At the same time we enjoyed handling Henry because he was a lot of fun. Together they were some team — hitch a great load to them and they would squat until their bellies nearly touched the ground and move the load if at all possible. It wasn't a bit unusual if Henry wasn't doing his share for Henrietta to give him a good kick in the belly and he would straighten up in a hurry and fly right. On this trail drive we didn't expect any trouble out of Henry with both Henrietta and Walter keeping an eye on him.

George, "my" horse, wasn't really my horse at all — he belonged to my Uncle Fred who as I said earlier was in the South Pacific retaking islands from the Japanese. While we were in Corpus Christi my horse, Pigeon, somehow got into poisoned grain and died as a result. Fred was headed to service but he still had George so he told Walter to let me have him for as long as I wanted when I came back to East Texas. So now I need to tell you about George's interesting background so you will know why he was such a character.

Back in the 1930s Fred was "horse crazy" as well as interested in motorcycles and such. As he began to receive income from the oil field developments he started breeding horses (as well as racing motorcycles). As he began to accumulate horses (now called quarter horses) he learned of the great ones to be found in Kentucky. So to head his breeding program he wanted a good stud and went looking in Kentucky for the stallion to breed to his Texas mares. Here he found Croesus — named this I guess because he was so rich in everything; appearance, intelligence, demeanor, and athletic ability. He had it all. Fred rode home in a railroad cattle car with Croesus. I have been acquainted with many great horses and friends of others including Triple Crown winner Assault and I don't think I have ever seem a better looking horse than Croesus.

As time passed, Croesus was a good stud horse and produced a lot of fine foals for Fred and others who used him on their mares. Fred decided he needed another stud to breed the mares produced from Croesus so he made another trip to Kentucky and came back with George. George wasn't his registered name — at this point I don't have the slightest idea what it was (probably a mouthful) — Fred always referred to him as his "George Pullen horse" (I think it was Pullen or something like that). So I eventually shortened it to George, and he too was a fine looking horse but not as flashy as Croesus. He was selected more for his conformation as a cow horse since this was what Fred was after in his breeding program.

A good cow horse has to have good cow sense and this meant he had to have an opportunity to develop it. Fred went to Raymondville where my Dad had his ranch and found a Mexican-American cowboy known for his cow horse training ability. He hired the fellow to come train his horses and moved the trainer's whole family to East Texas. Everything went well except for George. They said he was a little head strong but that would come out in time. Well while it was coming out he and the trainer had a difference of opinion about which side of a tree to pass it on and they hit it head on at near full speed. The trainer only broke a leg but George cracked his face from just below his eyes to just above his nostrils — and a horse's face is rather long. If it had been the other way around they would probably have shot George but they decided to take the trainer to the hospital and get a vet for George, but there may have been some that wanted to shoot the trainer.

The vet said he had never seen or heard of such a thing before but he was sure they could fix it. They took poor George to the vet's place in Tyler and I think they called in a professor from the Texas A&M vet school. They ended up putting a silver plate down George's face and sewing it up in place. George seemed to be doing fine until a few days later when it began to heal and of course itch. So George began to scratch it — by turning his face to the rear and scratching it with a hind hoof. In time he got the silver plate loose and caused a lot of bleeding. They sewed the plate back in place and moved George to Grandma's in Fred's stable. This time they built an elaborate contraption around him where he couldn't get a foot to his face or rub his face against anything either. George spent a few weeks in this predicament and the vets felt his face was healed so they let him loose in the pen for several days. He did well and began to look a little better and seem to enjoy life more. Fred, with the consent of the vets, decided to put him to pasture for a while to regain his health and get even more enjoyment out of life.

Things went well for a couple of weeks then one day George came to the barn with a bloody face. The vet's examination revealed the plate was loose again and his opinion was that George would never "adjust" to having it in his face. After some study and discussion Fred decided to have the plate removed and let George's face heal up without the plate. The face did heal — except for a slit a little over two inches long and about a half inch wide in the middle of his face. This left George with an opening which he also breathed through as well as his nostrils. Since he was disfigured to some extent it was decided that he would not be used for breeding and was "fixed," and retired to a riding horse. When Fred was selling off all his horses to go into service he remembered my interest in George from the past and my desire to ride him so he decided to "let me have him" for as long as I desired — since I was horseless at the time. When we moved back to East Texas in early 1943 I had a horse waiting for me.

By the summer of '43 George and I were fast friends — and remained so until about 1946 when my time became so involved with many other activities that Fred reclaimed George. I can truthfully say that George was the best riding horse that I have ever sat, and over the sixty-five or seventy years that I rode there was a number of good ones — the next best may have been my registered Arabian stallion, Chris, I used for a few years to breed my Arabian ponies. If I continued to tell the many adventures I had with George it would fill a book and now I am trying to tell about our trail drive — so I will get on with it.

The Saturday of the trail drive had not yet dawned when Walter woke Robert and me and told us to get with it. We dressed and went to the harness house where Buddy and William had already loaded two or three sacks of sweet feed, three sacks of cotton seed cakes, four or five bales of bright green hay and were in the process of putting in the five saddles and tack. It wasn't daylight yet but I noticed the trunk lid on Walter's car was raised all the way up and a wooden ice chest lying on the floor. On top of the ice chest was a five gallon galvanized water can. Walter was securely tying these all in place with a rope for our trip over to the cattle.

We all walked back to the house and found Ruby had a huge breakfast waiting for us in the dining room — except for Buddy who ate in the kitchen and chatted with Ruby as she brought food to our table and his. William told us that his mother had prepared us our lunch and it was in the ice chest in the car along with our soda pops that we would have during a break or two and for lunch. The water can contained a large chunk of ice and good fresh water for the day. Robert looked around and asked if we were going to pick up Sambo on the way. Walter laughed and said Sam had spent the last two nights with the cattle, horses and mules so everything would be safe and Ruby had packed him a breakfast that we were taking to him. As soon as we finished eating Walter and William got in their car and Robert and I got in the pickup with Buddy. We led the way in the pickup with the car following. Robert and I were ready to jump out and help if anything came loose in the piled up load in the rear, but we made the trip fine.

It was just getting daylight as we turned into the old place where the cattle were penned. Buddy turned off the head lights as did Walter so as to not spook the cattle and we parked next to the wagon. While William and Walter were harnessing the mules Buddy showed us how to unload and place the stuff from the car and pickup into the wagon as Sambo eagerly ate his breakfast and downed at least a quart of coffee. After Walter, William and Buddy had approved of the manner in which the wagon was loaded Walter and William hitched up the mules and we saddled the horses while Sambo went to the bathroom in a far lot.

When this was completed Walter called us all together around the wagon and he briefed us on his plan and explained everyone's role and duties. He had it planned to a "T" as if he was a general leading us into battle, and we were ready. The plan was, basically, that Walter would lead at a distance ahead of the procession in the car and turn traffic back or to the side. The wagon would lead the herd with the spare horses tied to it and Sambo working the herd with his magic feed bucket hanging from an arm. Robert and I would be riding back and forth and around the herd urging them on or slowing them down as needed and always keeping them from straying down a gulley, a side trail or the wrong road at an intersection. Buddy would follow us in the pickup to stop or reroute traffic with his red flag.

Not only did Walter have us ready but he had made arrangements with the sheriff's office for us to make the drive. The office had made copies of the Texas laws giving herd drivers certain rights and the penalties for infringing on them. A deputy was to be on duty in front of the drive and the local constable was going to be following the herd to give Buddy support if he needed it to do his job. I am sure these precautions were well worth it since we didn't encounter any problems with traffic on our drive that I knew of.

Walter had also located a small pasture about midway of our goal that had a large round water tank for livestock with easy access from the road that he rented from the owner for us to stop for lunch and let our outfit rest some. When noon came we simply drove the herd into the pasture, blocked the entrance with the vehicles and Sambo distributed a bunch of cake and a couple of bales of hay among the herd for those that wanted it but most lay down and chewed their cud after filling up on water.

It got pretty warm rather quickly that day, or so it seemed. Maybe it was because we were so busy on our horses and nervous because we were afraid we would do something wrong. We sweated and the dust caked on our face, ears and neck. Our lips dried and cracked some. Walter sent word by Sambo a couple of times during the morning for us not to push the herd so much because he didn't want to overheat the animals. No one worried about us pushing too much in the afternoon because we were all tired and took a leisurely pace as the temperature neared a hundred degrees.

We didn't have any really big problems during the morning. A few times it took both Robert and me to get a balky old cow or one that wanted to fight a little back in the herd and moving right. Our horses were well trained and had such good cow sense that they could usually size up the situation and take action like a cutting horse and our main job was to just hold on. Our horses were worked down so much by noon that we decided to use the spares to start the hot afternoon. Since we were both switching I felt that George wouldn't think that he hadn't done his job as the reason I was switching. When I told Robert this he laughed and said I was giving a horse too much credit for thinking.

As soon as everything got settled down for lunch we all gathered in a shady spot took off our gloves and started eating. As we satisfied our hunger, Robert and I took off our hats, kerchief, shirt and boots. We would probably have taken off more but we could tell that Walter didn't like the idea of us undressing out in public so we stopped there and tried to get a little breeze — which there was none — but we did stretch out and rest some. In about an hour the constable and deputy sheriff both showed up to check on us since they evidently had gone somewhere to eat lunch. Walter told them we would be going in just a few minutes. The rest of us took this as a hint and we started getting ready.

We found our relief horses weren't nearly as good as our others but since the cattle were pretty tired by now and knew the rules of the road we had a fairly easy time of it except for the heat, tired muscles and gnats. Somehow clouds of gnats had found our herd during our lunch stop and decided to travel with us. They would get in your eyes, ears, nose and mouth. I had never seen such pesky gnats — except maybe at Raymondville.

The afternoon dragged on and on. I caught myself dozing off every now and then despite the heat and gnats. I began to think we would never get there when I looked up and William was waving at us. When he could tell he had our attention he pointed up the road. We both stood up in our stirrups and strained looking forward. Then we saw Walter's car parked crosswise in the middle of the road and a gate on the left opened out toward the road. We both let out a little cowboy yell which caught Sambo's attention. We both pointed up the road and yelled to him that we were there.

William turned the team in through the gate and the cattle followed as they had been doing all day. As we got the slow pokes in Walter motioned for us to follow them in. He closed the gate as Buddy pulled up to it and parked the pickup. Walter got his car out of the road, parked it next to the pickup and spent a couple of minutes thanking the constable and deputy as they were ready to go on their way.

Walter and Buddy came in the pasture with us and directed the putting up of the wagon and team, the horses and tack and the feeding of the animals to be penned the rest of the hay and sweet feed and the left over cake put out for the cattle. Walter's house was only a few miles (maybe 3 or 4) from this place so he and William would go home from there and Buddy would take Robert and me back to Grandma's in the pickup. Sambo would stay with the horses and mules until they were taken back to Grandma's since Walter was concerned with their being left penned up next to the road with no one living there. He felt the cattle would be safe scattered out in the pasture. Sambo had plenty of food left over from lunch in the ice chest with a few soda pops and a lot of cold water. Walter said he would bring him a fresh supply of food in the morning.

Since the next day was Sunday Walter wanted us to return the wagon and team along with the horses to Grandma's on Monday. Buddy would bring Robert and me back to this new place and meet William and Walter. William would drive the team with the three horses tied behind the wagon and Robert and I would ride our horses. Without the cattle we could easily cover the ten or twelve miles to Grandma's in a little over two hours without pushing. Buddy would take Sambo home in the pickup and they would assume their regular duties of taking care of Fred's cattle at the new place.

When we got back to Grandma's after the cattle drive, Ruby had a big supper of fried round steak, mashed potatoes with gravy, fresh green beans and banana pudding cooked for us. With plenty of onions and radishes from the garden, we had a feast. We had never been so tired before in our lives so we soaked in the bathtub and went to bed. The next day we didn't go anywhere — loafed all day.

Monday we were ready to go again. Sonny, feeling like he had been left out of so much fun, begged to go with us so he could ride back in the wagon with William. Grandma and Auntie agreed so Robert and I put up no objections. As arranged, Buddy took us to meet Walter and William at the new place. They were already there when we got there and Sambo was eating the big breakfast they had brought him. Blanche and W. H. (William's mother and little brother) had come with Walter and William so when W. H. found out Sonny was going to ride in the wagon he set up a howl to do likewise. William ended up with a couple of passengers.

William was harnessing the team and Walter was going over the wagon in preparation for our return to Grandma's. Robert and I got the horses we were going to ride saddled, put the spare saddles in the wagon and tied the three horses to the wagon in order to travel. Walter put a chunk of fresh ice in the water can so we would have some cold water if we needed it.

We took off for Grandma's leaving Buddy and Sambo to do whatever needed to be done at the new place and then, they too, would head for home. We took it easy and got to Grandma's near lunch time and enjoyed another of Ruby's good meals. While we were eating Auntie said it was nearly the middle of August so she and Grandma had decided we would leave Saturday for Hitchcock, our last trip of the summer. I really wished William and Robert could go with us and have fun on the beach but it couldn't be worked out. It was then we all realized that our summer was drawing to a close.

We did have a good time on this trip, spending a good deal of time in Galveston on the beach and visiting kinfolks. Mother was making plans to return home in about a week and get us ready for school. Dad said he wished he could go to East Texas with us but he had to stay in Hitchcock and take care of his military duties.

Just two or three days after we were back at Grandma's from our trip, Auntie and Grandma took us boys to town (Tyler of course) where we met Blanche, William and W. H. at Caldwell, Hughes, Delay & Allen on the Square. Here Grandma "booted" us seven boys with new cowboy boots to start school. This had become a family tradition for the school season. Those in California would receive money as would Richard down in Austin. She and Auntie would take care of any others in another trip. Grandma did this up until we married and then she said we were on our own.

Maybe the weather didn't feel like it, but the summer of 1943 came to a close with the start of the new school year.

THE 1943-44 SCHOOL YEAR

After such an eventful and exciting summer, I expected the school year to be a lot slower paced and geared toward study. In some ways it met my expectations but not exactly in the manner I had imagined. It started off with a bang due to football and didn't slow down until around Christmas time. Things were pretty quiet until the end of the school year.

The year before I had attended school in Corpus Christi — a huge school to me — and since I was a transfer from a small country/oil field school my schedule was a little different due to some courses I had taken and some I had not taken. I was classified as a sophomore but took some classes with freshmen. Somehow I ended up in a P E class with the varsity football team — all juniors and seniors. This presented a problem for the coaches, but not nearly so bad as it did for me. I had a few good times but most of it was tough on me since I was somewhat small, not so fleet afoot and expected to meet the standards set for the others in order to make my grade for the course. I must have passed — probably due to one of the coaches selecting me for his goffer — while the others were taking a little rest I was running errands for him.

Many years later when I returned to Corpus Christi as the director of teacher education at UCC one of the natives was a professor there and when we got to know each other I related to him my experiences at the high school. Sonny Norrell laughed and said "Would you believe I was a junior in that class and remember you very well." He said he always felt like he needed to apologize to me for the way the team treated me — he did so on the spot. Somehow this created a bond between us and we became fast friends — both personally and professionally.

The coach I goffered for also helped get me a job selling cushions at the home football games in Buc stadium. We were paid on a commission basis for the number of cushions we sold and then a nickel each for gathering the cushions after the game. With the paper route, all these experiences helped to toughen up a small kid that always seemed to be younger than the others I was grouped with. This certainly helped when I went out for football in 1943.

I am sure it wasn't just Leverett's Chapel — since I have heard tales about White Oak, Gladewater and Gaston from some of their players — but back then the oil field high schools imported players. This was done similar to college scholarships or providing good jobs for fathers of potentially good athletes, all under the table of course. In the case of Leverett's Chapel a house on our property behind Coach Hill's house was used for some six or eight football players (who were usually good track and basketball players also) to live. They took their meals in the school cafeteria and had little part-time jobs at the school to make their spending money. There may have been another or two houses spotted around but I only knew about the one on our property and my Mother and Dad gave me strict orders to stay away from it.

These were really nice kids and most of them were from the same area in Oklahoma — in the case of the Medcalfs, Easleys and Bishops, more than one from the same family. If you were a local you had to be pretty good to play, and we had plenty of those too — the Gregories, McGintys, Pages and others. Due to the war this practice was coming to an end and after the war the University Interscholastic League imposed some strict rules regulating eligibility that ended it permanently, or so they thought. When I went out for football in September '43 as a junior and just turned fifteen in August, there was "Big John" Medcalf, "Cowboy" Bishop and one or two of the Easleys still playing. I think at the end of the season they all left for the armed forces as did some in my class that were a little over-age for juniors. My senior year was the first year that only locals played on the L C team.

I was too young, too small and too slow to make a good player but everyone was expected to play football unless they were physically unable to participate. If not a player then they would be expected to have some other role — such as a water boy, member of the band or at least in the pep squad. We ended the season with so few players that I got to play some in most of the games. I will never forget the first play I was in — it was against Overton on their field and we had the ball getting close to the goal when I was called for holding in the trenches. We failed to make a needed first down due to the penalty which probably kept us from scoring. When I came out two of the older players laid into me for getting the penalty and our quarterback told them to shut up — he said at least I was trying and that was more than they did a lot of the time. I did letter for the year and at least my family was proud of me.

It was planned that the first Saturday after school started, Sonny and I would ride our horses from Grandma's to L C so we would have them available to ride after school and on weekends during the school year. I was so sore from the beginning of football practice that I really wondered if I would be able to make the ride. But I had learned you had to suck it up and just do it — so I was ready. When we got to Grandma's and caught the horses to saddle them Buddy said that Sonny's Tony had a bad place just behind the top of his shoulders that looked as if another horse had bitten him. After we looked it over and doctored it, Buddy said a blanket rubbing it would be very painful and could cause infection. Sonny was very disappointed since Mother decided that I would ride George and lead Tony bareback. Sonny said he could ride Tony bareback but Buddy said a ride that far without a saddle would make even a full-blooded Indian terribly sore so he talked Sonny into being satisfied with letting me go ahead with the horses and him ride with Mother in the car — which plan Mother had made.

They were going to give me a couple of hours head start and then follow to check on our progress. This would give them a rough idea about when I should get to L C. If I hadn't arrived by the expected time, they would then give me a little extra time before coming back to check again. When we left Grandma's George was eager but Tony kept holding back for a while but pretty soon lined out and we moved on very well. We were just about to Overton when they drove up on us and found out everything was going well. They went on home and we made good time, arriving a little before they expected us. The ride actually worked out most of my soreness. The next morning we made Sunday school, church and back to Grandma's for Sunday dinner. Things were beginning to fall in place and our fall was going rather nicely except for the problems created by the war.

Robert wanted me to go with him and his dad to their ranch near Blanco in the Hill Country for Thanksgiving. He said we would be able to do some deer hunting in very good deer territory and I would be able to see some of Texas I had not visited before. Mother finally agreed and planned for her and Sonny to go visit Dad at Hitchcock during Thanksgiving.

I was able to get out of school a day early (along with Sonny and Robert) for Thanksgiving due to the long trips we were making. Charley, Robert and I left Grandma's about daylight Wednesday. This was during Charley's heaviest drinking days and as soon as we had his little '42 Ford coupe loaded for the trip he "loaded" himself — he reached in the trunk, took out a quart bottle from a case, broke the seal and poured about half of it down his gullet. He got seated under the steering wheel, set the bottle between his legs and as we slowed for Tyler, Jacksonville and Palestine he would take another slug from the bottle until it was empty. The further we got from Tyler and the more he drank, the slower he drove. I think the wartime speed limit was 45 MPH but by the time we got to Jacksonville we were down to 30 MPH and he held it there for the next 250 miles.

By the time we reached Buffalo Charley said he needed some coffee so we stopped and Robert and I got a quart of milk and a dozen donuts to snack on while Charley had his coffee. As Robert and I were using the restroom, he explained that this was the way his dad traveled by car. He only stopped for coffee, gas, the restroom and the fresh bottle as needed. Thankfully Ruby had prepared us a good sent off breakfast at Grandma's since all we had to eat the rest of the trip were the donuts until we got to the ranch at Blanco. When we got there a little after nightfall Nettie, the foreman's wife and a few years later to become Charley's second wife, had us a very good supper ready — consisting of fried round steak, mashed potatoes with rich gravy, and a platter of big golden biscuits.

Two or three miles before we reached Blanco we turned off the highway onto a gravel and dirt road, just wide enough for two cars to meet and pass each other. For about eight or ten miles we traveled on this road without meeting another vehicle and took another turn when Robert pointed to a leaning cedar post with a lonely looking mail box on top and said that was where Charley got his mail. Charley also added that this was the beginning of the ranch property. We went down this very narrow, winding, hilly and bumpy dirt road for another two miles or so until we saw the lights from the ranch house.

Since it was already dark and the only lights were those of the car and what came through the windows of the house, it was hard to tell much about the building — but my first impression was that it must be quite large. We parked in what seemed to be the back and entered a hallway. Charley pointed to an open door and said that would be our room (Robert and me) and the bathroom was across the hall. He then disappeared down the hall. We set our little bags on the floor, went to the bathroom and then got the rest of our stuff from the car.

Robert said I could have my pick of the bunks — there were two sets of a top and bottom — so I took the bottom one closest to the door and he put his stuff on the bottom bunk across the room. I was surprised that Robert didn't have a permanent room of his own at the ranch house even though he and his mother were living at Grandma Jernigan's where he went to school and he only visited the ranch three or four times a year. I didn't say anything about it — beginning to learn not to ask too many questions about people's personal lives unless they seemed to welcome them. As soon as we were settled in, Robert took me into the main part of the ranch house — which he and the others referred to as "headquarters" — showed me around some and introduced me to the foreman, his wife Nettie and their two children.

While we were eating supper Charley asked the foreman if he had heard anything from Richard. He said nothing since Charley had received Richard's postcard saying he would see them for Thanksgiving. The conversation about ranch and area happenings during the week Charley had been gone resumed and gave me a little insight into the difference between Hill Country and East Texas living. I also found out that the foreman and Nettie's son was about a year older than me and the daughter was about a half year younger — making the four of us very close to the same age. All of us were on our best behavior, trying to act like adults and impress each other.

Nettie and her daughter had prepared the meal and shared in the serving. Evidently there was no additional domestic help at the ranch and only two or three "day cowboys" most of the time — they lived off the ranch and would be at their own homes for Thanksgiving until Monday. Nettie assured us she was preparing a big feast for Thanksgiving the next day. Charley told her he had invited a couple of old single male friends of his to come have Thanksgiving dinner with them and hoped that wouldn't cause her too much trouble. She assured him that it would be no problem at all since she was preparing plenty.

I had been somewhat surprised when we drove up to the ranch at such a desolate location to see it had electricity. During the previous summer we had visited some of Dad's relatives a good way out of Waco and others near the Louisiana border and none of them had electricity. So I was really surprised to hear the jingle of a telephone on the wall that sounded just like our party line at Leverett's Chapel. The daughter jumped up from the table and ran for the phone. Evidently it was for her for she was talking a blue streak the next several minutes. I imagined the same thing was happening all up and down the line as it did at LC when the phone rang in all the houses with one — as soon as the phone quit ringing kids (and probably an adult or two also) would cover, with the palm of a hand, the part that you speak into and carefully, with the other hand, slowly ease up the listening piece and place it to an ear. Then, grinning from ear to ear, listen to both sides of the conversation over the telephone line.

During the time of the telephone conversation Charley explained to me that a group of the ranchers went together and put in a private telephone line to Blanco. This was my first knowledge of a co-op by individuals for utility service. After the war co-ops became very popular as a method to get electric and telephone service into rural areas. In about five minutes Nettie called out for her daughter to hang up since she had used "her allotted time."

After supper Robert gave me a tour of headquarters — the only residence on the ranch and it included the ranch office. The center of the building was a large rectangle which contained on one end a large front porch fronting the office, Charley's bedroom, sitting room and bath. The rest was taken up by a large room containing several seating areas and the dining room with a large kitchen. Robert explained that this had been some kind of a hunting club at one time but during the depression it fell on hard times and now the owners leased it out with a lot of acreage for ranching.

On the opposite end of the building from the office was an addition that housed the foreman's family. It contained three bedrooms, a sitting room, small kitchen and bath with a back porch. From each side of the center of the main building there were two matching additions that opened into the main room and each had a small back porch. A hallway connected the porch to the main room with two bedrooms opening to one side of the hallway and another bedroom and a bath opening on the other side of the hallway. The only difference in these two parts on the opposite sides of the main section was that the one Robert and I were staying in was equipped with bunk beds for hunters or cowboys while the other one had regular beds for visiting couples.

After this tour and look around, we were tired from our long day and decided to hit the hay — as everyone else had already retired to their own quarters. Robert tuned the radio in our bedroom to WOAI San Antonio and we drifted off to sleep listening to news from around the world.

The next morning we woke on our own and as soon as we were out of bed and dressed we could hear sounds and sense smells coming from the kitchen. A big breakfast, as well as some things for the Thanksgiving meal later that day, were cooking and making us hungry in a hurry. After a quick look around outside in the bright early light and cool morning air, we answered a call to wash up and come to the table.

Breakfast consisted of another platter of those golden brown biscuits, a mound of crisp bacon, a huge bowl of cream gravy and fried eggs to order. After we had eaten as much as we could, the foreman explained to Robert which horses — along with what gear — each of us was to use while we were there. Then he took us to a large gun cabinet in the main part of the big room, showed us where the key was kept on top and the guns and ammo that we could use for our deer hunting. He also said that Robert knew the rules and regulations about hunting on the ranch so he could explain them to me. He then said for us to have another cup of coffee before we got busy. All this time Charley had said nothing, was sitting at the table sipping coffee and watching us. After we sat down at our coffee he got up, walked to his office and returned with a small gun in his hands. He handed it to Robert and said he should take it with us every time we left headquarters since there were probably a few snakes still about. Then he added that Robert would find both size shells for it in the cabinet with the other ammo.

Then everyone got up from the table and headed in our various directions. Robert and I went to our room and he showed me the little gun that looked like a toy — a .22 and .410 combination with barrels only about a foot long and a stock not much longer. It would hold only one shell in each chamber — but pretty deadly for snakes. Then we checked out the horses, saddles, etc. so I would know where things were kept. We watched Sonny, the foreman's son, for a while as he fed and watered the assorted livestock penned up around in the various corrals. When he finished his tasks he came over where we were standing and put one of his well-worn boots on the bottom corral board and hooked his elbows over the top one in the same pose as Robert and I held. He then told us that his usual job on school mornings was to care for the horses and the day cowboys looked after the other livestock. Since the cowboys were taking off for Thanksgiving he was filling in for them as he did on weekends. He pointed over to a large pen with a good sized group of yearlings and said that they were being fed out for butchering during the winter for food at headquarters and some would be sold to individuals for their meat needs over the next few months. Another pen he pointed to was filled with cows and calves which he said were being doctored for various needs. Another pen had a bunch of poor looking cows that were headed for the auction in a few days to be sold since they had been barren that year and the ranch would let someone else worry with them or they would end up in one of the big meat companies for low cost cuts. One or two pens had only calves in it while another two or three had more cows in them. Only the horses had access to the protection of barns from their pens but most of the cow pens had some sheds with walls on the north, east and west sides for protection from the cold wind and rain.

Robert told us that later, after Thanksgiving dinner, we would saddle up and ride around the ranch some so I could get a better idea of the lay of the land but until dinner we would just knock around headquarters. Sonny said he would leave the riding around and hunting to us since he could get plenty of that when we were not there. Then a call came from the office for us boys to come into the house since we were needed there. Charley and the foreman were standing just outside the office front door on the porch and motioned us to come into the office.

We found out that Richard had phoned that he had been dropped off at the Texas Hotel in Blanco by a UT friend on the friend's way home for Thanksgiving and someone needed to come pick him up. A neighbor down the road had also called and reported that someone had run off the road and crashed their car or truck into the ranch's fence about a mile from the mailbox. Evidently the vehicle wasn't damaged too badly since it must have driven off under its own power. The fence wasn't completely down but some of the livestock might try to get out of it and get cut on the wire. Charley said the foreman and Sonny would take the pickup with repair materials and fix the fence before our Thanksgiving dinner. He said he wanted to stay at headquarters in case one of his expected friends called so he was sending Robert and me into Blanco in his car for Richard. He wanted me to drive due to our age differences but Robert would need to direct me to town and probably also on the return. We all headed for our assignments.

As we edged our way into Blanco I was keeping one eye on my driving and the other on the meager sights of downtown. The only person we saw was a sailor standing on the sidewalk under a sign that read Texas Hotel. He had a small bag in one hand and a book under the other arm. As we drew near we recognized Richard and he motioned with his free hand for us to pull over to the curb — which I did right in front of him. He circled around behind the car, opened the driver's door and said, "Scoot over stranger 'cause I'm gonna steer this ship." I put the gear in neutral, stepped on the brake with my left foot and moved over against Robert. Richard tossed his bag over the seat back and carefully placed his big book on top of the bag. Under his breath, as he took his seat below the wheel, he muttered that when you have to pay for those books yourself you take good care of them.

I knew Richard had joined the Navy and spent the three summer months in training but since he was back as a student at UT I was surprised to see him in a uniform — especially this far from the war. He looked over at Robert and asked "Beetle you and dad been treating Floyd O K?" Robert replied that I didn't deserve much but they were giving me their best. Then Richard looked up and down the street, made a U turn and headed back towards the ranch. Richard, all the way on the trip back, rattled away about his experiences at the Great Lakes in the Navy during the summer to impress us with what a big deal it was and the exciting times he was looking forward to during the next two years. I'll have to admit his tales made the return trip seem much shorter than our going to town had been.

When we drove up to headquarters we noticed the pickup wasn't back yet but another car was parked in front of the office. In the office we found Charley and his old friend from Dripping Springs. Charley greeted Richard and then introduced him to his friend. Then, with an arm around each of us, he introduced Robert and me to the elderly gentleman. After some small talk, without sitting down, we all went into the big room and sat around the large fireplace. Nettie brought in a large blue enamel coffee pot and sat it down on a folded cup towel to protect the ornate coffee table. Evidently the visitor had already been introduced to Nettie since as soon as she emptied her hands, Richard stood up and they embraced and exchanged pecks on their cheeks. Nettie's daughter was then placing a tray of cups along with sugar and cream on the coffee table and she and Richard exchanged hugs and kisses. The two females went back to the kitchen to work on Thanksgiving dinner and we all helped ourselves to coffee.

After we had finished our coffee Richard picked up his bag and book, walked into the bedroom next to the one Robert and I were using. We followed him in and I noticed a lot of stuff like pictures, books and things that must have been his so I assumed this was the room he used any time he was at the ranch. We sat around and listened a while to some more of Richard's stories until we heard some voices coming from the big room. Robert suggested we go see what was happening so we did.

The second of Charley's guests, a retired King Ranch foreman from Kingsville, had arrived and was visiting with Charley and the Dripping Springs man. We were duly introduced and joined in on the conversation group. In a little while the Kingsville man pointed an index finger at me and said "I've just made a connection." He then told the story that some ten years back he was helping another foreman with a roundup on the south end of the King Ranch when in camp one night after he had taken off his boots he was snake bit in his right ankle. They killed the snake and doctored his leg that night and doctored it again the next morning. All during the day his leg kept swelling and turning kind of purple so that evening the other foreman decided he needed to take him into Raymondville to see a doctor. The Raymondville doctor treated him and said he thought his leg would be alright if the doctor continued to treat it morning and night for at least three or four more days. After the visit to the doctor the two foremen stopped by to see my Mother and Dad for a few minutes on their way back to the ranch. After meeting and visiting with the foreman with the snake bit leg my parents invited him to stay in town with them so someone wouldn't have to bring him back over the rough roads both morning and evenings during the treatments. The two foremen decided that would be a big help and accepted the offer. The foreman said he was amazed what nice people my parents were to him and how he enjoyed his stay in spite of his pain and discomfort with the leg. He said he remembered very well sitting on our front porch with his foot propped up in a chair and watching me ride my pony round and round the block and my stopping every now and then to check on him. He wanted us to know how much he appreciated the hospitality of my family and he wanted me to give my parents his regards and to thank them again. I promised him I would give my parents his greetings and another big "Thanks." Charley followed this story with the comment that you couldn't find better people than Albert and Sister.

More conversation followed about snake bites and how ranch people cared for each other and were always eager to help those in distress. At this point our foreman and Sonny came in from their lodgings, all fresh and cleaned up from their ranch work, and completed our Thanksgiving group. Soon we got the signal to gather round the table for the Thanksgiving meal.

The ten of us took our places as indicated by Charley who placed the Dripping Springs man (Robert and I had assigned him this name in our talking about him) at the head of the table — probably due to his age. Charley took the other end (kind of the foot of the table) and sprinkled everyone else along the sides. He then asked Richard to give the blessing — he stood and gave the prayer. As Richard sat down the talking and serving really began. Sonny made an announcement that if anyone needed something not on the table to let him know and he would get it for he wanted his mother and sister to remain seated for the whole meal. His dad then spoke up and said if Sonny needed help then he would give it. The guests all kind of muttered approval and we began eating the traditional Thanksgiving fare of a huge baked turkey with cornbread stuffing and another platter heaped with the cornbread dressing as well as a big bowl of giblet gravy. Two or three small bowls of cranberry sauce (both whole and jellied) were placed among the other large bowls of sweet potatoes, corn, green beans and a few other vegetables and fruit salad. Another platter held an equally large baked ham ringed with pineapple slices, bright red candied cherries and baked apple slices. Sitting on the buffet behind Charley were two each of pecan and pumpkin pies with a spice cake ready for our dessert. True to their word Sonny and his dad were the ones that did a great job in getting coffee, pie and anything else we could want all during the meal.

The conversation was more or less dominated by the Dripping Springs man who wanted everyone to know that he went back a long way with the ranch and the headquarters building and was still a partner in the company that owned it. He told of the fine times at the hunting club during the '20s when the club was at its peak. As we finished our desserts he told us that during the all-male club's heyday at the end of dinner they would each have a glass of brandy and a fine cigar. Without a word Charley stood up and walked over to a large cabinet, opened it and placed ten "shot" glasses on a small tray which he then distributed one to each place at the table. He then took a bottle of wine from the cabinet and carefully poured a little glass for the four younger members of the group after Nettie's. Replacing the wine bottle in the cabinet he then took a bottle of brandy from the cabinet and filled the little glasses for the five men — including Richard. Setting the brandy bottle near his place and still standing, he lifted his glass and said "To our health, happiness and victory in the war……... soon." Everyone said yes and took a drink from their little glass. Again without sitting down he went back to the cabinet, took out an unopened box of Havana cigars and placed it on the table. With his pocket knife he pried open the top of the box and offered it to the Dripping Springs man. He took out a cigar, unwrapped it, reached for Charley's knife and cut off a little from one end of the cigar. He passed the box around the table followed by Charley's knife. Everyone took a cigar except for Robert, me, Nettie and her daughter. When all the cigars had been unwrapped and trimmed the Dripping Springs man took a shiny silver Zippo lighter from his pocket, lighted his cigar and then passed the lighter on. As the cigar smoke began to fill the air the Dripping Springs man pushed his chair back a little and said "This has been a great Thanksgiving day and dinner — one of my best. I want to thank you all, especially the ladies for such fine food and Charley for his warm hospitality." There were a few amends from around the table and then the talking and visiting renewed.

Richard tapped his coffee cup with a spoon and said that he had an announcement to make so all eyes turned to him. "Yesterday I gave Pat a ring so now we are officially engaged to be married in about a year.

Saturday morning her parents are taking her back to the university and are coming by the ranch to pick me up also so I would like all of you to meet Pat, my future mother and father-in-law and Pat's grandmother who lives with them. We are going back a day early since I have a meeting with my Navy group Sunday afternoon. Pat's parents want us to go to church together Sunday before they return home. The rumor is that at the meeting we are to get cadet uniforms in place of these swabbie suites. The new uniforms are said to be just like officers' — maybe a little less braid — so the next time you see me I may look like an admiral." As Richard sat down he received congratulations from several quarters and then an apology and regrets from the Dripping Springs man and also from the Kingsville man since they would not be there on Saturday to meet his intended.

In a few minutes the Kingsville man said he needed to start on his return trip if he was to make it in tonight but Charley cut him off with the statement that he should just stay overnight and get a fresh start in the morning. Nearly everyone chimed in that was the thing to do and the man seemed relieved to give in so he could — and as he put it — enjoy such wonderful company longer. The Dripping Springs man then said that if he didn't have hunting dogs at home that needed tending to he would also spend the night. Charley was the only one that expressed any disappointment over this situation.

Most of the group, especially the younger ones, pitched in and had the table cleared and helped with the dishwashing and other chores. The older members of the group took their places around the fireplace in the big room and shared more stories about earlier times. In a little while the dining room and kitchen were in good order so Robert and I went out back, caught and saddled our horses for a ride in the ranch. The others all did their own thing for the rest of the afternoon — mostly resting up after such a busy day. About dark we all gathered in the dining room for turkey, ham and cheese sandwiches with the exception of the Dripping Springs man who had headed for home while Robert and I were out riding. Charley had caught the Kingsville man up on the trail of my Mother and Dad since they had left Raymondville and their current wartime situation.

During the evening, after supper, we all gathered in the big room while the Kingsville man told us about his background before and during his more than forty years at the King Ranch. He had many interesting stories about the Kleberg family, the cowboys on the ranch and some of his friends who were Texas Rangers in South Texas. He didn't brag and boast like the Dripping Springs man did when he was telling his stories so this audience was well entertained and we encouraged him to keep the tales coming — until it was nearly midnight when we all headed for bed. I didn't find out how the story teller and Charley became friends to start with so after we were lying in our bunks I asked Robert. He said he had no idea so we would have to ask Charley later.

After breakfast next morning, as the Kingsville man was getting to his car to leave, he came back to where I was standing to give me a special invitation to come visit him in Kingsville and to encourage my parents to give him an opportunity to repay their hospitality. I promised him I would certainly encourage them to come visit him. Little did he nor I have any idea that in thirty plus a year or two I would come to Kingsville and live there for forty years. But, unfortunately, it was too late for him and I never saw or heard from him after my Blanco visit.

Robert and I spent most of Friday on the ranch riding around horseback and "hunting." We didn't do much actual hunting although we did carry the deer rifles with us. Robert explained that most of the deer hunters around there used dogs and rode horseback to hunt but Charley didn't want any dogs on the ranch for hunting so most people hunted on foot at this ranch. Robert and I opted for riding around on horseback, seeing a few deer, but not shooting at any so we weren't very good hunters. We did have a wonderful day riding through the hills, brush and creeks. One adventure didn't turn out too well but we laughed about it for many, many years later.

Getting along past midafternoon, it had warmed up and we were getting thirsty so when we came to this sparkling clear little creek crossing our path we decided to have a drink. Dismounting we tied our mounts a few steps from the creek and lay on our stomachs and "lapped up" the fresh water. When we finished we brought our horses over to get their fill also. While we were holding the reins letting them drink, Robert pointed over to the big roots of a tree growing on the bank of the creek. You could tell there was a hole under the root leading up into the creek bank. He said to hold his horse while he looked up in the hole. As he was bending over he said he could see something in it and it probably was a fox. He walked back to his horse, untied the little snake gun and went back to the hole. He stuck the barrel into the hole and pulled the trigger. Out fell about the biggest and prettiest skunk I have ever seen. Robert said "WOW! What a beautiful skin on that skunk. I must have killed him before he let loose with his stench because I don't smell anything." I asked him what he was going to do with it now. He said he was going to take it to headquarters and skin it and save the skin and that beautiful tail. He took a rawhide pigging string off his saddle and tied the skunk's hind legs together and hooked them over his saddle horn. The ranch horses were used to carrying everything from calves to firewood on the laps of their riders so they made no fuss over the skunk as we headed for the ranch headquarters with my horse following behind the other one.

As we neared headquarters, my horse began to hold back a little and I had to urge him on. Then I got a faint whiff of skunk odor and decided the skunk had slowly let it loose from the jogging of the ride and it had been so gradual that Robert and his horse didn't notice. About that time we arrived at headquarters and Sonny and his dad saw us — they took in the scene (and scent) and hollowed for us to stop. The foreman yelled to Robert to drop the skunk from his saddle, ride up to the tree that he pointed out, take off the saddle and blanket and hang them in the tree. He was to also hang his boots, his pants and shirt in the tree with the saddle and walk his horse to the barn for a bath. He said for me to come to the barn avoiding the skunk, Robert and his horse as much as possible.

Everyone in the house must have heard the commotion and came out to take a look and join in the laughing too. I never knew how long it was before they could use the saddle or boots again but I think they ended up burning Robert's shirt and pants. Charley had Robert bury the skunk pretty deep where he had dropped it, take a very long tub bath with sweet smelling salts and soap, as well as having a few choice words for him about his skunk hunting. Richard, who spent all of Friday studying in his room although it was a holiday from school, used "skunk boy" as his pet name for Robert during the rest of the time he was at the ranch.

Both Richard and Robert had this thing about giving everybody funny little names. As best I can remember, neither ever called me by one — I guess they felt Floyd was funkie enough. As for the skunk incident, Robert and I never talked about it until it began to get funny to us too — several years afterward.

Saturday morning we didn't do much except hang around headquarters trying to stay out of trouble and waiting for the arrival of Richard's girlfriend and family. Nettie had prepared a nice lunch for everyone so when they arrived we had another dinner party in order to get acquainted. We found Pat to be a very nice and likable but quite a bit reserved young lady. Her mother and dad were both very outgoing and easy to get along with while the grandmother was really a card. She kept us all entertained with her funny little stories and jokes about members of their family — whom we didn't know or ever get to meet. The grandmother took a good bit of wine during and after lunch which seemed to boost her spirits. I got the feeling that her family felt that Richard was quite a "catch" for Pat and very happy that they were getting married. I also ended up thinking that if they weren't wealthy they at least were pretty well off financially — which was good for a young doctor-to-be, considering his years of schooling and training yet ahead.

It was the middle of the afternoon before Pat's family, with Richard in tow, got off for Austin. The only time I remember seeing any of Pat's family was at Richard and Pat's wedding about a year and a half later in Austin at one of the large university churches. I visited Richard and Pat two or three times when they were in Dallas while he was in medical school and she was working (to support them and they were struggling) as a dietitian in one of the big hospitals. After that we drifted apart and it wasn't many years before they were divorced. I never really knew Richard's second wife.

Charley was in an eating, drinking and poker playing group of men that met Saturday evenings and spent most of the night together. They rotated their meeting place from one ranch to another each week but had the same Mexican cook prepare their meat and side dishes where they met. He was quite elderly and Charley swore he learned to cook from his father in a chuck wagon who was a noted cook from the old trail driving days. Since Charley would be gone for Saturday supper, Robert wanted us to go into town and have enchiladas at the Texas Hotel which he said made the best he had ever eaten.

The enchiladas were great but somewhat different from what I expected. We had our choice of several meats as well as cheese and we both chose venison — I wanted to at least be able to say I ate deer while I was in Blanco. They were heavily layered on the top with bubbling cheese and chili and a final statement with a mound of grilled onions that made them delicious. It would be a long time before I did have any that came close to being as good as those were.

I lay awake in my bunk for a long time that night probably due to eating so much heavy and spicy food, as well as drinking coffee at night — and also worrying about the long trip back home the next day. I was glad to hear Charley's car door slam closed about one in the morning so then I was able to slip off into some sleep. Everyone was up early and ready the next morning for another full day. The ranch family saw us off and we had pretty much of a repeat of the day coming down, except we were pointed north instead of south. When we got to Grandma's, Mother and Sonny were there waiting for me — so we ate some supper and then went on home to ready for another week of school

After Thanksgiving, with football season being over, school activities changed a great deal and I had more free time to spend on outside activities. At school, from November till school was out for the summer, I spent time with only two extracurricular activities — both carryovers from the fall. These developed from my regular classes and were called clubs. We had an activity period for club meetings each day except one day each week when we had assembly. Each club met twice a week so you could have two clubs. One of mine was the Industrial Arts Club in which we could work on our shop class projects or other little projects on our own with the supervision of our teacher Mr. Pittman. He would also stay after school for an hour or so in order that we have access to the shop tools and machines with his help and supervision. I spent most of my time making little gifts from wood for family and friends since I wasn't very good with the metal work.

The second club was the Airplane Spotters which developed out of the science classes from our studies of airplanes and flight. We learned to identify the many different enemy planes — and of course ours and our allies. We had a little tower built somewhat like half as tall as an oil derrick for our observations on a rotating schedule for an hour before and after school each day with Mr. Garrett, our teacher and then principal, with two or three club members always there with our government issued binoculars pointed toward the sky. We never saw any enemy planes for certain but did make a few reports while keeping watch over the great East Texas Oil Field. We did get a thrill each time we saw spotters like us in the war movies and really felt that we were contributing to the war effort. We received some very good training and experiences through this club and the hours we participated in it. We also received great benefits from the time we spent with Mr. Garrett (and Mr. Pittman) in these activities since some of us were missing a father figure at home during the war.

My outside of school activities consisted primarily with my chicken interests and gardening activities until school was out for the summer. I also spent a good deal of time riding George around the area enclosed by Kilgore, Red Level, Overton, Old London, Pitner's Junction and Pirtle. A few times I rode to Grandma's on a Saturday and came back Sunday afternoons. Most of the time my riding was with just me and George but sometimes it was with Sonny and Tony and a few times with Marcus or Novice up behind me — Sonny would never let one of my friends ride his horse with me since it made him feel left out. My one big adventure during this time came during a ride when I had Marcus up behind me on a cool but not a terribly cold Saturday morning.

After all my chores were done for the morning and I had worked some in Mother's rose bush beds, I saddled George and was headed from the house to go west on Don Leverett Road toward the Gulf camp. I had in my mind to visit the Westmoreland girls (cousins Billie Gene and Mary Elizabeth whose families both lived in the camp) and possibly show off some for them. Marcus called from his back yard (their combination house and his mother's café was located on the north east corner of our property) to ask where I was headed. When I told him, of course he wanted to go with me — so I agreed, not wanting to hurt his feelings. I let him put his left foot in the stirrup on that side, hold on to the saddle horn and swing up behind me. George squatted a little but he was trained well and knew how to brace for double up without any protest. We went west on the oil road with George eager to cover some territory. I held him at a rough trot — might as well give Marcus a little shaking-up for horning in on my plans.

As we rounded the big curve to the left at the Leveretts' home, Marcus — looking off to the right — remarked that it looked like someone evidently had cleaned up around the baby graves just inside the fence on the north side of the road. I said that was good for it had needed some work for a long time. There was something about this miniature cemetery, containing a few infant graves, that attracted our attention every time we went by — and still does. We then passed the Leveretts' barns and crossing the bridge over the creek swung back to the right as we reached the Still place, then passed the road leading north to Grandpa Jernigan's old farm place where my Mother was born. That road also passed between Grandma and Grandpa's property on the east side and that of the Charlie Christians' on the west side. The Don Leverett Road we were on also formed the south side of the Christians' property. As we rode by their homes, Marcus asked me if those people were my kin folks. I said yes that Mrs. Christian was my great aunt Ida, my Grandma Jernigan's sister. He said he thought so which made me wonder what and how he had heard about this relationship but said no more about it.

I eased George back into a fast walk as we neared the ninety degree left turn toward the Sexton City to Overton highway and took the right hand road angling off to the Gulf Camp northwest at about forty-five degrees. We rode into the camp and circled the two blocks containing homes and the company warehouses with offices a couple of times until we saw a school friend in his yard. We stopped and still sitting astride George we visited with him for a few minutes while a number of kids — including Billie Jean and Mary Elizabeth — showed up. One of the little guys wanted to ride so I asked Marcus to get down and put him up behind me for a loop around the camp. This turned into a long series of loops with kids — including the Westmoreland girls — up behind me. I called a stop when all had a turn and gladly accepted a Dr. Pepper offered by our friend. While I was busy ridding around all the kids, Marcus was visiting and entertaining "my" girlfriends which didn't please me. Without ever getting down from George I decided it was time for us to go so I told Marcus to get back up behind me if he wanted a ride back home.

I decided to return with a little change in our route. We rode straight south out of the camp on a little dirt road that led to the Sexton City to Overton highway. We then went east on the highway about a quarter of a mile until we came to the road running back north to the Don Leverett Road. I thought Marcus needed more rough riding so I had kept George in his rough trot all this time and finally Marcus complained that he was about to throw up his Dr. Pepper from all the shaking. I decided probably Marcus had about all he could take so I slightly pulled back on the reins while nudging George forward with my heels and put him in his "saddle" gait. George was one of the best saddling horses I had ever ridden and he could go for miles in it without breaking stride. Some people called it "single footing" and some horses naturally had it and some with their blood lines and training — like the Paso Fino of Peru — can develop it. George had it naturally and was some ride.

We were gliding along when we came to the ninety degree turn to the right and Marcus, all relaxed and probably half asleep from the easy riding, began to slip off to the left. He hooked his heels in George's flanks and this made George take off in a full run which really did send Marcus off to the left in the middle of the turn. I looked over my left shoulder and there was Marcus hugging my waist and dangling off in the air to the left. He didn't let loose so I came off with him. He fell in the middle of the road and I fell under the horse. As I was about to hit the ground I looked up and saw one of George's hind hoofs coming toward my face so I turned my head and it struck the side of my head just above and behind my left ear — that was all I remembered for some time.

Later Marcus told me what happened after he got up, and we all wondered how he and I came out of it with no broken bones — except maybe for the one in my head. George never slowed; he was headed home at full speed. Marcus said I was crumpled on the side of the road, partly on the hard oil surface and partly in the oily dirt on the shoulder. He couldn't tell that I was breathing and seemed out cold as a mackerel. He tried to talk to me but there was no response. He dragged me out of the road into the ditch where there was a little pool of water and splashed it on my face and head. Still no response so he decided I was dead and since there was no traffic he took off in a run just as George had done. He ran all the way home without seeing a car.

It took a few minutes to get enough breath to tell his mother what had happened. She decided to call my Mother first and see what she wanted to do. There was no answer so thinking my Mother could be out in the yard, they ran up to the house and saw our car was gone. Mrs. Carter did not have a car so Marcus ran over to the Garrett's and told him what had happened. They jumped in his car, stopped and told Mrs. Carter to call the Sheriff's office and stay at our house in case my Mother came home while they were going to check on me.

Meanwhile back at the accident scene, I must have come to just a few minutes after Marcus ran for home. I was still half sitting and half standing when a car drove by, stopped and backed up to where I was staggering around. A young man got out and came over to me, helped me stand up and motioned to the two other men to come help him handle me. The three, evidently oil field workers judging by their oily clothes, were headed to or from work. They cleaned me up some using water from the ditch and rags hanging from their hip pockets, got my story and when they found out where I lived decided the thing to do was take me home. They were amazed to find no blood on me. We must have met Mr. Garrett in his car on our way to my house but we didn't notice him nor did he notice us so he drove on and so did we.

The driver of the car steered it into our driveway and we saw Mrs. Carter sitting on the south porch steps with a worried look on her face as if she didn't know what to do. They gave her a brief report and she filled them in on events at her end. They turned me over to her and went on their way. After discussing my condition with her, she decided I needed to soak in the bathtub while we waited for someone else to show up. She drew me a tub of water, left me in the bathroom to bathe, leaving the bathroom door and the nearby outside door open so we could call back and forth then she resumed her post on the porch steps.

When Mr. Garrett and Marcus arrived at where Marcus had left me, they were surprised that I was nowhere to be found. They parked nearby and searched for signs of what might have happened. Then the deputy sheriff pulled up, parked and joined them. They saw car tracks in the soft oily dirt near where Marcus had left me and decided someone had picked me up and taken me away. Both cars then went to our house to see if anything had transpired there while Marcus and Mr. Garrett were gone. The deputy parked in front of our house while Mr. Garrett parked about halfway between our driveway and his house. Mrs. Carter was standing near the south door talking to Mrs. Garrett, Evelyn and Booger Red — Evelyn, a couple of years older than me, was the oldest of the Carter kids and Booger Red the youngest. This three had come to find out what all the excitement was about and discuss the situation with Mrs. Carter. A conference was held and the group decided they would all wait there until my Mother returned.

When Mother, returning from her gift buying trip to Hall Drug in Overton, was really surprised as she turned on the little loop oil road between our driveway and the highway to see the deputy sheriff and Mr. Garrett standing in front of the deputy's car talking with Mr. Garrett's car parked in a strange way near his house while the other group — except for Marcus who was in the back unsaddling and putting up George — was standing at our south door with it wide open. Sonny jumped out first but Mother was close behind. They were all ears to find what had happened.

Mother was shocked again when she rushed into the bathroom, and as she told it many, many times later, to find me asleep in the bathtub with only my nose sticking above the waterline. She had me get out of the tub, dry off and slip on a robe. Then Sonny led me into my bedroom since I was having trouble seeing. After I sat on the side of my bed Mother got her flashlight and looked in my eyes. She said I had a little chunk of oily dirt stuck under my left eye's lower lid. She got her tweezers, pulled on the lashes of that lid with her fingers on her left hand and with the tweezers in her right hand picked up the little chunk and knocked it out of the tweezers on the headboard of the bed. She then got me a warm wet wash cloth and had me hold it to my eyes. In a few minutes she returned with stuff to flush my eyes. She would dip a tablespoon into a cup of warm, slightly salty water, hold it in front of me and have me bend over hold my eye to the spoon and bat my eye lids to wash my eye area. She had me do both several times for she said the right would sympathize with the left and that would make them both feel better.

After catching her breath a little, she had me sit in a chair near the phone in the hall while she called our family doctor at home. Mrs. Hilegaman answered the phone and told Mother the doctor was in bed with a bad cold but would come to the phone. Mother explained the situation to him and answered his questions with mostly yes and no but turned a time or two and repeated the question and got an answer from me. She finished the conversation by thanking the doctor and telling him she surely would which made me wonder what she was going to do. She said the doctor wanted her to keep a close watch on me for a few hours, I could lie down to rest but not go to sleep until bed time and to call him to come out if I felt worse, other wise to wait until Monday to come in for a check-up. I then lay down on my bed and Sonny was put in charge of keeping me awake while Mother went out to report on the doctor's advice, give thanks to and dismiss our crowd and then prepare us a lunch of chicken soup and sandwiches.

Following the Monday examination the doctor said that I had an awful lot of bruises and probably a concussion which just went to prove I was a pretty tough little kid with a very hard head. On our way home Mother said "I guess it's time for you to stop riding George" — and noticing the shocked look on my face — quickly added "double." I kind of grumbled "That might not be too bad of an idea."

Later when Marcus and I were discussing our injuries, he said he had a lot of bad bruises too but he didn't need a doctor to tell him for he could see and feel them all too well. My head really did bother me for fifty or sixty years later although I never let on for fear friends and enemies would be assured that my head wasn't right — better to let them guess.

For many years afterward when I would laugh a lot my head would swell some on the left side and ache quite a bit so I found it better to not laugh a great deal. Gradually over the years the swelling and aching decreased somewhat and I learned to live with it.

Victory gardens were a big thing during World War II and we read a lot about them in all the publications where citizens were encouraged to participate as an aid in the war effort by supplying as much of their own food as possible. We were already much involved with gardening and canning at Grandma's, as well as having our own garden at our home so the publicity made me want to do more. Normally during the winter months we received a lot of seed catalogs for vegetables and flowers due to Mother's involvement with her flower activities, so this year I spent many, many hours poring over the stories and pictures in them. I became interested in many of the exotic varieties of vegetables, especially in the gourd and beet families. I ordered, planted and grew — some very successfully and others not so successfully — many, many different ones, all the way from those intended for ornamental purposes to medical usage.

I ended up with a very large eclectic garden which I shared with friends and neighbors — even feed beets for my animals. I spent a lot of time working it from the last really cold days of winter till the heat of late spring when we went to Hitchcock for the summer. When I left for the summer I still had a beautiful garden with the fence that enclosed it covered with a vast variety of colorful ornamental gourds and inside many luscious edible plants, many with fruits on them. I left it in charge of Mr. Garrett with Marcus and Novis assisting him. Mr. Garrett fell in love with it and then for many years afterward he kept a small garden in his back yard as an outgrowth of my victory garden. Several years after the war, some people told me they still remembered my spaghetti squash which was a hit as I shared it in the neighborhood as a novelty food.

So, in addition to my garden, the chickens also kept me very busy. Here too I went in for some exotic breeds and unusual practices such as the natural feather board brooder — which I touched on previously. Not always as successful as I had hoped for, I did have some great results and usually found (in my own way) a method to overcome most of the problems. Being so busy all winter and spring it seemed the end of the school year came quickly and we were at summer in such a short time — with many more adventures ahead in Hitchcock.

THE SUMMER OF 1944

As the 1943-44 school year neared its end, Dad learned the cottage he had rented for the summer of 1943 would not be available again. The couple decided to stay in Hitchcock for the summer. They were ready to start construction on their cabin in Colorado but due to the war the needed materials would not be obtainable so they postponed their project. Fortunately for Mother and Dad, the couple had a teacher friend who was going to spend the summer months with her parents in Arkansas so the couple made arrangements with her for Mother and Dad to rent her garage apartment in Alvin for the summer. It was very small of course, with a small bedroom just large enough for Mother and Dad but the little living room had a couch that made down into two half beds which Grandma and Auntie could sleep on and us four boys would sleep on a pallet spread on the floor where ever we could find enough left over space. This way we could visit during the summer as we had done the year before — just more crowded.

Mother moved down to Hitchcock/Alvin the weekend school was out since they needed her to go to work as soon as possible — with Sonny and me going to Grandma's. Since we were all very eager to visit with Dad and also get to the beaches in Galveston, we planned our first trip for the next week or two. On the way down on this first trip of the summer we stopped off in Houston and spent a couple of days with Uncle Willis and Aunt Loudella. As always, Uncle Willis showed us a very good time, despite the war conditions.

The first day we were in the small apartment in Alvin, Mother and Dad left very early the next morning for work at the Navy base and then

Dad came in again at noon to check on us to see if we had everything we needed. Seeing our car back in the driveway during the workday, the landlady also came up to the apartment to see if there was anything she could do to help. We had met her the evening before when we got there but this time she had her daughter Anne with her whom we met for the first time. The little apartment was bursting at the seams with people so Anne invited Sonny and me, along with Kenneth and Jack, to come down the stairs and see the backyard which she said we were welcome to use — there was plenty of room for us to play when we were there visiting Mother and Dad.

Sonny and the boys were soon involved in a game of chase while Anne and I each sat on facing concrete benches at a round matching table. I couldn't take my eyes off her, she was as cute as any girl I had ever seen and up to this time I had not been interested in any girls — but she was definitely stirring up my interest. She told me a lot of stuff, definitely liked to talk and I was a ready listener. I learned she was about a year younger than me but two grades behind — due to the adding of the twelfth grade. Her mother thought she was too young to date so she did not have a boyfriend but had a couple picked out that she figured she could latch on to soon. She was a little smaller than me but beginning to develop a very interesting figure.

Her dad was an officer in the Navy and currently serving aboard ship in the South Pacific. He had not been in the States for over a year and a half and they had no idea when he might get back. She had a grandmother and grandfather that lived in Galveston which she and her mother visited frequently. Her mother didn't have a paying job but spent most of her time doing volunteer work for the war effort. Anne helped her mother in a lot of these activities along with many of her school chums.

She talked on and on with me looking into those very, very blue eyes and that rather short platinum blonde hair pulled into a little stubby pony tail behind each ear with a blue rubber band on one and a red one on the other. A beach ball came rolling by and she reached out with a penny loafer and put her foot on it. She quickly got up, scooped up the ball and handed it to Jack, the smallest of the three playing toss with the ball. Jack ran around the table and standing behind me threw the ball to his brother keeping it away from Sonny. Anne put her hands at the waist of the loose fitting top, accenting her shape under her blue and white pin-stripe pedal-pusher outfit, and asked if I was going to just sit there all day or could we go upstairs and see what the old folks were up to. I jumped up and said I was ready — and I knew then I was smitten with Anne.

On the stairs we met Dad coming down on his way back to work. He said he wanted me to go with him and I would get to visit the base that afternoon. I had not been on the facility before so this would be a big treat. I told Anne goodbye and got in the car with Dad. On the way out of town he explained to me that there was a new policy in place where one civilian could be the guest of a serviceman stationed there between 9:00 am and 4:00 pm by having the guest sign in at the main gate with proper identification. If there was more than one guest at a time, the serviceman had to get passes for the visitors ahead of time through an office in the Administration Bldg. Dad said he would take me today, Sonny tomorrow and he had made arrangements for Grandma, Auntie, Kenneth and Jack on Sunday when the Navy conducted group tours on the base for civilians related to the service men stationed there.

After we were cleared through the Main Gate Dad said he needed to go by his office at the Brig for a few minutes then we would go to the Administration Bldg. so I could see where Mother worked. I stayed in the car while Dad was at the Brig. The building was not very large and kind of off by itself on one side of the base. We weren't there long and the only other vehicle there was a Navy Jeep parked next to us. We drove to the Administration Bldg., parked and walked in the main entrance. This place was a beehive of activity with sailors, officers, a few Marines and civilians both coming and going.

Dad guided us into an office opening off the main hall. There were six or seven desks scattered around the room with a woman either sitting or standing at each desk. He spoke or was spoken to by each as we headed for one in the back were Mother sat with a typewriter in front of her and stacks of papers on her desk. After she spoke, I said I didn't know she could type and she said she wasn't much of a typist but most of the forms had to filled out on a typewriter so she had to learn to do it pretty quickly. Dad told her he was showing me around the base and would be back for her when she got off work to go home. She nodded and went back to her work. We then went upstairs to another office where Dad said he had a desk to work at when he had business in the Administration Bldg. This office also had several desks with servicemen working at each except at Dad's and the one next to it which he explained was the one used by the officer in charge of the Shore Patrol and that he, like Dad, was usually somewhere else other than sitting in an office.

He said he needed to run some errands on the base and this would give me an opportunity to look around. He picked up a little stack of brown envelopes off his desk and we headed downstairs. As we entered the hall downstairs a Navy officer spoke to Dad and laughingly wanted to know if he was putting that young man with him in the brig. I could tell he was joking so I flashed him a big smile and he reached out to shake my hand. Dad said that I was his son and introduced us telling the officer I had come for a visit. The officer wanted to know if I would be there all summer like Mrs. Elliott so Dad explained I had come down with my grandmother and aunt for a visit but would be in and out during the summer. The officer apologized for asking so many questions and then explained he needed a young man to work in the Public Works Warehouse and I looked like I could fill the bill. He then asked how old I was and I told him I was fifteen, but quickly added "and sixteen in August." He and Dad talked some more. I was supposed to be sixteen to work for the Navy in their summer civilian employment program but they were so short on workers he could make an exception in my case since I would be sixteen before the summer was over. When they finally turned to me and asked if I wanted a job, I was overjoyed to say "Yes."

Dad left me in the care of the nice officer, saying he would be at the Brig when I finished up with my business. We went to another office where I was given some papers to complete — I had to run upstairs to Mother's office to find out the address of the garage apartment where I would be staying with them. Luckily I already had a Social Security card which I had gotten when I was delivering papers in Corpus Christi. When the forms were completed we walked over about two blocks to the warehouse for me to meet the manager. After our introduction, I sensed the manager didn't care much for me but with the officer there he was glad to quickly give his approval and sign off on my papers saying for me to be there at eight the next morning and, as my supervisor, he would orient me to my new job.

We then went back to the Administration Bldg. where I was left in another office for me to complete some more papers, have my picture taken and wait while a base pass was prepared. The officer congratulated me on my new employment and said when they finished with me in that office I could go to the Brig to meet my Dad. It seemed like forever waiting for the pass to be made but someone explained that the picture had to be developed to put in the pass and that took some time. Finally I was given my pass, told I was free to go, but be sure I reported to work the next morning at 8:00 am — they were sure I didn't understand military time being such a young civilian.

Almost walking on air, I decided to not disturb my Mother again at her work and hiked over to the Brig to meet my Dad. As I entered the Brig I saw a desk just inside the door with a Marine sitting at it checking off things on a paper form in front of him. He looked up and asked if I was the Warden's son and, when I nodded yes, he pointed over to some chairs in the reception area and told me to have a seat and he would be with me in just a few minutes.

After sitting down I looked around the room reading the signs posted on the doors, bulletin board, etc. Through an open double door I could see into a room where three or four tables were with four chairs at each. At one table four young men dressed in Navy fatigues sat reading while at the next table sat a Marine in his uniform with a big imposing Sam Brown belt holding an automatic pistol and a black night stick hanging down — looking directly at them. His manner gave you the impression he was all business. The prisoners were careful so their gaze didn't meet his, but a couple sneaked a look in my direction.

In a few minutes Dad came through one of the doors and said for me to come on and we would go get my Mother. He told the Marine at the desk that he was in charge until the next shift reported and we left in our car for the Administration Bldg. He noticed my base pass hanging around my neck, pointed to it and asked how things had gone. I told him all that had happened and he said he wanted me to do my best in anything they asked me to do and always remember my actions would reflect directly on my whole family. When we drove up to the Administration Bldg., Mother was standing near the front entrance talking to two other women. As I held the front passenger door open for her she also noticed my pass and asked me to explain everything again for her benefit. And, sure enough, she gave me almost word for word the same advice that Dad had given me.

That evening Dad took the whole bunch, two car loads including Anne and her mother, to his favorite hamburger joint for supper in celebration of my job. I was the hero of the hour and, although I felt a little embarrassed, I really did enjoy the limelight. When we got back to the garage apartment Anne's mother invited us all for cake and ice cream — with the adults eating in her house while us kids ate in the nice backyard. So we had a double celebration that was enjoyed by all.

The next morning it was rather hectic with the three of us getting ready for work while Grandma and Auntie were still in bed and the other three boys scattered about the small apartment sound asleep on the floor on pallets. Mother said she would make me a lunch to carry since we didn't know what my schedule would be or if I would have access to a place to eat. She ate her lunch at a cafeteria next to the Administration Bldg. that was open to civilians and my Dad ate at the servicemen's mess. Later that day I was certainly glad she had the foresight to prepare me something to eat. I learned I would eat when I got an opportunity and did not have a set lunch time.

Dad, always early to where he was supposed to be, had us at our work places about 7:30. I found all the doors to the warehouse locked. In a few minutes the other two employees that worked there came in a car together. We had seen each other the day before when I was there for my "interview" with the manager but we had not been introduced or talked to one another. Both seemed very old to me, the older one walked with a cane. They introduced themselves and explained that the older one was the bookkeeper and the other was the counterman. They unlocked the front door and we entered the building. The bookkeeper and I headed for the "office area" while the counterman was busy opening the other big doors on each end of the building. The bookkeeper and I then went behind the long counter, which more or less fenced off the office area from the rest of the warehouse, through the opening in it at one end which allowed us to walk past the manager's office. I was surprised when the manager opened the door to his small private office at his end of the office area, stepped out and spoke to us. Evidently he had gotten there earlier and was working in his office until we arrived. I soon learned this was the pattern that would be followed to start each day all the time I was working there.

The bookkeeper continued on to his desk in the front corner at the other end of the office area. The manager was looking me over so I stood there also taking a closer look around the office area — especially the line of filing cabinets on the back wall from behind the bookkeeper's desk to the door that opened into the manager's office. He stepped past me and pointed to the counter area on my left, directly across from his office door, and said "This is where we keep track of all the transactions that take place in the warehouse." There was a bank of files about two feet tall and six feet long sitting on the counter, covering it except for a few inches in front of the files. The cabinets held little drawers some eight inches wide and two high with labels on the front of each. He reached over pulled out a drawer, flipped up about half of the cards (the cardholders were hinged at the back side where you could get at any card) and pointed to the one exposed. He said, "Each item we stock in the warehouse has a card with a name, full description, number we should keep on hand and location across the top of the card. When we receive a shipment of an item we enter the date, number received and adjust the number we have on hand. When an item is taken from the warehouse, we enter this transaction also so that we always know what we have on hand. It will be part of your job to post these entries — standing or sitting on that stool here. That is why your position is classified as a clerk. Both the bookkeeper and counterman will instruct you in this process and some of the other duties you will have."

Again he stood looking at me for about thirty seconds, and then said for me to follow him. He walked to the other end of the office area and turned behind the bookkeeper's desk at a door in the corner next to the filing cabinets matching the one into his office at the other end of the filing cabinets. He opened the door and I saw it was a restroom with a lavatory and toilet. He said, "This is the head and it will be your job to keep it clean, Navy clean." He then entered the head, opened another door and walked to the other end of the narrow room with a table and two chairs on each side of the table. There were janitorial tools and supplies with some shelves filled with odds and ends. He told me this was where I would eat my lunch — I was not to eat or drink anywhere else in the office area or warehouse. This room was where I would work on any repairs that I needed to do to items in the warehouse and other work of that type. He motioned for me to follow him, turned and opened another door and we were back into his office where we had been the day before.

He closed the door behind us and motioned for me to sit in the same chair in front of his desk which I had been in the day before. As I more or less squirmed in the chair he sat behind his desk and began a long lecture about my duties and other things. He began by saying my position was classified as a clerk but he would call it more of a "flunkie job" since I would be doing any and everything any of the three told me to do. As time went by in my work all that summer, these words came back to me many times. During my whole employment I don't recall him ever addressing me by my name — he usually motioned for me to follow him, pointed at something indicating he wanted something done to it or just called me "Flunkie." He told me to do this or that while the other two would politely ask me to do something they wanted done.

After this introduction he began to detail some of the many duties I would be expected to do. Every day I would not only Navy clean the head, but I would clean, sweep, and swab the office area, the storeroom next to the head and his office. I would keep the drinking fountain located just outside the entrance to the office area sparklingly clean and sweep the warehouse out at least twice a week with the push broom. Dust and use the dust mop throughout the warehouse as needed. I would also be the delivery boy since some of the offices on the base would phone for things to be sent to them and especially the little machine shops in the blimp hanger just across the street from the warehouse. Then he told me that some of the items that had to be delivered would be too large or heavy for me to carry so it would be necessary for me to get a driver's license from the Navy so I could use the Reo dump truck (the only vehicle the warehouse had at that time) to do those deliveries. I then realized why one of the questions on my application had been could I operate a motor vehicle. Since I could drive our car I had responded yes and now was surprised to know I would be driving a dump truck. The manager told me to be careful with my driving since the young man that had my job previously was fired due to his running over things with the dump truck.

He was very emphatic as he explained that I would serve as the counterman during an hour every day when the bookkeeper and the counterman would go to lunch together. He said he would always be there in his office in case I came up against a problem I couldn't handle. After this bit of information I wondered when and where he would have his lunch since I was expected to eat in the storeroom before or after the other's lunch time. It didn't take me long to figure this out — for as I cleaned his office every day I found Vienna sausage cans, rattrap cheese remains and empty saltine cracker boxes in the trash can. He must have eaten the same thing every day for lunch in his office. I also realized he must have spent a night or two in his office each week since I would find signs in his office as to this activity. He then certainly shocked me by telling me that the warehouse was not scheduled to be open on Saturdays nor the employees paid to work on Saturdays but not having it open on this day sometimes hampered the work going on at the base so the three of them volunteered their time to work on Saturdays to help the war effort. He said I would not be required to do so but the base would certainly appreciate it. I didn't respond either positively or negatively at that time but showed up every Saturday all summer except a couple when Auntie, Grandma and the boys were there and we went to Galveston for the day. Since Dad went to the base seven days a week I would ride with him on Saturdays as I did during week days.

Then the manager said I needed to know something about our fellow employees but not to ask any personal questions in the future. After looking at me for a little while and not saying a word, he launched into this story of his life. He told me he was born and raised out in far West Texas where there was little water, a lot of sand and wind, very little grass for the livestock and not much food for humans to eat either. He was about in the middle of a bunch of kids and remembers best that he was hungry most of his childhood. He said his mother aged fast, lost all her teeth, most of her hair and could hardly walk when she died before aged thirty-five — on his fifteenth birthday. His dad spent most of their little money on drink, abused a new wife and beat the kids. Each older brother and sister had run away from home by the time they were thirteen or fourteen. He said he hung around to try to help the younger kids until he was seventeen and the World War started. He heard the Navy would give you plenty to eat, clothe and house you, pay you a little salary for spending money and show you the world. Sounded like heaven to him so he joined. He wasn't a war hero but was a good sailor and spent the next twenty years in the Navy.

He retired with his pension, married the widow of a Navy friend who had died in an accident, and she had two teen aged children from that marriage. With the money he had saved in the Navy and the little his new family had, they bought a small farm about twelve miles southwest of the blimp base. On the limited acreage they had, including an orchard, they raised vegetables and chickens which he peddled in the nearby neighborhoods along with the fruit from the orchard. It wasn't an easy living but he wanted nothing to do with the dry and windy West Texas and its scrubby livestock. He soon tired of the troublesome kids and sent them off to live with his wife's relatives. In a year or two the wife tired of him and ran off with a neighbor. His next door neighbor (small farm too) was the bookkeeper — a bachelor who had been crippled years before in a farming accident. In order for him to get the work done on his little farm, a nephew (now the counterman) came to live with him when the counterman was about fifteen years old and had remained. The manager and bookkeeper had become fast friends and with the counterman, more or less, like a family.

When World War II began, the manager went to the Navy to enlist but they suggested, due to his age and experience with the Navy, that he go to work as a civilian for them — which he did. When he became manager of the Blimp Base's Public Works Warehouse he hired his two friends to help him run it. He got an exemption for his bookkeeper's physical condition because he could do his job at a desk. The counterman, although a younger man, was 4-F due to a congenital heart condition but could pass the civilian physical exam.

Again he looked at me for a while without speaking. Then he said "Now you know all you need to know about us and we know all we need to know about you. If you do your job, what we tell you to do, and keep your mouth shut we will get along just fine. Any and everything that happens here stays here. You are to keep things to yourself. That includes the Warden and your mother as well as anyone else — Navy or civilian. Is that clear?" I nodded my head and as he starred at me I added "Yes sir." He stood up, held out his hand and I shook it. He said "You are now part of our Navy team to help the war effort. Go report to the counterman who will show you how to do your job as he has time to do so. After a day or two with him the bookkeeper will explain some things to you also so we can all get our jobs done correctly." He didn't say anything else so I turned and went out the office door to the counterman standing at his work station.

I thought about the manager a lot during that summer. I never did like him but at the same time I couldn't ever make up my mind whether or not I disliked him. But, I knew one thing — I never did like the way he looked at me through his office door when I sat working on the inventory files. As for the other two, I liked them both very much. They did everything they could to help me get my job done and to keep me out of trouble with the manager.

Before the end of that first week the manager said I needed to get ready to make deliveries since they had been postponed while I was being trained for the office work. He got a set of keys off a hook on the wall behind his desk and told me to follow him. We walked behind the warehouse to a shed attached to it. He unlocked the padlock on the driveway doors, pulled open one and motioned for me to do the same for the other one. He said for me to stand aside while he backed out this huge dump truck. He had me get in the cab beside him and he gave me a demonstration ride around the warehouse, showing me how the gear shift, brakes, etc. worked. When we got back to the shed, he turned off the engine, opened the driver's door and got out. I started to get out also but he said for me to scoot over under the steering wheel into the driver's seat and he came around and got in on the passenger side. I think it was about this time when my knees began to knock.

He talked me through the starting procedure and then we were ready to shift into a gear. Boy, what a time I had with those gears. I finally found reverse and we backed up a little, then I lucked into a forward gear and after some jerking and jumping around we moved into the street and around the warehouse back to the shed. The manager said for me to leave it parked there and I could come out later in the day and practice changing gears and looping around the warehouse. Tomorrow I would go to the Security Office in the Administration Bldg. to get a Navy driver's license. Two or three times that afternoon I came out for a practice session. Every time I passed the front door I saw the counterman looking out at me and the bookkeeper looking out the side window from the office area. I didn't feel like I was driving any better after these tries so in frustration

I drove the truck inside the shed, closed and locked the doors, then went into the manager's office and hung the keys back on their little hook. He watched but said nothing so neither did I — I went to the card files and worked there.

The next morning, as soon as I had completed my duties connected with opening the warehouse, the manager sent me to get my driver's license — over to the same office where I had been to get my base pass. I was directed over to a desk at one side of the room where a Marine sergeant sat at a desk. As I stood at the desk he looked up and wanted to know what he could do for me. I told him I was sent for a driver's license. He wanted to know who the driver's license was for and I told him it was for me. He kind of grinned (probably due to my age), pointed at a chair on the other side of his desk and said we would have to start with some paperwork. He took a form from a shelf on the wall from behind him, placed it before me and handed me a fountain pen that was clipped on his shirt front. He pointed to the blanks on the form and told me to fill all of them in to the best of my knowledge and to ask him any questions I had about them.

I completed the form without having to ask him any questions, handed it and the pen back to him and watched while he read over the entire form. He picked up a clipboard off his desk, placed the form I had just completed on it, retrieved another form from the shelf and clipped it on top of my form. He stood up and said for me to come with him and we would do my driving test. By now I was very nervous since I didn't know I would have to do this driving test. I followed him out of the Administration Bldg. to a parking lot on the back side of the building and he stopped at a Jeep painted the same Navy color as the truck I had driven the day before. It was parked in a space with a sign proclaiming "Reserved." He walked to the passenger side stepped up into the Jeep and pointed at the driver's side while saying for me to get in.

He asked me if I had ever driven a Jeep before so I told him "No, only my Mother and Dad's car some and a farm truck at my uncle's a little. He then asked me what I would be driving that made me need a Navy license. When I told him a truck at the Public Works Warehouse he whistled and then said I would have to take a test in it also. Now I really was nervous.

He showed me the ignition switch, the horn, gears, etc. then told me to start up and drive over to the warehouse and park out front. Since it was only two blocks back to the warehouse I made this drive without too much trouble and parked in front of the entrance. The sergeant said it is common courtesy to leave a walking space in front of a doorway and had me move over some to the right. I think he did this in order to see me back up and park again — a little straighter.

We went into the manager's office and visited a little while. By the conversation I assumed they were friends and just killing time while I sweated. After a few minutes the sergeant asked where the truck was I would be driving and the manager told him it was in the shed behind the warehouse. He said for me to bring it around and park it in front of the warehouse. I got up, reached for the keys on the wall and stood at the end of the manager's desk. Neither moved; they sat there visiting with each other and I realized I was supposed to go get the truck by myself. I hurried out the office to do so. When I drove up front and parked on the far side of the Jeep, I saw both were standing near the entrance. I walked up to where they were standing. The Sergeant took something from his clipboard and handed me a small blue card. Across the top was printed U S Navy Temporary Driver License. In the name line was hand printed William Floyd Elliott and in the date line was the day's date. Then the printed line VOID AFTER THREE DAYS followed by another printed line stating U. S. Navy LTA Air Station Hitchcock Texas USA. The last line on the card read Signed by and the signature M.Sgt. A. E. McKenzie, USN/MC.

I looked up and he told me I could come by his office tomorrow afternoon and get my license. They would have it made from a copy of the picture they took for my base pass. With that he walked over to the Jeep, got in and drove off. The manager smiled at me — this was the only time I remember him smiling at me all that summer.

The warehouse sat in a corner with a street on the front side (main entrance) dead ending into the street that ran along the side separating the warehouse from the blimp hanger area. On the hanger side there were large double doors that rolled open for easy entrance and exit of vehicles from a little gravel driveway leading up a ramp to the warehouse floor. Our office area was inside on the hanger side and ran from near the double door area to the front corner. On the side opposite the hanger there were matching double doors opening out back to a loading dock at a railroad track. The track ended just before it reached the street in front so the trains needed to back in with cars containing boxes of stuff for the warehouse. There was also a driveway on this side opening to the street on the front and running along the tracks in the opposite direction till it ran into the next street. There was also a driveway on the backside (opposite side to the front entrance) connecting the hanger side street with the track side driveway. These driveways, like the streets, were mostly oyster shell with some gravel and maybe a little sand and clay.

On the backside were two similar sheds separated by a walkway and door into the warehouse on that side. The smaller of the two buildings was where we kept our dump truck — which I found out later wasn't really ours, it actually belonged to the civilian crew that worked out of the other shed building and they let us use it to make big deliveries when needed. This crew was usually made up of four to six members, depending on the time of year and the constant turnover. The warehouse employees called them the "grounds crew" since they usually worked around the base on the grounds. They had a regular "boss" with two or three men and during the summer two or three school boys. The larger of the two sheds was their area where they left from each morning and came back to at the end of the day. They kept their "crew truck," tools and supplies in this shed. Sometimes when it rained they would hang out in the shed, supposedly cleaning tools, the truck, etc.

As I was carrying out the office area trash to the bins beside the driveway on the backside one morning I noticed the crew readying to get in their truck to leave for work. One of the boys looked up and waved. I stopped and waited to see if he needed something. He ran over and asked me if he had seen me at the Smith's house in Alvin a day or two previous. I said "Probably, since I am staying there for the summer with my parents while

I work on the base." He told me he lived a couple of blocks down the street and his name was Jeff. About that time someone in the crew yelled for him to come on that they were ready to go. He told me he would see me later and ran to the truck, hopped aboard and waving, they drove off.

Under the counter in the office area was a large pasteboard box in which we pitched burned out light bulbs. Each time someone checked out a pack or an individual light bulb they had to bring in a matching burned out bulb for exchange. This way the brass bases could be recycled. It was part of my job when the box was nearly filled to take the bulbs to the back, break out the glass and package the bases for shipment.

Nearly every time I did this I would cut a finger or two on the broken glass. I had seen some big rubber gloves on the shelves in the electrical section so one day I used a pair to protect my hands while I broke light bulbs. It happened that the manager walked by and saw me busy at work doing this chore. He stopped up short, frozen in his tracks, and I thought he must be amazed at my ingenuity in using the gloves. Instead he yelled at the top of his voice for me to stop. He said if any of the electricians saw me doing that they would probably have a heart attack. Then in many words I had never heard before, probably Navy terms, he described how stupid I was. As he calmed down some he instructed me to throw those gloves in the thrash and write them off the inventory as damaged and never tell anyone about it.

Every time I broke glass (without electricians' gloves) afterwards, I thought about the expression on his face that day and laughed a little — to myself.

After work one evening Dad asked me to wash the car to get the dried mud, salt and dust off it following a day or two of rain. I pulled a garden hose from the Smith's backyard and was washing the car in the driveway when I heard a honk in the street. I looked up and saw Jeff coming down the driveway with his wide grin and waving an arm. He had left the car he was driving parked at the end of the driveway. We began talking and he jumped in and started helping me wash the car. He said he was used to that since he usually worked doing that on Saturdays at a used car lot owned by his mother's boss. After we finished drying the car, we put the garden hose back in the yard and sat down to rest and visit at the round table and two benches. He told me a lot about himself and his family. He would be having a birthday in about three weeks and would be seventeen years old, making him about a year and a month older than me. He was also a good inch at least taller and probably fifteen or twenty pounds heavier.

His mother and dad were living in Houston when he was born with his dad working in the insurance business. Times were hard, his dad starting drinking, lost his job and when Jeff was two his dad left them destitute. His mother's mom and dad came, got them and moved them in with them in Alvin — where they had been ever since. His mother went to work for her current boss, just outside Alvin toward Houston. He had this little car lot where he bought junked and used cars, repaired them then would resale them with financing. Jeff said he made most of his money by financing the cars he sold. Jeff's mother was called a secretary/bookkeeper for the car business and a domino hall next door also owned by her boss. He also loaned money to the domino hall customers and Jeff said this made him a lot of money. I only saw the boss once or twice and I was at the car business only once during the summer but I decided there was more between Jeff's mother and the boss than just employment.

As dusk began to cover Alvin, Mother stepped out on the little porch at the top of the stairs and called me to come to supper. Seeing Jeff with me she said "Bring your friend to eat so we can meet him." I looked at Jeff and he said he would love to but he needed to take the groceries in the car to his mother and grandmother. I told him we would wait for him so to take the groceries and hurry back.

It seemed like only a couple of minutes till Jeff was tapping at the screen door. He was out of breath so I figured he had run all the way back — not bothering with the car for such a short distance. Mother and Dad both seemed pleased to meet "one of my friends," although I hardly knew him at that time but we were to become fast friends as the summer wore on.

Jeff explained that he, like me, was working at the base for the summer between his junior and senior year of high school. He told us that he had polio in the third grade and missed most of that school year so he had to repeat it. This was why he was a year older than me but we were at the same level in school. He was hoping, although he had one leg a little weaker than the other, to pass the Navy physical after graduation and join the service. If he couldn't make the grade, he planned to somehow work his way through college and be a teacher like his grandfather.

Jeff also told us that his mother didn't have a car but her boss let her use one from his lot to go back and forth to work. She also used it to take Jeff to work and pick him up when he didn't find a ride. One night a week, usually on Friday, she let him use the car to run around as long as he minded his Ps and Qs. Dad said that his schedule should match ours and he would be welcome to ride with us. Jeff was overjoyed with that news and we had another rider for the rest of the summer. Jeff repaid me by always including me in his running around on Friday nights. Mother and Dad didn't object to these outings since they considered Jeff a responsible and steadfast person since he was a little older and more mature appearing as compared to me.

I soon learned that there were a lot of things in the work-a-day world that I didn't understand. I'm sure my coworkers must have thought many times that I surely was stupid but they never let on as the manager often freely did. An example I will never forget was the term "quarter of an hour." Everyone knows that a quarter coin is twenty-five cents, don't they? This's what I thought, so a quarter of an hour would be twenty-five minutes, right?

One day the manager called me into his office. The ground crew's boss was with him and I wondered what was up so I just looked from one to the other until the manager finally told me that the ground crew's truck would be in the shop the next day. In order for us to have the dump truck to use the next day for deliveries they had decided that I would drive the crew in the dump truck to the pigeon loft where they would be working but didn't need the truck except to come back when work was over. I would go pick them up in the afternoon. The ground crew boss then said for me to have the truck in the back driveway at 8:00 sharp for the ground crew to put their tools, supplies, etc. and then themselves in the truck for the run down to the pigeon loft. The manager wanted to know if that was clear and I responded with a "Yes sir." The crew boss said "O K, see you in the morning." I returned to my file posting.

The next morning I made sure I had the truck in position at least ten minutes before eight and was standing by the driver's door waiting as the workers, including Jeff, arrived and prepared for the trip. The boss came out of their shed in just a few minutes and looked the truck over and said to the men to get in and then to me for us to go. He got in the cab with me and asked had I been to the pigeon loft before. I told him no but I thought I knew where it was. He told me to go there and park behind the building as he looked down at his watch. I did my best to drive without stripping the gears and putting on the brakes too hard for stops. When I parked behind the building I noticed he looked at his watch again, got out, told the men to unload everything. He walked around to my window and said for me to leave the warehouse at exactly a quarter till five and come back to that spot. I turned the unloaded truck around and drove to the warehouse to do my regular work.

Since the ground crew boss had made such a big issue about time I started glancing at the clock about 3:00 o'clock every few minutes until at 4:00 I told the counterman I was getting ready to leave for the pigeon loft. I got in the truck, and watching my watch, left at exactly 4:35. When I drove in behind the pigeon loft, the crew seeing the truck began putting their tools and supplies in it. The boss came storming from the doorway of the pigeon loft. He addressed me in something similar to the language my manager had used the time he saw me using the rubber gloves while breaking light bulbs — just as loud and long also. All the crew began getting their tools and going back to work, none saying a word. I noticed a sailor had followed the boss out of the building and was standing near the doorway watching. I sort of kept my eyes on the sailor while the boss waved his arms, pointed at the truck and the men scattered about working. Since I knew he was describing how dumb and/or stupid I was, I just kept mumbling yes sir. When he finally ran down or was completely out of breath, he walked over to the men, pointed at his watch and was giving them some Navy language too — I think.

After the boss was out of hearing range, the sailor came over and said a few nice things to me, like don't take it personally, give some people a little authority and they think they have to yell at everybody, etc. He added that in his opinion it was much better to be early than late and he thought I did alright. His support came just in time for I was having trouble keeping from breaking down and crying. I am sure I had tears in my eyes as he invited me to come back to the pigeon loft for a visit sometime so he could show me around. The last thing he said was if the boss made any trouble for me over this incident to let him know and he would back me all the way. I thanked him as he turned and walked back to the building.

After the men had worked only about five additional minutes, the boss called to them to load their equipment and get in the truck. Without any further bidding from the boss, I got in the truck and readied for the return trip to the warehouse. After the boss's command of "Let's go," I drove off. As we neared it, the boss in a somewhat subdued voice, told me how important it was to keep a careful schedule when you were responsible for overseeing and supervising others. He said my miscalculation on time had cost the Navy the equivalence of an hour's work by one man — causing the Navy to lose that amount of work and the cost of it. He said nothing further as I stopped in front of the shed and they all unloaded.

I put the truck in its shed and went into the warehouse where I began to busily help the others shut down for the day. I felt that even the manager seemed friendly to me. When I came out the front door Jeff was already there, waiting for me. Jeff kind of held back as we walked over to the Administration Bldg. to meet Mother and catch our ride home with Dad. He said he was sorry for what happened at the pigeon loft and that was just how his boss acted some times. The members of the crew had discussed the boss's "fits" and a couple wanted to "call him out" for a fight but the oldest member talked them out of it. He said the boss had a nice wife and a couple of little kids and something like that would probably cost him his job. After the thing today they decided in the truck on the way back for the oldest one to talk to the warehouse manager and ask him to help since he seemed to be the only friend of the boss they knew off and was also a friend of the oldest member of the crew. Jeff also said he didn't think it would do any good for me to discuss it with my parents but that was up to me. After thinking about what he said I decided he was probably right so I never discussed it with anyone. I don't know what happened after that but I do know that I never saw nor heard about the boss having another "fit" during the rest of the summer.

I made at least one more trip to the pigeon loft that summer but most of the time the supplies from our warehouse were picked up in their Jeep by someone working at the loft. I never got the opportunity to tour it the way I had been invited by the sailor there on my first visit, but I did peek around a little on my second visit and got a look at some of the birds and facilities. They were adding a shed room across the back of the building and a civilian crew was tamping the dirt preparing to install a concrete floor with a couple or three drains in it. I had brought a load of materials for them to use on the project.

The civilian crew boss asked me to wait around for a few minutes so he had time to check the materials with his concrete man. After he was through he called me to come to where they were standing. He had a slip of paper that he had jotted down a note to our counterman for three or four items they had decided they needed. He handed the note to me and gave me my instructions. As I started to walk to the truck, he stopped me and handed me a set of keys with one between his fingers. He said "You won't need the truck to haul this little batch so take my car over there and hurry back." I looked in the direction he pointed and saw a black 1940 or '41 Buick sedan so I headed for it. I tucked the slip of paper securely in my pocket and got in the car. I placed the key in the ignition and turned it on and looked for the starter on the floorboard. At that time most cars had a dimmer switch on the left side of the clutch that you stepped on to switch the lights from bright to dim and the reverse. To the right of the brake petal and toward the one for the gas was usually a similar switch to activate the starter — but there was none. I then looked on the dash since I had seen a Ford one time with a push button for the starter placed there but could find none. In frustration I glanced toward the boss as he headed toward the car. I looked again on the floorboard, moving my right foot around to see better, when my foot accidently hit the gas petal and the engine fired up. I was able to depress the clutch, get in low gear and drive off just as the boss was at the side of the car.

I made the trip without further incident, back in just a few minutes with the needed supplies and even got a thank you from the boss as I handed him his keys. I was learning on the job.

During my senior year in high school my English teacher, Miss Littlejohn, introduced us to research writing. I wanted to do my paper on pigeons and under her guidance started my research. With her direction I kept narrowing it down until I ended up with it being on their role in warfare — and brought it up to World War II. Few people at that time had any idea that pigeons were still used in warfare. To me this was a very fascinating study and I always thought I would raise and race homing pigeons at some time in my life but at age eighty-six I haven't gotten around to it yet.

In a very short time it was nearing Jeff's seventeenth birthday. When we were going home from work on a Wednesday before his birthday on Friday, Jeff invited me to his birthday "party." He explained that his grandparents and mother were preparing a family dinner for him and wanted him to invite me. Along with the five of us his uncle, aunt and two cousins would be there too. He timed his invitation well so that Mother and Dad were there to hear it first hand and said that was very nice for his family to include me. I had not been to Jeff's home before so this gave me an opportunity to meet and visit with his family.

On the way home from work on his birthday, Jeff asked if he needed to come pick me up for the party. I told him I would just walk the two blocks and promised not to be late. As soon as I had bathed and put on fresh clothes, I headed for Jeff's house.

I noticed three cars in the driveway — Jeff's grandfather's Plymouth, a beat up old Ford and a late model blue Cadillac convertible with the white top down. I found out later that the Ford belonged to his uncle's family and his mother's boss had let her bring the convertible (which he had been driving) home that evening for Jeff to use since it was his birthday.

After I met all the members of his family, we assembled in the backyard for an outdoor dinner of fried chicken, potato salad, corn-on-the-cobb, pickles, fresh onions, radishes and hot rolls. Then, of course, there was the big birthday cake with ice cream to top it off. Jeff's grandmother said she had been saving back a little sugar for months to make this cake and icing and added it would probably be some months before they had a cake again.

We had a great time stuffing ourselves while Jeff's mother and grandmother guided the conversation along so that their family learned about me and my family and I learned a lot about their family. By the time we had finished eating and visiting, I had found out that both his uncle and aunt worked at the same defense plant in the bay area on different shifts. They also lived nearby to their work. The girl cousin was a few months older than Jeff and had just graduated from high school. She was going to a business college in Alvin and was planning to go to work at the same plant as her mother and dad when she finished the one year course. The boy, a few months younger than me, had just finished his sophomore year in high school and would be a junior when school started. He was working around their neighborhood this summer doing yard work and odd jobs for the neighbors. They seemed like very nice people and made it plain that before the war they had a struggle to make a living and were now enjoying having a good income but were saving most it for after the war when times might be hard again.

After everyone had finished their cake and ice cream, we all pitched in and helped clean up the table and put all the tables and chairs back in their places. Jeff said we would take a spin in the convertible and see how it felt to be a big shot. The four of us teens headed for the car and Jeff pulled the driver seat forward and pushed us two younger boys in the back seat as the girl went around the car and took the front passenger seat. He started the car and drove up the street going very slowly by the Smith's so if anyone was outside there or at the garage apartment we could wave at them. I was glad that my parents didn't see us, but I really didn't know why.

We made a loop or two around town and then Jeff headed the car out of town on the highway toward Galveston. Jeff said we might as well make a night of it and Jill, the girl, asked if anyone had any money with them. I checked my supply and said I had a little over eight dollars, then Jeff said he had the twenty dollar bill his grandfather had given him for his birthday. She said that ought to be enough for us to have a great time. Out on the highway the wind was really blowing on us so James and I ducked down some behind the front seats to keep the wind off us as Jeff cruised down the causeway toward Galveston where we headed straight for the seawall street and followed it to Stewart Beach. We turned around and went back the way we came slowly taking in the sights from a different direction.

Jill directed him to pull over near the carnival rides so we could take that in. She took the twenty dollar bill from Jeff so I handed her my eight dollars too assuming she would be in charge of the money. She just smiled and thanked me as Jeff and James headed toward the rows of booths with the types of games we expected. We fell in behind the two and we all walked along with the crowd with none of our four stopping to play or be taken in by any of the hustlers. When we got to the end of that row we were at the entrance to the roller coaster. I had never ridden such a big roller coaster and really didn't want to ride this one but Jill walked up and bought four tickets. I was watching Jill while Jeff and James were looking up at the huge maze of timbers and I heard James say "That is some ride — I can't wait to get back home and tell my friends that I rode it." Jill pipped up "It's the world's largest wooden roller coaster according to the ads and I believe them." I was trying to keep my Adam's apple from taking a dive to my stomach as I realized there was no way to back out without losing face. I was kind of pushed by Jill into the front row of a car and the other two fell in behind us. It was a slow pull up the first "hill" which seemed to take forever. At the top we could see for miles — water, waves, land, streets and lights everywhere. Then, all of a sudden, it felt like the car fell out below us as we raced down. The hills didn't seem to get any better, they just kept on taking my breath away. I was certainly glad Jill was so friendly since I had never clung so tightly to a girl before. She just smiled and laughed at me.

When we got to our starting point, Jill handed the gateman another two dollars so we could stay in the car and go again. By then I was so sick and weak I didn't care anymore because I didn't think I could stand up and walk so I endured it a second time, but this time I was afraid I would throw up on Jill. By some miracle I kept it in check, finished the ride and was able to get off with the others — as they gushed about what fun it was. I think the people lined up to get on the car, watching us get off, probably wondered if I was that green color naturally.

We took a turn through another part of the park and headed back toward the entrance when Jill stopped and yelled "Let's ride the Loop de Loop!" I looked at this contraption and saw what appeared to be a small airplane cabin, without a tail or engine, hanging down nearly to the ground with the door standing open exposing four seats — two on each side facing each other. Looking up, about forty feet in the air above this one stood another matching plane, but with the door closed. They were connected with some metal structure that allowed them to spin when power was applied. I turned "yellow" at this sight and said "There is no way I am getting in that thing." Jeff and Jill just laughed at me but James said he was with me on that so Jill handed the attendant a dollar bill as she and Jeff slipped into the little plane.

I spied an empty concrete bench midway in the walkway, nudged James, pointed to it, walked over and sat down. James followed me and we watched as the top plane slowly made a half circle and the two swapped positions. Three grownups got out of the one on the ground and were replaced by four kids a couple or three years younger than James and me. We looked at each other with surprised expressions on our faces. As we looked back at the Loop de Loop we saw the planes slowly making a circle and began to gain speed as it went into the second and third circles. It kept getting faster and faster until about the sixth or seventh circle when it began to slow down and then stopped with Jeff and Jill's plane in the grounded position. We walked over to meet them as they headed toward us in a rather wobbly walk. They were laughing at each other as they each caught a hold of James and me to steady them.

We were all laughing by the time we left the amusement park and as we neared the car Jill said "I know where we can go now" — and we walked past the car. About a block later she turned into a brightly lighted entrance and we walked into a very large dimly lighted room with many tables of seated people. She kept on going to her right and I saw a more lighted bar across the end of the room with people standing and seated on bar stools. Jill moved down the bar until she found three empty stools and sat on the middle one placing Jeff on her left and me on her right, leaving James standing between and behind her and me. I kept looking around for the police to come and get us since we were underage to be in a bar — but I soon learned there was no such thing as being underage at that time in Galveston.

In a couple of minutes a burly bartender with a bald head stopped in front of Jeff and asked what we were having. Jeff gave him an order, then Jill and she nodded her head at James and said what he would have. The bar tender moved down in front of me and said "You?" I wasn't able to tell for sure what the others had ordered and the only drink I could think of by name was a whiskey sour so I said "Whiskey sour." James and I were all eyes taking in the scene while we waited for our drinks. Jeff and Jill were talking but I couldn't tell what about due to the noise being pretty load with so many people around. In a few minutes the bar tender set a tray with our drinks on it in front of me and James. He placed Jeff's and Jill's in front of them, picked up the tray, placing mine in front of me and then James's in front of him.

The drinks were all very colorful with mine being the smallest. My liquid was kind of a murky color with an oversized toothpick loaded with little chunks of fruit standing up in the middle. I took a swallow and it nearly gaged me so I ate the good tasting fruit off the toothpick. The bartender would come and stand in front of me every now and then with his elbow resting on the bar near a bowl of eggs sitting on the bar. I had picked up one and was looking it over when he came to rest once. James asked him what the eggs were for and he replied "Eating." Then he went on to say that some people liked boiled eggs to eat with their drinks so he (probably actually meaning the bar) provided them complimentary. In a little bit he looked back at us again and said "You can have one if you like." As James and I cracked, peeled and placed the shells on a napkin the bartender came back and placed a couple of little shakers on the bar and said "They taste better with a little salt and pepper."

He looked over at Jill and Jeff and asked if there would be anything else.

Jeff said give us another, Jill nodded but I said "I think I will pass," then Jill pointing at James said "He will too." James and I ate another egg each while they finished their second drinks. Jill put down a dollar bill as a tip, picked up our check and paid it at the cashier's stand then led us out the door headed for the car. As we walked Jill told us about the party they had at that place after her high school graduation ceremony. Nearly all the boys were leaving for the armed forces right away and they all wondered what lay in the future. She ended up by saying that most got pretty drunk but she was thankful nothing bad happened. I wondered all the way home what she meant by "nothing bad" as scene after scene flashed behind my closed eyelids of things that could have happened.

The next morning I was rather slow in getting ready for Dad's and my Saturday work at the base. Mother was eager to get started on her Saturday cleaning and washing before she had any visitors since she used that day each week to do our laundry and cleaning of the little apartment. She finally rushed me out to get in the car and leave with Dad. On the way to the base he asked if we had a big night out. I told him about our visit to the amusement park but made no mention of the bar we visited. It didn't do any good for on the way home he said that he didn't want me going to Galveston with anyone except our family. He looked me straight in the eyes and asked if I understood him and I could tell he knew all about my adventure in the bar. I answered him in a weak but promising tone of voice "Yes sir." Evidently a sailor or marine that knew me and my Dad had seem me there and made some remark to him about it. I thought what a small world.

For some reason, during the course of my work, I began to make a lot more deliveries across to the blimp hanger. I guess more of those people found out that we would deliver so they started using our service. Since the truck was so big and I still felt nervous driving it, I never drove it into the hanger. I would park it at a corner of the hanger and use a hand truck or dolly to push the big boxes and packages of material to go to places in the hanger. Jeeps and trucks would zip past me and I could tell that some of them wondered why I parked there and not inside the hanger as they did. I just couldn't get up enough nerve to drive into the midst of so much activity inside the hanger. I noticed an officer riding a Cushman motor scooter, painted the same Navy gray as the Reo and the other Jeeps and trucks, would always wave at me or beep his horn. I had no idea why, so one day as I was visiting with a sailor in one of the shops where I was making a delivery, I asked him did he know who the officer was. He said yes that he was Lt. Byrd — a very friendly and popular officer on the base. He went on to tell me that he was the courier pilot that flew to Corpus Christi every day one or more times to get and take base orders back and forth as that was the command center for Hitchcock. He had one of the few airplanes on the base and kept in on a runway in front of the blimp hanger ready at all times to take off if needed. With this information I started waving back at Lt. Byrd since I was now sure that I wasn't doing something wrong as to the reason for his waving or honking.

One day while in the hanger I noticed his scooter parked near the shop where I had just made a delivery. I stopped and was having a look at it when Lt. Byrd walked up. He said "Well, what do you think about my scooter, kid?" I said I thought it was pretty nifty and I hoped to get me one when I went off to college. And I added "As they say in their ads, it's cheaper to operate than shoe leather." He said that I seemed to know a lot about it and I told him I had sent off for their literature as well as the King Midget cars I had read about in Popular Mechanics magazine. This turned into our discussions about scooters, motorcycles and cars. Several times after this he would drop by the warehouse and give me a magazine about motorcycles, cars and such.

One day I was in the hanger when Lt. Byrd walked by and in a low voice said "Hang around a little while and watch the excitement." He then walked off without another word. I wondered what was happening so I briskly started to the other end of the hanger as if I had been sent on an errand, turned and started to go back. About that time I heard this loud buzzing and knew it was an airplane. It increased until it was a deafening roar and a rush of air when an airplane flew just above our heads through the hanger. It was Lt. Byrd's plane and he had flown through the hanger!

All the sailors and civilian employees cheered and began laughing. I heard a sailor near me say "Lt. Byrd won't be laughing when the old man gets through with him for that stunt."

I went back to the warehouse and was telling the counterman what had happened. As I started to walk to the files to record the day's transactions, he caught me by the forearm and in a very low voice said "Don't tell anyone else that Lt. Byrd told you something was going to happen." I didn't see what difference it could make but I did as he had requested. The next time I saw Lt. Byrd he seemed kind of subdued but the incident was never discussed between us. I did notice that he still had his First Lt.'s bars on his uniform.

A few days later Lt. Byrd came by the warehouse and asked to speak to the manager. The manager, as always, in his office listening to everything going on at the counter, came to his office door and motioned for the Lt. to come around the counter and into his office. They were in the office for a while and when they both came out the manager walked over to me and said "Go with Lt. Byrd, he needs your help for a few minutes." I wondered what was up but only answered with "Yes sir" and followed the Lt. outside. When we approached the parking spaces he pointed to a bright and shiny Jeep and said "How do you like my new ride?" Before I could answer he said "Get in and I will take you for a spin." I still wondered what was up because I didn't think he had come over to just give me a ride, but I kept my mouth shut and climbed in. We rode over to the motor pool and he parked in the vehicle yard, got out and motioned for me to follow. As we rounded the line of vehicles, there on the end was his scooter. He reached in a pocket took out a key, handed it to me and said "The scooter is yours to use at the warehouse. The manager said you would be responsible for it and house it in the warehouse when you weren't using it. Take good care of it." Before I could even thank him he wheeled and headed for his Jeep. I walked around the scooter a couple of times looking at everything and touching it here and there to be sure everything was tight and in order. I sat down on it, put the kickstand up with my toe, balanced it carefully and bounced on it a couple of times and inserted the key. As I turned on the key I kicked the starter and the engine came alive. I grinned really big, gave it some gas, picked up my feet and rode out of the vehicle parking lot. As I went through the gate

I noticed Lt. Byrd was still sitting in his Jeep, watching me with a big grin on his face.

My sixteenth birthday finally rolled around. It too was an outdoor dinner similar to Jeff's but in the Smith's backyard. Mother's cousin Verna and her family, along with Mrs. Smith, were responsible for most of the food and work since Mother had a full time job. Grandma, Auntie and the boys didn't come down since they were making their last visit for the summer in a couple of weeks. Mother invited Jeff, and through him his two cousins, but that was about all. It turned out to be a yard full and everyone seemed to enjoy it. As the party was winding down Verna had to stand up and announce that Floyd had turned sixteen and probably never really been kissed so everyone was to give him a kiss. I was really embarrassed with even the males giving me a peck on the forehead or cheek. Only Jill gave me a big juicy kiss on the mouth and everyone laughed. Anne, after her mother, was last and she just gave me a peck on the cheek, but we both blushed and everyone applauded.

The summer of 1944 was drawing to a close and we were getting ready to go back to LC for my senior year and many new adventures. But now, some seventy years later, there are times when I wake up at one or two in the night and wonder what became of the people of my summer of 1944 — Lt. Byrd, the warehouse manager, Jeff and his cousins and ….. especially Anne.

THE 1944-45 SCHOOL YEAR

As August and the summer went slipping by, I began looking forward to returning to East Texas, school, friends, relatives, my horse, chickens and life in general at LC. I am sure Mother too wanted to be in her own home, visiting friends and relatives and again assuming the full time role of mother to two boys without a father who was engaged in the war effort. We would have to leave him behind for an indefinite period of time. With the war still going full speed we had to look forward to an unknown future and make the best of our opportunities.

The Allies were pushing the big offensive in Europe since the decision had been made that they would crush the enemy there first and then destroy the Japanese forces in the Pacific. On the home front Americans carefully followed the war's daily news with their radios and newspapers, getting both the good and bad from the many fronts. The American forces, along with their friendly allies, were slowly closing the ring around their enemies in Europe — but it was a slow and bloody endeavor. In the meantime we all did what we could to help the war effort.

My first knowledge of the Texas State Guard came one Friday afternoon in August when an Army truck parked in front of our warehouse and a guy in Army fatigues came in and asked where he could find a couple of men that he was supposed to pick up. I recognized the names of the two as being members of the ground crew that Jeff worked with. I told him they were back of the warehouse if they had come in yet and offered to show him where they usually "hung out." He said he could probably find it and thanked me for the information. A few minutes later he and the two (dressed in fatigues like the first man and each with a bag in a hand) came back through the warehouse, got in the truck and they drove off. I finished my closing duties and waited for Jeff to go with me to the Administration Bldg. to meet Mother and Dad for our trip home.

On the way Jeff explained to me that the two who left in the Army truck were members of the Texas State Guard and were going to Camp Wallace for a week-end of special training. He said he thought they went for training or maneuvers every other week-end and had drills one evening every week. He had two friends in his class at school who were also members of that same group and had told him what it was all about. He told me that when the Texas National Guard was taken into the Army at the first of the war, the Texas State Guard was formed for home defense and there were units throughout the state. He wanted to join the Navy when he graduated from high school and now he had decided he would join the State Guard when he started back to school to feel like he was helping the war effort some and to get a little military experience for later. His grandfather had agreed that the training would be good for him. His two friends had been in the State Guard ever since they turned sixteen (minimum age to enlist) and now Jeff wished he had done the same. I said if I were to stay at Alvin for my last year of high school I would probably join too since I had just turned sixteen. Neither Mother nor Dad said anything but I knew I would have to have their permission to do so.

We left Alvin early in the morning on the last Saturday in August for East Texas to give us a week or two to get ready for school to start. Sunday morning Mother laid out our dress clothes and announced for us to get ready for Sunday school and church and then to Grandma's for Sunday dinner. Despite our half-hearted grumbling and complaining, we complied. We were really happy to be going to familiar places and visiting with old friends.

In my Sunday school class the teacher noticed three returnees after some time of absence and asked each what we had been doing while being gone. Gene Weaver told of working on his grandparent's farm in Corsicana and then I reported on my working for the Navy at Hitchcock. Pete Fuller then related that he had been training mostly on week-ends with the State Guard so had been missing church. I had my mind mostly on what he had told during the rest of the lesson. As soon as Sunday school was over, I cornered him for more information on the Guard and we "sat out" church on the rock wall in front and he told me all about the company stationed in Overton. It met every Tuesday evening in the American Legion building and most week-ends at various places. We were still busy talking when church let out and Mother came checking on me. I promised Pete I would be there early Tuesday so he could show me around and help me join up. Of course I had some explaining to do on the way to Grandma's but Mother seemed to be very understanding and did not discourage me about my dreams of joining the Guard.

While we were at Grandma's, I checked on George and he looked at me as if to ask "What happened to you?" We had moved him and Sonny's Tony to Grandma's at the beginning of the summer so we would have them there all summer before we knew anything about my staying in Alvin and working at the blimp base. I promised him I would ride him back to LC the next opportunity I had — maybe the next Saturday or Sunday. Later when we were leaving for home I imagined he had his eyes glued on our car until it was out of sight.

Monday we were busy getting things back in order after our long absence. I didn't visit with anyone until it was almost dark when Marcus Carter came to the front door calling me. I met him outside and we talked for a good while, sitting on the front steps. He asked me if I knew football practice had started that afternoon and when I admitted not knowing he said that was what he thought since I wasn't there and he had seen our car at the house on Sunday. I told him about the Guard in Overton and that if I got in I probably wouldn't have time for football too. He was very disappointed to hear that since he was looking forward to us playing together with Novice Davis — making up what the year before we called the "terrible trio." We called ourselves that because we weren't very good but probably not terrible either. Marcus said he wanted us called that this year for the havoc we would cause the opposing teams since he thought we had great potential. I told him he would probably be very good but Novice and I would never be any good since we didn't take football very seriously and I had might as well not waste my time on it. He said if we really tried and put our minds to it we could be pretty good also so I didn't try to argue with him any more about my playing. He told me that two-a-days started tomorrow and gave me the times, etc. I decided I would just not show up and let it go at that.

The next day we worked around the house all day with me working in the yard mostly getting rid of weeds and overgrowth that had occurred during the summer. My garden was pretty well gone so I made no attempt to revive it, deciding to wait until spring and renew it then. I had my mind on seeing Pete at the Guard meeting late that afternoon and getting very excited about it. I discussed it with Mother and she said it was all right with her and Dad. She told me to go into Overton in the car when I felt like it was time.

About 3:00 PM I decided to quit my work in the yard and went inside to bath, put on fresh clothes and get ready to go to town. I left around 3:30 and was at the American Legion Hall well before 4:00. There were a lot of men there, nearly all wearing Guard uniforms, milling around, talking and smoking except for a small group in the front left of the building standing or sitting around a couple of domino tables watching a game on one of the tables. They tended to be quite elderly, dressed in old overalls or kackies, smoking pipes or cigars, some drinking a coke, others a strawberry, orange or such and most laughing and carrying on about the game in progress. As I timidly edged my way into the building, one of the guys in uniform asked if he could help me. I told him I was there to meet Pete Fuller. He said Pete should be there any minute and if I would hang around the front door I would see him when he came in. As he motioned toward the front door, he added, "Here he comes now." I thanked him and saw Pete about the same time he saw me.

He said he had come from football practice which had just started but the coach let him off for the Guard meeting and three or four team mates would be right behind him. Overton too had started two-a-days as had LC. He said the coach was very accommodating for the players that were also Guard members. Pete directed me over to a table in the back near the corner explaining that this is where we would find the company clerk who had all the papers needed and see that I was properly signed up. Nearby was a door with a Quartermaster sign over it that I would get my stuff issued from later. I found out that there was much more than just signing up. After completing a lot of paper work, I had to go for a physical exam by the old doctor in his office above Pure Drug, get issued uniforms, equipment (including a big rifle and bayonet but no bullets) and it seemed like more than a dozen other things. After the exam by the doctor, he signed my paper as approved but told me I needed glasses. He then wrote out an order for a pair of "military style" glasses and instructed me to go to the optical place in Kilgore and get fitted for the glasses — further explaining that I would have to pay for them myself since they would be my personal property but would get them at a deeply discounted government price since they were for use in the Guard. After all this I was finally taken to a big fellow with a lot of stripes on his sleeves who assigned me to a squad. I had expected to be assigned with Pete but my squad was made up of seven or eight new recruits and we would go through some basic training before we participated with the others. Two of them were New London High School students, a couple of older men from Henderson and the others from different places in Smith, Gregg or Rusk counties. After meeting each other we were directed outside to a little space between the Hall and the building next door. A corporal gave us the background of the Guard, its mission and our responsibilities as members. He said the Captain would administer our oath at the next meeting in front of the whole company if our papers cleared us for the organization. He was very business-like and made a really good talk. He told us to study the booklet given us that explained the Manuel of Arms and learn all of it for the next week. It was about this time that I realized the Guard wasn't going to just be a lot of fun but we were expected to work our tails off. Then our leader took us to the alley behind the Hall and introduced us to "military drills."

After about an hour or so of this a whistle called us along with the other squads from different activities to general assembly and closing exercises for that evening's meeting. The big man with all the stripes on his sleeves was the one that called the assembly to order and conducted the business. During this session we heard from our company Lt. and Captain. They explained what activities were scheduled for the month of September and how important it was for everyone to attend all functions and activities if at all possible. The schedules had been carefully worked out to allow for school and most workplace calendars so there shouldn't be too many conflicts and a closing reminder that those who would like to sabotage the oil field did not take holidays. Our squad leaders gave us a mimeographed set of papers with the scheduled calendar of events and instructions on what to do to be prepared with when and where.

After we broke ranks Pete came over to where I was and said he was headed back to school for a few minutes to meet with their coach and the other football players. He said if I had any questions or needed any other information to phone my squad leader whose name, address, and phone number was listed on the handout. I thanked him for his help and said I would see him next Tuesday. He said to study my handout and notice that we had a meeting all day Saturday and to be ready. He then added that the following weekend was the only free weekend we had during September — and with that he waved, turned and hurried off with about four others I recognized as Overton High School students. I gathered all my stuff, took it to the car, loaded it on the back seat and headed for home and a late supper.

As Mother warmed my supper she had me recite everything that had transpired at the Guard meeting injecting a question every now and then for more details as I recalled it all for her. She was particularly pleased to know about the glasses — thinking maybe this would get me to wear them now since I hadn't done so since about the eighth grade and she knew I needed them all the time. She said we would go see about them the next day and maybe they would be ready in time for school to start. We chatted while I ate my supper and Sonny was sitting also at the table with a funny book in his hands but his eyes were mostly going from one of us to the other as he listened to the conversation. As I finished and Mother began to gather the dishes up, we heard a knock on the front door — Sonny jumped up saying he would get it but Mother slowed him down with an arm around his neck and told him to let me do it.

Sonny was standing by my side as I opened the door and I was surprised to see a classmate, Charles Bufkin, standing there just grinning. I couldn't help showing my surprise but was able to greet him and invite him in. He said he had to get on home but wanted to see me for a couple of minutes. As we stood there I replied "What about?" He said that I had not been at football practice and they needed me since they were short on experienced players. I told him I wasn't very experienced like Billy Cox, James Lloyd Billingsly and himself — they would be the big stars with Billy at quarterback, James Lloyd at receiving and running end and Bufkin as the powerhouse fullback. He said they were short a center and coach Shanks had told Billy and him that he had thought that I would probably do there but since I hadn't showed up he would have to look elsewhere. Marcus had overheard the conversation and told Bufkin and Billy that I was home and he had talked to me.

We both just stood there a couple of minutes looking each other in the eye and I was turning things over in my mind while I am sure he was wondering what else to say. Finally he said "Floyd, we need you, the school needs you, don't you want to play? Billy and I talked it over and we want you, we need you." I slowly came up with "I wonder what Coach Shanks thinks?" Bufkin blurted out "He sent me to get you" and with that he turned and walked off. I just stood there until Sonny tugged on my arm and said "What you gonna do?" I said "I don't know" as I closed the door. We walked back in the kitchen and sat down. Mother had cleaned up from my supper and said "Sonny you need to bathe and get ready for bed and Floyd doesn't need to be far behind you." She didn't say any more so I was pretty sure she had heard all that took place at the front door and would leave it up to me to make my own decisions. I knew I had a tough night ahead of me.

After I was ready for bed I walked into the kitchen to get a drink of water from the milk bottle I kept in the refrigerator. Mother was sitting at the kitchen table reading her Bible but her eyes followed me to the refrigerator and stayed on me until I closed the door, then she said "Sit down a minute, I have a couple of questions I want to ask you." As I sat down across from her I was thinking here it comes now but she only wanted to know if I knew any of the people at the Guard meeting. I told her that besides Pete I knew two of the other Overton High School football players from seeing them around town and playing ball against them the year before and there were two men from our church that I recognized but didn't know their names. She seemed satisfied with that and did not ask another question. So, based on the briefing by the corporal, my squad leader, the Lt.'s and Captain's remarks and what Pete had told me I pretty much outlined for her all I knew about the Guard.

The two commissioned officers evidently worked for the same independent oil company, lived in the same company camp (a little behind the Dickerson place just off the Sexton City/Pitner's Junction highway) where the Guard vehicles and equipment too large for storing in the

Legion Hall are located, were engineers and graduates of Texas A&M. The Captain must have been the superintendent of his oil company for the East Texas field and between that company and the Guard he must have worked day and night. Due to their essential work to produce oil for the war machine they were not in the army but were putting their military training and experience to use through the Guard. Several of their company employees were also members of the Guard. Their company evidently helped support the Guard considerably by heavily contributing of their resources.

The troops were made up of ten to twelve high school age boys, a dozen or so in their twenties or early thirties with the rest mostly from the late thirties to probably around fifty-five. At least two or three of the early twenties were ex-servicemen who had been discharged due to injuries or wounds but could still pass the Guard medical exam and wanted to continue their contribution to the war effort. Many of the older ones were veterans of World War I and over time we heard many, many stories from them about their overseas service back then.

I went to my room and got the handout from the meeting and gave it to Mother to read. Then I left Mother reading it and feeling I had answered all her questions that I could, went to bed. For a while — maybe an hour or two — I lay there thinking about the start of my new school year and how I would handle it. Finally, I must have drifted off to sleep — before I heard Mother go to bed.

Early Wednesday morning I awoke to the smell of bacon frying and glanced at my unset alarm clock. It was seven on the nose. I got up, dressed and made the bathroom — then to the kitchen. Mother just smiled and said she thought I might want a good early breakfast to start the day. As I sat down she put a pan of her fluffy biscuits on the table, a plate with two over easy eggs and some bacon at my place, went to the refrigerator for a bottle of milk to set next to the empty glass already sitting by my silverware. I said a soft "Thanks."

We didn't talk any while I ate my breakfast, Mother just watched me

— taking a sip of coffee every now and then. When I finished eating I simply said I was going to brush my teeth and then I thought I would go see about football practice. Mother stood up too and said "Good, when you get back we will go to Kilgore and check on the glasses." As I walked down the hall to the bath, I was wondering what she meant by the "good." The tooth brushing? The football? Both? Mother never wanted me to play football but she never put up any objections since she knew how much my Dad wanted me to do so ever since I was in the sixth grade and we started organized football in school. He had pushed me every year and every year I had a little less interest since I didn't think I would ever be any good — being a little undersized for my grade and no speed demon either. Maybe Mother thought it would help me develop physically since I had grown quite a bit during and after football season last year. Could be but now I was going to play because there were others who wanted me to and I felt too that they needed me. So, I pushed Sonny aside as he was trying to get in the bathroom as I was trying to come out — with a feeling that I had important things to do and headed for school.

It was good to see so many old friends and feel like I belonged here with them. One of the first things I noticed was that we had a lot more players than I expected. I mentioned that to Novice and he said if I had been there yesterday I would know why. He explained that the coach had revamped things by bringing all the freshman up with us instead of the previous practice of just using the largest ones and those with great potential. The 7th & 8th graders would play what had been called Jr. High, and the 9th grade would be with the high school team. There was a good crop of 9th graders and this increased our numbers considerably.

One problem this increase in numbers created was a shortage of equipment. Since I hadn't been there the day before when equipment was passed out, I had to get mine from the left overs. I did fairly well till it came to shoes, I finally came up with a matching pair but they were a mess. With the war going on we just couldn't get any new equipment and the old stuff was falling apart. I didn't want to complain so I got an extra pair of shoe laces and tied these beat-up shoes on my feet and tried not to be late on the field for practice. Everything went pretty well during practice and then we had closing exercises with wind sprints and such. This nearly did me in but I was still standing (barely) when the coach announced that everyone could go in except for — then he would call a name, the number of laps and what for. The last name called was mine, five laps for missing practice yesterday. Bufkin spoke up with "But Coach, he wasn't a member of the team yesterday!" Coach shot back "He should have been!" I said "Let it go Bufkin," turned and started a lap. I decided I would run those laps if they killed me, and believe me, I surely felt like I was going to die but I drug them out till I finished and headed for the showers. As I passed through the gym door I saw Coach Shanks standing outside where he could see me finish my laps. I thought to myself that he is probably thinking I won't be back for the afternoon session. But I said to myself "I will show him. I will be back and I'll be early!"

When I got to the house — remember we lived just across the highway from the school — I stepped into the living room and dropped in a chair, closed my eyes and let the room spin a little. In a few minutes I felt like I had landed on earth again so I looked around the room. Mother was sitting in her favorite rocking chair knitting something or other. She didn't say anything until she was satisfied that I was fully with it. She softly asked "Rough practice?" I said "You better believe it." She went back to her knitting and in a few minutes she added that when I felt up to it we would go to Kilgore. I told her I was ready so she said to go get Sonny from the back yard and head for the car.

We ordered the glasses, bought groceries at Safeway and stopped by a drug store on the way home. After our lunch of sandwiches and potato salad Mother suggested I lie down and rest a while — which I did since the afternoon football practice wouldn't start until 4:00 PM. Sure enough, I was the first one for the practice. I was there waiting for the coaches to unlock the gym when they got there. That afternoon practice and the next two days went pretty smoothly, and I rounded out the week with a very busy Saturday with the Guard out on a farm northeast of Overton where they met quite frequently for drilling and such. We set up day camp and while we were busy with our activities the company cook (Rowland York's dad, Rowland being one of the Overton football players) and his crew cooked our delicious steak lunch with biscuits and gravy from scratch. I learned this was one of the treats to be expected with our Guard activities.

I was very, very tired when I got home again Saturday night. I told Mother that I would wait until the next week-end for Sonny and me to ride our horses home from Grandma's. She said that would be fine since there was no rush. We went to bed early, getting ready for another week back home and the start of school. We made church and Grandma's for Sunday dinner and then spent the rest of the day just taking it easy.

Monday was registration day at school. Mother took Sonny to enroll him while I went to the high school and picked up my packet at the library to fill out. I was undecided about an elective I needed to take and decided to confer with Mother about which I should take. I proceeded to go back to the house and wait for Mother and Sonny to return from his getting enrolled. They were on their way home and we arrived about the same time. Mother studied the elective possibilities and promptly recommended the typing one offered. I told her that none of the boys took typing and I would be out of place with a bunch of girls. She said surely in this day and time boys would be taking typing since it had gotten to be so important in all lines of work. I said if I took typing I would look like a sissy. Mother said that was foolish, with me a football player not many would say I was a sissy. She said if someone did just invite them out on the football field to take a round or two with you and see who was a sissy. Then she added, "Besides, not long ago your Dad and I were discussing my struggling with learning to type for my Navy job when he said the boys in the Marines that could type always got the better assignments — so it would be a good thing to have." I didn't have much of an argument for this so I gathered up my papers and went back to school and finished my paper work — including registering for the typing class. I never regretted this move since this class turned out to be probably the most useful class of any I had in school when I finally got serious with my college classes and a career. The next day when I went to the typing class, I found there were three other boys in it. One, a senior like myself, and two juniors. None of us fit the sissy mode.

Since we had finished two-a-days, our one practice for the day was long and grueling — lasting until dark enough to turn on the lights some evenings. We were toughening up and getting into pretty good shape by now — starting to run some simple plays. Coach assigned a freshman player to each of the seniors and the starting juniors, both offence and defense, to shadow them so they would begin to know something of the position and were called the backup. These were not necessarily the one that would substitute for that player in a game situation. Coach Shanks tried a lot of things to give a player the opportuniy to understand the game better. In this case sometimes he would have the backup in a practice play so a player could see how the play looked to the coach. In those days we didn't have films, TV and such as today where kids see so much sports and know so much about them. Most of my team never saw any football games other than the ones they played in until after their playing time was over.

I was tabbed the starting center and had Dan Page assigned as my backup. Dan proved to be very good at any task he was asked to perform. He had desire, ability and willingness to work to get better. Although Dan and I were never very close, I feel I need to tell you a little about him and his football career. On Wednesday that first week of practice after two-a-days, Coach announced we would have a scrimmage with and at Kilgore on Saturday (although Kilgore was a much larger school than LC and in a higher level of competition, we were always able to give them a pretty tough time in a scrimmage to start off the season). He gave us the schedule and plan for the trip, with the addition that everyone must go. Then at Friday's practice he announced his appointments as team captains. The first was Billy Cox, quarterback, Charles Bufkin, fullback, and then to my great surprise I was named as the third one. Although we three were thought of only as offence, due to our positions, Bufkin and I both played defense full-time so we were both on the field most of the time.

When Saturday rolled around and we were in the gym getting our gear together to get on the bus, Steve Hughes (another very promising freshman and the running buddy of Dan Page) came up to me holding out Dan's equipment bag. He said "Dan asked me to get you to put these on the bus for him. His dad won't let him go to the scrimmage until he hoes the garden this morning. He plans to flag the bus down near his house at Laird Hill." This kind of hit me the wrong way so I told him to put the bag on the bus himself and turned back to my packing. Steve put his hand on my shoulder and walked around to my face, then said "Dan said if I did it the coach might throw a fit but felt like if you did, you're being a senior, a team captain and him your backup, the coach wouldn't say anything." I could tell he was pleading, almost begging, and this weakened me so that I said to set the bag down and I would get it on the bus.

I don't know if the Coach noticed me carrying two bags on the bus or not but nothing was said about it. I did notice that as the bus slowed near Laird Hill to pick up Dan the coach turned and gave me a questioning look. When the door opened Dan stuck his head in and asked the coach if he could get in. The coach, in a rather gruff voice, responded with a yes. I don't remember Dan even playing during the scrimmage that day but this always stuck with me that Dan would overcome difficult obstacles to play. It was about this time Coach moved Dan to the quarterback on the offensive practice team to prepare our defensive unit to face upcoming teams. I think the next year, as a sophomore, he was the team's starting quarterback until he graduated. After I graduated and went off to UT Austin, I didn't keep up with Dan but I knew that he and Steve went to UT and played there after I left. I know there were also at least two from their team that also played at LSU — so that high school team evidently was a very good one. Dan always impressed me as a natural athlete with a born desire to play.

Just a few weeks ago during a visit to the Texas Hill Country I was rummaging through some books about Texas at a very good bookstore in downtown Kerrville when I came across the LONG LIVE THE LONGHORNS! — 100 Years of Texas Football by John Maher & Kirk Bohls. I thought it would be some interesting reading so I bought it along with four or five more books. That night in my motel room I was looking through it and reading about the 1951 team when I found: "...Quarterback Dan Page came off the bench to help Texas pull out a 14-6 win over Rice... Turnovers doomed the Longhorns in an 18 — 6 loss to Baylor. Page, though, then revived Texas's dormant passing game with a couple of touchdowns, including a 61-yarder to ALL SWC back Gib Dawson, to stun TCU. Texas's 32 — 21 victory dealt the eventual SWC champion Horned Frogs their only league loss of the year." I said to myself "That sounds like the Dan Page I knew — always ready when called on."

I don't remember much about individual games during that fall of 1944, but there is one I will never forget. It was the very first game of the new season and we played at Van. They were having homecoming or some similar program and as part of it they had their Queen kick off the ball to us as part of the ceremony at the beginning of the game. The "queen" in her brilliantly white evening dress with a very large bright red corsage on her left front shoulder got a pretty good foot into the ball, and as I was standing on the right end of the receiving line it sailed just over my left side and stopped dead on the ground. I turned, jogged over to the ball and scooped it up. Without looking back at the kicking line-up, I threw it back in that direction over my shoulder. As I turned to retake my position I heard this loud gasp coming from their stands. I looked toward the kicking queen just in time to see the football strike her in the middle of her corsage, knocking her backward into a sitting position. I knew then my name was MUD.

I know they must have kicked off to us and we downed the ball in a fairly good position for the first thing I knew Billy was tapping me on the shoulder saying "Set the huddle!" I was still so embarrassed I didn't know what I was doing as we broke huddle. I got over the ball and at the signal I centered it — way over the back's head and as he scrambled for the ball we lost only about twenty yards on the play. I glanced over at our bench for I was sure the coach would be motioning for me to come out. Billy, calm as always, grabbed my arm, tugged me back in position to set the huddle again and things began to make sense. Billy said "OK, lets get it together," then he called the play and I asked, as I always did as a part of my little ritual, "Who gets the ball?" Billy would answer with the name and I would look at that individual and ask "Lead?" He would move his left or right hand to indicate which direction and if no lead he would put both hands to his midsection. I did this not because I was so stupid I couldn't remember the plays but it helped keep everyone alert as they recalled the play in their own mind and maybe everyone would be on the same page. We played on, and if I remember correctly we won this nonconference game to start the year.

The only other game from that year that I can now recall is the one with Arp. W A, my first cousin, was playing on that team so we had a little personal rivalry going before the game. Dub was about six months older than me but he was held back a year in about the second grade so that year he was a junior and I don't remember him playing the year before.

I never thought of him as much of a talker but when we got on the field for this game he was a real chatterbox. Evidently he was kind of the team cheerleader on defense. He kept it going all the time and directed most of it toward me. Since he was at a tackle position he was loud so I would get the benefit of it at my center position. He was saying such things as "Hey big boy center show us something — we thought you were a hot shot but all you do is hang over the ball!" And other similar stuff.

His talk began to have its effect on me and I soon had enough of it but didn't want to let it show. Finally, near the half, I had to do something so I cornered Billy on the way to the huddle and said "I've had enough of that loud mouth tackle and want to shut him up. Let me pull, stand him up and Bufkin pop him a good one. OK?" Billy glanced over at the bench as if wondering what the coach would think and then turned back to me and said "OK." He mapped it out in the huddle and I bent over the ball with a little laugh. When I charged Dub I didn't get a very good hit on him and he got his hands in my armpits and held me so that I didn't get him turned much and Bufkin blasted into both of us as we were turned just a little. We both went down and Bufkin thundered over us for about three yards on sheer power. As Dub and I came up, we both had a face full of dirt and a bloody nose — he said "I sure hope y'all don't call that play again." I just grinned at him, but I had enough of that play also. Years later we would laugh about that game and call that play the "Elliott Earth Quake."

One other incident I do recall now occurred while we were playing Overton at our place. I was the only football player from LC in our Guard company while there were several from Overton in it. During the game a few of them were good naturedly kidding me that led one of their oversized guards to think it was open season on me. He never said anything but kept laying an elbow or knee into me every chance he got. Finally while I was pinned down in a pileup in the line he took a couple of pokes at my exposed face. A couple of my fellow guardsmen happened to see this and they grabbed him and drug him back about five yards, yanked him up and dressed him down good — even threatening to break his neck if he didn't lay off me. A ref nearby said to one of the guardsmen "Good show." Needless to say, I didn't have any trouble from that fat boy again.

The Sunday following the Saturday scrimmage turned out to be a beautiful fall day so Sonny and I rode our horses from Grandma's to LC that afternoon. I remember enjoying this ride very much since it had been months since I was on horseback. I knew I wouldn't have time for much riding due to football and Guard so I sat back and enjoyed the colors and sights. Old George must have sensed my laid back mood so he too settled into a slow pokey walk also taking in the scenery. It wasn't long before Sonny said "If you guys don't pick up the pace a little we won't get home before dark." I didn't think so but I just said O K and pushed George into a little faster walk. We were home in plenty of time to eat our supper before dark and put our animals away for the night.

I kept up my football until the season was over and the Guard began to absorb more and more of my time. Policies were changing in the military as the focus of the war was changing. Now more and more of the servicemen killed overseas were being shipped back home for burial. This meant many more military funerals. Our Guard unit was being asked to furnish Honor Guards for many of these services. A squad, we called it the burial detail, was formed to be ready to service military funerals on short notice. Most of the members were high school students since they were readily available and would usually volunteer for this duty. The Lt. selected about ten of us to be in this squad and I, along with Pete Fuller, was selected as a member. Since I was one of the few members of the burial detail that had access to a car all the time (Mother saw to that) I was assigned as driver of the truck when the unit was called out. My duty was to drive our car over to where the trucks were parked, get a truck, and pick up members that needed a ride on our way to the Legion Hall where we assembled. Eventually I was put in charge of the vehicles (called the motor pool) and promoted to corporal, my highest rank until I went off to college. I had a lot of fun with my new duties, like driving the officers around in their Jeep and getting a Scout 45 (motorcycle) to use in checking on our vehicles when we were traveling and running errands for the company, etc.

It wasn't all just fun because we did a lot of serious training and worked pretty hard at some of it. But for us sixteen year olds it was a glorious time. We not only had our weekend training sessions camped out but we also would go to Camp Fannin near Tyler to take part in some of their regular Army training. We crawled under live machine gun fire (just eighteen inches above the ground) with our not only hearing the bullets screaming above us but also seeing them, since every fifth one was a tracer. We also dug fox holes, got in them and had tanks run over us and then we would stand up and throw mock hand grenades (a sock with sand and a big firecracker sticking out) on the tracks of the tank. And, of course, the rifle and bayonet training. Exercises such as these impressed the seriousness of our training. We even had some minor injuries and mine was one of them. As we stood in ranks with our rifles and bayonets, somehow the fellow in front of me let his get loose. I instinctively reached out with my left hand to keep it from striking me and the bayonet stuck in my hand between the index and next finger. Not a bad wound but it bleed a lot so I was taken to the doctor. He sewed it up, bandaged it and said I would be fine. I had mixed feelings as I assumed the role of walking wounded. I got a lot of attention but also felt a little guilty since I should have grabbed the rifle a little further down rather than let the bayonet strike me.

After football season the Guard took up most of my non-school time, and being on the burial detail a lot of my school time also. The most notable thing that happened during my senior year outside of football and the Guard was that for Christmas Mother somehow, somewhere found me a new Smith-Corona portable typewriter with elite type. That little machine served to encourage me with my typing class and later, as it was always available at all hours, for me to work on projects. Many years later I traded it in on another Smith-Corona portable — an electric model.

As the school year drew to a close, we prepared for our graduation ceremony. Due to the wartime situation it was held in the afternoon. Afterward, early that evening, a fellow graduate — Gene Weaver — was killed in an auto accident. This, with the funeral in Overton and internment in Corsicana, made for quite a sad week. So we ended our school days at LC on a rather downbeat note as we all scattered for the next phase of our lives.

R. L. GOOD JR. AND MY FIRST YEAR OF COLLEGE

Recently I heard a commercial on the radio for Good's Pharmacy in Tyler. This commercial started me thinking about R. L. Good, Jr. — as I always do when I drive past the business on Beckham St. R. L.'s dad was called Ralph so most people referred to Ralph, Jr. as R. L., except for his mother who usually called him Ralph Louis.

My family and the Good family became close friends while we lived in Tyler during 1938 and 1939 — my fourth and fifth grade years. Our families attended the First Baptist Church and R. L. and I went to Gary Elementary School. Our parents were in the same Sunday school class just as R. L. and I were — my little brother and R. L.'s sister were also about the same age. During this time most of our social activities outside of the family were involved in church activities — I joined the church and was baptized at the age of ten.

After we moved back to LC from Tyler and I started the sixth grade, we continued to go to Tyler for shopping and visiting and we would drop by to see the Goods — usually at their business. This continued until I was grown and married. I remember seeing R. L. only once or twice during high school mainly due to the war conditions. About the time we were ready to graduate from our high schools Mother ran into Mrs. Good at a meeting or some gathering and they learned that both R. L. and I were planning to attend the University of Texas in Austin.

I had made a reservation at one of the dorms on the UT campus and Mother found out that R. L. (having friends on campus and being up-to-the-minute on such things) was booked in at private housing called Triangle H Courts, about three blocks off campus. A few days later I got a call from R. L. inviting me to room with him since he didn't have a room-mate as of that date. We went over to the Good's to discuss the housing situation and all decided it would work to everyone's advantage if we roomed together. I also found out that R. L. had a "new" (1942) Ford to take to school — and the car had an interesting story behind it.

I called it new since it was only about a year old and had been built completely from new parts — there weren't any new civilian automobiles after 1942 until the war ended and the 1946 models came out. At this time gasoline and tires were rationed and tires hard to find even if a person qualified for them. This car had aircraft wheels with wide tires and the body a beautiful baby blue — the most "cool" ride I had seen in those days. The previous owner had been an administrative assistant or personal secretary for some bigshot at Ford Motor Company and he had it built for him while working there. Evidently he was a draft dodger and his time was about up so he decided to make a run for Mexico. When he got to the Dallas area he sold his car to get enough money for an exile in Central America and not be so noticeable. R. L.'s dad heard about the car from a friend in Dallas and bought it for R. L.

This might sound as if R. L. was a little spoiled and I guess he was in some ways. After R. L. and I had lived together for a little while I began to understand their situation better. R. L. was a hard worker and spent nearly all his spare time working in their drug store from the time he was twelve until he went off to college. As soon as he graduated as a pharmacist he returned to the store and worked there until he died — a very young man with a family. R. L. had a heart condition — congenital I think — that required him to take a lot of medication daily. He looked very robust, a little on the fleshy side, and usually slightly flushed. He knew he would be 4F when we registered for the draft and he could make his plans without worrying about military service (which I had been looking forward to since Pearl Harbor). Well the car was an eye-catcher where ever it went and I think this was the way the Good's wanted it for R. L. He did not act spoiled as I would probably have done if my folks had treated me the way his had done him.

Compared to me, R. L. was a suave city slicker, with a lot of friends already on the UT campus. His family had moved into the country club set and had a lot of social contacts in the city of Tyler. I think R. L. felt it his duty, after finding out that I too was going to UT, to look out for his little country friend. After seeing his car I decided I needed to stay close to him and his friends. My Dad was still in the Marines at the time so my Mother and brother took me to Austin and saw that I was settled in at the Triangle H and had everything I needed in order to start college.

R. L. and I started the school thing, going through orientation, registration, etc. At orientation they let the Inter-Fraternity Council make a presentation and explain what to do with the Rush Week packet in your materials that were sent to us. R. L. wanted to know which rush parties I had signed up for so we could coordinate mine with his. I told him I didn't know what a fraternity was so I had not signed up for any. He found out how really naïve I was so he decided he had better sign me up for the same rush parties that he had mapped out with his friends.

It happened that the first rush party we attended was at the Sigma Chi house. During the activities three of the Sigma Chis took me aside and told me what a good fellow I was and they wanted me to pledge Sigma Chi. One of them I especially liked said if I pledged, he was asking to be my big brother. Well I liked them and they sounded as if this would be a good place to be so I said I would pledge. They whipped out a form to sign and there I was a "fraternity pledge." On the way back to our place, R. L. asked me what I thought about Sigma Chis and I told him I liked them and had signed up to pledge them. His blood pressure really rose then as he said he was trying to help me and there I had signed up to pledge them without letting him know what I was doing. He said he thought I understood that we would go to all the rush parties and then decide which fraternity we would pledge. He further explained that the fraternity couldn't let it be known that I had pledged them until after rush week was over so for me not to tell anyone and we would go through all the rush parties as planned but at the end he was going to have to pledge Sigma Chi also in order to look after me. We did go through all the rush parties and I learned how to say "thank you" and I would consider their fraternity when we got around to talking about pledging them. At the end of rush week, sure enough, R. L. also pledged

Sigma Chi — and that is how R. L. became a very good Sigma Chi for the rest of his life.

The reason I say a "good" Sigma Chi is because he finished his pledge period with flying colors, was initiated and became one of their staunch members and later a very supportive alumnus. On the other hand I wasn't a very good Sigma Chi except for maybe a part of my pledge period. I loved the fraternity and spent the rest of the year partying and of course did not make my grades in order to be initiated. As I look back now I know I wasn't ready for college without some supervision from a stronger authority than R. L. and my fraternity friends. R. L. gave up on me after the first semester and I moved into the fraternity house where I lived the rest of the year. I was barely seventeen, very little experience with social life outside of my extended family, lived a rather sheltered life in the country (mostly an oil field) and there wasn't much going on during the war years besides school and keeping things going around home. When I left for college, I really wanted to be in the war and my parents wouldn't consent — and the war was about to pass me by. While I was at the university, my Dad got out of service and returned home — then took a job as a game warden for a while before going to work as a policeman in Overton.

I must admit that I did benefit from my first year at UT in many ways and the year was not a total loss except for formal education — and the expenditure of my educational savings. I met some very great people. The two who impressed me most were from San Antonio, had gone to high school together and were rooming together. During the spring semester we were suite mates in the annex and got to know each other well — they being model students, pledges and individuals. As for me and my roommate, we were better known as the party boys.

Jack Crittenberger was from a military family — his father (a graduate of West Point) was a general in the army at that time, a brother (also a graduate of West Point) was a colonel on the staff of General Patton and another brother had been killed in action during the Italian campaign. Jack was preparing for his turn to go to West Point and sometimes questioning if that was what he really wanted to do (and I wondered how anyone could question such a future). I never saw nor heard from Jack following our year together as freshman at UT. The second one was Tom Frost. It was easy to follow his story after his graduation since he followed in the footprints of his father and grandfather as the head of the Frost banking empire. I visited in each of their homes in San Antonio while we were students and was amazed at the grace and acceptance their families extended to us visitors. It was a great pleasure and benefit to be around these two during the time we were associated at UT.

There were so many others that it seems I spent the entire year just getting to know people and having a good time doing so. Some of the fraternity members were veterans who had returned from service and some others were still in a service. One, Glenn DeVinney, was about twenty-five or twenty-six and had been in the Navy for five years. He was now being sent to the university in some program for especially talented servicemen. Glenn was big, strong, smart and had been around the block a few times. He wasn't my fraternity big brother but once I moved into the annex for the spring semester he took me under his wing and "looked out for me." He didn't have many close friends but I was glad I was one. Glenn had this little game he loved to play with someone and he was amazing with it.

Glenn would ask a person to take a blank sheet of paper and in a column number from one to twenty-five. He would then ask them to list a word of four or five letters next to each number. After this was done, he asked the person to go down the list, call out the number and connected word. Without ever looking at the list he could then tell what word went with each number. Once he was tested on this he would ask the person to test him on matching a number with the word. He never missed. It was fascinating to see him do this, but he wasn't through. He would then ask the person to turn the paper over, again make a column of numbers with matching four or five letter words — different words from before or some of the same words in a different order — and do the same feat again. He once told me the hardest part was wiping the slate clean and starting over. I would marvel over his ability to do this and tried it a time or two for myself but was an absolute failure. I asked him how he ever learned to do this and he told me that he had spent years on the rear end of carriers as a lookout for approaching enemy planes. Here he worked on this "game" to keep his sanity.

There were many others that I found very interesting also, but as I look back I now realize there weren't many girls that left an impression on me. As a fraternity pledge we had to go to a lot of sorority parties as well as fraternity affairs. If my memory serves me correctly, across the street in front of our fraternity house (it was old in 1945-46 and replaced soon after the war ended) was the Tri Delta house and immediately behind our house was the Zeta one. We always had a lot of interaction with these two and we dated a lot of their pledges but I don't recall ever being serious about any of them.

Only one girl stands out from this freshman year and I guess this is because she was so different from the others. The one I went with most was a girl in one of my classes (a class I did occasionally attended in order to see her), Yvette De La Grave. Her dad was high up in the French diplomatic office in Mexico City and her family spent World War II in Mexico. She was very independent (did not believe in sororities or fraternities) and wanted to be very "American." We were never serious about each other but did enjoy going together to movies, sporting events and such. Not many students had cars and her attitude was "Who cares? We can always ride the bus." She would tell me I didn't need to be such a plutocrat — just enjoy myself. Well, I did learn to enjoy myself and forgot all about going to class. But as I said, I wanted to get into the war and it was soon to be over and I was being left behind.

Years later I was Vice President for Student Affairs at Texas A&I University and part of my job was to work closely with the sororities and fraternities on campus. When asked if I had been a member of a fraternity in college I would reply no — since I was never initiated — for I decided it might be better to keep my little secret and never be accused of showing favoritism. I did end up being the sponsor for the APOs (usually referred to as the Boy Scout fraternity) for a number of years since they were a service fraternity as well as having social activities.

But, back to R. L. — he remained in the Triangle H with a new roommate — his folks didn't want him to go to the fraternity house since that would offer too many distractions. R. L. was a good student, not the brightest but a hard worker as in all his endeavors. We didn't see each other much at UT the rest of my time there except for fraternity functions and riding home with him a few times. R. L. finished college and pharmacy school, went back to Tyler and worked in the family business, married and had a family.

I would run into him every two or three years but no more often than that — usually at a Kilgore/Tyler Jr. College football game. The last time I remember seeing him was at a Billy Graham Crusade in Tyler's Rose Stadium about 1960. He was an usher and we only got a chance to wave and then to speak to each other — no real opportunity to visit. I was proud of R. L. and would have liked to have told him so myself and that I was glad to be his friend. I would also have liked to tell him that I hadn't done too badly since at the time I was the high school principal in Overton and some of the people considered me a pillar of the community.

Two or three years after that last meeting, I found out R. L. had died a few months previous.

AND, THEN .....

The primary reason I wanted to get home as early as I could from my first year at college in the spring of 1946 was that Mother and Dad had acquired a new Buick, the first to arrive in Overton following the war. Since everyone that had the money seemed to want a new car, the dealers had worked out a rating system and had a list of returned servicemen (based on their discharge points) who would receive priority on purchasing the new cars. Charles Rambo, having entered service a little ahead of my Dad, was the first on the Overton Buick list. Dad was second. When the first Buick arrived it was a beautiful maroon four door Super model. Charles had his mind set on a two door Sedanette — more streamlined and youthful looking — so he passed over it and Dad snapped it up for our family car. Charles got his shiny black Buick just a few weeks later.

As soon as I could exit Austin for home at the end of the 1946 spring semester, I did so. UT was still on a wartime tri-semester, or maybe a quarter system, calendar with Dean Nowattley and me agreeing to my skipping a semester while I matured a little more at home. This gave me a few months to save up some money while working as a painter and carpenter's helper for Wm. Cameron Lumber Co. as they had jobs available through contract work with Humble Oil. I had depleted the funds my parent's had set aside for my college education and all I had to show for the year was a badly battered freshman academic record. They decided I might be more responsible if I helped a little more to pay for my education.

Things seemed to begin to come together for me that summer as I made many new friends, mended some fences socially but also created some new problems at the same time. I had this relationship that had developed between me and a female cousin of William's (on my Jernigan side) on the Florence side of his family. We spent some time together during the

1945 Christmas holidays since she was spending the year with her (and William's) grandparents next door to William's family and going to the junior college in Tyler. Her family was in the process of relocating or something. We were the same age and had seen each other some as children. William's mother, Blanche, taking the role of matchmaker, was pushing our connection. When I came home for Easter, she was ready and it seemed all my activities were centered around her niece. We exchanged pictures and promised to write when I went back to school. We did write and somehow she developed the idea we were engaged — many years later at a family funeral I recall her mentioning she still had my "love letters." Before the semester ended my passion had cooled and a friend suggested the strategy I used in my first breakup with a girlfriend. Don't write but tell her face-to-face that you have to call it off for some time since there would be years of schooling ahead of you with no means of support other than your family — and they made it clear they would cut you off if you quit school. After a few tears on both sides it worked and I was free to enjoy my summer. A few months later her engagement announcement was made and I began to wonder if she had already found another boyfriend at the time of my little show.

With the war over, my interest in going into the military service had waned and I was enjoying the life of this new era. I was working, had spending money, even saving some, free use of our new car and not worrying about the future. I became close friends with the two Rambo brothers, Charles and Howard. They had just returned from the Navy and were enjoying their adjustment to civilian life. Both were living at their widowed mother's home along with their sister Katherine and her little boy. Katherine's husband was still in service and hoping to make a career of it — I think. Charles was the older son, twenty-five or twenty-six, with Howard about to turn twenty-two. Katherine fit somewhere between the two boys. Charles was the flashy, dominate character of the family and loved to tell stories about his time in the Navy where (according to him) he spent most of his time operating traveling crap games and skimming off profits which he loaned out at interest. He may have come home with a bankroll — paying cash for his new Buick. Howard was quieter, more serious and I thought very dependable. Katherine and Howard were much alike, even in looks — both blondes with brown eyes.

Mrs. Rambo, Fannie B. to everyone, ran a little dress shop on one of the busy downtown blocks facing the railroad tracks where Hall Drug, the bank and Busy Bee Café were also located. Called "Fannie B's," it sold ready-to-wear dresses, a few accessories, with its specialty being custom made dresses by Fannie B. She had raised her kids with this little shop and they worshiped her for the sacrifices she had made for them.

I first became acquainted with Charles and Howard when they opened a watermelon stand early that summer. Charles had seen such a set-up in Southern California or the Pacific islands and adapted it to East Texas. They served cold watermelon slices along with whole melons for take-out. Rambo Gardens, as they called it, cooled the melons in barrels of iced water, had some picnic tables and benches with lights strung around and music playing from a record player. It was a huge success, especially with the young people since it gave them a place to hang out in the early evening until it closed nightly about ten PM. I helped them some when they had a rush, needed someone to go get extra ice, and such things so we bonded rather quickly.

Charles, with his new Buick, was going steady with his longtime sweetheart Gladys Utsey. They were doing most of their courting that summer with the watermelons (married a year or so later and divorced in a few years). Howard didn't have a car and was kind of playing the field by occasionally double dating with a friend. Pretty soon, I became that friend.

Hanging around the Rambo Gardens, I was able to renew some friendships and make a few new ones during the summer. Most of my guard buddies had gone to the services when I left for college the year before. But there were some from my church who had gone off to college and were home for the summer. Bob Lloyd had been at SMU and now we renewed our friendship. He also struck up an acquaintance with sisters Joyce and Billie Jean McCord — falling in love at first sight with Joyce. The problem being Joyce was only fifteen and she was always with her older sister, who was nineteen, already out of high school and working as a teller at the bank. I'm sure the McCords were hoping to get Billie Jean married off soon but one of the town's most desirable young bachelors had eyes only for the younger sister. Bob got me to double date with him and Joyce (Billie Jean as my date) since the McCords (very strict parents) wouldn't let her go on a date unless her older sister was with her. Surprisingly Billie Jean and I took to each other (could be I "more or less" fell in love, to some extent, with every girl I ever dated a few times). We followed this procedure for several dates until the sisters were tiring of chaperoning each other and I wanted to include Howard — and six, three couples, didn't fit very well even in our nor the Lloyd's large sedan. Billie Jean came up with a solution. Bob and I would pick up the McCord girls in his car, he and Joyce would drop me and Billie Jean at Rambo Gardens where we would get in my car, load Howard and go for his date. I hated this deception, but that is what the girls wanted so who was I to complain? I had fears Mr. McCord would find out what was happening and probably shoot Bob — and me along with him.

Back then young love seemed to change with the moon. It wasn't long till Bob and Joyce broke up and went their separate ways — but Billie Jean and I continued dating (with her commandeering my high school ring, whatever that meant — and about a year later it was destroyed when their home burned). I think I liked the idea of being linked with an "older woman" so we drifted along in our relationship. It was about this time that Howard discovered a new girlfriend.

There were three good drug stores in Overton at that time — Hall's, Pure (sometimes named Overton since it changed hands a few times over the years) and Davis's. Davis Drug didn't have a fountain at that time and was the smallest of the three. Pure Drug was the middle sized one being most centrally located on a corner and had a good sized fountain. We hung out a lot in front of it on the corner but the fountain and other services never attracted as much business as Hall's, the largest and favorite of most people. Hall's was headed by C. P. and you could sometimes find three generations of his offspring in the place. There was a large gift department, headed by the senior Mrs. Hall, offering beautiful free wrapping which attracted the moneyed crowd. The large fountain was the draw for the young people. C. P., that sly old fox, always had two pretty and very popular high school girls (from Overton but always one of his pool from New London) working behind the counter during non-school hours. Each worked a couple of hours after school maybe twice a week and about four hours on Saturdays. There usually was one good looking and very popular boy also there on Saturdays — and he probably was a well know athlete too. After the 1946 high school graduations, the New London girl went off to college on a scholarship and C. P. selected Joyce Petty to take her place. Joyce had just completed her junior year and would be a New London senior in September.

New London also had a "drug" store, McConnico's, across the street from the school. Charlie was not a pharmacist, nor any of his employees, so they did not fill prescriptions — just sold patent medicines. He did sell a lot of school supplies, sundries, notions, gifts, etc. They had a beautiful and busy fountain which offered sandwiches, drinks, ice cream and such. Usually the fountain was manned by Charlie, or other adults — only occasionally did a younger family member work behind the counter. Today the fountain is part of and fully operational in the New London Museum — dedicated to telling the story of the 1937 School Explosion.

Howard was helping his mother at this time in her business by doing her post office, bank and other errands during business hours while Charles took care of the daytime watermelon business. Fannie B's was only two or three doors down from Hall's so Howard stopped in at Hall's for drinks and snacks during the day. He took an interest in Joyce and asked her for a date. Naturally she refused the first few times — due to the age difference and worker/customer relationship. So he had a selling job to do, convincing her he wasn't an old, tough and hardened sailor from the war but still just a kid like her friends. One day Joyce's mother was in the drug store while he was pleading his case. She came over, introduced herself and joined in their conversation. It ended up with Mrs. Petty inviting him to a Sunday school social the next Sunday evening at their church. As he told me later, "What could I do but accept under the circumstances? So I asked if I could bring a friend and she said yes. So please be my friend and help me out." I almost laughed in his face, but I could tell he was very serious so I agreed.

The following Sunday evening I drove into the New London First Baptist Church parking lot with a very nervous Howard as passenger. We circled the cars already parked and stopped on our second round. We saw Joyce come out of a side door between the auditorium and Sunday school addition (where she had been looking for us). Now knowing where we were going, we parked and walked in her direction. She had a big inviting smile on her face and met us halfway. She escorted us to the door she had emerged from and as we entered we were welcomed by her mother. Joyce introduced me to her mother (I don't ever remember meeting Joyce but later she told me about asking a friend of hers who I was after seeing me driving around in Overton and this made her feel like she knew me). Her mother in turn took us over to a table and introduced us to Mr. Petty and Granny (Mr. Petty's mother who lived with them).

After this Joyce took us over to the serving table and prepared each a paper plate with cake and ice cream. We sat at a card table, eating our food as first Joyce's little sister, aged four, came over for a visit — not in the least bashful or hesitant in letting us know what she thought of the situation. Soon the other sister, thirteen year old Rosalynn (Bo), came over to fetch Jerry but decided to sit down and visit also. In a few minutes the brother, Ed (between Joyce and Bo age-wise), came over to meet us and then did take the two younger girls to the other end of the room where games were being organized and started. While we finished our refreshments, several adults came over, introduced themselves and welcomed us. After the food we were taken around and shown the church facilities. As we were standing around watching the going-ons, we both decided this was a good time to leave before we were involved in more church activities. Howard rather awkwardly suggested we needed to leave and Joyce did not attempt to discourage it so we thanked her mother for inviting us with Joyce walking us to the parking area. Without further fanfare, we left. As soon as we were on the road headed back to Overton Howard said "What a relief to get that over. I've worried about it for days and days. Now maybe I can relax a little."

We went to the watermelon stand and relieved Charles and Gladys so they could get some supper and do some watermelon-free courting. Howard was still talking about Joyce as we had time during our tending to the watermelon sales. He told me that ever since he first noticed her she had struck him as the ideal All-American girl, just what he had dreamed of as a girlfriend. I had to agree she was certainly a very nice looking, friendly school girl with a great personality. I wasn't as impressed with her as he appeared to be but, of course it was his girlfriend (or at least the one he wanted to be) we were talking about and not mine. He then told me he had asked for a date while we were at her church and she had agreed to a "little" one. This first date was for the next Friday when she finished work at six PM to go and have a watermelon supper at Rambo Gardens. There were other conditions also; it was to be a double date with Billie Jean and me. Billie Jean would get off at five, so Howard and I would pick her up first and then Joyce when she got off at Hall's. After our "supper" we were to take her home since she had to pack and get ready for an early Saturday morning departure with her family for a Galveston vacation. He said he had agreed to her terms without consulting me since he felt we were in this thing together. I said O K this time but not to count on me to have so much to do in the future with his dating. This first date worked out well and for the next couple of months we double dated a few times each week. Each couple considered themselves as going steady, the practice back then.

As the summer drew to a close, we drifted apart in preparation of my leaving for Austin, Howard starting to Kilgore College, Joyce returning for her senior year at New London and Billie Jean resuming her banking work. I decided to end it with Billie Jean once and for all on the same grounds as with my first serious relationship, but this time I waited until I was back in Austin to do so — by letter. It was on my first trip home from Austin (probably Thanksgiving) I learned Billie Jean was engaged to Scott Baskin, one of the many returning from the war, living with his sister and her family in Overton while attending Kilgore College. I always had a great deal of respect for Scott, he was a fighter pilot during the war and a first rate person and friend also — I felt that Billie Jean had done quite well in selecting her mate. After he finished Kilgore, they married and moved off. I never saw Scott again but did Billie Jean and her sister Joyce many years later when both were widows and we were all at an Overton High School reunion — my being there as an ex-teacher.

On that same trip home, I found out Howard and Joyce had stopped dating also at the end of the summer. The story I got was that he was too serious about marriage and she wanted none of that and was happy looking forward to the many activities and dates of her senior year in high school. Howard was dating Billie Jean Westmoreland (a close friend and almost ex-girlfriend of mine from LC). In a few months they married, had a little girl and divorced in a few years due to an unhappy marriage. Billie Jean raised their daughter on her own, never remarrying, while Howard shortly remarried and had another family.

During the summer term while I was lying out of school in Overton, I received an unexpected, but quite interesting, letter from the business manager of the Sigma Chi house in Austin. He explained how the fraternity, needing more living space, had leased the large old house across the alley from our annex and behind the Hirsh's Drug on the corner of Guadalupe. He said in the budget for the operation of this additional property for the coming year they were providing for a position as an assistant to the business manager to live there and help with the overall management operations of the fraternity properties. He further explained that no salary went with the position but free room, board and all fraternity fees and assessments were included. Due to the help I had given him during my past semester living in the annex I was his first choice as the person to fill the position and to let him know as soon as possible if I was interested and would return for the fall semester.

After I shared this letter with Mother and Dad they were very excited since this would cover nearly all my living expenses — with tuition practically nothing at that time and most textbooks available through the fraternity library or contacts. They wanted me to jump at this chance for a second opportunity at going to the university, even though I would be on scholastic probation during the semester. I responded positively to his letter and thanked him very much and just wanted to know when he needed me there. This firmed up my plans for the end of the summer, making my parents happy to know that I would be resuming my college education and not be a financial drain on them. Dad had given up his dreams of being a part of the FBI or Texas Rangers and had settled in as the chief of Overton's small police force, giving into Mother's wishes that they settle in at their Leverett's Chapel home for life and not be subjected to moving around as Dad's dreams would entail.

Naturally Mother and Dad wanted to know what help I had given the business manager for him to want me as his assistant. I shared some of my relations with BM (short for business manager, as I had come to call him since he had a difficult name for my East Texas tongue to pronounce) but withheld some, thinking they would rather not know about. As a pledge I was always volunteering to go out of my way to please the members, especially those with extra authority, so BM allowed me to do some little things for him and gradually the tasks got larger with more responsibilities.

The bedrooms in the main house were all on the second floor and attic where some of the actives lived. BM had an office on the first floor that contained a little sleeping alcove and private bath with a huge bathtub on curved legs. Almost every week he had a late night poker party in his office for his "group." Late one afternoon while I was hanging out at the fraternity house he was running short of time and called me to please come into his office. He asked me would I take his car, go to the store, and get him a case of beer and a washtub of crushed ice from the ice house. I replied "Sure, what brand of beer?" He handed me his keys, some money and said whichever brand was on special and the tub was in the trunk of the car. In just a little while I was back with the goods and waited till his office cleared to find out where it went. He told me to put the beer in the bathtub, cover it with the ice and hang around for his poker group to come — in case he needed me to do anything else. This turned into an every poker game job with me as his right hand man in handling his collection of money and dispensing beer, mixing drinks, etc. This led to my helping type up some of his reports — using my portable typewriter when he had other work on his office machine. We worked well together so my pledge duties all began revolving around "helping" him.

BM was a small man (barely five feet tall and hardly weighing a hundred pounds) in his upper thirties with very thin blonde hair and wearing thick lensed horn rimmed glasses. A full description of him would call to mind a "book worm." He was a graduate student at UT working on his dissertation for a Ph.D. — in economics I think. He was a sometimes part-time instructor and graded papers for some of the professors. He was paid a very small salary for his work at the house, but got his room, board and such free from the fraternity.

In early August I began to hint to Mother and Dad that I wasn't really looking forward to returning to Austin and resuming my pre-med studies. They quickly came up with the idea that what I needed was a visit to Dallas with Richard and Pat so they would have an opportunity to counsel and encourage me about my career plans. We loaded up that weekend and headed for Dallas. After a day or two they left me with Richard and Pat for a few days stay and they returned home with me to follow later on the bus to Tyler where they would pick me up. This plan worked very well since it provided me with a look into the lives of a young married couple, living in a small efficiency apartment, with Richard attending medical school while Pat was their primary financial support by working as a dietician in one of the hospitals. Richard also helped out some by working as a nurse or nurse's aide in the hospitals (as a lot of the medical students did then) when he had a little free time. Their living area was rather cramped so I heard some of their private discussions and arguments as I tried to sleep on their nearby couch.

The result of this visit was the opposite for which my parents had hoped. I came home with a definite decision that a medical career was not what I wanted. As I told Howard following my visit, I would rather work in a field requiring manual labor as I was presently doing rather than go through the training necessary to be a doctor and the demands you had to face in such a career. He tended to agree with me since he had some experience in the medical field while serving in the Navy.

I told Howard, and then later my parents, how I had followed Richard around in a lot of his activities (except for class lectures) and had some rather eye opening experiences. One of the first that (I sometimes think I can still "smell") is deeply inscribed in my memory is of our visit to the lab where his anatomy class worked. He walked over to this huge vat, raised a section of the cover, reached in with a metal rod with a hook on the end and pulled over a cadaver. As he propped it up in the pool of formaldehyde he said he wanted me to meet "George" — his current project in class. As he pointed and probed with the metal rod he explained what he had been doing on the body. The odor alone was enough to make me want to throw up but looking at this mutilated human was just about too much. I also spent Saturday night with him in the emergency rooms of Parkland Hospital while he pulled a twelve hour shift. I think I watched as at least three of their patients died — one from stab wounds and two from car wrecks. The next morning over breakfast before we went to bed, well after the sun was up, I told Richard that I would take my hat off to him (if I had one on) for the work he had done the night before. I said I just couldn't believe he had done what he had that night. He said "Just remember, someone has to do it and if it is your job, do it right."

When I got around to telling Mother and Dad that I just couldn't look forward to the many years necessary to be a doctor and I didn't know at this time what I wanted to do, they were so shaken, it made me feel quite guilty. I felt as if I was crushing their dreams and it was their future we were talking about rather than mine. For two or three days we all moped around and finally one evening at supper my Dad looked at my Mother for a minute or two, turned to me and said "It's up to you to decide what you want to do and we will help you all we can." Then Mother added "But we do hope you will go back to college while you decide." I told them I planned to leave for Austin pretty soon since I had written BM that I would be there well before the semester starts. I also told them I planned to register for some different types of courses and steer away from so many science classes for a while. That night they went to bed in a happier mood than I had seen them in for the past couple of weeks or so.

Although Mother and Dad had accepted my decision about college with relief and felt that everything was going to be alright, I was filled with doubt, worry and anticipation for the coming move back to Austin. What had been a light hearted exit from Austin to a summer of work and fun at home was ending with the beginning of a one of the most depressed and sad periods of my young life. The last two weeks before I left Overton was a very dreary and dragging time for me.

In one of the letters from BM, he mentioned for me to let him know how I was coming to Austin, when I would arrive and he would pick me up in his car. He had also noted that he had the front bedroom in the Old House (the newly leased expansion house, which we always afterwards referred to it as the old house after that, but officially used the street address as the title) converted to a small version of his office/bedroom in the main house for my use and had it completely furnished and ready for me. I had not thought of anything other than my parents taking me back to school in our family car so this led me to checking on the train schedule. It turned out Overton was on the direct line to Austin and the train made very good time — so a plan emerged in my mind. Since I only needed my clothes, I would use a couple of suitcases to move and take the train. On second thought, I included my typewriter since it had proven so handy in the past. My primary reason for this change in plans seemed to be so I wouldn't have a full day of parental preaching and advice. Of course, it was usually a two day trip for Mother and Dad with a night in a motel since Dad could always find something he needed to do in Austin. They were very pleased when I presented my plan to them, thinking I was taking the train to save them a trip.

Actually I wanted to escape; escape home, my parents, friends and, really, I didn't want to return to college at this time. I had started writing Billy Cox about the time I had returned home and inquired about what he thought about the Marine Corp — since I was still thinking about joining at that time since my college career had started so poorly. He was serving in China at the time and his thoughts were that the Marine Corp was good to be from but hell to be in. He suggested something in one of the services that would give me training useful in civilian life since it looked like we would be returning to a peaceful situation now that the war was over. My last letter to him told of my current situation and I was trying to decide whether to return to Austin or leave it all behind and go into the service. His last letter was very plainly spoken, or rather written. He said to get my ass to Austin and forget everything else; a college education was the most important thing for me at this time. He convinced me to follow through on my plans and return to Austin.

Some fifty years later, as I sat in Billy's funeral service, all of our old correspondence flowed through my mind. It took a while but I came to believe he had given me very good advice back in those days. He followed it himself since as soon as he got out of service he went to the University of Houston with the aid of his veteran's benefits, completed a degree in petroleum engineering and was very successful in his long career in the oil fields and his offices.

When I boarded the train for Austin, holding my portable typewriter case in one hand and waving goodbye to Mother and Dad with the other, I was still undecided about my future but now at least I would be away from home for a while.

I arrived back in Austin the last day or two of August and it seems that the university was adapting back to the regular semester system, so school didn't start till about the middle of September. This gave me time to settle in and gave BM an opportunity to orient me to my new duties. Since I had completed my pledge period but had not been initiated, I was kind of in a limbo status to some degree. The pledge master seemed to want to make me his head pledge and push some of his duties off on me. He and BM had some conflicts over the assignment of my duties. BM, more or less, won out on this issue and I ended up just being responsible for making out the pledge work schedule (for serving in the dining room, desk and phone duty, etc.) and sometimes relieving the pledge master on checking on the pledges to be sure they were reporting on time and doing their jobs. But there continued to be a lot of stress about my status with several of the actives since some thought I should be treated the same as the new pledges. BM had to fight this issue all semester — which was rather stressful for both of us.

Since I was on scholastic probation I had to go through a special advisor during registration. I decided to take a liberal arts program and my advisor helped me select my classes in that area as well as the ones to meet the requirements, or conditions, of being on probation. I had to retake at least two classes which I had previously failed so I choose the second semester of freshman English (literature) and the same semester of freshman history (American). I chose these because I didn't really fail to pass them but just quit going to class my last semester, so I failed all that semester (record wise). These two were required courses in the liberal arts degree plan also so I thought I was killing two birds with one stone. My advisor pointed out my degree plan would require two years of a foreign language and I might as well get started on that — we decided on French — a huge mistake. My advisor then went down a list of courses I could take and one of those was anthropology. I asked what it was about and she read the interesting description. We put it down on my list of classes. She then said that I was required to take a P E activity course also, so we selected one from the many offered. The advisor pointed out this was the minimum I would need to pass (with a grade of "C" or better) in order to get off scholastic probation but she would suggest I take a somewhat easy course in addition to these to give me a little breathing room in case I needed to drop one. We looked over the possibilities, and after asking me a few questions, we settled on a three semester hour freshman introductory course to physical education, which she suggested should be "easy" for me. After wishing me luck with my classes, she pointed down toward the long department lines on the main floor of Gregory Gym and told me to go sign up for those classes.

We got the fraternity housing off to a good start but my classes turned out to have some problems. The biggest problem was the French class. I should have dropped it the first day and added some other class. The instructor had his own way of conducting class. He would use no English and did not allow the students to use English either. I don't think I even recognized my own name when he called the roll. My ears, nor my East Texas tongue, were capable of handling French. I may have had a little French blood in my veins — from my great grandmother Elliott who was supposed to be a descendant of the French Evangeline group that settled in Louisiana — but my body didn't seem to know it. I stayed in the class thinking it would get better. At midterm I was reported as failing so I quit going to class and then this was reported to the dean and this meant we had to have a little talk — he dropped me from the class as failing.

The next big problem was my English class. This instructor, as I could tell at first glance, was an overage, underweight, sour puss woman. Later I found out she was a bitter, man-hating and vindictive one also. She was cloyingly treacly (which I later learned meant disgustingly or distastefully sweet) that first day in class and I fell into her trap — I guess you might say I was her fall guy. She outlined her philosophy of education somewhat, explained her approach to our studies, what she would do and then what she expected us to do. She told how she would help us and how we could help ourselves. Then she got to the point where she asked if we had any suggestions or experiences which might be included in our discussion on our work in this course. Any activities or methods we knew of that had helped us in other classes would be welcomed. She looked around the class seeking a response, but received none. She looked directly at me and I took her expression as desperately wanting me to say something. As I was to do so many times in the course of my education, I talked when I should have continued to listen. I suggested an activity the instructor used in the same course I had taken the year before which I thought had benefited me a great deal. As I was thinking of patting myself on the back for coming to her rescue with this suggestion, I noticed a little smile on her face — then her eyes narrowed into thin slits, and maybe her ears moved a little backward on her head as she lit into me about how she would never ask her students to do such a time wasting activity. She didn't call me names but she gave some descriptions and associated them to me and then she fried any instructor that would use such methods. I was so humiliated I know I must have blushed to such an extent as to light up the room a little more. After a three or four minute tirade she then smiled sweetly and asked if there were any other suggestions. There being none she gave us a reading assignment and dismissed the class. I moved out as quickly as I could but I felt a couple of pats on the back as I exited the room (the kind you might give a sacrificial lamb) and looked no one in the eye. I should have dropped that class the first day also — but, sad to say, I didn't.

My other classes did not present any special problems. The history course was one of the dullest, boring and uninspiring that I was to ever sit through. The instructor, evidently a graduate student himself, mostly just read uninteresting facts, dates and names as he kept his eyes pointed toward the clock hoping to make it move quicker and end the period. The P E courses, while not very notable, were kept interesting by the participants. It happened that both courses were basically filled with varsity athletes and I became acquainted with many who later were to become somewhat famous. Two I especially enjoyed were Bobby Layne and "Rooster" Andrews.

The only course that I really enjoyed was the Introduction to Anthropology. I rarely missed this class, applied myself far more than the others and had my best grade in it. I felt I surely earned a better grade than a "C", but the professor — a rare type but probably one of the three best that I ran into during my days as a student — graded on the curve and there were a bunch of sharpies in this class so I guess I was lucky to come out average. The rumors were he would be fired for his religious beliefs (an avowed atheist and very outspoken about it and many other sensitive issues in those times) at the end of his current contract. He did expound on many issues unrelated to our course content but we found his lectures very informative and interesting.

Another interesting part of this class was the girl sitting across the aisle from me. She was very nice looking, but most people would not say a beauty compared to a lot of the campus queens, and she made the mistake of smiling at me every morning at the beginning of class. Grade wise she turned out to be one of the top three in the class. This really surprised me for I observed she never took notes and just followed the professor with her eyes, soaking up his every word and motion. I was amazed after our first quiz for she received a ninety-eight on her paper (there were no ninety-nines or one hundreds), one of only two. I asked her to go with me for a coke after class that day and she said she couldn't just then but maybe some other time. I followed with a "Such as?" and her reply was maybe four o'clock that afternoon at a drug store fountain near her private dormitory. We did have our coke and visit that afternoon which got to be almost a weekly event. Neither of us considered we were "dating", just friends visiting, but as far as I know this was the nearest thing to dating either did during the semester.

We talked and talked, mostly about school and our classes but a little about our past experiences. The thing I remember most was her method of study. She had a strict program she had developed in high school and rigidly followed it at college. She was a straight "A" student in high school and expected to be so in college. At the end of the semester our anthropology professor posted our grades. Sure enough there she was in the top ten per cent with an "A", mine was one of the higher "Cs", but a "C" none the less. There was the same percentage of "Ds" as "Bs" and "Fs" as "As", just as the professor had promised.

Several years later, as a graduate student in education, I wrote a paper entitled "A Sure Fire Method of Study" based on her program (which I had tested myself in some courses with success) and received an "A". Much later I used the information in this paper in my many lectures on educational psychology.

The 1946 fall semester at UT was a very trying one for me, but somewhat enjoyable at times. It now seems to me, with the following first half of 1947, it was a kind of bridge from one stage of my life to another — from just drifting to a period of goal oriented preparation for a role in life. Again, it was the people I was associated with that brought the times of enjoyment, as well as, those moments of despair.

Glenn DeVinney was located in an obscure little cubby hole of a room in a rear corner of the second floor in the old house. He liked being rather separated from the others and not in the suite situation of the annex as in the previous year. We didn't run around together much anymore; but we still visited a lot with him stopping by my room/office nearly every day, sometimes just sitting around reading while I was doing other things. I still counted him as one of my best friends for he always seemed eager to take my side when one of the actives wanted to lord it over me. There were three or four living in the old house who had been members of my pledge class that wanted to assume that role. Most of the older actives didn't give me much trouble since they knew they would have Glenn to deal with also.

My room/office was on the left side of the hall entrance (probably a parlor from days past) with the extra-large living room (the original dining room included with it) being on the right. The kitchen had been converted to a snack bar (our meals were taken in the main house) and an attached bath in what was once a large panty. A door opened into my room from the hallway, which I kept open at all times when I was there. Another door in my room opened into a bath which separated my room with the bedroom next door which shared the bath. This room, a little smaller than my room/office was occupied by only one active which was the most expensive room in the old house. This active, a junior that had not been in school the previous year, turned out to be my closest friend that semester — and not just because we lived so "close" to each other either. He was another who didn't like to be cooped-up with other people, similar to Glenn but not at all like him in appearance, and was willing to pay extra for it.

Garth, a family name I think, wasn't so terrible tall but being so thin it made him look tall (he probably was around six feet at most), tanned, slow talking with deliberate movements and his western wear looked the part he was — a western Texan. He was from an old ranching family located near Santa Anna. He had missed the previous year of school due to his father's heart attack, or maybe a stroke, in the summer of '45 and had to stay at home to tend to the ranch for the family since other help wasn't available. The ranch still belonged to his grandmother but his dad was in line to inherit the family enterprise, so it was his baby — but the grandmother made no bones about it, she still ran things. He had come back to school a little early and we had an opportunity to get to know each other before the rush at the beginning of the semester. We hit it off from the start and remained fast friends until I left UT — after which we had no contact. I always wondered if he had something physically wrong with him since, as far as I knew, he hadn't been in the service and didn't seem to be worried about being drafted. As I got to know his family better this feeling was strengthened, but also an idea there could be some "in" with the draft board about it. Probably, I worry too much about such things.

Garth was a huge Longhorn football fan and we made all the home games together and one out of town — and nearly two (more about that later).

I also made a couple of visits to their ranch with him as well as our trip to Dallas/Denton. I was able to take these periods off since BM worked out a schedule where either he or I would be on duty on weekends and he didn't care for football so I could plan around the football program. My contacts with so many of the players (and want to be players) in my PE classes made my interest in their activities soar. Garth was so surprised that I knew so many of the players and he liked to pal around with them too.

He had come back to school in the family car, the folks back home having the ranch pickup to use and grandma's car (she didn't drive), so we had wheels — he would need it in a couple of weeks to return home for some planned movement of cattle. When he told me of his need to return home soon for this I told him about my "trail drive" and some of my experiences with horses. He was surprised to find I was such a kindred spirit when it came to horses and such that he invited me to go to the ranch for a few days with him. I talked with BM about it and he said since we had everything in the old house ready for the semester and we would be back just in time he would cover for me while Garth and I made the quick trip to the Ranch. We left on Thursday and returned on Sunday — leaving the ranch before daylight that morning in order to be back in Austin early that afternoon when the guys would start moving into the old house.

This was a very exciting and pleasing trip. I met all of his family, including grandma, and they accepted me warmly, especially appreciating my help with the ranch work. Dorothy, Garth's sister, was there and also aided with the ranch work. She was just a few months younger than me and would be a freshman at TWU the next week. What a cowgirl she turned out to be, riding circles around Garth and me — showing out for my benefit I think. We got all the work done Friday and early Saturday afternoon so we went to a big dance Saturday night. We picked up Garth's girlfriend and this left Dorothy and me as a couple also — and as it turned out, we both enjoyed this very much. I wasn't much of a dancer — to be honest two left feet, but I got by with a lot of hugging while supposedly dancing. We had a great evening at probably my first ever western dance.

The next day after Garth and I left, his mother, dad and grandma took Dorothy to Denton in grandma's car to move Dorothy and her belongings into the dormitory. I thought this would be the last time I would see Dorothy. In about ten days I received a letter from her (she had Garth's address) telling me all about their trip to Denton and her beginning school at TWU. She closed the letter by saying how much she had enjoyed being with me over the weekend and hoped to see me again, really soon. I was shocked since Garth had told me she was engaged to a guy in the Navy and her family was very happy because they thought he was such a good "catch" for her. At first I thought I would just ignore her letter but then I decided to send a short note, pretending to be very busy. But, other letters followed, which I enjoyed so much that I wrote some too.

The first out of town game we went to was Rice in Houston, I think. It was an afternoon game as most were at that time and we left early that morning, got to town about noon, located the stadium, had a hot dog or two with a beer and showed our student IDs for admission. We enjoyed the game and as soon as it was over we headed back to Austin since we didn't have anyone in Houston either wanted to see. It was a long full day but we both enjoyed driving and talking — just the two of us.

The big out of town game that Garth wanted to make was UT vs OU in Dallas, along with visiting his girlfriend in Denton. He was planning big on this trip but didn't want his parents to known about it. He decided if he took me with him to go with his sister, she would be in on it and there was less likelihood that his parents would find out. Of course I was willing to sacrifice a weekend to go to a big game and have another hot date with Dorothy. We could each have two tickets on our student activity card so we could also take our dates free. We were early in line for the tickets as soon as they started issuing them Wednesday.

Garth had some friends going to school at North Texas and they said they would always find him an empty bunk in the dorm if he came up — so we planned to stay in Denton near the girls. We arrived on Friday evening, contacted his friends, got beds in their dorm for the two nights and then picked up the girls. They were living in dorms with a midnight curfew on Friday and a one am one on Saturday so we had to watch our time so they wouldn't get reported to their parents. Friday evening we had hamburgers, went to a movie and checked out Denton. The next morning we headed for Dallas to be there before noon and eat lunch near and before the game.

We picked out a Colonial Pig for our lunch. While we were eating inside, a fellow came in, asked around if anyone had tickets for sale to the game. Garth and I looked at each other, knowing what the other was thinking — the girls didn't really care about the game and we could listen to it on the car radio — so when he came by our table Garth asked "How much?" He replied ten dollars each. We both reached in our pocket and held up our tickets. He wanted the four and handed us each a twenty dollar bill. The girls looked a little puzzled but we just smiled at each other. After lunch we drove over to a high hill in Oak Cliff for good reception on the car radio, parked and listened to the Longhorn Band play until the football broadcast started. I doubt if anyone watching the game enjoyed it any more than we did.

After the game we drove through downtown Dallas to see some of the celebrating going on. As we drove up to a red traffic signal and made our stop at the street corner in front of the Baker Hotel, I saw Mr. and Mrs. Donald Leverett crossing the street. They were looking straight at our car. I slumped down on the floor of the back seat as the other three turned to see what I was doing. The Leveretts walked on by and after the light changed we drove on. I had to explain that their home was next to ours (our thirty acres had come off their property and the community was named after his family) and if they told my parents they had seen me in Dallas when I should have been in Austin, I would probably be in deep trouble.

We made the Denton curfew that night and made it back to Austin Sunday. Our friends in Austin thought we were at the game in Dallas, and none of the parents ever knew we were in Dallas — as far as we knew.

The last week of October or early November, Garth got a letter from his girlfriend that told him she and Dorothy had worked out some deal to go home for a weekend and they wanted to see "us" very much if we could make it there too. He was fit to be tied, so we made arrangements to go to the ranch at the same time. We had a great weekend and I couldn't believe how lovey-dovey Dorothy was toward me. Evidently her parents noticed also because Garth got a letter from his mother asking him not to bring me back for Thanksgiving, or any time when Dorothy was home — since she felt we shouldn't be around each other in the future. Garth shared this information with me because he thought it was so funny, but I wondered what Dorothy may have said to her parents to upset them so. I assured Garth I didn't intend to cause any friction in his family and I would certainly abide by their wishes.

For Thanksgiving we shut everything down at the fraternity house and farmed out the residents living too far away to go home for the holiday into Sigma Chi homes (alumni and such) in Austin. Garth didn't need to worry about my wanting to return to the ranch since my parents were counting big on my being at Grandma's for our extended family dinner. Mother and Dad felt like I was having great success with my college life and wanted to share me with the rest of the family. Little did they know how I felt — as if everything was crumbling in on me. On the train toward home I did my best to buoy my spirits so I could put on a happy face and be as gay (somewhat different usage back then) as possible. It was a good holiday and I returned to Austin with a resolve to work harder — but my heart and soul didn't seem to be fully committed.

My English professor, that dear old soul, told us she always held a private fifteen minute conference with each student about this time of the semester. The objective, according to her, was so she could evaluate the student's work so far and make any suggestions that might help the student in his or her studies. We were to sign up for a time and date on the schedule sheet she had posted outside her office. After class there was a rush to sign up in order to get a prime time since the professor had indicated this was mandatory for a grade and, if missed, no makeup unless you were seriously ill in a hospital. As much as I dreaded this ordeal, I stood in line and signed up.

My conference didn't go very well, I remember that sickening smile on her face the whole time as I squirmed in my chair and gripped its arms — for fear what I might do with my hands if I let them loose. She cut me and my work to pieces in such a sweet tone you would think she was stroking a cat. The only exact words I now remember were "Mr. Elliott your grammar is terrible." I came to believe at least this was true, so maybe all the other bad things she had said about me were also true. If this was the case, maybe I was the worst student she had ever had and I didn't deserve to be taking up space in a university. But, as I exited her office, all I was concerned with was controlling my tears, the heat in my face and the roaring in my ears.

Somehow I managed to get to my room in the old house, sit at my desk and stare at the wall for quite some time. I was convinced I was a failure and needed to do some thinking about what I was going to do now. After today I knew I wouldn't be able to get off probation since the best I could hope for was a "D" in my English class, but I was passing all the others so I could come back but would still be on probation. I was neither fish nor fowl at the fraternity and I had no further desire to be initiated and come back here. I simply didn't want to come back for another semester of stress and strain that I had put up with during this current one. My options seemed again to be the same as a year ago — return home, get a job and mark time, or go into the military service — which at this time didn't really want new recruits since they had a surplus of those wanting to stay in the service and a few returnees. While I was in this deep funk, I heard my bathroom door open and Garth walked in without saying a word. He pulled up a chair and sat down facing me. After a few minutes passed without either of us saying a word, he stood up, strode to the bathroom door and turned back toward me. I lifted my eyes up, looked at him and I knew he must be seeing my tears — but I didn't care. Again he paused a couple of minutes, then said "I have had my mouth set all afternoon for a big plate of El Mat enchiladas but they would taste even better if I had a friend to share them with me. I'll go back through, lock my door, you do the same and I'll meet you at the front door." I told him I didn't think I would be very good company right now. His reply, "There is no one I had rather be with right now." He walked into the bathroom; I heard the hall door to his room close and looked up at him standing in my doorway. I stared a minute or so as he just stood there. I wiped the tears from my eyes, got up, walked through the doorway and closed the door behind me.

We didn't talk much going to, eating or coming back from supper at the El Mat. Garth didn't ask me any questions about what had happened so we just made a little small talk about the happenings around the old house and the residents. When we got back to the old house I was surprised to see BM sitting in the living room all by himself. I thought something must be wrong but he said since he didn't see me at the supper table in the big house he thought he would walk over and see how things were going. I told him that as far as I knew everything was fine. Garth spoke up with "I owed him a mess of good enchiladas so we had 'em tonight." BM just smiled, said "You country boys" and walked out.

In two or three days I was settled down in my thinking, decided to go through with the semester and complete this one through grit alone. The semester had a little over a month to run since the school was now on the old schedule — the Christmas and New Year holiday period, a couple of weeks of class and then final exams. The only decision I had made was that I didn't want to come back to UT for the spring semester. I felt obligated to share this with BM so the first time we were alone, I told him so. He just thought a minute or so, then asked what I was going to do. When I responded with "I don't know right now" he said "I — we — will really miss you." No more was said about my leaving until he drove me to the train station for my trip home for Christmas. The last thing he said to me was "You will come back won't you?" I responded with a "Sure."

Just before the holiday break a friend from another fraternity showed up at my room one day. He brought me a printed invitation to a formal dinner and dance on Christmas Eve at the Longview Country Club being given by him and a few other UT boys for their friends from several colleges. I really wasn't in the mood for such gaiety but he said he was hand delivering it so he could get a commitment from me. He was a year or two ahead of me at school but through our fraternity activities he had taken an interest in me since some of his family, living in Kilgore, were friends of my grandparents. He always introduced me to his friends as a "good East Texas neighbor." There really wasn't any excuse for not accepting, except I needed a date — as he had pointed out. I accepted, he wrote me on a list he had (with the comment that I completed his table) and thanked me very much. I gave it very little thought until I started packing to go home and remembered to include my tux — yet not fully committed in my mind to going to the party.

Again on the train traveling home for the holidays, I was in deep thought most of the time during the long and crowded trip. I didn't want to spoil my family's holidays with my problems so I resolved to act as happy as I could. I was becoming quite adept at putting on a happy face — even if I felt terribly bad, inside. I just couldn't completely give up the idea of going into the armed forces. I kept turning over my choices — the Navy, Marines or maybe the Air Force.

My first day at home found me in Overton to see who was around that I could visit. I stopped in at Hall Drug for a cherry Coke and there was Joyce Petty behind the counter with her sparkling smile and a twinkle in each eye. I spoke to her and she responded with a warm greeting. We didn't talk much but eyed each other as I sipped my Coke and she went about her duties. Then it hit me, she would be a great one for a date to the dinner/dance — good looking enough to make the guys jealous and a fine mixer. Also I figured that she and her mother could outfit her in just three days if anyone could. The first chance I got when the fountain was kind of deserted, I asked her if she was dating anyone I knew. She just smiled and replied "No one in particular." About that time someone sat down two or three stools from me and she turned to serve them. In a couple of minutes she came back and with a funny look in her eyes, asked me if there would be anything else. I could take her question more than one way so I choose what I hoped she intended. I replied that I had an invitation to a formal dinner dance on Christmas Eve in Longview and would like it very much if she could and would go with me. She reacted as if this was more than she intended, then smiled, said she would love to, I could give her the details later and she would call her mother to start thinking about a dress for her. I was the one a bit surprised this time but felt it worked out better than I imagined it would so I just said "Thanks, we can talk more tomorrow," turned and walked out the front door. Later I wondered if I had paid for my drink.

I checked with her each day, including the day of the date, going over our plans. By Christmas Eve we were talking like old friends again. I found out this was the time her family had always celebrated their Christmas together but due to Joyce's big date they were going to move it to Christmas Day. Early that evening, when I went to pick her up, the whole family (even Granny) was gathered in the living room to see us off. They acted as if this was her very first date. Other than Mrs. Petty, everyone wanted to be introduced to me — evidently not remembering that we had met about five or so months before.

For some reason Mother and Dad wanted me to stop in Kilgore at my aunt Ruby's (mother's sister) house to swap cars. Joyce didn't go in with me but Dad came out to supervise. Funny how these things stick in your mind for years and years. We took Ruby's Hudson, leaving our Buick for Mother and Dad. They along with Ruby and her kids, later that evening, were going to Grandma's to spend the night and be there and ready for the big Christmas. I think Carl Jr. and Lanell (the kids) were at the Jeter's (their other grandparents just down the street) for the Jeter's Christmas.

Dad had to remind me not to stay out all night, told Joyce how pretty she looked (they were acquainted since he was then the police chief in Overton and in Hall's almost daily) and then told me there were two dozen fresh eggs in the refrigerator from Ma's that I was to bring with me in the morning to Grandma's. He watched us drive off.

It was a perfect evening as far as I was concerned, since I normally didn't care much for such affairs — being a terribly bad dancer and at that time not liking to spend a couple of hours over dinner and conversation. The company at our table was very nice and the conversation good. Joyce was the only one at our table still in high school but she held her own with her poise, personality and looks. After finishing dinner, during the dancing, I mostly had my arms around her and let her do the dancing. Since we were strangers to most of the people we spent a lot of time sitting, talking and getting better acquainted. Two or three people, finding out this was our first date, said we certainly made a nice looking couple. I began to feel very comfortable with her.

When I took her home that night, as I thanked her for the evening and trying to tell her good night, she brushed me on the lips with a very soft kiss, said she had a good time too, good night and rushed inside. I walked to Ruby's car and went home — thinking maybe life wasn't so bad after all.

I stopped in Hall's nearly every day during the week between Christmas and New Year to "see" her. I think people were beginning to notice, but I didn't care. We didn't have another regular date during the holidays, but we had an almost date. One evening I was there waiting till time to eat some supper at the Busy Bee (Mother and Dad had gone with someone out of town and Sonny was visiting a friend) when she was called to the phone for a call. She came back and was telling Nelda that Ed, her brother, was in Henderson and had a flat on their car. The spare was also flat so he was going to be late picking her up. She asked Nelda if she could walk home with her (Nelda's home only about three or four blocks away) and wait there until her dad could come get her or Ed was able to get the tire aired up and come for her. Nelda said sure, but me being the gentleman I thought I was, said "Let me take both of you to supper next door and then I will take both of you home." Nelda said that sounds great for you and Joyce but it's my night to fix supper for the family so I need to get on home or my name will be Mud." I came up with "Just a slight change of plans, 'we' will take Nelda home, eat at Busy Bee, and then make the run to New London." They looked at each other, Nelda quickly nodded, then Joyce. I told them my car was parked out front and I would be in it when they were ready. In about fifteen minutes they came to the car, we dropped Nelda at home, then came back to the same parking space.

We had another nice meal together with good conversation and headed for her home. This time I was the one who initiated the kiss.

On the train, headed back to Austin, my thoughts more and more turned toward my returning home at the end of the semester — and not joining a branch of the armed forces.

As we were driving from the train station to the old house, BM suggested we not tell anyone of my plans to leave at the end of the semester so he would have some time to think about replacing me without being hounded with people that might want my job. This sounded great to me also, I wouldn't be working under a lame-duck atmosphere. He would handle the change in his own way.

I finished the semester as best I could without too much pressure on myself or others. I wouldn't know my grades till they were mailed to my parents since I planned to exit Austin as soon as I finished my last exam. I had accumulated some junk so I found a sturdy wooden box to pack and ship it home and took only one suitcase and my portable typewriter with me on the train. I told Glenn goodbye in his room, went by BM's office, left my keys and a note pad with some notes he might need and then Garth took me to the station. We took my box into the express office and left it for shipping. We had about thirty minutes until time for my train so Garth waited with me and we talked. I invited him to come visit me, he halfway promised to do so when it was summer, but as we bid each other goodbye we both knew this was probably the last time to see each other — and that proved to be the case.

My trip home and reception were rather ordinary. I had not written anyone since leaving on the second of January, my parents only knowing that I was coming in as soon as the semester was over. When I got off the train in Overton, I went into the depot, used the pay phone to call the house and got Sonny. I told him I was in Overton at the depot and I heard him yell to Mother. In a few seconds he said "Mother said we will be there in a few minutes" and hung up. The man in the express office said my box would be there tomorrow afternoon on the same train I had come on today. I walked outside and looked around some, feeling rather strange. I didn't feel like I was home but in some distant place yet everything looked familiar. I wanted to get back on the train and go further but seemed tied to this place. I saw our car turn the corner and head toward me. Sonny jumped out to help me with my suitcase and wanted to know why I didn't just wait a couple of hours for Dad to get off and come home with him. Sarcastically I said "I couldn't wait to see you" and playfully punched him on the shoulder — as he grinned really big. Mother wanted to know how was my trip, how were things in Austin and was I hungry, all in the same breath. I told her I had a good trip, everything was fine in Austin and I could wait for supper. We went home, Mother finished preparing our meal and Dad came in for the night. He was surprised to find me in the backyard visiting with Sonny's horse and the dogs. He said I could have caught a ride with him when I told him I had come in on the train that afternoon. I thought to myself maybe I don't want you to know everything I do in Overton.

At supper Mother and Sonny filled me in on our family happenings then Dad got me up to date on the things (and rumors circulating) around Overton. He ended his report with "I dropped in at Hall's on the way home and Joyce wanted to know if you would be in between semesters. I told her we were expecting you any day." I just acknowledged his interesting report and excused myself saying I needed to get some clothes together for tomorrow. I was a little afraid he might keep talking about Joyce or some other of my friends if I hung around so I didn't want to appear too interested in his little encounter at Hall's.

When I woke up the next morning, Dad had already gone to work. It seems their schedule was to get up about four thirty, Mother would prepare their breakfast to be ready at five and then Dad would leave for Overton about five thirty. Mother would usually read the Dallas Morning News and Tyler Morning Telegraph with another cup of coffee until between six and six thirty when she got Sonny up to get ready for school. She always had another good breakfast for him to make the school day on. Dad's early morning schedule didn't vary — seven days a week. On Saturdays he usually came home up in the morning or about noon. Sundays Mother and Sonny would meet him at the church for Sunday school and church services then to Grandma's for Sunday dinner, unless something unusual had happened during the night that Dad had to work on. Dad ate lunch at one of the Overton restaurants Monday through Friday to be visible to the public (Mother met him once or sometimes twice a week for supper also) since some of the town people resented his living five miles away at Leverett's Chapel and not a City of Overton tax payer. I think this, along with some other factors, finally led him to leave this job after several more years and go to work for the Leverett's Chapel ISD as the building maintenance supervisor — from which he retired after getting enough years in to do so under the teacher retirement system in 1972. They built a new home in Overton and retired there. Joyce and I bought the LC properties consisting of the home and about eight rental houses on the property.

My first full day at home was sunny and unusually warm for the middle of winter. After Sonny and I ate breakfast and he got off to school, soon Mother appeared at my bedroom door wearing a jacket, hat and work gloves then said "I am going to clean out some flower beds in the front yard this morning. I could use a little help if you are up to it." Well I knew this simply meant she wanted me to work in her flower beds so I said "Sure, let me dig out some work clothes and I'll be right with you." We worked until almost noon, taking a couple of breaks to warm up and have something to drink during the morning. Mother stopped her work, put up her tools, and told me to finish the small bed I was working on and then come in to get ready for lunch. I didn't say anything, just nodded my head and went on with what I was doing.

Mother had her timing down pat, as I watched her put the bowl of chicken salad on the table alongside the chips, lettuce, pickles, onions, bread and drinks, we heard Sonny call from the door that he was home. Mother still fixed lunch for him every day — he walked across the highway for it as we had done ever since I started in the first grade. Sonny, trying to make small talk as we ate, asked what I was doing with my time. Mother answered him with a report on our morning's work. I told him I was going into town later after lunch to get my box at the train station. He asked if I had time and could to stop by Gordon's to get him a sack of horse feed since it was getting low. He said Gordon knew the kind and would put it on Dad's account. This reminded me that Dad had leased a place nearby and stocked it with some Black Angus cows. I said "I didn't even ask Dad yesterday how his cows were doing." Sonny said that he could tell me since he was the one that hayed 'em and gave 'em some cake every other day. "They eat a lot" and grinned. Mother said she and Dad had ridden around the pasture on Sunday afternoon in Dad's old Dodge coupe to check on them. She said they all looked good and they were expecting a good calf crop — starting very soon. As we got up from the table, Mother turned to me and said that I may have noticed the car had some red clay dried on it from the last rain and I could wash it off while the weather was fairly warm and I had on my work clothes if I would. I said "O K" and followed Sonny out to get a bucket, hose, soap and a wash rag.

After I had done a fair job of cleaning the car, I came in, bathed and put on some fresh clothes. Mother saw me walking down the hall and commented "My you look nice, going somewhere?" I said I was getting ready to go to town to get my things at the train station and pick up Sonny's horse feed. I asked if she wanted to go. She answered in the negative but added that she needed a couple of things from Davis Grocery that I could pick up for her. She went to the kitchen and returned with a short list and said "Just charge them."

On the way to town I mapped out in my mind the route I would take. First to Davis Grocery, Gordon's, and then to the train station before my last stop at Hall's. I visited with Mrs. Davis (Mr. Davis must have been in the back store room where he sometimes "hide" to read) and found out Novice was stationed in New Jersey at an Army base taking some type of training but was having trouble with stomach ulcers. After the Davis grocery stop I drove up the street past the ice house to the feed store. Gordon was in an unusually talkative mood for him — being married to Bonnie, my Mother's first cousin he considered us "close enough kin" to confide in me, I guess. He inquired what I was doing home, what I was planning to do and such. I visited with him and he finally came around to why so many questions and his interest in what I was going to be doing. He told me that a new man in town (John Crager) had bought the ice house, and as his next door business owner, he was helping John with a few things. One problem they each faced was that the bookkeeper for both businesses had to be replaced since she had moved with her oil field employed husband to South Texas where he had been transferred. Gordon explained further that his business had slowed down some so Bonnie had decided she would do their bookkeeping for the store since she had had some business college way back but had never needed to work. The ice house business was slowing down some too he said with people getting refrigerators to replace ice boxes more and more. He said Albert (my Dad) had told him that I had been doing some bookkeeping on my job in Austin so he was wondering if I might want a few hours work a week. He had mentioned me to John that morning (after finding out from Dad in the coffee shop that I was home) about the job and John sounded interested so he was going to tell my Dad when he came in but I had shown up first so he had gotten the word straight to me.

I thanked him and said I would walk next door, meet Mr. Crager and discuss the job with him — mostly just to please Gordon. Then he told me John wasn't there since he had to go to Tyler on some business, but would be there the next morning. I thanked him again and went to the depot to retrieve my box. After loading it in the trunk of the car I drove over to Hall's Drug. I went in and sat down at the fountain — looking for Joyce. Nelda, down at the other end behind the counter, turned, saw me and rushed over to speak and take my order. As we talked and I sipped on my cherry Coke, I casually looked around and asked if Joyce was working. Nelda laughed teasingly and said "I wondered when you would ask." Then quickly "She isn't scheduled to work again until Saturday." Seeing the disappointment in my face she added "There is always the phone" and hurriedly reached for an order pad, wrote down Joyce's number and handed it to me.

I left the drug store in low spirits, now realizing how much I had looked forward to seeing Joyce again. I was really surprised at how disappointed I was in missing her. I went on home and took my box into my room and started unpacking it when Mother stuck her head in the door and inquired if everything was alright. I acted as if her question was about the box so I responded that it seems to be fine. She then said she was stepping over to the Deason's to visit with her just a few minutes before getting supper ready.

Since Sonny was at school, late for some reason, I was alone. I took out the slip of paper Nelda had given me, walked into the hall, rang the bell on the telephone (still a party line), gave the operator the number and waited for an answer. When the hello came, I asked if I could speak to Joyce. I was told that it was Joyce speaking, to which I responded "This is Floyd." From her came "Well, I was wondering if you would ever call or if I wouldn't hear from you at all." I decided Nelda had called her to sound the alert that I was in town and to expect a call from me. I wasn't very smooth talking on the phone but finally did get around to asking her to go for a milk shake after supper, promising to get in early since it was a school night. She replied that she would be ready any time I got there.

Our supper went about the same as yesterday except tonight I could tell about my visit with Gordon and that I was going to see John Crager in the morning about doing some bookkeeping for him. Dad said that might be a chance to get some good experience since there wasn't a lot of work around town at that time. So as soon as I finished eating, I asked if it would be alright if I took the car for a couple of hours and went to town. Mother said that would be fine and gave Dad a look which he understood to mean not to ask me any questions. As I said thanks and excused myself, Sonny looked up grinning and asked if I needed him to go to keep me company. I assured him I would be fine and the three of them laughed a little as I walked into the hall and put on my jacket.

My first date with Joyce after returning home turned out really well. I saw all of her family at her house before we got off for the DriveInn in Overton which now was the big hang out after dark. We sat in the car, drank our milkshakes and talked. Actually Joyce did most of the talking, she loved to talk and I equally liked hearing her talk about what had been happening with her and her friends since I had been gone. We decided we would have a big date Saturday night; first dinner at Jay's Café in Henderson, a movie at the Crim in Kilgore and then back to the DriveInn in Overton before calling it a night and me taking her home. As I told her good night at her front door, with her family closely watching from the living room, we both said we were looking forward to Saturday night.

The next morning after Sonny and I had breakfast and he got off to school, I got ready to go see John Crager. I waited around till a little after eight before I left so I wouldn't get to the ice house before they were ready for the day. I needed not worry about arriving too early since the trucks had all loaded and left on their first deliveries. Since it was still winter there were only two trucks loading out and one of these made only one route with a single load while the other made a short afternoon run also. I parked right in front of the office and could see all the way through it.

I saw this one man sitting at a desk in the center so he could see in all directions from his vantage point. He watched me get out of the car, got up, opened the front door and met me in the doorway. He stuck out his hand and said "I'm John." I replied with "Floyd Elliott, Mr. Crager," as we shook hands. He said "Call me John, come on in and have a seat," pointing at the chair beside the desk where he had been sitting. He closed the door behind us and retook his seat behind the desk.

I didn't rush him because I sensed he wanted to take his own time. He was quite a bit larger than me, about the same size as my Dad I judged, but looked a few years younger than Dad. He started out with "I feel like I kind of know you since I have visited with Gordon and your dad about you." I just nodded my head and he went on. "In fact, Gordon and your dad had coffee with me this morning while I ate breakfast about six-thirty in the Bee. You were the main topic of discussion." Still I just nodded and let him continue with the lead. "Gordon and I had talked about you as possibly being interested in my little bookkeeping needs and then this morning I found out that your dad might have some work he could use you to help him with also. So we decided we needed to see what you thought, but your dad had to go to Henderson to appear in county court on the sentencing of some fugitive he was involved in the arresting of and couldn't be here this morning — so he left it up to me to explain my part and then he would do his with you this evening." I replied with an "O K" this time.

"I met Elouise a couple of years ago in Dallas and found out about Overton through her. We visited back and forth until we decided to get married a few months ago. Both of us had been married before, and I am sure you know a little of her past history as everyone in town seems to since her family is an old one here. She had her own beauty shop and family home here and I wasn't doing much, so we decided to settle down and live here. I looked around for something to do and found this ice house was for sale. With some help from my brother J. C. and the veteran's program, I was able to swing the deal. I didn't intend to work a whole lot, just do a little managing. It has turned out to demand more of my time than I had planned. We are getting by now since our busy season is over until the weather warms up some, but I didn't want to assume the bookkeeping work and could use a little more help here on the dock also. That's where you entered into the picture when Gordon told me you had come home from college, had some bookkeeping experience, was a hard worker and probably wouldn't mind a little work on the dock. I decided what I could use right now was someone to take care of the dock from two pm till closing at six and do the bookkeeping in the office at the same time while not busy with sales off the dock."

As he finished his last sentence the front door opened and a young man came in, turned to a cash register on a table against the side wall to my right, rang up a sale, put the money in the cash drawer, closed the drawer, and walked back outside. John went on with "That was Johnny, he works the dock from six am until two pm when he is replaced by one of the two drivers, usually the one that is making only one trip in the mornings. Right now I want to get rid of that driver, he gripes and complains too much. I don't want to do any dock work myself, so if I had someone to cover the dock after Johnny gets off, I would let that driver go. I am basically saying I can offer you about a half-time job, four hours a day, six days a week, working in the office and keeping an eye on the dock to take care of the few sales we have there during that time. And, after talking to your dad this morning, I know he would like for you to go to Kilgore College and take a couple of courses this spring semester to see how you like it there. Having been in and out of college for a total of about three years, I think his idea has merit, but that's for you two to decide on."

He went on to tell me what he paid the route drivers (including the commission on their sales), Johnny's pay and the pay for Travis Grindle (the engineer who operated the equipment, maintained it, "pulled the ice blocks" and ran them through the scoring machine). My salary would be a little more than half Johnny's pay since I would have more responsibility, such as minding the office and bookkeeping. He asked if I had any questions at that point. I shook my head, said I didn't think so, and quickly added, "I probably don't know enough to intelligently ask any questions right now." He nodded and said, "It will take a little time. Now let me show you around and introduce you to Johnny and Travis."

We went through all the buildings, observed the machinery working and visited with the other two employees. I had bought ice off the dock before to make ice cream at home and for the Rambo's watermelons but had no idea how much stuff was in the building behind it. When we looked in at the "cooler room" he asked me if I wanted a coke as he pulled one out of a case. When I said yes, he pulled out another for himself. We went back into the office and drank our cokes as he chatted some about what he had done and where he had been during the war. Then he told me of a project he was working on to rejuvenate the old golf course at the City Park. I told him I had played golf only once and didn't know much about it. He said he loved it and felt the course at the park had great possibilities.

I said I had a question about the bookkeeping, since I didn't know much about that — just the way we had done it at the fraternity house and when I had worked for the Navy one summer. He said the books were very simple and from a shelf behind his desk pulled down a couple of large account books. He showed me how it was done since he had been doing it for a few weeks. I felt sure I could do it alright and told him so. He said he would work with me to begin with until I felt completely confident.

We walked outside, stood around and talked a while and finally he said "You talk it over with your folks and if you think you would be comfortable working here, I will be pleased to have you." With that we shook hands, I got in the family car and headed home.

After I got home, I asked Mother if she had anything she needed me to do. She replied with a "No", but then added she would love to know how my meeting with John Crager had gone. I welcomed the opportunity to tell her for it gave me a chance to recall and turn it over in my mind. Afterward she simply said that it sounded good for me if I would like to do that. I told her what John had said about Dad had something he wanted me to do for him and I was wondering what it could be. She said we would wait until he got in for supper to discuss that and let him do it, but she did tell me that they had talked a lot last night about they both wished I would patch up my poor college record some by taking a few courses at Kilgore College. I had not even thought of such a thing until John had made a slight reference to it today. I realized I had some thinking to do so I told mother I was going into my room and straighten up some papers on my desk. She said she needed to get busy on our lunch for Sonny would be in pretty soon.

I just piddled away the afternoon waiting for supper and Dad to come in for our "big" evening conference. I did go over to Mrs. Carter's combination home and café to visit with her and Evelyn (the oldest of her four kids and only daughter, married to Cowboy Bishop and home for a visit) and get a report on Marcus who was now in the Navy and serving somewhere in the Pacific. They told me he was doing fine and seemed to enjoy his work. Mrs. Carter went into her bedroom and brought out the last two or three letters from Marcus for me to read while she and Evelyn made a pot of coffee and got out some cookies for us. After this visit I crossed Don Leverett Rd. and went in what used to be Davis Grocery to say hello (now run by the Lambs from Arkansas who had bought it from the Davis family). Mr. and Mrs. Davis "retired" and bought a home in Overton. In less than a year they had bought another store in Overton and were now running it. Mr. Davis never retired again, worked in that store until he died several years later. He said the store business gets in your blood and just won't go away. After his death Novice and his mother continued to run the store until she passed away. The store was then sold, Novice getting three-fourths of the proceeds and his older brother Wendell (living in Oklahoma) a fourth — the proceeds from the sale of the house were divided evenly. Novice had been raising cows on leased land so now he bought a farm, moved the cows and his family on it and "messed" with cows the rest of his life. The last I heard Patsy, his wife, still lives there with maybe some grandkids and probably their kids — the way life in East Texas goes on.

When I got back to the house, Mother was already preparing supper. I went into the kitchen and sat down at the table. She waited for me to tell her what I had been doing. Before I started that I asked her if there was anything I could help her with. She said "Yes, go wash your hands in the bathroom and then I will give you some potatoes, carrots and onions to peel and cut up. I've decided to make a pot roast for supper so it will be fresh out of the oven when your Dad gets in." I did as she directed and when I got back to the table the vegetables were lying there on newspapers with a couple of knives and bowls neatly arranged around a large cutting board for me to get to work on as I told her of my visit with the Carters and Lambs. She was washing a big piece of meat in the sink and placed the meat on some cloths on the drain board to pat dry. She got out her big cast-iron skillet, put several pats of butter in it, placed it on the stove and turned on the gas flame. She then generously salted and peppered the meat, put it in the skillet and browned it on both sides. She turned off the gas and as I put vegetables from the cutting board into the bowls she would take them to the sink and rinse them off before she put them in the skillet with the meat. When the vegetables were all loaded in the skillet she handed me a cloth for each hand and asked me to lift the pan and place it in the warm oven. She said, "In a little over an hour I will put in a pan of biscuits to cook and then pretty quickly supper will be ready — Albert's favorite."

Again Mother's timing was right on the money. Supper was ready just a few minutes after Dad's and Sonny's arrival. During and after our meal we were involved with small talk, mostly what each had been doing. Mother surprised us with a hot, fresh sweet potato pie for our dessert that had baked while we ate. Mother had some coffee with hers but the three "boys" opted for a fresh cold glass of milk.

Dad said one thing he forgot to tell us was that he had run into Randolph Watson at the court house in Henderson. He said that Sonny and I probably didn't remember him but he had married Ellen Rhode — one of the LC teachers that had lived with us for two or three years and taught Sonny in the second grade. Sonny said he didn't remember Mr. Watson at all but he would always remember Miss Rhode because she was his all-time favorite teacher. I said I remembered her too and had seen her a few times — and she always calls me Sonny and thinks she taught me. Mother said she is sure it must be confusing for teachers to keep pupils straight with so many over the years.

Dad said he had visited for a while with Randolph and found out that after he had gotten out of the Marine Corp. he had attended some graduate school and now was teaching government at Kilgore College. Dad said they had discussed my college career and both thought I was too young to have gone off to the university at sixteen and could now use some catch up on my college classes. Randolph reinforced Dad's idea that now I should try Kilgore College at home before I gave up on college. He said he had talked that idea over with John Crager also when talking about my working at the ice house because John had been to college some before the war, some during the war and even some after the war. He had decided he didn't want to follow an academic career but seemed to be plenty knowledgeable about academics. He told Dad he didn't think I should give up on college now and he wanted to encourage me to keep trying and would do so if I worked at the ice house.

So with the four of us sitting around the empty supper plates and dirty dishes, looking back and forth at each other, Dad went on to say that he and Mother had discussed it last night and had come to the conclusion that they would ask me to sign up for a couple of morning classes in Kilgore and work in the afternoons at the ice house. I could use the car to go to class and Mother could take me to work if she needed the car and I could come home with Dad. That way I could apply myself to my classes and yet have spending money and time to "run around" some. Everybody was pretty quiet at this point so I injected "Talking to John Crager he had said you had some work you wanted me to do. How does that fit into this picture?"

Dad said "There is no rush on it. On Florence St. facing the railroad right-a-way there is an old house that the City is afraid is going up in flames during dry weather since it has been vacant for many years. It has a train load of great lumber in it. They have put it up for sale for the taxes due on it but no takers. Now they will give it away if someone will put up a one thousand dollar bond that it will be completely removed and the lot cleaned. I figure we could do that and use the lumber to build a couple of houses on our property next to where I let Floyd Williams build his new house. I already have two water connections there and electricity would be no problem. With my help on week-ends and my vacation time you could do most of it. I would pay you the same hourly pay you would be getting at the ice house, but we wouldn't start until your classes were over for the spring semester and then we would have all summer while you weren't going to school.

Sonny excitedly said, "Since it will be in the summer after school is out, I could work on it too!" Both Mother and Dad smiled at him and Mother said, "Yes we can work that out also — later."

Dad added "Since your pay for work at the ice house would be more than you need for spending money, the pay from the building project would go into your education fund for when you went off to school." I looked around and all I could do was to say "Looks like you have covered all the bases and sounds like a good plan to me. First thing in the morning I'll go back to see John, tell him I will take his offer, and then head to the college to see about enrolling."

I looked at Mother, she had her eyes closed but I saw tears coming from the corners, Sonny was grinning and Dad said, "You should have enough money in your bank account to pay your tuition and buy your books." We got up from the table and started clearing it.

Things seemed to fall in place the next day. I visited with John again and we decided I would start work at the ice house the next day (Saturday) and when I got to Kilgore College I found that day to be the last day of regular registration. The people in the Registrar's office were very kind and helpful — even seemed glad to have me. Since no advance preparations had been made for my registration, we had to start from scratch. They said someone would phone Leverett's Chapel School to get a copy of my high school record mailed today and based on that I would be admitted. They stamped on my papers Conditional Admissions and I went through the process. I decided to retake the same English literature course again for I was sure I had made a "D" in it and I wanted to retake all my classes that had an "F" or "D" on record in order to get my grade point average up to at least a "C". When looking for another class to take I noticed a government one taught by Randolph Watson and decided I would try for it since he might help me a little considering our backgrounds. When I went to the government table to sign up, the lady said it was a sophomore course and with conditional admissions she couldn't verify that I was a sophomore. I pulled out my UT Activity Card from the previous semester and handed it to her. It didn't say sophomore on it anywhere she could tell, but somewhere it said third semester student so she let me register for the course. I knew I probably didn't have nearly enough semester hours to qualify as a sophomore, but what are a few semester hours between friends? I paid my fees, got my books from the bookstore and headed home — ready to begin classes on Monday.

I didn't call Joyce, and I hadn't talked to her since our milk shake date when we had made plans for our big date Saturday night. I thought I would just let that rest until Saturday morning when I would go to Hall's for a sandwich lunch and then to the ice house early for work.

That afternoon before supper I wrote a long letter to BM, especially thanking him for all the help and kindness he had shown toward me. I then brought him up to date on all that had transpired since my return home and our plans for the summer. I felt I at least owed him that much. Later, after supper, I wrote a letter to Garth, just as long, thanking him for his friendship and the good times we had together. These messages effectively ended my connections with UT and Austin. I felt more remorse than I thought I would.

At supper we had another good family meal with me reporting on the progress I had made concerning work and school. Everyone seemed more relaxed and feeling things were going to be alright.

Saturday was a great day, the best I had in a long time. I got to Hall's about eleven and Joyce was there. I told her I had a lot of news to tell but it would mostly wait till we left for Henderson on our date. I said I would pick her up between seven and seven-thirty due to my new job.

I ordered a chicken salad sandwich (Mrs. Hall's specialty, she personally prepared the chicken salad at home) with the trimmings and a vanilla shake. As I ate, and Joyce was back and forth, I quickly told her about my job at the ice house. She was surprised. When I finished my meal, I just waved to her after I paid my bill and headed for the car. I arrived at the ice house about a quarter till twelve, parked in the back and reported for work. John was surprised I was so early. Johnny showed me the ropes around the dock and the coding for sales. He used a J for his sales, John used a C for his and the others who used the cash register also used an initial. None used an F so I adopted it. By one o'clock we had gone through all the dock procedures and I was ready for some books and the office. John said we would hold that till later in the day since he was ready for some lunch. Everything went fine the rest of the day and John said he would let me have that afternoon shift all alone come Monday.

That night I picked Joyce up as promised and we drove to Henderson;

making small talk on the way. We parked almost in front of Jay's on South Main just a half block off the square. We chose one of the booths to the right side of the entrance. I commented on the heavy curtains which you could close for privacy if so desired but opted to leave our booth open to view and be viewed. The menus, with a pitcher of ice water, fresh glasses, silver wear and napkins were already on the table and in only a couple of minutes a young girl was at our table holding out a tray of warm rolls freshly baked. We each picked one and put it on the small plate with a couple of pats of butter which the girl and placed before us as she said, "Your waitress will be here in just a few minutes to take your order." We both buttered our rolls and then looked at the menus. I said, "I'm starving so I think I will have their big chicken fried steak with a baked potato." Joyce folded her menu and said "I'm not that hungry so I think I will have a BLT with some potato salad." We both went back to our rolls while they were still warm and taking a few sips from our water. We didn't talk, just watched each other enjoying our rolls and just smiled a great deal.

After the waitress came, took our order and went to turn it in, Joyce said, "O K, so what's the big news?" I replied that my job at the ice house was the first part but that it was designed so I would be able to go to school some also. I told of my registering for two courses at KC the day before and that I would be starting classes on Monday. She had a few questions and we talked back and forth until our food arrived. I was hungry so I attacked my food with a fresh supply of those delicious rolls — not able to remember ever having such delicious food. I decided the company had a lot to do with it for, with a mouth full of steak, I realized I was head over heels in love with the girl on the other side of the table. It was at that moment I knew she was the one, the one I wanted to spend the rest of my life loving, taking on together whatever life had to offer — hand in hand. Of course I didn't want to tell her that for fear she would laugh, so I just chewed my food, adoringly watching her nibble on her sandwich.

We did drive over to Kilgore but when we drove by the Crim we decided we weren't interested in that movie and had rather just ride around and talk. She asked that we go by my aunt's house and then the Longview Country Club — remembering our first date on Christmas Eve. In Longview we parked in front of the Country Club, just holding hands and watching the people come and go. We must have sat there an hour or more as she got into a talkative mood and told me about so many things — all I could do was love her more.

As we didn't go to the movie as planned, neither did we go back to the DriveInn in Overton. We went back to her house, sat out front for a while and said our good nights at the front door. After our good night kiss, she looked me in the eyes and said, "You are so special, please don't get away from me," turned and went into the house. I didn't know what to think, I was just kind of dizzy and seeing with things blurred. As I drove off, I realized — maybe, she is serious too.

Monday I met my two classes at KC. Things were getting a little restless when it was time for the government class to start and no instructor had shown up. About five minutes later two men walked through the door, the older of the two walked up to the teacher's desk, looked around and nodded at a few of the students. He said, "As some of you already know I'm Pop Christenson and am director of the Arts and Science Division here at the college. This large distinguished looking man here is Mr. Randolph Watson, who was to be your instructor in this class. This morning the president appointed him to the newly created post of dean of men so we had to relieve him of some of his teaching load and unfortunately your class was one of them. So we will need to get another instructor beginning Wednesday. I promise you it will be a good one — even if I have to teach it myself. So let's give Mr. Watson a hand and best wishes on his new assignment. We all clapped, Mr. Watson waved a hand in appreciation and left the room. Pop Christenson said, "Class is dismissed" and hung around a few minutes talking with students.

I had no idea of what an important role these two men would play in my future. Neither taught me in the classroom, but Watson was the Dean of the College that hired me later as an instructor of history and psychology and Christenson was my director — and I am glad to say also both were very good friends. Randolph Watson was later promoted to the post of president and served many years in that capacity developing the college.

That spring semester was a busy one for Joyce since it was her senior year, with the many end of school activities such as the senior play, banquet and prom, senior day, etc., but after that night at Jay's, as far as others were concerned, it was "us" for the next sixty-eight years — we were married just a year and a few months later. I finished the semester (with a B in the government class and a C in the English — realizing that with a little more effort I would have had a B in it also) and this boosted me into thinking that I would be ready in the fall to tackle bigger stuff. When the weather began to warm, Dad completed the deal on his old house in Overton, traded his car for a new pickup and I started work on dismantling the old house on Tuesday, Thursday and Saturday mornings when I had no classes to attend. We went into summer planning for the fall.

GOING ON .....

After completing the 1947 spring semester at Kilgore College I was working in the mornings on Dad's project of reclaiming the materials from the old house in Overton and moving them to LC to use in constructing a couple of rent houses. I continued my job in the afternoons at the ice house. Joyce had graduated from high school and continued her part time job at Hall's during the summer. About once a week we had a real date, at least a couple of times a week I would visit her in the evenings at her house and we went to church together on Sunday evenings. Our dates usually consisted of going to the Pine Grove teen-age hangout near Turnertown, where there was a juke box, soft drinks, a small dance floor and booths for sitting and visiting — both indoors and outdoors. I didn't (and couldn't) dance very well, so we just mostly hung around with the others, sipped Cokes and talked. This was a nice, clean, well run place where no alcoholic beverages, cursing or bad behavior was allowed.

We had talked a lot about our future and trying to decide what to do about the coming school year. Joyce's parents were adamant that they wanted her to go to college, get an education so she would be able to support herself if she needed to in the future. She had decided on preparing to be a teacher and told me a little story on how that came about.

In the Petty's New London neighborhood, about a block from their house, lived Mrs. Etheridge and her three daughters. I think Mr. Etheridge had been killed in an oil field accident since Mrs. Etheridge was a widow. She was a hard worker but had a difficult time raising her daughters on her meager earnings doing housework and taking in laundry to wash and iron. I heard Mr. Petty once refer to the time the men of their church put a new roof on her house when he found out it was in such bad shape. The girls were also hard workers and very bright. The oldest and Mrs. Petty, being somewhat close to the same age, were very dear friends but since

Mrs. Petty married at fifteen and started a family when very young they were living much different lives. The elder Etheridge girl graduated from the New London High School, and having nothing else to do, took a year's post graduate secretarial services course which the high school offered (as some high schools did at that time). She did so well in this program that the school hired her as the high school office secretary. She worked at this job until the next girl graduated and wanted to go to college for training as a nurse. In order for the second girl to go to college, the older one got a good job (based on her experience at the high school) in Houston and the family moved there.

The oldest daughter was the primary bread winner and sent the two younger ones through college. The youngest one made a teacher, and all, the mother and three daughters, still lived together as a family unit for a time. During this period, one summer while Ed and Bo were at church camp, Joyce and her mother visited the Etheridges. Joyce, observing that while the oldest sister was working five days a week in an office, the middle sister was doing very physical and hard shift work in a hospital, while the youngest one was on a three month vacation as a teacher. Those were the three most common vocations for women at that time. Joyce said, as far as she was concerned, the choice for her was a no brainer — she would take teaching.

As for my plans, I wasn't sure at that time other than to finish college and try to provide a living for Joyce and me. I probably wasn't motivated enough at that time to really want to make a lot of money but felt I wanted to do something that helped people. Mother and Dad were encouraging me toward business since they felt I was getting some good experience at the ice house. More and more I was leaning toward teaching. I even considered majoring in business and getting teacher credentials also. Next to doctors, Mother and Dad probably respected teachers as professionals. Of course teachers didn't make much money so most people knew men teachers didn't do it for financial reasons if they could do something else. The problem was I didn't really like business and preferred the study of history and government above all others.

Most of Joyce's classmates where going to Kilgore College in the fall, while a few were headed to North Texas State in Denton for some reason.

Joyce and I were thinking that I would probably go off to school since I was somewhere just over a freshman in transferrable semester hours or go back to Kilgore for the fall semester and then go off for the spring semester. Joyce decided she would like for us to go for the fall to North Texas where we would have some friends. North Texas was fine with me since I didn't plan to go back to UT and had no other favorites and it was a highly regarded teacher's college. Her parents had told her they could send her off to a state college (due to tuition costs) if she worked and saved her money in the summers. We made the necessary applications and dormitory reservations.

When she discussed it with her parents and they found out we were both planning to go to the same place, Mrs. Petty balked. She said she didn't think that was a good idea (not exactly in those words) and they decided Joyce needed to go to Kilgore for her first year. Well this didn't upset us much so we both decided to go to Kilgore for the fall semester and we made the necessary switch in our paperwork.

I spent a lot of time talking with John Crager while working my shift at the ice house and also I usually came by once or twice during the mornings on my way to or from LC with a load of building materials and had coffee or a Coke with John and Travis. Other than Joyce these two were my closest "confidents" concerning my school affairs, family relationships and love life — especially John. When I told them of our plans John suggested I check with the registrar at the college for he said he thought that if you went to a senior college before or during your attendance at a junior college you could transfer more than sixty hours to a senior college. I did confer with the registrar and she told me it was true and after reviewing my record said I could go both fall and spring semesters and then transfer all of it to the senior college of my choice. After discussing it with Joyce we decided that both of us would go to Kilgore for the year. After I reported to John on this he was happy since he told me he wanted to keep me at the ice house as long as he could, but he didn't want my work there to interfere with my education.

John and Travis Grindle both turned out to be life-long friends. While I was in college John was elected to the Overton Board of Education and after I graduated he was instrumental in the school making a position for me teaching science and physical education in the elementary school. At that time there were no men (other than the colored janitors) working in the elementary school and John keenly felt the students (especially the boys) needed a male as an example and influence on them. He and Mr. Davis (of Davis Drug) campaigned for them to make a position for me and this is the reason I was able to begin my teaching career in my quasi hometown. Travis was about John's age. Married and had several children. He had an artificial leg, never would talk about it and surely didn't let it slow him down. He didn't talk much about anything but was a very good listener and any advice he gave me always turned out to be very solid. He believed in hard work, truth and Christian values. Later he was elected justice of the peace for the Overton area and was a very respected and appreciated office holder for many years. I taught a couple of his children, coached another and was high school principal to a fourth. He was always a very supportive parent of his children's teachers. I was very lucky to work with such people as these for the year and a half at the ice house and later as part of the school system for twelve years.

We started the school year at Kilgore in September. It was a very good year in our lives. We loved the school, our classes, our teachers and all the activities associated with the college. Since it was a little late in the summer when Joyce made her final decision on where to go, she did not sign up to try out for the Rangerettes, band or other big time groups. Since freshmen were required to take a P E course (unless meeting certain exemptions) she signed up for a dance class taught by Gussie Nell Davis, the Rangerette director. Late in the semester Miss Davis asked her to join the group since some dropped out when football season was ending and some had completed their college career by "catching" a husband. So Joyce was very busy the spring semester participating in the many activities associated with that program. Since I was still working half-time at the ice house and taking a full load of college classes, I had to limit my extra curricula activities. The only big activity I participated in was the spring Ranger Roundup — as student manager. At that time it was the major talent show of the year and continues to this day except now it has changed into a showcase for the Rangeretts, with several performances and a name change. My job was to coordinate the many people and parts during production and to introduce the college president.

Both New London and Leverett's Chapel belonged to the Kilgore College District so bus service was provided where both Joyce and I lived, she rode the bus most of the time — 7:30 in the morning and 4:00 in the afternoon. Since I had to be at work at the ice house in Overton by 2:00 pm, I usually took our car except when Mother needed it and then I too took the bus in the morning with her picking me up in time to get me to work in the afternoons. Some days Joyce got through also by noon and I would take her with me and drop her off at her home on my way to work. We only had one class together, but we spent a lot of time together during the entire school year.

The class we had together, American history with Miss Ruth Parks as the teacher, was my favorite that year. I, and of course Joyce, did well in all our classes but I excelled in this class. It lead me to major in history and some fifteen years later I was teaching this same course at Kilgore College with Miss Parks as my department chairman. This was the only period (two years) in my long teaching career where I taught American history — my major on my bachelor's degree and minor on both master's and doctor's degrees.

As the 1948 spring semester was winding down, I told Joyce I thought we should not wait any longer for I wanted us to get married, live together during the summer and go off to school as a couple in the fall. She said that sounded great but she didn't see how we could finance such a move at that time. I told her I would do some checking and for her to think about us getting married as soon as school was out for the summer. I was planning to get a full-time job working in the oil field during the summer.

That evening when I came in from work, Mother was putting our supper on the table but had set only two places. She said Sonny was at a track meet and would be in late and Dad would eat in town prior to a city council meeting and probably be in very late. When we began eating I wanted to talk to her about Joyce and I getting married, but couldn't think how to begin. Finally, following a somewhat extended period of silence, I just came out with, "I've been thinking of getting married." She was quiet a little while, her expression unchanged and asked, "And then what?" I didn't hesitate or stutter but probably talked too fast and excited as I told her that I wanted to get married as soon as school was out for the summer, get a job in the oil field to save some more money and go off to North Texas in Denton for the fall semester. I continued, somewhat slowing down my explaining, with more details. I told her I felt I had saved enough money through the work I had done for Dad on his building project combined with my earnings from my ice house job I had banked also to get us by until next summer when we could come back home and us both work again. Again she was silent for what seemed a long time but probably was just a couple of minutes, then she finally said, "Seems as if you have done a lot of thinking on this and we probably could work it all out. I haven't told you before but you have an educational insurance policy maturing in November in the amount of a thousand dollars that I took out when you were about one or two years old and have paid on it for something like fifteen years. Besides your insurance policy we plan to help you some when you go off to school again."

This time it was my turn to be quiet since I didn't know what to say. I wanted to reach out and squeeze her hand or hug her but we never were big on demonstrating our affections so I just sat there with tears in my eyes. Then she said, "Have you or Joyce said anything about all of this to the Pettys?" I told her we had not and I would leave it up to her as to when and how after we were a little more settled about our plans. Then she said I probably should get an engagement ring to give her and she could use it as an announcement to family and friends. I told her I didn't know anything about buying jewelry so she said that tomorrow when I come in from school before going to work she would go with me to Ergle's Jewelry in Overton and with Mr. Ergle help me pick out a ring. Then she added, "Don't say anything about all of this to your Dad or it will be all over town before we want it to be. I'll tell him myself in a day or two with orders to keep quiet about it until I tell him it's alright for him to spread the word." We smiled at each other and I think maybe she winked at me.

The next day we made our visit to the jewelry store with Mr. Ergle (they were members of our church) being very nice and helpful to us. Mother suggested a wedding set she particularly liked and Mr. Ergle said it was a very good deal for two hundred and seventy-five dollars. He added that the diamond wasn't very large but the quality was very, very good. Mother wrote out a check for it and said that was her gift to me.

I could hardly wait for it to get late enough for Joyce to get home from school to call her. When the time finally arrived I called from work and told her that I was really hungry and wondered if she could go eat supper with me when I got off from work. She said she needed to shampoo her hair but she guessed she could if we wouldn't stay out too late. I told her I wanted to go to Jay's and she said, "In that case, we can take as long as you wish, the hair can wait." Maybe she had begun to wonder if something was up — could have been the tone of my voice.

That night as we were shown to a booth at Jay's, the hostess asked if we wanted the curtains closed, I nodded yes and grinned really big which brought a nice smile to her face. This was when Joyce looked me in the eyes and said, "What's the big deal?" I didn't say a word, just kept grinning, reached in my pocket, pulled out the ring box and set it on the small roll plate in front of her. Her eyes got big, she opened the box and let out a "My Gosh! Really?" I said, "You need a ring to get married don't you?" She replied with a "But two?" and I said, "Yes, we need to be engaged for a week or two first don't we?" About then the roll girl pushed the curtains apart wide enough to hold the tray toward us as Joyce put the engagement ring on her finger and held it out for the girl to see. The roll girl smiled big and said, "How beautiful — you are one lucky girl." We thanked her but said we would pass on the rolls for a few minutes so she turned and left — after reclosing the curtains. Joyce handed the ring box back to me with the wedding ring still firmly in place with the comment that I had better hold onto it until we were ready to get married, but she was going to wear the engagement ring — all the time.

When the waitress came to take our order Joyce asked her to leave the curtains open and there also stood the roll girl with her tray. She wanted to see Joyce show the waitress her ring as a couple of other waitresses came over too. One of them said we know how to sing a happy birthday song but not a happy engagement one so we will just say congratulations. As soon as the others left, we gave our waitress the order and talked, and talked. And then we ate a little.

That night sitting in our car in front of her house, I told her what I wanted to do. Basically, get married the Saturday before the week of finals, take our finals and then go to work full time for the summer — in the mean time I would continue my work at the ice house. I was sure John could find someone to take on my dock time, probably another student, and I would continue to keep the books on the side until he could get a bookkeeper. She was thrilled with this plan and said she could hardly wait to tell her parents. She wanted to know if I had said anything to my folks and I told her about discussing it with Mother and the ring story. Her next thought was that her parents would be thrilled to know that I intended for both of us to continue college and then teach.

She decided she couldn't wait to tell her family so she asked me to come in with her while she told them. I said that it would probably be better for her to tell them alone so I wouldn't hamper their discussion. She thought I was being chicken but I persisted, we kissed and she fairly ran into the house. I drove home almost in a daze, with all that had happened in one day.

About thirty minutes after I got home and was getting ready for bed, the phone sounded our ring. I answered and it was Joyce. Her mother wanted to know if we (Mother, Dad and I) could come over tomorrow night for dinner at the Petty's and talk about the wedding. I said to give me a couple of minutes to check with my parents. When I told Mother and Dad, he was the first to respond with, "What time?" I said I would see and went back to the phone. I came back with, "She said 7:00 o'clock." Then Mother, "Tell her that will be fine and we will see them then." I relayed the message and Joyce and I talked for a few minutes. I wanted to know how things went when she told her parents and she indicated everything was fine.

The dinner the next evening was a great success. This was the first meeting for our parents and they all four seemed very happy over the developments. The only thing the Petty's wanted to be sure of in my plans was that we have a church wedding and they wanted Brother Bratton to do the ceremony. He was their ex-pastor now living in Baytown, the one who baptized Mr. and Mrs. Petty (as well as Joyce, Ed and Bo) when they got religion some years back and helped lead Mr. Petty to become a deacon in their church. Mr. Petty had checked with him that day after seeing that the church was available and found Reverend Bratton was busy with a revival the weekend I had selected but was free the next one. So, the Pettys were suggesting that the date be set for the Saturday after our finals and we were free from school for the summer. Dad said he didn't see the need to rush so and thought a week later would work well since I didn't have a job yet to go to and could continue with my current job at the ice house and work for him in the mornings until I did find other employment. Everyone agreed to this date (which would be May 28) and then decided for an early evening ceremony at the church, located across the street and a half block down from the Petty residence. Mrs. Petty said that helped her considerably time wise by having three weeks to prepare for the wedding rather than just two. She also said she would love to have the reception following the wedding outside at their home if there were no objections. Mother said she thought that would be beautiful and offered to help her in the preparations in any way she could to decorate the church and the yard for the ceremonies.

The dinner evening ended on a high note with everyone very satisfied with the plans. Joyce had announced her selection for maid-of-honor and said she would talk to her the next day. I said I would like for Ed, Joyce's brother, to be best man and went into the den to ask him — where the other Petty kids were eating at the time while the "grown-ups" had their dinner in the dining room. The plans worked out well. Mrs. Petty was able to get an engagement announcement in the next Overton Press and progress followed.

The only tiff occurring during the wedding preparation period was over the pick of ushers. One evening as Joyce and I were going over the plans she told me the names of all the attendants, including the ushers. I really didn't have any objections to her (or probably her mother's selection) but one I didn't know (their distant relative) and one I didn't particularly care for at that time (who later became a relatively good friend). I accidently said something about this to Mother and she was quite miffed about it.

She said that the groom should choose the ushers. I didn't intend to start a spat but I mentioned it to Joyce and the first thing I knew Mrs. Petty had called Mother with an apology and asked her to have me ask the ushers and give her a list. I simply used the same ones except I replaced the above mentioned two with a Jernigan representative (Robert) and an Elliott one (W.A.), my two closest cousins — since Sonny was already one of the originals.

The wedding, and associated activities, kept getting bigger and bigger. Joyce's friends gave her a bridal shower early and then Mrs. Petty's close friends and some church women had a coffee at the church parlor for Joyce at which they planned a larger shower for her. Mrs. Petty showed the ladies the pattern and material she and a friend were using to make the bridesmaid dresses. Someone asked about Joyce's dress and Mrs. Petty told her that they were going shopping for it again tomorrow since they had not found one yet that satisfied both of them. After the details for the shower were completed and the work divided up, the group departed for their homes.

At the coffee Joyce met some of the women for the first time. One of these was Mrs. Sonny Lea (he was the operator of the "Company" service station across the street from the New London Humble camp) who was only about four years older than Joyce. Soon after Joyce and her mother arrived home the phone rang, it was Mrs. Lea. She said she knew they were full of coffee but she wondered if they would drop by her house in the afternoon for a Coke because she had something she desperately wanted to show them. Of course, they accepted under these terms. When they arrived and entered the Lea's beautifully appointed home, Mrs. Lea was very glad to see them and suggested their Cokes could wait a few minutes while she showed them what it was she wanted them to see. After they were seated she took the top off a large oblong box with a lot of tissue paper spilling out. She then stood up, held this beautiful wedding gown in front of her and said, "This was my dress and when I heard you were still looking for one, I thought it would look great on Joyce and I would love for her to have it." Mrs. Petty exclaimed, "You are so kind to offer but Joyce is a few inches taller than you and I am afraid she couldn't get in it." Mrs. Lea insisted and Joyce couldn't resist the urging to at least try it on.

After she had it on, her mother couldn't help saying that it was surely beautiful and it made her even more beautiful, but they had not planned a formal wedding and it was probably way too fancy for their needs. But Mrs. Lea wasn't ready to give up yet, so she continued with the statement that the bridesmaid dresses she had seen that morning would complement this dress beautifully. And it was not at all unusual for the women to be formally attired and the men to wear business suites in weddings today. Some very big and fancy weddings she had been to lately even had the men attired in western cut and stitched suites. Since you are doing the bridesmaid dresses I thought you could put a little lace here in the front on the bottom and the train will take care of the back for height. She then held the train up in the back to demonstrate.

So the wedding dress was set — a gorgeous and unexpected development. But I must tell you the rest of the story about this beautiful Lea/Elliott wedding dress. After the wedding Mrs. Petty had the dress and train cleaned with fresh tissue and boxes. She returned it to Mrs. Lea (at least six months pregnant at the time) and said they couldn't possibly keep it because it was her wedding dress and meant so much to her — and she might have a daughter that someday would love to wear it to her own wedding. Mrs. Lea thanked her and said she would keep it. The Lea's expanded their business to include butane and propane sales and deliveries with their headquarters in Kilgore. They moved to Kilgore, bought the Spear home (my Auntie's in-laws) when the Spears moved to the Potter mansion (know now as Nine Acres Estate). When we were looking for a home in Kilgore in 1962 as I was to teach at Kilgore College and Joyce in the Jr. & High School, the Spear place was on the market again since the Leas had built them a fine new home and our realtor insisted on showing their old place to us. As we looked through the second floor we saw the son and daughter's name with Room scrawled in crayon on the doors of their bedrooms. Since there were several spare rooms there we noticed the same writing proclaiming Playroom # 1 and another Playroom # 2. Joyce went in #2 and there hanging on a hook on the closet door was the tattered wedding dress. So we assumed that dress was never used for another real wedding. The Lea's son, Larry, gained some notoriety later as an evangelist, church founder and author.

Back to May, 1948, everything went off very well for the warm-up activities, wedding and reception. The weather was fine, the bride the most beautiful and the groom at least passable. All through the reception I kept urging Joyce to get a move on, go change and us sneak off since we planned to drive to Galveston that night for our honeymoon. Well that didn't work too well. I had put our car (Mother and Dad's since I didn't have one) hidden behind the Curry's house about a block away where I could have access to it to blast off when ready. Someone had found it and Sonny (having keys) drove it to the front gate of the Petty's and other members of the wedding party loaded it down with lipstick, crepe paper and tin cans. Thank goodness they didn't have time or were too soft hearted to open the trunk and disturb our bags stored there.

We made quite a racket when we left. I had to stop at the first service station (it was closed) and try to clean some of the lipstick off with wet Kleenex. It just made a mess, red smeared all over the windshield and windows. I finally gave up after getting the tin cans and crepe paper all off the Buick. We drove on and by the time we reached Lufkin we were dead tired. We decided we could never make it to Galveston that night so chose to look for a motel. We drove in at one named something like Lodges in the Pines; I went into the office and the sleepy looking woman behind the counter said yes, they had a vacancy and if I had to I could go look at it. She wasn't very enthusiastic about showing it but did get a long flashlight and lead the way. The cabins were typical of motels of the day, small rooms with very small baths on the back and an open front garage between each unit. The best I can say is it did appear to be very clean and no bugs in sight. On the way back to the office I told the lady we would take it for one night. She looked at me and then Joyce in the car and said, "Ya'll look pretty tired so if you want to stay a second night we knock off a dollar fifty if we don't have to change the sheets and clean the room." Without comment I handed her the seven dollars she had quoted as the price, got in the car, drove to #7 (I remember the number because for some reason Joyce wrote it down on a piece of paper she kept for many, many years) and we spent our very first night together.

We didn't really unpack much, we took in Joyce's little boxy suitcase that I think they called a makeup-kit in which she had her gown and stuff for the night. I just slept in my underwear — with my new pajamas still packed in the trunk.

The next day we zoomed through Houston before noon and into Galveston about 12:30. We had opted for no breakfast since we wanted to get on to Galveston to find us a place to stay. We not only had not provided for our lodging ahead of time but we did not realize that this was the Memorial Day weekend — bringing huge crowds to Galveston. Both of us were used to vacationing with our parents in Galveston but neither knew anything about making reservations in advance. We drove down the seawall seeking a room in one motel after another. We got the same story at each, booked up for days. As we neared the end of the beach, we were really getting worried. The Jack Tar was about our last hope. Before we even said anything to the lady behind the counter, she knew what we were going to ask and starting shaking her head. I said, "Nothing?" and she replied, "The report is everyone is overbooked, sorry." I turned to Joyce and said, "I don't know what to do, maybe try back close to Houston or somewhere else nearby." The lady could tell we were getting frantic so she asked, "How many nights did you want to stay?" I replied three or four according to the cost. She looked at us with pity in her eyes, I think realizing we were honeymooners. I noticed I had lipstick on my left sleeve and glanced out to the car and could see the rosy hue still on the windows.

She said give her a minute or two and she would see what she could do. Turned out she had a friend that was an agent for a real estate firm that rented small apartments near the beach by the week and sometimes someone didn't show so they would have a vacancy that they could rent for a shorter period since they had a forfeited deposit to help cover part of the vacancy. We eagerly waited as she plugged in her headphones and dialed a number. On the second ring she got an answer. She said, "This is Mary, I'm looking for a place for a three or four day rental for a couple. …pause… They look like nice kids, good car and clothes. …pause… OK,

P and a half, in fifteen minutes. I'll tell them." She told us her friend had an apartment at the address on the slip of paper available for three days. We would have to go look at it and discuss cost with the agent. She would be there in fifteen minutes and will only wait another five minutes for you to show since she had other things to do. No funny stuff and you understand I am sticking my neck out for you so don't let me down. She then told us how to get to the address from where we were. We could have hugged and kissed her but we thanked her with our whole hearts and bolted toward the door and then the car. Joyce looked back, smiled a big smile and waved at the figure waving to us through the office window.

The agent was very nice, showed us this upstairs two bedroom apartment with a nice kitchen and bath, charged us ten dollars a night (paid in advance) and asked us not to mess up more than one bedroom. We gladly agreed. It ended up that we didn't use either of the bedrooms since there was a screened-in porch on the back with a bed where we slept each night with the sea breezes blowing on us and we dressed in the bathroom. The rides and carnival things were only a couple of blocks toward the beach so as soon as we brought in our bags we walked down there and stuffed ourselves on hot dogs, chips, a big dill pickle each and cold drinks — we had been starving.

Back at the apartment, as we were putting up some groceries in the kitchen we had picked up at the convenient little neighborhood grocery store only a block away, I remembered the small envelope Auntie had handed me at the reception just before we left on the trip to Galveston. She had said, "I think this will come in handy. We want to help you so don't forget to call on us when you need it." I wasn't sure who "us" meant but Auntie was always special. I thanked her and being very busy put it in my shirt pocket, later sticking it in the ash tray in the dashboard of the car at the motel in Lufkin (no one was allowed to smoke in Mother's car so the ashtray was always clean — Dad chewed tobacco and kept a tin can on the floor in front of the driver's seat with a small amount of dirt in it to spit into). I went down to the car, retrieved the little envelope and took it upstairs. I said, "In all the excitement leaving last night, I forgot about this" and handed it to Joyce. She opened it and in a little gift card was folded a fifty dollar bill, with a note, "For some extras, with love, Grandma and Auntie." We were overjoyed since we were now down to only a few dollars in cash and Mother's Gulf card for gasoline. Now we really could have some "extras."

As the sun began to get a little low in the west, we donned our bathing suits, took our beach towels and drove to a parking area on the seawall. We walked down to the beach, across the sand and into the warm salty water. We were enjoying the waves when Joyce let out a little scream, grabbed her left hand and ran for the beach. I thought she must have been bitten by something or stung by a jelly fish. I ran after her to help as she stood holding her hand with the other one. I said, "What is it?" She held out her left hand, firmly squeezing her ring finger with her index finger and thumb of the right hand. She told me she felt her rings slipping off and thought she was going to lose them but was able to grab them and make it ashore holding them on.

We knew they were a little too big but she didn't want to leave them at the Ergles' shop to be sized until after the wedding and we were back from our honeymoon. Now she was really afraid to wear them for fear she would lose them. She looked at the little pocket on the front of my bathing suit and wanted to know if I thought they would be safe in that pocket while we swam. I thought they would be but to be sure I said I would take them to the car and lock them in the glove compartment for double safety — since the doors of the car would be locked also. As I was digging around in the glove compartment hiding the rings in a back corner, I saw a bag of Bull Durham roll your own with it tightly tied by the familiar little yellow string. I returned to the water where Joyce sat in the edge letting the waves wash back and forth over her legs and feet. I assured her everything was fine and we resumed our swim. As it began to get dark we retrieved our beach towels, dried off some and returned to the car. We folded the beach towels to sit on in order to help protect the seats and then Joyce wanted me to check on the rings. I unlocked and opened the glove box door, peered in and assured her again that everything was fine.

After we had washed off and dressed again at the apartment, we walked again past the carnival area until we spied a fried chicken shack. We ordered a basket of chicken and fries to share and each had a glass of iced tea. It wasn't Mother's tasty fried chicken but was plenty good for our hungry stomachs. We strolled around some and then realized how tired we were from our long day. We returned to the apartment and as we passed our car on the street, Joyce said she was worried about her rings being there. I said OK, we will take them up with us. I also got the bag of Bull Durham and she wanted to know if I was going to roll my own. I told her no, just wait and see.

Upstairs I told her to sit down on the side of the bed on the porch while I went into the kitchen. I found a paring knife in one of the drawers and took it with the rings, Bull Durham bag and sat down beside her. I laid the rings in her lap, cut the yellow string with the knife and pulled the string free from the bag. I asked her to hold her rings together the way they would be on her finger and then I took one end of the string and tied the rings together. I asked her to slip the rings on her finger, then I had her hold her hand in front of me and I tied the yellow string around her wrist. The string was just barely long enough for a knot. I wanted her to test it so I had her move her hand around and move her fingers some too. It was a tight fit and I told her I would have to cut the string to get the rings off. She said for me not to worry about that, she would just wear them like that until we got back to the Ergles'. She did it too! For many, many years after that any time we saw a Bull Durham sack we would laugh over the fond memories it would bring back.

Neither of us was much of a coffee drinker at that time, so for breakfast each morning we had a glass of milk and a couple of fresh donuts from a little bakery next door to our grocery store. We would eat lunch out at a seafood restaurant along the seawall and have sandwiches for supper in our apartment. The first full day in Galveston (Monday) we rented a bicycle built for two for four hours and rode around — mostly on the seawall. This turned out to be so much fun we rented it Tuesday for all day so we could hope on and off anytime we wanted and go for a spin. Normally the power peddler (male) rode on the back seat and the lady in the front doing the steering. Joyce didn't like steering so I rode in the front and provided most of the peddling while doing the steering also. Joyce said women were supposed to be the "back seat driver" and use vocal directions.

After we turned the bicycle in during the early afternoon, we took the car and went to ride the free Port Bolivar ferry. We had both ridden this ferry many times with our individual families but this was our first time to do it together. We made the roundtrip and when we got back to the Galveston dock, Joyce asked could we do it again. I said, "Sure, you sound just like a little kid on the carousel." She went on to say that her family sometimes rode it two or three times when they were there. I told her we could ride it as many times as she wished. On our second trip an older couple kept looking at us and we could tell they were interested in the left hand with the yellow string. Finally the woman leaned over to Joyce and asked her if we were on our honeymoon. Joyce smiled and nodded. The man proudly spoke up and said they were celebrating their 40th wedding anniversary that day. We both congratulated them and then they wished us good luck on our marriage. This was not the only ones we noticed showing interest in the yellow string on her hand. Several were bold enough to ask about it during the couple of days she wore it in Galveston. It didn't bother Joyce much for someone to ask about it either — which kind of surprised me.

Joyce and I made this ferry trip many, many times over the years — many times on our wedding anniversaries. Our last trip on the ferry together was in September of 2013. She was too ill to travel on our 66th anniversary, May 28, 2014, but we did celebrate; by having dinner at the Longview Red Lobster — eating seafood, with Joyce seated in her wheelchair between her nurse and me. She passed away the following July 12.

Wednesday morning, the day our rental on the apartment was up and the day we were headed home from our honeymoon, dawned cloudy and we slept a little later than the previous two mornings. We had our breakfast, packed the few belongings we had with us and loaded the car. We dropped off the key at the rental office, made a last loop down the seawall and headed out toward the highway. By the time we were on the causeway a light rain was falling. We drove through mist and a little rain most of the way back home. By the time we were back in Lufkin, the skies had cleared and it was a beautiful sunny day. We were hungry so we stopped for a hamburger a short distance down the highway from "our motel" and waved at it as we drove by (as we were to do for many years until they built the bypass around Lufkin and we would from time to time drive through town in order to go by that little motel).

We arrived at the Petty's about midafternoon and the whole family was there with the exception of Mr. Petty — who arrived from work not very long after we did. Most of our wedding gifts were still piled about the living room and Joyce looked through them again for a short period of time as I gave the rest of the family a report about our stay in Galveston. Mrs. Petty said she was preparing a big spaghetti supper and wanted us to stay and eat. It sounded very good to me but Joyce said we probably needed to run over to my folk's first, see them a few minutes and check out our new place — the garage apartment at Mother and Dad's. We decided we would come back for supper and take some of the wedding gifts with us to go back to "our apartment" afterward.

Our apartment was only "ours" for the summer. The band director at LC and his wife rented it from Mother and Dad and he wanted to go back to college during the summer and finish his master's while his wife was still working on her bachelor's. Since Joyce and I could use it during the summer they would not have to pay rent for the three months we would be in it. This seemed to make everyone happy — maybe Joyce the least because this left her very close to Mother and Dad and us under their easy observation (especially since we didn't have a car and depended on them for transportation to work, etc.). Joyce continued to work on Saturdays at Hall's except for the couple we used to go to Denton and Commerce. Her mother with one or two siblings usually came over most days for a visit or to take her somewhere.

My work schedule had been determined before we married and went on our honeymoon. Humble did not have enough jobs for sons of employees going to college to include sons-in-law so Mr. Petty had made arrangements for me to work for the Bert Phauf company (a labor contractor for Humble) in a gang working out of the New London District but the work was in the Carthage field, an hour's drive away. We commuted from New London as a gang in the pusher's pickup daily, Monday through Thursday — four days a week. It was an hour's travel each way with the company paying us for one hour and one hour was on our time. This meant we actually worked (including travel) forty-four hours a week and paid for forty. This schedule made for long days but meant we had three days a week off which the whole gang liked. I continued to keep the books at the ice house and occasionally worked a Friday or Saturday if they were short-handed.

My gang did the things oil field roustabouts do, just about anything that needed be done on the leases, in the camps, along the pipelines and occasionally in the gasoline plant. Every working morning, we arrived at the Humble camp just south of Carthage, transferred to our gang truck with all of its tools and equipment and went to our assignments. The gang was made up of four regulars (the pusher, his assistant and two others all living either in Arp or Troup, and all related by blood or marriage — making their commute even longer than mine) and two "college boys" as we were called (me the youngest at 19 and a 20 year old just out of the Marine Corp and starting college in September). The four regulars were all farmers turned oil field worker and still farmed and raised livestock part-time. We got along really well — the college boys learning from the older men and giving them their due respect — if we didn't we figured we would get a shovel whack across the ear. Being mostly raised in the great East Texas Oil Field, this was my first real experience in the workings of the oil business. I learned a lot — about people too. What a great summer this was!

We had made plans to go off to school in the fall to North Texas State in Denton so the next thing we needed to do was find housing there for our move in September. We planned to take off very early one Friday morning in June and scout out an apartment to rent. We would rely on Mary Ann and Jerry Jack Jordan to assist us in this since they had married in the spring, had a small efficiency with Jerry Jack working full time at a cleaners during the summer (as he had done part-time through high school at New London — both he and Mary Ann had graduated with Joyce) while Mary Ann was going to school. He planned to return to school in the fall.

Our first trip to Denton didn't prove to be very fruitful but we did see a lot of it and looked for an apartment all around in the college area. We would be without a car and didn't plan to have one for some time — saving our money for more basic living expenses. Housing was very scarce since there were a lot of married veterans returning from service and to college. We made a second trip a couple of weeks later with a name and an address to check on. Through the grapevine (I think my Dad and John, since they kept up with everything going on in town) we learned that a new shop teacher had been hired at Overton High School and he and his wife were and had been attending North Texas. The super sleuths put two and two together and decided the couple would probably be vacating an apartment so they got the name and address from the school secretary for me. We went back to Denton the next weekend.

We left LC early Friday morning and arrived in Denton about midmorning. We found the address and also found the house to be a very large and very, very old one. An attractive and obviously pregnant young woman answered my knock and I told her we were looking for a Mays K. Whitten. She turned her head and called out over her shoulder, "Kenneth, someone to see you." Then a nice looking young man, wearing carpenter's overalls without a shirt, came to the door and stuck out his hand to shake mine and said, "Hi, I'm Kenneth." As I shook his hand with my right, I held the slip of paper up and glanced at the name. He laughed and explained that he went by his middle name. I told him that I did too, introduced Joyce as my wife and then myself. The young woman introduced herself as his wife, Mary Jim, and shook hands with us too, inviting us into the living room. This was our introduction to the Whittens, to be lifelong friends.

As we four sat in their living room, I explained how it came about that we were calling on them. Mary Jim explained that she managed this house for the owner's and their apartment was already spoken for by one of the building's renters in a smaller apartment and that apartment in turn was promised to a friend of the current renters. She added that as far as she knew every apartment within walking distance of the college was rented by word of mouth at least a semester before it was to become vacant. They could tell we were very disappointed with this news. Then Kenneth spoke up with an idea how he might help us. In one of his building trades classes they had visited a construction site near the college where they were building an apartment complex that was supposed to be completed for occupancy by September. He had met one of the supervisors and through him might find out who was going to handle the renting of the apartments. Mary Jim added that sounded like a good idea and she wanted to go also to see the building construction going on.

Kenneth put on his work shirt, Mary Jim locked up their apartment and the four of us got in our car with Kenneth directing me to the property. We parked where we could see the work going on while Kenneth went looking for the man he knew. In a few minutes he was back and walked near the construction company sign, bent over picked up another sign, turned it toward us and pointed to a real estate name and phone number on the sign. As soon as he could tell I had jotted down the number he laid the sign back down on the ground. As he got in the car he explained that the supervisor told him they had just delivered the sign they were to put up when they had time.

We went back to the Whitten's apartment, Mary Jim offered to make the call and we gladly agreed. She came back from their bedroom with the information neatly written on a piece of paper and handed it to me. As I read it she explained that the real estate office was downtown and she would go with us if we wished. I asked if Kenneth wanted to go and he said he was repairing the back screen door and needed to finish it and would do that while we were gone. We drove the few blocks to the office and found the lady handling the rentals. She showed us a picture, the floor plans and the rental rate charts. And she said they were to be ready by September 1 in plenty of time for the fall semester. We decided we wanted the smallest size apartment due to the cost of a larger one and filled out an application. Mary Jim said the rates were not bad for a new apartment compared to the going rates at that time. The agent said if I put up a deposit she was sure we would be in line for one. I pulled out the required fifty dollars and laid it on her desk. She quickly wrote me out a receipt and handed it to me with my copy of the rental application. We left the office very happy with the results of our trip this time.

On the way back to the Whitten's apartment I invited Mary Jim, including Kenneth, to have lunch with us since they had been so helpful. She accepted with the condition that we check with Kenneth back at the apartment since she didn't know what he had planned. After checking with him he said that sounded fine if we could give him a few minutes to shower and change clothes. He was very quick and he also said he was very hungry. He had attended his only scheduled early morning class and then came home to do a few repairs before he returned to college to work in the library all afternoon. Mary Jim explained that he had to take one class each six weeks while he was registered for his thesis also, busy working on it, to finish his master's by the end of summer. She had finished her bachelor's and was working on a librarian's endorsement. She did not plan to work this school year since her baby was due in early fall.

We had a very enjoyable lunch of chicken fried steak and all the trimmings at a restaurant that was a favorite with the Whittens. After depositing them at home we went by Mary Ann and Jerry Jack's apartment and had a good visit with her since she had finished her classes for the day but he was still at work. She told us she was pretty sure she was pregnant and was to see a doctor next week. She said if she was Jerry Jack was going to quit school and try to get a job with Humble since they just couldn't make it going to school with a child. We told her we hoped it worked out for the best, since we didn't know what else to say. We headed straight home from the Jordan's; wanting to share our good news with our parents at New London and LC. As we drove toward East Texas, I asked Joyce if she noticed anything in particular about Kenneth's speech. She said she only noticed that it was a little different from the usual, but not all that different. I told her that it sounded so much like my Dad's I felt like I was listening to Dad when Kenneth was talking. Joyce said, "Now that you mention it, they do sound a lot alike — even use some of the same expressions when making a point."

I was silent for a few minutes, then I told her the story Dad had told me about his speech when he was a little kid. He was slightly tongue tied and his brothers were always making fun of him. Once he went crying to his mother and she took a look in his mouth. She called Allen, his brother two years older, and Fred, two years younger, and carefully examined their mouths also. She had Allen bring her sewing basket to her, took out her scissors, had Dad put his head in her lap with the nose up and mouth wide open. With the index and thumb of her left hand she took hold of his tongue, held it toward the roof of his mouth and with her right hand using the scissors clipped back about a half inch of the tissue that held his tongue to the bottom of his mouth. She then told him, as Allen and

Fred watched open-mouthed, to fix some warm salty water and rinse his mouth until the bleeding stopped. Dad said his mouth was a little sore for a day or two but his speech improved a great deal.

We loved our little garage apartment and the time we spent there. Joyce taught me to drink my iced tea unsweetened which I do even today. We had one table top fan and we moved it from room to room with us — sleeping under it each night. The garage apartment still stands, barely, with some of the very unstable furniture remaining from our stay. Since our three or four day honeymoon was so short, this time in the garage apartment was almost like an extended honeymoon. During the summer we visited (with both sets of parents) our "new relatives" we now had. We made trips to Cass County, Blooming Grove and several other places way out in the country to see Joyce's relatives. Down on the Sabine past Carthage we visited many of Dad's relatives and did some overnight fishing, as well as all around Smith County to see both Dad's and Mother's many kin. It seemed a wonderful way to start a marriage.

We were having a great time, thinking everything was all set for us to begin school at North Texas in Denton when in the first week of August "the letter" arrived. We were shocked, dismayed and a little stunned, when we were notified by the real estate company handling the rentals on the apartment house where we had reserved "our" apartment that they were only going to rent to "faculty and other professionals" and returning a check for our reservation fee. We went running to Dad to ask what we could do. After he read the letter a couple of times, asked to see our receipt and after studying both he said, "They can certainly rent to whom they wish and since you don't have a lease yet they can deny you an apartment and probably could get away without refunding your deposit but at least they are doing that." We were disappointed to say the least. Since it was Saturday when we received the letter we decided we would go back to Denton again the next Friday, visit the Whittens, see if they had any ideas and look around the campus again just for good measure.

The next day being Sunday, we went to have Sunday dinner after church at the Petty's in order for me to meet the Huggins — friends from the Corsicana oil field long before the Pettys were married and both families moved to the East Texas oil field. Mr. Petty and Mr. Huggins were partners in a new auto agency they had set up in Hawkins to handle the new Kaiser-Frazer cars — they were trying for a Ford agency but the Ford people weren't setting up new dealerships yet and had suggested this route for the time being (but it wasn't long before their business went broke from poor management by their employees so they only sold a few of the new cars before they closed their doors). I think this was the day Mr. Huggins brought over the first car they had received and he was using it as a demonstrator. It was my first look at a new Frazer.

Of course our news about the failed housing situation in Denton was a shocker to everyone also. When someone finally asked what we were going to do, Joyce and I answered almost in perfect unison, "We don't know." After a few moments Mr. Huggins looked at me and asked, "Is there some specific reason you need to go to North Texas?" I replied that the only reason we had selected it was because it was a teacher preparation college, we liked it and some of our friends had gone there. He then told us that as far as he knew the college East Texas State in Commerce was the same type college and forty or so miles closer to your homes, this being the reason his daughter and her husband, Fred Gray, had gone to East Texas when he got out of the Navy. I spoke up with I thought East Texas College was in Marshall since our church had had "youth preachers" from there some times in the summer. He replied that the college in Marshall was East Texas Baptist College, a private college where one of Mrs. Huggins's nieces had gone.

He then went on to explain that the reason he brought all this up was that when Fred got out of the Navy he wanted to go back to college on the G I Bill (having two years at a junior college before the war) and make a coach. Ruth completed a couple of year's college work while he was in the Navy and wanted to finish her degree and be a home economics teacher. Mr. Huggins, enjoying the attentions he was getting from the group, took time to roll his cigar around a couple of times in his mouth and went on to explain further. He said they too ran into a crowded housing situation so he, being the good provider he was, found a little run down shack near the college, bought it and Fred reworked it into a nice little cottage

— quite cute now. They were both graduating at the end of the summer, had teaching jobs and planned to rent the little house to a student or two for the school year but they wanted it back for the next summer so Fred could work on his master's and administrator's certification. I was kind of stunned at first after hearing all this, so I asked the first thing that I could think of on the spur of the moment. "How much rent will be needed?" Mr. Huggins replied with "Thirty dollars a month for you two." I said this is a little less than half the cost of the apartment in Denton and Mr. Huggins said that it was not new and that he expected rent was much less in Commerce than Denton since Commerce was much smaller and more rural.

I said we would just switch our plans for Friday and go to Commerce instead of Denton to see the house, town, school, etc. Huggins then drew us a map how he drove to Commerce then turned the paper over to make another map showing how to get to the house. He also said he would drop Ruth and Fred a card to be expecting us. The Pettys also decided they wanted to see Commerce so they decided to take us on Friday in their car. Huggins then said "Who knows, if I can get all my oil pumped by Friday morning, Maude and I may show up also and we will make a party of it."

Well, we made the trip Friday, found everything great — the school seemed to be about half the size of North Texas and Commerce (downtown business area) didn't seem much larger than Overton and definitely not any larger than Kilgore. We were pleased to find the little house was less than two blocks from the south east corner of the campus. It was built very similar to the garage apartment we were living in at that time, except it rested on the ground and only a step or two up to get in the front or back. Out the back door it was only a couple of minutes to the college walking. The campus was beautiful, the students friendly and the surroundings very rural looking. The Huggins didn't show up but we had a very good visit with Fred and Ruth — they reminded us very much of Kenneth and Mary Jim who would become fast friends of ours in Overton and later in Kilgore. We told the Grays we definitely wanted the house and I gave him thirty dollars in cash for the first month's rent which he could give to Huggins — if he was to get the rent. Fred said they would be moved by the first of the month and we could move in by that day for sure. They would just leave the water and electricity on and we could have it changed over as soon as we were settled in — the keys would be under the front doormat.

Mr. Petty treated us all to a big meal at the only restaurant we found downtown. Fred and Ruth said they had not eaten there during the two years they had been in Commerce. The only time Joyce and I ate there during the two years we were living there later was when Mr. Petty was working in an oil field somewhere nearby and came to town on his expense account and took us out to eat. College students didn't eat out much in the 1940s and 50s.

Well, six days could certainly make a difference in college plans back then. Again we were all set to begin a new college school year at a new college (to us), a new house (to us), in a new town (to us). We felt like our luck had definitely changed for the better.

AND ON . . . . .

As we looked forward to closing this chapter of our lives near the end of summer in 1948 and opening a new one in the fall, we were young (Joyce nineteen on May 9 and I just turning twenty in August), a newly married (three months) naïve couple, full of shared optimism, hope and ambition. The binding force was that we wanted to do it together. We knew our future was out there and we wanted to "make it" together. We really never thought in terms of me and you but in only "us" — we can do it.

The last Thursday of August I worked the final day with my oil field gang, bid them a sincere and warm good-by and walked over to the Petty's where Joyce waited with her family for my return and then us to our little apartment at LC. Joyce, her mother and Bo, had spent the day in Tyler doing their last minute (which takes them all day) shopping for returning to school, which of course meant clothes — and especially shoes. I knew their pattern, once around the stores in the six blocks facing the "square" to see what was there, and then another complete turn buying the "bargains" they had spied and then the third round to pick up any additional items that were needed to complement the bargains and those that they "just had to have." They were experts in frugal shopping, Mrs. Petty depression experienced and trained.

That evening Joyce prepared us a small pot roast with potatoes, onions, carrots and some brown gravy, our last "cooked" dinner in our first apartment. We ate on Joyce's drop leaf kitchen table she had found stored in the barn and sat on the two straight back, cane seat chairs retrieved also from the barn. The table was a more or less drab olive green when she found it and she turned it into a gleaming, brilliant white with several coats of paint. She then painted the shaped outer edge around the table a striking Chinese red. The corners of the drop leafs were decorated with delicate little blue flowers. The chairs were painted a matching white

— she said this would brighten things up in the kitchen. She had pushed the band director's wife's brown table and chairs into the corner so we could use her "creation" our first time. She had candles on the table, our iced tea in crystal glasses and our food on china (borrowed from Mother) — our California Ivy pottery wedding gifts securely packed for moving on Saturday. She wanted us to celebrate — and we did. Friday was packing day and she planned for us to finish the leftovers for lunch.

Fred and Ruth were taking their furniture with them to their rented house near their teaching jobs so we were equipping our "new house" with hand-me-downs. We had a bed, mattress and springs as well as a chest of drawers, a small desk with a straight chair and a big stuffed chair we had gathered from relatives that we stored in one of the garages underneath our apartment ready to take to Commerce in Dad's truck Saturday, along with the kitchen table and chairs.

After breakfast Friday we returned Mother's dishes and began loading Mother and Dad's car (trunk and back seat) with everything we were taking to Commerce except for the furniture that would later go into Dad's pickup. We left a few wedding gifts at the Petty's which Joyce decided we wouldn't use in Commerce and save them for later when we were more settled. By the time we had eaten our lunch and cleaned up afterwards, we felt satisfied we had everything ready to go except for a few things we would pack in a suitcase when we were ready to leave the next morning and take it with us in the pickup.

About two p.m. I decided we had enough time to drive over to Grandma's for a short visit with her, Auntie and anyone else that might be there. Mother decided she would also go — which filled the car since we had the back seat piled high with clothes, bedding and such. Sonny volunteered to stay home and hold down the fort. We had a good visit at Grandma's and dropped Mother at home just in time for Joyce and I to get on over to the Petty's.

Mrs. Petty had planned a "going away" picnic party for us in their front yard for Friday evening. She had invited the Mitchells (from across the street), the Currys (the man who worked with Mr. Petty and lived just down the street), the grocery store Alfords (store and living quarters both just around the corner), along with the newly married Reynolds and Mallard couples (living in the Petty's garage apartment and little house in the back). This turned out to be a very nice affair and it seems everyone enjoyed it very much.

We got up early Saturday morning, had us some breakfast and started in cleaning the apartment to leave it in pristine condition for the band director and wife when they returned the next day or two. Mother and Dad had followed their very early morning schedule with Dad going to town in the car to check everything out in his office, jail and such with some time for the Busy Bee and probably another or two coffee drinking places. Mother came upstairs to the apartment to check on our progress and get a report on the previous night's party. As she left she said she would get Sonny up for his breakfast so he would be ready to help me with loading the truck as soon as I was ready. Our timing and progress was going great and as we checked the weather outside we were pleased to see it was warm, sunny bright and a beautiful day.

About nine, Sonny and I loaded the furniture in the truck, securely tying everything in its place. We put in a couple of treated canvas tarps that Dad used for tents when we went to his uncle's place down on the river to fish — just in case we ran into rain somewhere up the line. We had just finished the loading when Dad drove in from town. He gave Sonny his "orders" for the day, ending up with telling him Dad and Mother would probably be back by dark or soon after. Our plans called for Joyce and me to lead the way in the truck with them following in the car. On Mother and Dad's return trip home Mother would drive the car and Dad his truck.

As Joyce and I got in the truck, Dad reminded me for about the third time to take a left at Highway 80 in Mineola and stop at the old restaurant about midway of the block. He wanted us to eat lunch there so he could visit with an old friend of his from Tyler who now owned the restaurant. Dad had a good visit with his friend since, soon after we arrived, the owner's wife relieved him of his cashier's duties and he came over and sat at our table, drinking coffee, while we ate and he and Dad talked (as Mother said later — "Like a blue streak"). When we finished and headed out the owner said the meal was on him but Dad put a dollar on the table for the waitress and laid a five dollar bill near the cash register when he went by. It was a very good meal, made even better since it gave Dad so much pleasure.

The rest of the trip to Commerce went fine also, no problems with our load or heavy traffic to deal with. The roads north of Mineola and Quitman weren't very good but we got by alright and arrived in Commerce early afternoon. Mother and Dad were relieved to see we had such a nice little place to live but were amazed at how small it was. It may have been as large as their garage apartment but definitely no larger.

Dad and I set about unloading the furniture while Joyce and Mother worked on the things in the car. Mother had insisted that we wait until we were in Commerce to stock our kitchen with groceries so everything would be fresh. When they had cleared the back seat, they took the car to the big grocery store downtown (which was really kind of up for us since we were on the low side of a long hill leading to town) about six blocks from our house. There was a small neighborhood store a couple of blocks from our house where we would go most of the time, after that initial stocking, since we would be afoot and hand carry all of our groceries. We didn't have a refrigerator and had to depend on an ice box, but we had a card in the front window which meant we would have home delivery of ice and the price was penciled in near the weight so we would know how much to leave for the ice man.

In about three hours we were all set up, ready to start living in our first really home of our own. After Joyce made us a pitcher of iced tea in her new kitchen and when we were all refreshed, we drove around the college and most of the town. This was Mother and Dad's first ever visit to Commerce and only our second one so we were all exploring it. I think Mother and Dad were both shocked by Commerce being such a "country" or rural type of place and having such a nice college. They both expressed the opinion that we had made a good selection where to begin our married lives and work toward our futures. Dad began to get a little restless to start back home so we returned to our little house, bid them farewell and they headed home with Mother in the lead. We sat down in our "living room" which was an area in front of our kitchen table of only about six feet by maybe at most seven feet since the front door opened into it also.

We had the stuffed chair (with back turned toward the walkway from the front door) with a little side table and another little table, we called our coffee table, in front of the chair. The little desk was tucked into the front corner. This just about took up all the room so for two of us to sit in the living room we had to turn around one of the kitchen chairs for the second person — or the little straight chair at the desk. Sitting in the stuffed chair you could look out the one window in that room on the front and see two or three houses across the street and some of the street running in front of the house. The only other window in this side of the house was a small one over the kitchen sink with some cabinet on each side of it. There was a back door in line with the front one — so I guess the often used term in East Texas of "shotgun house" would describe our castle.

Since the front door was in the middle of the front wall, the bedroom was even smaller than the living room and kitchen since the bathroom was also located in this portion. There was a small clothes closet (about thirty inches wide) with a curtain instead of a door. There was a door on the bathroom which was tiny, only a homemade shower and toilet. For a lavatory we used the kitchen sink. There was a matching window to the one in the living room in the middle of the front bed room wall and a very small one in the bathroom over the toilet. We placed our bed length wise against the front wall under the window and had just enough room on the other walls to place the chest of drawers and dresser.

The wall separating the living room/kitchen from the bedroom/bath was a single one (no framing) with a doorway, but no door. We sat in our new home's living room, surveying our domain, feeling very lucky and appreciative to have our own place — and each other. We looked at each other, really realizing for the first time that we were actually "on our own," without a car and no parents to go running to for help if we needed it. We were not afraid — just thoughtful.

After spending our first night in our little house, we were eating breakfast when Joyce said, "I noticed a little Baptist church about three blocks toward town, in the Y where the street forks, yesterday when your mother and I went for groceries. I would like for us to go to church there this morning if you will." She looked awfully serious so I simply replied with an O K. She then said she thought the sign said Sunday morning service at 10:30 a.m. and wanted to know what time we would need to leave since we were walking. I told her fifteen minutes to walk it should be plenty. We dressed in our Sunday clothes and still had a little while to kill.

Our timing was good and I was afraid we might be overdressed since the building looked a little seedy to me but as we got near I could see all the men were dressed in black (or at least very dark) suits and the women also looked as if they were dressed for a funeral. We were warmly welcomed by the people there and those arriving. There weren't many young people and very few children. We took our seats toward the back and joined in the service. I wasn't familiar with the hymns but I didn't sing much in church anyway, so I just mumbled a little. I thought the sermon, full of hell and brimstone, seemed to last forever. Finally there was a strange invitational with some witnessing and something like confessionals for several minutes by some of the members. Eventually we were able to leave after more prayers by individuals.

As we walked toward home Joyce turned, looked back at the church and seemed to be studying it. She said she had something to tell me when we got home. I asked her what it was but she said to just let it wait till we got into the house. As soon as we got in the house I asked her what was the big secret. She said that was not our kind of church even though it was Baptist. She went on to say that we were Southern Baptist as in the Southern Baptist Convention and that church, according to their sign, was A Primitive Baptist Church. I told her I didn't know there was a difference in Baptist churches but that was certainly different to what I was used to. She fixed us some Sunday dinner and lectured me about the Southern Baptist Convention. After we ate we lounged around awhile since we didn't have anything else to do. Later in the day we walked over to the school and toured the campus on foot, returned home for a cold supper and got ready to check on our registration the next day on campus.

Monday morning at the registrar's office we found that our transcripts had been received so we ordered our registration packets. We were told we could register Wednesday afternoon at 2:00 p.m. and our packets would be ready for us at our place of registration. We were given an outline of course offerings with a trial schedule to complete and have ready at registration. We had already received college catalogs containing degree plans and such for us to study and use to make out our trial course schedules. We were told that if we needed help in selecting courses, an advisor would be available at registration for assistance. We took this material home with us and spent the rest of the day studying the catalogs and course offerings so we would be prepared for registration.

The next morning after we finished our breakfast, Joyce said she was going to wash a few things and hang them out to dry on the clothes line in the backyard and wanted to know what I would be doing. I said I thought I would walk over to the campus and visit the library. I wanted to get acquainted with it and this would provide me with some newspapers and magazines to read since we had been so busy and I hadn't had much time for any reading lately. She said that sounded like a good deal to her. That way I wouldn't be in the way while she got some other little jobs out of the way.

I looked around the campus on my way to the library and saw very little activity. I went straight into the library and wandered around a little, looking here and there as I went. Soon a lady approached me and asked if she could help. I told her I was new on campus and just looking around to get acquainted with the library for the start of school. She said if I would follow her over to the circulation desk she would give me a printed guide to the library which had some very helpful information for new students and had been designed for freshman orientation, but sometimes transfer students didn't get it. As she handed me the little booklet off the counter, she said she was glad I came by and got one. I told her I was also glad to get it since I was sure it would help my wife also since she too would be a student. The lady insisted that I take my wife a copy also and turned one of the copies to the diagrams showing the layout of the two floors of the library. I thanked her and used the guide to find my way around the building, looking at some of the reading material as I browsed about. I finally settled down in the magazine section for about an hour as I read (or rather looked at) a couple of magazines.

I decided to go outside and stretch my legs. As I went out the front doors

I decided to take a closer look at the lion statue in front and read the plaque on it. As I bent over to read the plaque, a young man leaning on the far side and smoking spoke to me. I apologized for disturbing him and explained that I was new to the campus and just looking around. He said I didn't bother him at all and introduced himself as Capp, "That's cap with two Ps — which was my mother's maiden name and my parents hung it on me, so I have always needed to explain the two Ps." We both laughed (since I thought he meant for it to be funny) and I introduced myself. He wanted to know all about me, where I was from and such, so I gave him a little overview with him injecting questions every now and then and seeming very interested. I began to wonder why all the questions and he finally explained that he was responsible for issuing textbooks to students at registration and he had just gotten word one of his three student workers would not be there to work so he needed a replacement. He went on to explain what the job entailed.

The college had a textbook program in which they issued the student textbooks for his courses and he was assessed a three dollar fee each semester at registration. At the end of the semester the textbooks were turned in and the student charged for any damage or losses. Capp was not a full time employee of the college and only worked at this job at the beginning and end of each semester. He had done it for a few years, as a close friend of the man in charge of the college library program he did it mostly as a favor — beginning when he was a student. He had continued to do it ever since he graduated with a degree from the college. Since graduation he held a job as assistant manager of the two theaters in town and still helped with the textbook program.

Capp explained that he and his crew would begin at one o'clock setting up the basement in the library to issue textbooks the next day. If I wanted to work, I would work until everything was ready — usually eight or nine PM. Then we would do our registering at eight the next morning and be ready at nine to work until five PM, and then eight until five the next day. When Capp asked me if I would be interested, I told him I surely was. He said we would walk over to the college personnel office and sign me up as a student employee. He told me the pay for students was thirty cents an hour — which shocked me since I had been making a dollar twenty-five in the oil field. I tried not to let on since I had nothing else pressing and could certainly use what money I earned, and of course I felt I would get some good experience also.

Capp left me in the hands of the personnel people who had me fill out a lot of paperwork, issued me an early registration permit and told me to report to the library as instructed by Capp. I decided to go by the library on the way home to look up Capp. I told him I was all set and he said, "That's good," then added that the job had some advantages he didn't mention — such as you will get your pick of the books for yourself and tonight about six the head librarian will bring a tub of fried chicken and all the fixings for us, so don't worry about your supper. I said, "O K" and I would see him at one PM — planning to be there at least fifteen or twenty minutes early.

Joyce was sitting at the kitchen table, reading an old magazine and glancing out the front window every now and then when I came through the unlocked back door. I kind of startled her and I could tell she was relieved when she recognized for sure it was me. I couldn't wait to tell her my news about what had happened at the college. She was very attentive as I related the happenings over the last couple of hours and what would be happening over the next couple of days. Finally I said, "And I am really hungry." She said she thought she would fry some bacon with a can of pork and beans to go with it since that was one of my favorite quick meals. She also knew I loved slices of fresh onion to go with mine and she liked sliced tomatoes with hers so I said since I will be working with others this afternoon maybe I should skip the onions. She looked at me, laughed and said, "Now you are thinking of others when many times you ate onions and I had to endure them." I laughed too and said, "Yes, but you were in love with me and that counted a lot." She stopped laughing and grunted, "I guess so."

We had our lunch and discussed our plans for the rest of the day. She said she had thought we would have sandwiches for supper and now she would have one alone. I told her that since the college was not in session today, I had read a sign that the library would close at six PM tonight. I suggested that she go with me after lunch and plan to spend the afternoon in the library until five-thirty or six, then walk home while there was plenty of bright sunlight, lock the doors and wait for me since it would probably be well after dark when I got through with work that evening. She thought a few seconds and said that sounded like a good plan and started cleaning up from lunch. Capp had told me we would be moving chairs, tables and lots of books so to wear work clothes when I came back. I put on a pair of pants and a matching shirt that were old but clean and neat looking. Joyce put on some of her school clothes and we headed for the library.

We made the evening's activities fine, but Joyce was a little jittery when I got home. I told her I was worried about her all the time she was home alone since this was the first time she had been alone at night since we were married.

The next day I left early to register and go to work which left Joyce alone again to make her registration time in the afternoon and finish the process. Capp worked out staggered lunch times for us and I chose an early one so I could check on Joyce. I hurried home and we had a sandwich together and then we walked to the library together where she would wait until time to report for her registration. I was advising her on what to do and not do to get the process done. While I was talking she put an index finger over my lips to hush me and said, "I am not helpless, I think I can handle it just fine. You go do your job and I will take care of myself." With that she turned and headed up the steps to the library and pointed to the stairs going to the basement which had a sign "TEXTBOOKS" and an arrow pointing down the stairs.

Around three o'clock I was stacking some books near the checkout tables when I felt a tap on my shoulder. I turned and it was Capp. He said in a voice loud enough for several around us to hear, "Mr. Elliott would you please go over to the second table and help the next lady in line, the one in the red dress and with blonde hair?" I looked over there and saw Joyce standing in line. I smiled at Capp, just nodded my head, walked over and took Joyce's schedule card. Without a word I started my circle around and through the maze of books, getting her books from here and there. I could tell there were some eyes on me but I was all business. When I had her books clutched in one arm, I carefully stacked them in one of the paper bags we expressly used for this purpose. I handed the bag to her, she said "Thanks," then blew me a kiss. I heard a little laughter after Capp told some of those near him, "His wife." I asked Capp how he knew that she was my wife. He said, "I have my sources, but actually I saw you two walking to the library after your lunch break and the way you two acted, I put two and two together."

Friday Capp had me work three hours during the morning to be sure there was enough help to cover those registering late. When I went home after working my shift and for lunch, I had a warm feeling of having accomplished a great deal during the week. We were both registered for a full load of classes that perfectly fit our program goals. We both had great schedules, my classes were all in prime times (beginning at eight and through by eleven each morning) and Joyce had only a lab on Tuesday and Thursday afternoons from two till four with all her other classes in the mornings. Of course back then college classes were mostly fifty minutes long on Monday, Wednesday and Friday or Tuesday, Thursday and Saturday. Since that was how it had always been, we thought nothing of going to college on Saturdays. Some years later someone came up with the bright idea of increasing the Tuesday and Thursday classes by twenty minutes and dropping the Saturday ones, as now is the case with most colleges — some offering special classes only on Saturdays.

About midafternoon I suggested we walk to town and take in a movie since we had everything done that we needed to do with all of Saturday and Sunday to get ready for our classes on Monday — and we would have a few dollars extra since I had worked a little at the college. Joyce said she was ready so we struck out for town. This was our first time to walk to the main part of town. It was a little different from getting in a car and covering the distance in a few minutes. Our street came to a dead end about six blocks from our house and that street was kind of the back side of a couple of blocks of main downtown. About a block to the left it formed one side of the downtown square, which was just an open parking area; with four blocks facing it (three of these were business fronts while the fourth was the side of the biggest bank in town). That same street continued on west and formed the highway to Greenville while to the right it dead ended after two blocks into a street going south that wound around some and eventually headed east to Sulphur Springs.

We turned left and walked west till we reached the west side of the square (the south west corner) turned right (north) made that block then turned right again (east) and after another block started down what we considered the most important downtown two blocks. The bank now faced us, being across the street on the north east corner of the square — a rather unusual layout for a down town. We walked by a furniture store, then a gift shop and stopped in front of the theater to study the bill boards (and also glance across the street and down the two blocks of businesses to the east). By the bill boards advertising coming attractions, we saw there were five showings each week: which were Friday/Saturday, Sunday/Monday, Tuesday only and Wednesday/Thursday. It was Friday and the marque listed two features while the coming attractions also listed a double feature for next Friday and Saturday so we assumed the Friday and Saturday fare always included a double feature.

We just wanted to go to a movie so I walked up to the box office to purchase two tickets. I said, "Two please" and she looked at me and asked, "Either of you a student?" I replied that we both were. I then noticed a sign in the window of the box office showing three ticket prices; adult, student and child. She charged us the amount for two student tickets, punched the machine which fed out our tickets and some change in a little silver tray passing through a window cut out of the glass front on the booth. I pocketed the change and kind of looked around holding the tickets so the young lady in the booth smiled and pointed to the double doors to our right. Joyce headed that way and I followed. I opened a door for her and we saw a young man standing inside the doors, he said, "Good afternoon," held out a hand for the tickets and with the other held open the door for me. We were surprised to see a doorman taking tickets since in Overton and Kilgore the ticket booth girl tore the ticket and handed you the stub. As the doorman handed me the ticket stubs, he asked if we would like for him to show us to our seats. I asked if the tickets were for certain seats. He said, "No, you may sit where you wish." I told him I thought we could find seats for ourselves, which we did.

After the movie we went to the pharmacy next door which had a fountain counter much like Hall's and we each had a milk shake. Joyce said it had been a long time since she had drunk a milk shake on that side of the counter. We really enjoyed it. As we exited the pharmacy, we looked at the other "picture show" across the street and saw the lights were now on it with a few people going in. It displayed two western feature titles, a serial and comedy on its marque. The young man who had served us at the fountain counter came out on the sidewalk and took out a cigarette to light. Noticing our interest in the theater (and probably our talk while in the pharmacy) could tell we were new to town. He volunteered, "That's the Bloody Bucket, and it's only open Friday nights and most all day and night on Saturday. We call it the bloody bucket because it is a shoot 'um up." We both nodded and thanked him as we headed back the way we had come. This time we crossed the street in front of the bank and took the shorter route beside it to the street in back of that block which took us to our street. The sun was disappearing and beginning to darken in the east as we turned on our street. We walked a little faster to beat the darkness and gain the safety of our little home. It would be only a few weeks before we began to feel pretty safe walking around campus and town after dark in our new place.

We were up very early Monday — eager to start our classes and the new semester. Saturday morning we had scouted our closed classrooms in the open buildings on the campus so we knew where we were headed Monday morning for each class. We had designated a couple of meeting places for us after classes and before returning home for lunch — by the lion at the library (if raining in the covered main entrance) and the lounge of the Student Union Building. Monday we met our MWF classes, I waited for her at the lion and we walked home together. When we got home for lunch we were still excited about starting our classes and looking forward to the other classes the next day. We ate sandwiches for lunch and Joyce said she planned to cook our supper of macaroni and cheese with green beans (one of our most often repeated meals during our school days). After lunch we cleared the table, spread out our textbooks and started looking through them and reading our class assignments from that day's class meetings.

As we were thus engaged, we were startled to hear a knock on our front door. I walked over to the window, looked out and saw a car parked in front of our house. I opened the front door and was rather surprised to again see Capp standing there with his hat (actually a cap) in his hands.

He said, "Hi, sorry to bother you, but I wanted to talk to you before I did anyone else." My first thought was that I had done something wrong while working at the library and he had come to ask me to straighten it out. I said, "Come on in," pointing at Joyce said, "This is my wife Joyce, Joyce this is Capp who I have told you about." They both said "Hi, glad to meet you,"– or something to that effect. I took a couple of steps over to the desk, pulled the straight chair up to the table, asked Capp to have a seat, and sat down in my chair at the table.

Since both Joyce and I looked at Capp expecting him to speak, he cleared his throat and said, "You helped me out with the textbooks by doing such a good job, I decided to give you first chance at another job — if you are interested. We are losing our doorman/usher rather unexpectedly due to some illness in his family back home and he wants to leave as soon as possible. I immediately thought of you and told him I would check with you this afternoon."

I immediately remembered the young man when we went to the theater Friday. Joyce and Capp were both looking at me now. Joyce was expecting me to respond to Capp by saying something. I said I could be interested, but I would need some more information. Capp said, "That's why I came right over. If you want me too I will give you all the details here so Joyce will be in on the information for your decision and then, if you are interested, I would want you to go with me to meet Doug, the manager and my boss, for his approval — just a formality." I quickly replied, "O K, sounds good, tell us some more, especially the pay, how many hours on what days, the duties and such."

Capp looked at Joyce for a second, then turned back to me and said, "We pay a little better than the college. You would receive fifty cents an hour, the number of days and hours would be somewhat adjustable at this time. If you assumed Marc's current schedule it would be Tuesday through Saturday nights from six till eleven PM as the floor man and also 12:30 till 5:30 PM on Friday and Saturday afternoons as the relief projectionist. This was what Marc liked and had worked for us the past two years so we had worked out this schedule for him. I had no idea if you knew anything about a projection booth and might have any interest in it, but we can eliminate it if you want and have it picked up by another of our projectionist at the "bucket" or hire someone new since we have an abundance of students looking for work. As far as the job of the floor man; it is to take tickets, usher, call down rowdies and misbehavers, relieve the ticket and concession girls for restroom breaks and handle any emergencies. After seeing you work this week I think you could do that."

He paused then, either to catch his breath or give me a chance to ask any questions I might have. I said, "A friend of mine (Bruce Gillespie) was a relief projectionist in Overton and I have spent some time with him in the booth, so I know how to make change overs and splice film. Working in the booth would be no problem, but working that number of hours at night worries me — since Joyce would be home alone five evenings each week." Joyce spoke up with, "At first thought that worried me too, but it might encourage me to study in the evenings since I will be here by myself." Capp said he knew we didn't have a telephone either because he had checked before driving over, and suggested that with the extra pay we could have one and that would help relieve our anxiety since she could call me anytime or vice versa. We both nodded thoughtfully. Then Joyce spoke up saying "I am agreeable, so don't let that stop you if you want to take the job, it's your decision — it might be nice to not have you underfoot too much," and laughed. We both knew she was joking about the last part of her statement — so we smiled. We sat for two or three minutes and I said, "I think we should give it a try so let's go see your Mr. Doug." Capp laughed and explained that Douglas was his first name and he didn't like Mr. Matthews so for me to call him just "Doug," as did everyone else.

We bid Joyce goodbye for a little while, got in Capp's car, he made a U turn in our street and we headed "up" toward downtown. Capp parked in front of the pharmacy since all in front of the theater was marked off with a curb painted red with white lettering of NO PARKING. Between the theater building and the pharmacy was a brown wooden door with the street number at eyelevel in white. Capp opened this door and inside was a stairway going up. He left the door open and led the way up the stairs. On the landing at the top of the stairs was a little fence and hallway outlining the opening for the stairs. We walked past two doors on our left and turned right to another door in the wall which let us into an office. There were windows all along the outside wall from which we could see the street below and the "bloody bucket" directly across the street. Capp told me to have a seat while he got Doug. He left the office door open, took a few steps down the hall and I heard a door open without any knocking. In just a couple of minutes, I heard more steps, this time approaching the office. I watched as Capp came back into the office with a man, about my size (a little smaller than Capp) and looked to me as being in his late forties or early fifties. His hair was kind of a sandy color with a good bit of gray.

Capp introduced us, we shook hands, then Capp sat down in the chair beside me while Doug edged around the large desk and sat in the chair on the other side. Doug looked at me a minute or two then said, "Capp tells me you are a good worker and we happen to need one." I could tell he was expecting a comeback so I said, "I always try to be a good worker when there is a job to be done." He said that sounded like someone they could use and asked me if I had any questions for him. I told him I thought Capp had been very informative and I probably would have a lot of questions later. I went on to tell them that my wife and I had gone to the movie Friday afternoon and was very impressed with it and felt like it would be a good place to work. Doug beamed and said he was glad we had enjoyed it and Capp would familiarize me with the facilities and operations — and Capp was my boss but he would be available anytime I needed help or information. He went on to say that he lived in the apartment next to this office so he usually was either in the theater, office or apartment and I was welcome to talk to him anytime. He stood up, I thanked him for seeing me and he said he hoped to see a lot of me in the future. Capp told Doug that he was going to show me around the theater and explain some other things to me and if Doug was satisfied he would put me to work tomorrow evening (Tuesday) to start my first week. Doug said that sounded good to him — so, for us to get busy.

After touring the whole facilities (including the bucket) and discussing the operations, Capp took me home and apologized to Joyce for keeping me so long. Then he told her one of the benefits of being an employee's spouse she would have free admission to both theatres at all times — only having to pay the federal tax (which at that time was six cents at the bucket and eight cent at the main theater if I remember correctly) while the employee didn't have to pay even the tax. After Capp left I filled her in on what had happened and we talked and talked until we realized it was well past our supper time. We ate a snack and talked some more. We had to remind ourselves that we were there to get enough education to start making a living, getting a home and starting a family. Joyce, started laughing, and said. "Do you realize I can go to the theater five times a week, see seven features plus some extra stuff for less than fifty cents?" I laughed too and asked her if she really wanted to do that and she said she surely did, and I think she actually did all the time we were in Commerce — for she dearly loved most movies.

Sometimes I think I could write a whole book about my experiences during the two years I was working at the theaters. I also think maybe I got as much education from that part of my college years in Commerce as I did from attending classes. My duties changed somewhat over time but overall my work was enjoyable. I was given more and more responsibilities, especially for the bloody bucket which at times was much less enjoyable than those at the main theatre but both Capp and Doug were always very good and helpful to work for and with. At one time as we neared graduation and looking for a job, we thought about trying to buy an old theater near Alto that was for sale (of course getting a loan from our families). Thank goodness we soon gave up on this dream and did get the jobs in teaching where we wanted for it wasn't long before theaters everywhere were closing due to the popularity of television.

It was my employment with the theaters (almost equivalent to a fulltime job for the rest of our time in Commerce) which enabled us to finish college without being a financial drag on our parents. The Petty's gave Joyce the money for her registration and fees each semester with mine doing the same for me, as well as some gifts in cash along the way. We were not spendthrifts so we did get by. I always had Sundays off and usually Mondays so I was able to take care of things on those days if I planned accordingly.

We really did enjoy our school work. To me the junior and senior level courses were much more interesting than the first two years. My grades were excellent and of course Joyce was mostly a straight A student from start to finish with only a couple or so Bs which earned her honors when she graduated. My first two years weren't very good even after retaking some freshman courses but I could point with pride to those after we were married.

Our first trip home from school was for Thanksgiving. Since I was working at the theater, I didn't know how that would work during school holidays so one afternoon I asked Capp about our schedule during those periods. He said if I wanted off to make a trip home any time he was pretty sure he could get some of the others to cover for me or either he could do so in an emergency. I said the periods I was concerned with were Thanksgiving, Christmas, Easter and between semesters. He said those times would be easy to cover since the other local students would be out of school also and always glad to get a little extra work.

Since we had no car and knew no one from our area going to school there, we checked on the bus schedule and found we could make good connections between Commerce and Tyler. We called Mrs. Petty long distance (one of the very few such calls we made on our phone) telling her when we would be in Tyler to see if some of her family could meet us. She said they certainly would and was happy to know we would be in for Thanksgiving. The bus trip was a rough one with two changes of buses on the trip. One had a couple of hours layover — which turned out to be a good thing since our bus was nearly an hour behind schedule by the time we got there. We left Commerce mid-afternoon Wednesday and were supposed to get into Tyler around nine-thirty. It was almost eleven when we got there and the Pettys were about ready to give up on us (we were also by the time we got there). With it being the day before a holiday, all three buses were overflowing with people (many with bad attitudes and tempers). The poor drivers were overworked and about to give up and walk away a time or two it seemed. One driver threatened to stop and get a policeman if one fellow didn't quieten down. We finally got to Tyler — quite a relief.

Then another type of problem popped up, one that would plague us on many holidays, for decades. Which family would we spend the holiday celebration meal or night with; the Elliotts or the Pettys? This time it was solved by us going to Grandma's for the big noon meal gathering and then to the Sheppard's with the Pettys (of course, with Mrs. Petty preparing the meal and taking it to her parents' place in Kilgore) for the evening dinner — most holiday meals found us partaking of two. Christmas would always pose a special problem, especially after we had children. This first Christmas that we were married we spent the night on Christmas eve at Grandma's with cousins galore — Joyce was really amazed when the youth choir from Grandma's church in Tyler came out the fifteen miles from town to sing carols for us and help us enjoy hot chocolate, cookies, fruitcake — and an abundance of paper bagged fresh holiday fruit for them to take home.

Since we got in so late on Wednesday night from Commerce, our first Thanksgiving together, we spent the night at the Petty's. About midmorning the next day (Thanksgiving) Mr. Petty drove us over to Mother and Dad's for us to go with them to Grandma's for Thanksgiving dinner. On our way to Grandma's I related what a bad time we had on the bus getting home for Thanksgiving. Dad said he was sure that Mr. Bennet (the Overton blacksmith) had told him that his son Don was coming in for Thanksgiving from Commerce where he was going to school. Dad said he would check with him since Don must have a car if he was driving in. Joyce and I both knew of Don but neither had ever really talked with him. He was the quarterback on the Overton football team and I had played against him but didn't remember ever seeing him otherwise. Joyce said he had come in Hall's a few times when she was working but was only told by Nelda who he was. So we left it to Dad to check with Don's dad.

Both of our Thanksgiving dinners went well and gave us an opportunity to visit with many of our close relatives. Since we had dinner Thanksgiving night with the Pettys (Sheppard's house) we again spent the night at the Petty's. We made a point to spend the night Friday and Saturday nights at Mother and Dad's so they wouldn't feel slighted. Mrs. Petty took us over to Mother's and Dad's about noon after we had visited with the Alfords, Currys and Leas. We ate lunch with Mother and Sonny, borrowed Mother's car and spent all afternoon visiting some of our friends around New London and Overton. We had dinner Friday evening with Mother, Dad and Sonny. Dad told us he had talked with the Bennetts, father and son, and Don had come home in his own car and was going back Sunday about eleven a.m. He told Dad he knew who we were but did not know we were in school in Commerce. He said he would be going back alone and we were certainly welcome to ride with him; but there was a reason he was leaving so early. He was a big fan of Jimmy Durante and was going through Dallas to attend a concert Durante was giving in Dallas at the auditorium in the State Fair grounds. The concert was scheduled for two p.m. and would be over about four and he planned to be at Commerce around six.

I told Dad we were not big fans of Jimmy Durante but we could certainly go to the concert with Don in order to get a ride back to Commerce since we imagined the buses would be very crowded again on Sunday with a lot of people trying to get home after the holiday. Dad made arrangements with Don's dad for Don to pick us up at Dad's office Sunday morning.

Saturday morning while we were eating breakfast with Sonny (Mother and Dad following their early morning schedule), Mother said she and Dad had talked about us all visiting Ma and some other relatives at Ma's. Dad had called his brothers Allen and Fred and they were going to call some others. What they wanted us all to do was go to Ma's for lunch. Mother would fry up a bunch of chicken, make up a big batch of potato salad with some other fixings and we would take it to Ma's. This sounded good to us. Mother said she didn't need any help so we were free to take her car and go visit the Pettys until time to pick up her and Sonny and then Dad on the way to Ma's.

When we got to the Petty's we found the Huggins there and had a good visit with them. We gave them a report on the house and our school experiences — also my work. They said Fred and Ruth were getting along fine in their new place and jobs with Fred planning to build them a new house himself after he finished his schooling the coming summer. Huggins said he planned to sell the little house we were in after Fred and Ruth finished school and give them the money to put in on their new home. We left the Petty's, went back to LC for Mother, Sonny and the food. On our way to Ma's we picked up Dad in Overton and found quite an assembly at Ma's. We had a great lunch and visit with our Elliott relatives. Joyce met many of them for the first time and I saw some I had not visited with in years. This trip home for Thanksgiving turned into a very nice experience for both of us — and made us really look forward to coming home for Christmas.

We had a really nice trip to Commerce with Don Bennett. I rather enjoyed the Jimmy Durante show but Joyce later said it was too much slanted toward men with the rough jokes and the flimsy dressed women dancers and singers that were a part of the show. Don was very polite but did not talk very much. We traveled with me on the front seat with him — Joyce on the back seat. I tried making conversation with him but ended up with me mostly asking questions and his answering them without offering much detail. After a while we rode for long stretches without much talking. He gave me the impression that he didn't like to talk while driving so I didn't do it much on this trip. I tried to pay for his ticket to the Durante program but he refused to let me so I paid for ours only. When we neared Commerce I asked him to stop at a service station and let me fill the tank for him but he refused to let me do that also saying we were his guests and it was a pleasure to have us with him. I gave him directions to our house and as we arrived we invited him in for some supper but again he refused saying he was going to be right on time for the evening meal at the dormitory.

About all we found out about Don was that this was also his first year at East Texas and he had come on a basketball scholarship from Tyler Jr. College. He told us he had a girlfriend still going to school there and planning to follow him to East Texas if he was still there the next year. He told us the car was their old family one and his mother didn't drive so when his dad got a new pickup they decided to let him take it to college. He had only a much younger sister at home so the family used the pickup for the family's transportation. I never remember seeing him in Commerce the rest of the time we were there but Joyce thinks she saw him a couple of times on campus and once he spoke as they passed. We considered him rather unusual for a person his age and background.

Some fifty-seven years later, soon after we had sold our home in Kingsville (2005) and settled down somewhat in our house in Kilgore, I began an interesting practice of eating breakfast at McDonalds about five-thirty most mornings — as I had done at Lydia's in Kingsville for many, many years. It wasn't long until I was joined by four or five other diverse retirees (another ex-faculty of Kilgore College, an attorney, a physician, a career army man and a teacher now driving a school bus part-time — plus a couple or two floaters). One morning we noticed a similar appearing man at a nearby table that seemed to be interested in our talk but also trying not to let us know he was interested in us. This was repeated two or three mornings with the "stranger" leaving before we broke up. I knew he looked somewhat familiar but for the life of me I couldn't place him. This soon got the better of me so the next time he was there; I picked up my cup, walked over to his table and asked if I could sit down. He grinned and said, "Please do."

I introduced myself and he responded with he knew who I was. Then he told me he was Don Bennett and figured I wouldn't remember him. I said that I did remember him very well; he was the star quarterback at Overton while I played at Leverett's Chapel and later he was kind enough to give my wife and I a ride to college in Commerce. He said he had followed my career through his little sister (Susie) who I had taught in Overton in the fifth grade and had been her high school principal. He said her group at school reunions kept up with me and she always relayed the information to him thinking we were friends because he had told her we had both gone to East Texas after going to different junior colleges. He also said he had run into Pete Fuller in Overton who told him the two of us had been recalling our State Guard days (which Don was not a member) since we were again both members of our old church in Overton. We sat for a minute or two.

Finally, I said, "Since you know something of my life tell me about yours. Where did you go after high school?" He paused a few seconds, took a sip of his coffee and told me a tale that wasn't very happy. As my group left, one at a time, I introduced each to Don and the next day he was a member of our group. We probably continued our visit for an hour or two telling the other what we knew of mutual friends and such. Not ever being close to each other in the past, we now became somewhat friends for at least three or four years — although we were very far apart on all our beliefs (religion, government, economics, etc.). He had some very unusual ideas (ideals?) and was a very active member of the Republic of Texas (a controversial extreme right wing organization at that time). Don had been instrumental in getting the old Overton Hospital bldg. as the headquarters of the organization with him as the treasurer. He made the headlines a time or two when the organization was being pressured by the government and sued by several individuals. It finally collapsed from within and Don didn't live long after that.

Following our Thanksgiving holiday, we quickly settled back into our school schedule until time for the Christmas break. We planned to take only a week off from my work but had about two weeks off from school. As it turned our Mr. Petty was running a survey in the Talco field which was not too far from Commerce so he planned his work and travel schedule so he could come by for us on his way home and give us a ride. All during our tenure in Commerce, Mr. Petty always was able to find some reason where he would "need" to come by Commerce (a very out-of-the-way place) every couple of months to take us out to dinner and assure himself we were doing alright.

As soon as we had a little time with Mother and Dad at home in LC, they said there was something they wanted to talk to us about. I said we were all ears, so why not now? Mother explained that she had mentioned to me once that she had an educational insurance policy for me in the amount of a thousand dollars. It had matured and was in their bank account. Dad picked up the story then by telling us that since I had gone to work and had been paying nearly all of our expenses, if I felt I would continue working at the rate I was now that they would not need the insurance money for my schooling. I was afraid they were going to say they needed the money now and just wanted us to know they were going to use it. But instead Mother said right now it seemed we needed a car very much and they had decided maybe we should use that money to buy one and make our college life more comfortable. Joyce and I looked at each other with surprise and then pleasure on our faces, since we had thought it would not be until we graduated and both were employed that we could afford a car.

We realized Mother and Dad had been thinking a lot about this and it was an indication of the pride and satisfaction they felt with our progress and achievements. We thanked them and assured them we felt my job was secure for as long as I wanted and that we were not wasting our money. Dad said he wanted me to look at a car George Melton (the used car dealer in Overton that had a rock solid reputation and was a pillar of the community) had mentioned to him at their early morning coffee meetings a couple of times as being ideal for us. Dad said he had looked at it but was not too impressed but George felt like it was just what a college couple needed and wanted us to see it. Dad and I made plans to meet at George's car lot the next morning as soon as he opened (Joyce opting to leave the car business to us and she wanted to go Christmas shopping with her mother).

I was surprised when George showed me the car. It was a small tan car (similar to the tiny Austins we were used to seeing occasionally and just as dated looking), appearing to be an early 1930s model. George explained it was a 1948 model English Ford Anglia import with only eight hundred miles on it. You could tell by the smell and appearance it was almost new. It was a tough looking little number with pigskin leather seats, some wood trim, etc. in the interior. He went on to explain a man had bought it for his family in order to get a new car and with three or four kids found it was completely impractical. He had traded in to George for a full sized well used sedan much more suited to his family. George insisted I take it for a spin with Dad as the passenger. It drove like a new car and had some interesting features such as little lighted and blinking turn signal arms that flipped up from the sides to indicate your turning direction. It handled well on the city streets but on the highway it handled a little differently due to a very short turning radius in the steering unit so it required careful handling at highway speeds.

Back at the car lot George explained that its owner had just left it with George to sell for him and get as much as he could with an asking price of a thousand dollars. I asked about parts and repairs and George had checked with the local Ford dealer and found out all Ford dealers were authorized to work on them and the Ford distribution center in Dallas had parts stored in their warehouse. Dad said, "If he wants a thousand do you think he might take eight-fifty?" George said he had no idea but he had not gotten any offers so we could try. Dad looked at me and said, "I think it might be something you could use, what do you think?" I said I agree, so Dad told George to try the seller at eight-fifty but let him know we wouldn't go any higher and let us know what his answer was. George said if you have a few minutes have a seat and I will try to call him now and we may know what he says. We sat down in George's little office building as he went to his desk, looked up the number from some cards on his desk and made the call.

We watched as George carried on the conversation and took a little break while the owner discussed it with his wife. The answer was yes if the buyer was sincere and dependable. We heard George reply that it was a 100% good offer. They ended their conversation and George said, "It's a done deal if you put up the money." Dad pulled out his checkbook, making out a check, leaving the pay to line blank for George or the owner to fill in. George pulled out the transfer papers and filled in the forms with the answers I gave him. While George completed the paper work, Dad wrote another check to me for one hundred-fifty dollars and said for me to deposit that to our account for our school expenses. George handed me two sets of keys and said I would get the papers from the state in the mail but to keep a couple of pages he handed me in the glove compartment to show I had purchased the auto. I left George Melton Motors driving my "new car" headed for the bank — as Dad left in his pickup headed for his office.

I drove back to LC, gave Mother and Sonny a ride and after leaving them at home drove over to the Petty's. Joyce, her mother, Bo and Jerry were still shopping but Mr. Petty and Ed were home raking and sacking leaves. I drove up, honked and they came running. They inspected it and each took it for a spin with Ed going over to John Paul Sutton's house and taking him for a little ride too. As the girls drove up from shopping, Ed pulled in right behind them. They all got out about the same time and Mrs. Petty asked Ed what he was driving and he said, "Joyce's new car." They all shrieked and ran to the little car with Joyce inspecting it from front to rear bumper. She said she loved it and wanted to drive it. I showed her how things worked and she backed out of the drive and took it for a spin as others had done. When she came back she said it had a mind of its own about where it was going. Mr. Petty said you will get used to it because it was designed more for London traffic than the open spaces of Texas and be thankful they built the imports to the USA with the steering wheel on the left and not on the right as they do in England. Joyce then took her mother, Bo and Jerry for a ride through the Humble Camp.

We got another important Christmas present for ourselves; a female cocker spaniel puppy, a strawberry blonde that we named Sugar. We thought this little bundle of joy would be company for Joyce since she spent a lot of time at home alone while I worked. She said she was always busy with the washing and ironing necessary for my white dress shirts that I had to wear to work and all the other household duties but a puppy would be nice for those winter evenings to talk to and cuddle. Sugar sure came to love that.

So, we had a wonderful Christmas at LC and New London and returned to Commerce to finish our fall semester and begin the one for spring. We were beginning to feel like Commerce was home.

Since we now had our little car, gasoline was twenty cents a gallon and we got about thirty five miles to the gallon we did some driving around in our spare time. We made the trip home every two or three weeks — usually when I had only one day (Sunday) off. I would trade one of my week-day afternoons with the projectionist for him to work for me on Saturday night — sometimes there was a little "boot" involved. We would normally leave Commerce about seven in the evening and make the two and a half hour drive to New London and spend the night (Mother and Dad usually went to bed early so we did not want to disturb that routine).

We piled our laundry basket full of dirty clothes and put it on the back seat of the car — Sugar soon learned this was a nice place to nap on our way. We saved the laundromat charges to apply to our gasoline purchases by washing our clothes at the Petty's or Mother and Dad's on Sunday. As soon as the Pettys left for Sunday school we would go over to LC and then with Mother and Sonny, meet Dad at church and then to Grandma's for Sunday dinner. We would then again visit with the Pettys, have supper and leave for Commerce around seven-thirty or so. There were a few variations to this schedule. We were young (and thought we were carefree) so we loved this visiting with our relatives. We did these trips all during the rest of our college years at Commerce — extending our stays during holiday periods.

Not long after the spring semester began, the projectionist asked me if I was interested in a good deal on an apartment. I told him I wasn't looking for one right then but would be for the summer since we were losing our house at the end of the semester. He said their next door neighbors were moving at the end of this month or the next, depending on when he had to report for work at a new position in Dallas. He and his wife were interested themselves at first in the apartment since it was larger and nicer than theirs but they had decided it would be too much trouble to move for just three or four months and pay ten dollars a month more rent also.

His wife and Joyce had become friends as a result of going to the movies together and our visiting back and forth. She had suggested he mention it to me since she would like us for neighbors, even if for just a short time. I told him I would talk to Joyce about it that evening when I got home.

This apartment had many advantages over our current residency and only one real drawback — rent was ten dollars a month more. The size and arrangement of rooms were the best of the improvements but location was also an important factor — our car now lessened the location factor somewhat but it still loomed large in importance since we were still going in many directions at the same times. The apartment occupied by the projectionist and his wife was almost identical to the one we had at LC, a tiny kitchen and living room occupying about half of the space with a bedroom and bath the other half. There were two narrow little garages underneath and a stairway on the left (facing the front of the building) just like the LC one. A previous owner (prior to the Love's) had extended the building more than double its size by constructing a foundation with two floors and an apartment on each. The upstairs one (at the head of the stairs across the landing from the original was the one that would be available) and we soon got a look at it from the current renters.

Joyce fell in love with it at first sight inside. The rooms seemed huge to us compared to what we were used to. You entered a little hallway from the landing with a wide doorway straight ahead into the kitchen (which was kind of like an alcove but furnished with a refrigerator and real cook stove), the door to the left led into the living room and the one to the right into the bedroom. The bathroom was located on the far side of the kitchen wall with a door on each end opening into the bedroom and living room as well as a little window on the outside wall. The living room actually extended a couple of feet on the front past the front wall of the downstairs apartment and the original apartment above the garages. This wall had a door leading out to a covered balcony about four feet wide and the length of the wall. It also had double windows which let in a lot of light along with the double windows on the other outside wall.

This overhang arrangement not only increased the size of the upstairs apartment, gave it a usable balcony and created an attractive front appearance but also provided a covered patio and entrance for the downstairs apartment. The back yard of the main house, being the front yard of the three apartments, was attractively landscaped with many plants and usually a lot of blooming flowers — even in the cold months. The Loves, an elderly retired childless farming couple, a year or two previous had sold their farm, bought this property with the proceeds and were living on the rental income. They also rented a room in their house to a lady who worked at the college and boarded with them. The projectionist had told me that Mr. Love spent most of his time working in the yard as the weather allowed or sitting in his rocker on the back porch keeping an eye on the apartments.

We met the Loves and told them we were interested in renting the apartment when it was available. They didn't appear much impressed with us and especially when they learned we had a dog. We quickly got the impression that Mr. Love was not easy to get along with — might even say he wasn't filled with love (as the projectionist's wife put it). He said he didn't want any dog digging up his flowers and plants or messing up the place. We assured him Sugar was housebroken, well behaved and very lovable. We invited them to come see our house, Sugar and our yard. We even offered to put up a deposit which they did not charge at that time. The one thing that we believe finally decided him to rent to us was that I told him I had helped my Dad build and keep up rent houses since I was a little kid and I would help him without charge if he needed me to help with repairs on his house and three apartments. Later after we moved in I realized what a mistake this was for he knew practically nothing about plumbing and was coming for help very often. But we made a deal on the spot, gave him a month's rent in advance and started thinking about moving. Later Joyce said she had decided Mr. Love was only trying to be hard-nosed about it because he seemed really happy to get the first month's rent ahead of time.

The thing about the location that was so important, it was about midway between the campus and downtown. It was only a good two to three blocks each way and there were good sidewalks and street lights. Our little house had been the only one in our block on that side of the street and no sidewalks for a couple of blocks. The block facing our house had four houses on it but there was a good skip on each side to any other houses which made this location seem rather lonely at night, especially for Joyce alone. And too, the new apartment had neighbors across the stairs and below us besides the Loves and others nearby.

We hated to tell our parents we had obligated ourselves for double rent for probably three months. Joyce called her mother to tell her family about the new apartment and mentioned the rent stuff but that we felt we could handle it. In about a week her mother called back and said she had seen Huggins and mentioned the new apartment. He wanted to know all the details and when he found out we might have obligated ourselves for some double rent he told her to tell us to only pay him for the time we were actually in the house. Since we were moving somewhat for their convenience he didn't want us to pay double rent. Huggins went up in our estimation of him and we always felt a warm spot in our hearts for him. We did pay double rent for about two weeks while I made a slow move in our little car by tying furniture on top and behind it. We decided to leave our ice box and old clunky stove behind since Huggins had been so nice about the rent and we didn't need to move them. He could let them go with the house when it was sold if he wished.

By the first of March we were snug in our new apartment. We were especially happy that we had made the move when I was involved in two or three overnight out-of-town trips with the college debate team. The spring semester I had signed up for the required high school teacher's speech course. Dr. Pope was the professor for my class and also the coach for the debate team. He selected me and James Grammar from our class to be on the team. I recall two college tournaments we attended; one at Stephen F. Austin State in Nacogdoches and another at Baylor University in Waco. There was probably one or two more but the reason I remember these two so well is due to the fact that James and I placed in the top three in these and it was against nearly all the colleges in the state.

As a result of these experiences, James and I being together in other classes during our two years in Commerce we became fast friends, close like family. James was a navy vet and he, Orel and their little boy Billy lived in the ex-servicemen's Quonset hut village on campus. We babysat Billy some and they kept Sugar a few times for us. Billy thought Sugar and our little car belonged to him. Every time he saw us he wanted to take Sugar for a ride in "my little car." Orel was a full time at home mom, many times keeping other kids for moms in the "village," but I think we were the only ones that Billy ever stayed with for more than a few minutes. After they and we graduated they returned to Alto, their home town, and in time James became the elementary school principal and remained so for decades. They were probably the only couple from those two years that we stayed in touch with over the years.

Joyce had connected with three or four other married female students through the Baptist Student Union and they hung out together some at the BSU. This was good since I had very little free time for socializing and there were programs at the BSU they enjoyed. One of the "girls" (as we called them) was an unmarried mother of a two year old but fit in well with the rest and was really Joyce's best friend (after our next door neighbors moved). They had met in the art course for elementary teachers and shared many common interests — her grandmother lived with her and her little boy in a small apartment near the college (she walked to school while the grandmother took care of the child). About the time our next door neighbors (across the landing) moved, the BSU got a new director, Dr.

Height, and he ended up as our new neighbor. To us he was almost elderly, probably only in his late forties or fifties but with gray hair at the temples.

Through her activities at the BSU and our coming and going at the apartment we got to know him a little. We found he was a divorcee which at that time was very unusual for a Baptist preacher and probably accounted for his now being a BSU director. We thought he was very quiet and subdued for a Baptist preacher compared to the ones we had known. Joyce had an elective course left in her degree plan so she decided to take a Bible course taught by Dr. Height (Bible courses taught off-campus by state law but given credit by the college) during the first six weeks of the summer. Since she had attended church and Sunday school for many years, she was somewhat familiar with the material and later said this was the dullest course and him the most uninteresting instructor she had had in school. She also later confessed that she had thoughts of trying to get her friend and Dr. Height romantically interested in each other but now she knew she didn't want to be a match-maker.

We carefully planned our academic courses so as to not waste any time in completing our degrees. I completed my Bachelor of Science degree requirements with dual majors in history and secondary education and a minor in government at the end of the 1949 fall semester. I opted to stay in school and immediately began my graduate work in the 1950 spring semester. I was pursuing a master's degree in history and government. Joyce was on an elementary education program designed to graduate at the end of the summer session with us both planning to begin a teaching career in September. I would lack six hours completing my master's but planned to do so during my first year of teaching.

The college placement office had sent me a notice about the services available to graduating students when I filed for my graduation in the fall of 1949. Since I was not interested in getting a teaching job right away, I waited till the spring semester had begun before starting my paperwork for the placement office and have Joyce do hers along-side mine since she would be graduating at the end of the summer. We would be contacting school districts personally in the area that we were especially interested in, but the placement office would handle our recommendation letters and evaluation forms for us through that office and notify us of vacancies.

Dad had told us that if we were able to get jobs around home (Longview, Tyler, Jacksonville or Henderson area) he would help us get a house of our own. He knew how to get one built at minimum cost — with him contributing his labor and much of the material coming from his own stockpile of stuff. This offer had Joyce planning strongly on us following this plan. When I received a couple of job offers (almost sight unseen) she insisted I turn them down. One was in Midland (one of the highest paying districts in the state) but they did not anticipate a teaching vacancy in Joyce's field and no other schools in the nearby area. The opportunity I was most interested in was due to the support I received from Dr. Saylor, my favorite professor in my master's program. He wanted me to go to UT, finish my Ph.D. through a teaching fellowship in the government department that he could swing if I agreed to come back to ET in two or three years to replace Mr. Tartar who was retiring. He had even talked to the president of the college (Dr. Gee) and gotten his tentative approval. Joyce liked all of it except coming back and living in Commerce. She said she couldn't "see" us living in Commerce permanently since she had all of it she wanted and planned to raise our kids near home, their grandparents and other relatives — if we could do it at all. So we concentrated on the area close to LC and New London.

Our prospects began to look really good after Easter when Joyce found out a second grade teacher at New London had decided to retire and they would have a vacancy. The principal and superintendent told her she would be their first choice if they were to fill the vacancy from outside. But changes were taking places from within and it didn't work out in Joyce's favor. The kindergarten teacher was to finish her degree at SFA during the summer and wanted a regular teaching position due to the salary difference. At that time kindergarten teachers were not required to have a degree nor be certified so there was a big pay difference. The board decided to promote the kindergarten teacher to the 2nd grade and hire an elementary substitute teacher for the kindergarten position. This left Joyce out in the cold with a promise that if anything else developed she would probably be their first choice.

In the meantime John Crager had talked to me about how he wished I could teach in Overton and wanted to tie it into getting a man in the elementary school. With Mr. Davis, another trustee, they had talked with the superintendent about it. The elementary school principal was Miss Dorothy Harris, a middle aged lady that had grown up in Overton and as a young woman just out of college began her teaching career there. Miss Harris didn't "cotton" to this idea but finally came up with a proposal that fit in with some of her own ideas she wanted to do. She wanted to departmentalize the 5th and 6th grades somewhat by having special teachers for music, art, science, math and maybe another two or three. She didn't want to have P E in this group but since she was being pressured she ended up with a program she felt would satisfy the superintendent and board members by including P E for the 4th, 5th and 6th grades. She knew there was enough talent and interest by her current teachers to fill in as the needed special teachers with the exception of science in the 5th and 6th grades along with the P E in the three grades. Her plea to the superintendent was that the "added" teacher be fully certified and qualified to teach these courses in the elementary school — she probably thought that they had some local Overton graduate who they were wanting a job for and to expand their athletic program into the elementary school at the same time. Undoubtedly she was shocked when she found out this was partially true but the man was a graduate of L C (the arch rival of Overton in all sports) and not really known by the coaches.

We learned that there was a possibility of a vacancy in the lower grades also in Overton which we hoped would materialize and Joyce would have a chance at it. But we were also informed that the board had a policy of not hiring husband and wife as teachers (a holdover from depression days) and the board did not plan to change it since it had come up when Kenneth Whitten was hired and later Mary Jim applied for a librarian's position. So Joyce was still looking for her a position and I needed to be sure I could qualify for the one coming up in Overton.

I checked with the certification office at ET and was told that since I was already certified as a high school teacher I could also be certified for elementary teaching with twelve semester hours of method or content courses in elementary education. Since these could be graduate courses, if I shifted my major on my master's degree to general education they could also count toward my degree. So I changed my major on my master's and found four courses on the summer schedule that would fill both needs. I studied the college catalogue very carefully and found there was an undergraduate course in teaching physical education in the elementary school but it was not offered in summer school. I found it listed in the courses offered by correspondence and enrolled for it before the spring semester was over and completed it during the first six weeks of the summer. So I felt this would help me organize the elementary P E program if I got the job. I was ready if everything fell in place for the job I wanted.

Joyce noticed a posting in the placement office for an elementary teacher at Gaston ISD (between Overton and Henderson at Joinerville, location of the East Texas Oil Field discovery well) now consolidated with the New London ISD to form the West Rusk CISD. She went over to see the principal at home that Saturday but he was not very interested. He indicated that they were very selective with who they hired and went only with referrals from the placement offices. She was very disappointed. Two or three days later she went by the placement office to see if there were any new postings. She was very surprised to see the principal (Grady Coates) from Gaston sitting at a table going over her folder. He looked up, saw her and rushed over and asked if he could talk to her for a few minutes. They went to an interview room, he told her he was very interested in her qualifications and wanted to ask her a few questions. Later Joyce said she wanted to act hard to get but she thought better of it and they had a good visit. It ended with him assuring her she would be getting a contract in the mail within the week and all she had to do was sign it and return it by mail. That night I asked Capp to fill in for me for two or three hours while we drove over to Greenville and had dinner at the Steak House. We felt like celebrating since it seemed as if we were set for the fall.

That weekend we told Dad we were 95% certain we would move to Overton or New London (about halfway between Overton and the Gaston school). He said John Crager had told him he was sure I would be teaching in Overton come fall since he felt he had enough support now to get me hired for the position that was coming. He also said that he and John had discussed our residence and both felt it would be better if we lived in Overton and became members of the community. He also pointed out that if we lived in Overton (within walking distance of the school) only one of us would need to commute and not need a second car. So Dad was ready to build us a house in Overton if we gave him the go ahead. We told him to go do as he pleased since we were certain it would be fine with us (knowing that if anything went wrong with our plans he could probably sell the house at a profit).

Dad had already located a lot he was interested in, next to where Dr. York (head of the new state hospital they had opened in the closed Rocky Mount School at Sexton City) had built him a very modern looking cottage on Bradford Street. It was only about three or four blocks from the Overton schools as the crow flies but it was six blocks if you went on the streets. This was caused by an old creek bed that ran south east from downtown and was used as a drainage ditch. The only street crossing the ditch southwest of the school at that time was Helen. In order to get to the school by car from the lot you had to go a block west to Helen, then three blocks north to Henderson and east a couple of blocks to the school. Since it was fairly well settled around the school, he felt this would be the best located of the building sites available. He went ahead and purchased the lot in our names — the first real estate we owned.

Gulf Oil Company was downsizing its camp just out of Overton and had put several buildings up for sale by bids. Dad had placed bids on three of them but was the high bidder on only one — a very sturdy storehouse measuring about thirty feet long and sixteen feet wide. He decided it could form the basic part of our new house, had it moved to our lot and started to work on it using Sonny as his helper. They tore the roof off, removed the windows, doors and the back wall; then they extended the building eight feet on the back side, putting all this newly sized building under one roof and put in new windows and doors. The new windows included a six foot by eight foot picture window in the living room which Joyce "just had to have" — she sketched the design, with forty-eight individual panes of glass and it was custom built at my Uncle Fred's cabinet shop in Tyler.

Dad drew his proposed floor plan for us to study and make suggestions. We studied and studied his plan and every time we thought of a change we came back to his plan, we decided it was ideal for us — his years and years of building houses had paid off for us. We had a kitchen, bath and bedroom across the back with the living and dining rooms across the front. Some people would say we had too much space in our living and dining rooms compared to that in the back half; but Dad knew, and we appreciated it later, as a young couple we enjoyed the space for friends to come visit — and we had a make-do spare bedroom in the living room with the use of a couch that made into a full bed.

Dad spent all of his vacation and spare time that summer (with Sonny freely volunteering his summer) to build our new house. Since we were so busy working and finishing summer school, we could only check the progress every couple of weeks. We got out of school a week or ten days before our jobs started so I was able to put in some time on the house as well as moving. The house was livable when we moved in but not yet finished. We, Joyce and I, finished the interior at night and weekends — taking two to three months with all our school activities. The walls were sheetrock inside and I textured them (having never seen it done before) and painted them the colors Joyce selected. We had inlaid linoleum put on the floors in the kitchen and bath with wall to wall carpeting on the rest of the floors. What a nice sight it was when finished. Sonny had graduated from high school in May so he started to Kilgore College in September and Dad got some rest with only his full time job and cows as a sideline. We moved into our new home with only a fifteen hundred dollar mortgage at the bank, a couple of hundred dollars in our checking account and paying for the rest of the materials, etc. from our salaries as we went along.

Joyce had her contract approved by June the first, with a contingency clause that she must have completed her degree in elementary education and be properly certified as an elementary school teacher completed by the start of school. Mr. Coates wrote her saying she was assigned to a 4th grade class, giving her the room number and telling her he would be glad to show her through the school and answer any questions she had by appointment any time before the general faculty meeting and teacher orientation. She responded thanking him and asked for an appointment following the July 4th holiday. She wanted time between seeing her room and the start of school to begin assembling things to decorate her room.

I didn't have anything in writing concerning my job until about the middle of July when I received a letter inviting me for an interview with the superintendent and principal around August 1. When I showed up for the interview I was told that the principal was normally on vacation from a week after school ended till two weeks before the start of the new school year but in this case she had returned early for our interview and to complete the plans for the new schedule of classes. The superintendent handled the interview very casually, trying to make Miss Harris and me as comfortable as possible. I had been told she was a tough old gal and would probably skin me alive if given a chance. She turned out to be very nice, maybe too nice, but couldn't hide her surprise when she found out that she had known my Dad for years as the policeman and had not made a connection in the names. It also turned out that I slightly knew one of her sisters through her brother-in-law (as he was an older brother to one of my Overton friends).

Although not very formal, the meeting was rather structured by an outline used by the superintendent he and Miss Harris had probably worked out together beforehand. He gave me a lot of background information about the Overton schools (especially the elementary one) as well as Miss Harris — through summarizing her contributions during her over twenty years' service to the school district. He briefly noted that they were modifying the upper grades' curriculum somewhat and this called for the addition of a new teacher and this was the reason they were interested in talking to me and to give me an opportunity to see if I was interested in being considered for the position. This sounded a little bit like a round-a-bout way in getting down to the facts but I felt it was alright since he wanted everything to be above board.

Miss Harris then explained the new curriculum for the 5th and 6th grades as well as adding a P E period in the 4th grade. The new teacher would be responsible for three periods of forty-five minutes each for boys in each of the three grades. She explained that each grade had two classes so the girls' P E would be handled by the two women teachers for each grade (probably alternating by the week or six weeks). The activities for these classes would be planned by the three teachers of the P E classes and the boys' teacher would be responsible for coordinating all P E activities. This teacher would also be assigned four thirty minute science classes (two for each of the 5th and 6th grades) for the day during the enrichment periods — music, art, science and math.

"For the time being, we will call this position the Boys' Science and P E Teacher," the superintendent added after this and wanted to know if I had any questions at this point. I replied that I didn't have at the moment but I was sure there was much more information I would need and I felt that I had spent a lot of time preparing for an opportunity such as this. Miss Harris said she had noticed I had a rich background in science and felt I could handle the job well. The superintendent added that this along with my preparation for teaching elementary P E was what had them interested in me. I told them I appreciated this confidence and would certainly like to have a try at the position. The superintendent then asked Miss Harris if she wanted to share any more information at this time. She responded with a yes and said there were a few things I probably would like to know. She then glanced at a couple of sheets of paper (I am sure she had notes she had specifically prepared for this interview) and began to explain more fully the duties of the Boys' Science and P E Teacher.

She said the teacher would not have a home room or the duties assigned to one but would be assigned a desk in the teachers' workroom adjacent to the principal's office and would be there during homeroom period for assistance to the office staff at the beginning of classes. He would also be kind of a first aid person for all the grades since he had some training for this in his P E classes. Besides hall and bus loading and unloading monitoring during the day, he was to be assigned an hour's lunchroom duty while the 4th, 5th, & 6th grades were having their lunch and then mentioned a few other duties such as ordering, maintaining and storing the P E equipment, etc. I realized she intended to keep this person very busy — and under her eyes.

Since I had already submitted an application for a teaching position and had all my papers from the placement office in order for them I didn't think there was anything else for me to do. When the conversation seemed to be near an end, I decided to ask if there was anything else they needed from me. The superintendent used this as a way to end our interview. He said the board would meet in three days and they would take the superintendent and principal's recommendations on the curriculum change and addition of a new teaching position under consideration. Then I would be hearing from him as to the status of my application. Nothing was said about salary and I didn't ask.

The next few days seemed to drag but the day after the board meeting, just a few minutes after I got to the apartment for lunch the telephone rang and it was Dad. He said John Crager told him at coffee that I was hired during the board meeting. They both felt I would want to know as soon as possible so he (John) asked Dad to call me since he didn't think it would be proper for a trustee to do so. In just three days I got a contract by mail — I signed it and got it back in the mail the same day.

We really celebrated that evening by taking off from work all night and going again to Greenville for supper and some shopping. So here we were, two employed young teachers ready to embark on our careers.

EPILOGUE

Joyce and Floyd settled into their new jobs, new home and into a somewhat different lifestyle. They planned on waiting a couple of years before starting their family; but sometimes nature has its own plans and after experiencing some bouts of early morning sickness Joyce consulted her doctor in January, 1952, and he pronounced her two months pregnant. So on the advice of this physician she retired "in a family way" from her teaching position in March. On July 19 a son arrived. For the next ten years Joyce spent her time as the busy mother to him and his baby sister who arrived on June 27, 1956.

Floyd continued his career with the Overton Independent School District; teaching three years in the elementary school, three years in the junior high school, three years in the high school and then three years as the high school principal. At this point he moved his career into higher education; first in Kilgore, then Corpus Christi and finally Kingsville.

Joyce and Floyd spent slightly over sixty-six years together — enjoying their marriage and loving their ever-expanding family.

This book is dedicated to Joyce because

She lifted me from the depths of despair,
My faults and troubles she did bear.
We sailed through life on a silvery cloud,
She so lovely, and me very proud.
I loved her beyond words, all her life,
Since God chose her for my wife.

CPSIA information can be obtained
at www.ICGtesting.com
Printed in the USA
BVHW042211120619
550887BV00004B/31/P